SOME ACROSTIC SIGNATURES OF
FRANCIS BACON

PROLOGUE

The greatness of the prize induced Œdipus . . . to accept the condition and make the trial: who presenting himself full of confidence and alacrity before the Sphinx, and being asked what kind of animal it was which was born four-footed, afterwards became two-footed, then three-footed, and at last four-footed again, answered readily that it was man; who at his birth and during his infancy sprawls on all four, hardly attempting to creep; in a little while walks upright on two feet; in later years leans on a walking-stick and so goes as it were on three; and at last in extreme age and decrepitude, his sinews all failing, sinks into a quadruped again and keeps his bed.

This was the right answer and gave him the victory; whereupon he slew the Sphinx. . . .

The fable adds very prettily that when the Sphinx was subdued, her body was laid on the back of an ass: for there is nothing so subtle and abstruse, but when it is once thoroughly understood and published to the world, even a dull wit can carry it.

OF THE WISDOM OF THE ANCIENTS, by Francis Bacon, 1609. Translation by Spedding, 1858, XXVIII. *The Sphinx*, or *Science*.

SOME
ACROSTIC SIGNATURES
OF FRANCIS BACON

BARON VERULAM OF VERULAM, VISCOUNT ST. ALBAN

TOGETHER WITH SOME OTHERS
ALL OF WHICH ARE NOW FOR THE
FIRST TIME DECIPHERED
AND PUBLISHED

BY

WILLIAM STONE BOOTH

BOSTON AND NEW YORK
HOUGHTON MIFFLIN COMPANY
The Riverside Press Cambridge
1909

TO MY WIFE

WHOSE CONFIDENCE AND SYMPATHY

ENABLED ME TO COMPLETE

THIS BOOK

PREFACE

Iᴛ is ungracious to destroy a pleasing illusion, and this book is not written with that purpose. It is written solely in the interest of Science — in this case, the Science of Biography.

By the simple process of cancelling one inference against another I came to the conclusion that what was left of the biography of Shakespeare was a few facts about the Actor, and the work of the Poet. I had already read and thought much about what we know of the work and the mental habits of Francis Bacon, and, like others, had been struck by the many seeming points of contact — and with one or two which were more than seeming — between his work and that of Shakespeare.

As a mere step in a scientific enquiry I turned to see if Bacon could have signed his name to works for which he was supposedly responsible, by some such cipherer's trick as that of Francesco Colonna, and after some methodical tests I found that he, or others, had done so.

I confess that I was daunted at the outset of my work by the personal obloquy that has been heaped upon scholar and charlatan alike by the men who are content with the inferential method of writing literary history; but, reflecting that life is short and that a little obloquy does not do much harm, I decided to make known these acrostics in the hope that their discovery might lead men to approach the problems of biography in a more scientific spirit.

The man who in recent years has expressed in the bravest words the spirit in which we should approach such a problem as that with which this book deals, is Gaston Paris, in a lecture delivered at the Collège de France in 1870, when the German armies were surrounding the walls of Paris, and French patriotism was scouting German science. He said: —

'Je professe absolument et sans réserve cette doctrine, que la science n'a d'autre objet que la vérité, et la vérité pour elle-même, sans aucun souci des conséquences bonnes ou mauvaises, regrettables ou heureuses, que cette vérité pourrait avoir dans la pratique. Celui qui, par un motif patriotique, religieux, ou même moral, se permet dans les faits qu'il étudie, dans les conclusions qu'il tire, la plus petite dissimulation, l'altération la plus légère, n'est pas digne d'avoir sa place dans le grand laboratoire, où la probité est un titre d'admission plus indispensable que l'habileté. Ainsi comprises, les études communes, poursuivies avec le même esprit dans tous les pays civilisés, forment au-dessus des nationalités restreintes, diverses et souvent hostiles, une grande patrie qu'aucune guerre ne souille, qu'aucun conquérant ne menace, et où les âmes trouvent le refuge et l'unité que la cité de Dieu leur a donnés en d'autres temps.

'Cette disposition d'esprit, qui est et doit être la mienne, je désire qu'elle soit la vôtre en quelque mesure.'[1]

Bacon was ahead, not only of his own time but also of the present, when he wrote (*De Augmentis*, book vi, Spedding's translation) of the methods of teaching and of the transmission of knowledge. He styles the first difference of method *Magistral*, or *Initiative*. 'The magistral method teaches; the initiative intimates. The magistral requires that what is told should be believed; the initiative that it should be examined. The one transmits knowledge to the crowd of learners; the other to the sons, as it were, of science. The end of the one is the use of knowledges, as they are now; of the other the continuation and further progression of them. Of these methods the latter seems to be like a road abandoned and stopped up; for as knowledges have hitherto been delivered, there is a kind of contract of error between the deliverer and the receiver; for he who delivers knowledge desires to deliver it in such form as may be best believed, and not as may be most conveniently examined; and he who receives knowledge desires present satisfaction, without waiting for due enquiry; and so rather not to doubt, than not to err; glory making the deliverer careful not to lay open his weakness, and sloth making the receiver unwilling to try his strength.'

Scientifically speaking, there can be no such thing as orthodox or unorthodox scholarship. Such phrases belong to the bygone age of the ecclesiastical pedagogue. The man who allows his inferences to crystallise into an 'orthodox opinion' is on the highroad to oblivion, or is courting the ridicule of posterity. Literary history is a science. It is a matter of facts. No lasting history can be built on opinion, and no scholarship which is afraid of enquiry can retain respect.

---

[1] *La Chanson de Roland et la Nationalité française*, in 'La Poésie du moyen âge.' First Series, third edition, 1895, pp. 90–91.

The main conclusion we reach after examining many first known editions of works of obscure authorship is that it is unsafe to base our scholarship on any man's inferences or reports. We must see the original document, and study it in the light of the literary practice or habit of its time.

I take this opportunity to express my gratitude for suggestions, criticism, and encouragement, to my friends Mrs. Lucien Howe, Mrs. G. H. Parker, T. T. Baldwin, R. A. Boit, W. B. Cabot, W. C. Chase, J. Koren, C. E. Merrill, Jr., Alonzo Rothschild, W. L. Stoddard, and H. F. Stone.

Mere thanks are inadequate to express my debt to my friends John A. Macy, G. H. Parker, and R. T. Holbrook, who have greatly improved my manuscript by their painful reading and generous criticism. I am indebted to the latter friend for much of the text with which the third chapter opens. In its early stage my work was materially aided by Mr. H. G. Curtis, who lent me his superb copy of the first edition of Selenus, and I have derived constant inspiration from the works of the late Rev. Walter Begley, a remarkably fertile scholar with an accurate imagination. My one regret is that he is dead, and that I cannot show him what is, after all, so far as I am concerned, but the testing of some of his brilliant theories.

The openhandedness with which rare books were placed at my disposal by the Boston Public Library, the Library of Harvard University, and the Library of Congress has lightened my work; and by their skilful handling of typographical problems the gentlemen of The Riverside Press have helped me to make the truth still more plain; but I value not less my Publishers' ready and generous cooperation.

                                                    W. S. B.

Cambridge, Mass., March 13, 1909.

CONTENTS

CONTENTS

PART I

INTRODUCTORY AND EXPLANATORY

SOME ACROSTIC SIGNATURES OF FRANCIS BACON

CHAPTER I

AT THE OUTSET

In printing this book I wish to present, as concisely as I can, some acrostics which have come to my notice. Each of these acrostics is accompanied, wherever possible, by a photographic facsimile, from the earliest known edition, of the page to which it refers; and accompanying each facsimile are a few words of description to enable the reader to see the acrostics clearly.

Most of the acrostics show the name of Francis Bacon, his title, and armorial motto; a few show the names of his brother Anthony, Ben Jonson, John Milton, and Leonora Baroni. In a few cases, where the acrostics are not structural signatures, they seem to have been used to lend point to compliment or satire.

I have made my book in two divisions. *Part I* consists of a short historical review of the few important aspects of the subject; a careful explanation of the method by which the acrostics are made, and are to be found; and a score or so of other acrostics and structural signatures. The reader can thus familiarise himself with a habit which has prevailed among many writers through many centuries.

Part II is devoted to the signatures, directions for finding them, and to the facsimiles of the pages in which they are to be found.

The reader who intends to follow me through *Part II* will find it necessary to master thoroughly the chapter on *Method* in *Part I*, and to familiarise himself with the practical *Specimens* which lie next to that chapter.

To seek letters in alternate directions on each succeeding line will require a little practice; and at first it will not be found easy to fix the attention on initials, on terminals (the first and last letters of a word), on capitals, etc., as the case may demand. Patience will be needed, and some intelligent direction of the imagination, and the analytical faculty.

The discovery of these acrostics was the result of study in the cryptography of the sixteenth and early seventeenth centuries, that is to say, in the cipher codes which were the tools used by ambassadors, intelligencers, and men who were directly or indirectly in the service of the governments of those days.

Every student of history and of literature is aware of the abundant literature of cryptography, and of the constant part that ciphers played in diplomatic and semi-official despatches between officials and their agents at home and abroad. The student of alphabetical ciphers quickly becomes aware that acrostics and anagrams are close variants of more recondite mathematical arrangements of types, or letters to be seen in ciphers. He will be inclined to regard all such uses of letters as sprung from a very ancient habit — that, namely, of using signs to express meaning. The official cryptography of the times of Elizabeth brought into play a very high order of intelligence. To decipher a difficult despatch, which had been intercepted, required not only a keenly developed analytical faculty, but often a wide knowledge of languages and mathematics. It would follow naturally that a man learned in the art of ciphering would find it easy to make an acrostic or an anagram. His occupation would suggest to him many a trick for hiding his name, if he wished to do so. The art drew into its service chemistry, curious cabalistic mysticism and ingenuity, astrology, mechanics, and, as has been remarked above, languages and mathematics. I shall show later that the use of an acrostic as a structural signature, before the days of the title-page and printing, is of great antiquity. Its more general use in the late sixteenth and early seventeenth centuries is seen in the weaving of the name of a patron or friend into a poem. The use in both ways seems to have spread at that time, with the influence of Italian genius, throughout the more polite literatures of Europe. Elizabethan literature is liberally strewn with acrostics and anagrams.

Students of talent or genius often found their best means of support in the service of the nobles and gentlemen about the Court, and their fortunes often depended upon the good will of their patrons. Such men were Spenser, John Davies of Hereford, and Ben Jonson, to give three well-known writers as examples. Such men have given us a large part of our literature, and it does not surprise us to find them making use of the devices and courtly literary tricks and amusements of their day. Who does not remember Malvolio's attempt to find his name in cipher in the forged note which Maria let fall in his path? Most readers of *Volpone* have noticed the acrostic which Ben Jonson ran down the side of the 'Argument' to that play. Thomas Howell's *Devises* contain many good acrostics; and indeed what student of Elizabethan and early Jacobean literature could not find enough specimens to fill a large volume?

So far as they are *known*, however, they are almost always to be *seen* woven in verse; especially in complimentary verse, where they were regarded as an ornament. They were one of the legitimate amusements of the day. J. R. Green, in writing of Elizabeth (*Short History*, 1890, p. 374), alludes to the 'love of anagrams and puerilities which sullied her later years.' A clever anagram, or acrostic, was one of the bye-paths to Queen Elizabeth's favour, and Green's unnecessarily contemptuous remark is confirmed by the author of *The Arte of English Poesie* (Arber's edition, 1895, p. 123), who, 'seeing this conceit so well allowed of in France and Italy, and being informed that her Majesty took pleasure sometimes in deciphering of names, and hearing how divers Gentlemen of her Court had essayed, but with no great felicity, to make some delectable transpose of her Majesty's name,' says, 'I would needs try my luck, for cunning I know not why I should call it, unless it be for the many and variable applications of sense, which requireth peradventure some wit and discretion more than of every unlearned man, and for the purpose I took me these three words (if any other in the world) containing in my conceit greatest mystery, and most importing good to all them that now be alive, under her noble government.

'Elissabet Anglorum Regina.

'Which orthography (because ye shall not be abused) is true and not mistaken, for the letter *Zeta*, of the Hebrews and Greek, and of all other tongues, is in truth but a double SS. hardly uttered, and H. is but a note of aspiration only and no letter, which therefore is by the Greeks omitted. Upon the transposition I found this to redound:

'Multa regnabis ense gloria.
'By thy sword shalt thou reign in great renown.

'Then transposing the word (ense) it came to be

'Multa regnabis sene gloria.
'Aged and in much glory shall ye reign.

'Both which results falling out upon the very first marshalling of the letters, without any darkness or difficulty, and so sensibly and well appropriate to her Majesty's person and estate, and finally so effectually to mine own wish (which is a matter of much moment in such cases), I took them both for a good boding, and very fatality to her Majesty appointed by God's providence for all our comforts. Also I imputed it for no little good luck and glory to myself, to have pronounced to her so good and prosperous a fortune, and so thankful news to all England, which though it cannot be said by this event any destiny or fatal necessity, yet surely is it by all probability of reason, so likely to come to pass, as any other worldly event of things that be uncertain, her Majesty continuing the course of her most regal proceedings and vertuous life in all earnest zeal and godly contemplation of his word, and in the sincere administration of his terrene justice, assigned over to her execution as his Lieutenant upon earth within the compass of her dominions.

'This also is worth the noting, and I will assure you of it, that after the first search whereupon this transpose was fashioned, the same letters being by me tossed and tranlaced five hundred times, I could never make any other, at least of some sense and conformity to her Majesty's estate and the case. If any other man by trial happen upon a better omination, or whatsoever else ye will call it, I will rejoice to be overmatched in my device, and renounce him all the thanks and profit of my travail.'

His opinion of his own amusement is worth hearing. He says, 'When I wrate of these devices, I smiled with myself, thinking that the readers would do so too, and many of them say, that such trifles as these might well have been spared, considering the world is full enough of them, and that it is pity men's heads should be fed with such vanities as are to none edification nor instruction, either of moral virtue, or otherwise behooveful for the common wealth, to whose service (say they) we are all born, and not to fill and replenish a whole world full of idle toys. To which sort of reprehenders, being all holy and mortified to the world, and therefore esteeming nothing that savoureth not of Theology, or altogether grave and worldly, and therefore caring for nothing but matters of policy, and discourses of estate, or all given to thrift and passing for none art that is not gainfull and lucrative, as the sciences of the Law, Physic, and merchandise: to these I will give none other answer than refer them to the many trifling poems of Homer, Ovid, Virgil, Catullus and other notable writers of former ages, which were not of any gravity or seriousness, and many of them full of impudicity and ribaldry, as are not these of ours, nor for any good in the world should have been: and yet those trifles are come from many former siecles unto our own times, uncontrolled or condemned or suppressed by any Pope or Patriarch or other severe censor of the civil manners of men, but have been in all ages permitted as the convenient solaces and recreations of man's wit. And as I cannot deny but these conceits of mine be trifles: no less in very deed be all the most serious studies of man, if we shall measure gravity and lightness by the wise man's balance, who, after he had considered of all the profoundest arts and studies among men, in the end cried out with this Epyphoneme, 'Vanitas vanitatum et omnia vanitas.' Whose authority if it were not sufficient to make me believe so, I could be content with Democritus rather to condemn the vanities of our life by derision, than as Heraclitus with tears, saying with that merry Greek, thus, —

> 'Omnia sunt risus, sunt pulvis, et omnia nil sunt.
> Res hominum cunctae, nam ratione carent.

'Now passing from these courtly trifles, let us talk of our scholastical toys,'[1] . . . and so he passes to them.

[1] *The Arte of English Poesie.* Quoted from the unnumbered cancelled pages which are to be found in a copy bearing Ben Jonson's autograph. Arber says that so far as his knowledge goes this is the only copy known to contain these cancelled pages. It is in the Grenville collection in the British Museum. (See Arber's edition, 1895.) I have followed Spedding's plan in modernising the spelling of my quotations from this book; and have inserted a few commas to make plainer the meaning for those unused to the punctuation of this period.

CHAPTER II

THE USERS OF CIPHERS

As the study of ciphers in their relation to the literature of their day has hitherto been allowed by scholars[1] to remain largely in the hands of credulous persons and charlatans, it may be of interest if I give a short account of the class of men who were expected to be responsibly conversant with the art and practice of ciphering. The class may be represented by two well-known men whose work is open to all students — Anthony Bacon, the brother of Francis, and Sir Henry Wotton.

These two men were contemporaries, and each was engaged during the larger part of his life in supplying his sovereign with information about the secrets of foreign Courts. Each had capable educated men in his immediate personal service, or going to and fro, with express despatches, between London and different correspondents on the Continent and in Scotland. Each had served a similar apprenticeship to what was then regarded as the first step in the diplomatic service, for a young man of good birth and with his way to make in the world. Anthony Bacon built up so important a service as an intelligencer for his friend and patron Essex, that Queen Elizabeth came to carry on her official correspondence through Essex, to the embarrassment of her responsible minister Burleigh, and of his son Robert Cecil.

Wotton's letters bring into use many ciphers, and constantly allude to other cipher despatches. He frequently enclosed a cipher code for the use of his correspondents in reply. His despatches show that part of the recognised business of an ambassador to a foreign Court was to intercept the despatches of the envoys of other Courts, and to regard philosophically the interception of his own by another. Provision was often made for this by the despatch of a

[1] So far as I know, Mr. W. W. Greg stands alone in his careful and intelligent examination of the work of so-called decipherers in this field. See his article on Bacon's 'Biliteral Cipher and its Applications,' in *The Library*, 1902, series 2, vol. iii, pp. 41–53. I allude elsewhere to his admirable edition of *Henslowe's Diary*, in which he has now given to us the text free from the forgeries of some misguided scholars.

false message in one direction and a true one in another. Messengers were waylaid and sometimes left for dead, and Wotton himself half-humorously excuses himself for keeping in his employment an unprincipled ruffian, with the reflexion that by so doing he was preventing the employment of the fellow against him.

On page 63 will be seen one of the simplest methods of sending a message in cipher. It is from the first printed edition of Selenus's *Cryptomenytices et Cryptographiae*, published at Luneburg in 1624. This book is in large part an exposition of the *Steganographia* of Johannis Trithemius, and of the *De Furtivis Literarum Notis* of J. B. Della Porta, earlier and rarer works. We read in Mr. Logan Pearsall Smith's *Life and Letters of Sir Henry Wotton* that ' Wotton vainly attempted to procure by means of bribery one rare manuscript for his patron Lord Zouche, the *Steganographia* of Trithemius, which was the earliest treatise on cipher writing, a dangerous book to possess, and therefore much prized.' Wotton was at this time travelling in the guise, and honestly so, of a well-born student not too well supplied with means. He seems to have studied hard, and, within the loose lines of what was then considered personal honour, he was using the hospitality accorded to men bearing good introductions, as a means to obtain state secrets for the good of his own government.

At this time, ' for young Englishmen of birth the main object of travel was almost always political. By observing different forms of government, by penetrating into the secrets of foreign Courts, they both prepared themselves for the service of the State, and procured information likely to be useful to the Government at home. They acted as informal spies on foreign princes, and on the English political exiles; and attempted to fathom the plots, and discover the warlike preparations, that were perpetually threatening England from abroad.' They travelled by licence, without which none could go abroad. 'They were restricted to certain countries, and to certain periods of time. Their movements were more or less determined by orders from home; and it is plain from Wotton's letters that he was acting under instructions in his various journeys. Francis and Anthony Bacon, Robert Cecil, Raleigh, Essex, and indeed almost all Wotton's contemporaries, eminent in politics, spent some years on the Continent in their youth.' [1]

[1] Smith, *Life and Letters of Sir Henry Wotton*, vol. i, p. 9.

A few years later Wotton was taken into the service of Essex; at this time, however, he was corresponding with Lord Zouche. He was killing two birds with one stone in thus improving his mind by travel and study, while laying the foundation for the future political advancement which came from useful service, as an intelligencer, to Essex's party. His letter to Zouche, which was in Pearsall Smith's mind when he wrote the paragraph just quoted, is dated at Vienna, January 15, 1591 (style of Rome). It runs, 'I have herein sent your Honour a supplication written by Johannes Sturmius, under the name and in the cause of Gifanius, to Maximilian the Emperor, very worthy the sight in a dangerous matter, of high prejudice, which I have added on the back side. If I had writ it in Latin, my letter intercepted might bring me into the like peril. Your Honour likewise receives included Johannes Trithemius his preface to his book of Steganography, which I have caused to be written out of a book in his Majesty's library. I came a little too late, or had lighted on the work itself, which yet I despair not to help your Honour unto; it is a notable piece of work for a statesman, but an instrument of great ill, if the hand be not good that holds it, as the author disputes in his preface; I promise nothing because your Honour shall, I hope, not find me false. If I chance to send it, you are wise (my Lord) to keep it secret: otherwise the bare having of the book is to call in our state many eyes about us to observe our actions, which is needless to tell you.'

He found later that neither bribes nor persuasion served to debauch the custodians of the book, and he failed to obtain a manuscript copy of it. It must be remembered that in those days the word *book* applied to manuscript as well as to printed works, and it is quite possible that the copy of Trithemius's work was itself in manuscript. Racetrack gamblers still make 'books' in manuscript.

Mr. Pearsall Smith's brilliant work is an admirable example of literary biography. He does not stray from his documents to let his imagination play around inferences, often so speciously used as 'internal evidence' by writers who cannot make available facts fit their theories. His work is at once both history and romance, and redeems from commonplace the trite saying that truth is stranger than fiction. His imagination leads his documents, but never outstrips them.

Those were days when letters were carried by posts or couriers over roads ill-protected, and often dangerous. Letters were also often carried and passed on from one merchant to another to their destination, much as they are to-day in the out-of-the-way parts of Mexico or Brazil. Despatches of an important political nature were, as now, generally in cipher, and were carried by special agents, or couriers. The times themselves were full of romance and uncertainty. As Pearsall Smith says, ' The definite and comparatively commonplace character of our news makes one of the most obvious differences between the life of modern days and that of former centuries. News has for us lost half the wonder and uncertainty it possessed for our ancestors, when echoes of great battles, and rumours of the deaths of Kings, travelled mysteriously over Europe; when travel-stained couriers galloped through the gates of old walled cities with, in the phrase repeated by Wotton, " lies in their mouths and truth in their packets "; and when to know the news of the world, to gain the confidence of the well-informed, to study the masked faces of statesmen, and to rob the posts, was a profession in itself.'

Until recent commercial times, when the invention of the telegraph has made it necessary to condense our message into a few words (a necessity not felt in the days of Elizabeth), few private persons were supposed to have need of secrecy or of a cipher in their daily life. We often use both to-day, though we are apt to forget it.

From the days of the Phœnicians to the times of which I write the art or trick of sending messages by cipher was devoted to the use of princes or their servants. The so-called Morse Alphabet itself has come to us almost without change from the biliteral cipher system described by Joan Baptista Porta, and adapted to his own use by Francis Bacon.[1]

The ' wig-wag ' system used in armies is of extreme antiquity, became embodied in a cipher method, and is to be seen in Porta's *De Furtivis Literarum Notis Vulgo. De Ziferis.* (Naples, 1563), p. 33. Our common telegraph code, in which one word is made to stand for another, or for whole sentences, is to be seen in its prototype in the same book, on pages 114 to 133. The principle of the Yale lock is very old, and was embodied in a cipher in former times. Indeed, a lock itself was made, and a good drawing of it may be seen on the last page of Selenus's *Cryptomenytices* (Luneburg, 1624).

[1] *Tractatus de Dignitate et Augmentis Scientiarum*, 1638, p. 166.

Secret commerce no longer disturbs a civilised government; but in those days it is easy to see how readily suspicion might fall on a plain citizen, who by the possession of cipher codes might be taken for a spy in the pay of an enemy of his government. In the trial of Somerset it was regarded as an aggravation of his offence that he was possessed of a private code in which were the names of James I and his family. High as his position was as the King's favourite, he was still deemed by Sir Francis Bacon, the King's Attorney-General at the time, to have had no proper use for a cipher in his relations with the unfortunate Overbury. To quote Bacon's words in his charge, 'And like Princes' confederates they had their ciphers and jargons.' In the draft of the same charge previously submitted to the King for comment, Bacon had said, 'I mean to show likewise what jargons there were and ciphers between them, which are great badges of secrets of estate, and used either by princes and their ministers of state, or by such as practise against princes.'

This restriction of the common use of ciphers to public servants and their agents naturally had for its corollary the tacit prohibition of their use for purposes which were not in the interest of the Government; and the man who so used them did so at his peril if found out. The feeling about them seems to have been much the same as it would be if a private in the ranks of the army were found in possession of a code during wartime. He would be haled before his superior officer and would be required to submit to a searching cross-examination.

We use the very words 'cipher ' and 'decipher,' to-day, with little thought of their connexion with the cultivated officials and their scholarly servants and protégés who have given us so large a part of the splendid literature of the period. Another familiar word is used in an interesting relation to this lost art — the word 'frame.' We frame a reply to a question. Francis Bacon uses this word in such a way that it betrays his intimacy with the official use of ciphers. He is writing to his friend Tobie Matthew, who had been allowed to return from his banishment, and was making himself useful at Court: ' If upon your repair to the Court (whereof I am right glad) you have any speech of the Marquis of me, I pray place the alphabet (as you can do it right well) in a frame to express my love faithfull and ardent towards him.' This letter was dated March 27, 1621 (1622). (Spedding.) Matthew had been banished because of his relapse into

Catholicism. Being the son of the Archbishop of York, and having powerful friends, he received light punishment. The 'Marquis' was Buckingham.

I shall have occasion to put the alphabet in a frame in my chapter on 'Method,' so the explanation may be deferred. It is, however, an interesting example of literary usage and exposes a knowledge of the art of ciphering both in Francis Bacon's and in Matthew's mind. Matthew must have been conversant with the art, for he spent many years of his life in dangerous correspondence with recusants at home and abroad. In this letter, the knowledge common to both of them permitted Bacon to use the phrase as a well-understood metaphor.

This is a proper place to give Francis Bacon's own words on ciphers, as he deals with them in his *Advancement of Learning* (Spedding, vol. iii, p. 402): 'For Ciphers, they are commonly in letters or alphabets, but may be in words. The kinds of Ciphers (besides the simple Ciphers with changes and intermixtures of nulls and non-significants) are many, according to the nature or rule of the infolding; Wheel-ciphers, Key-ciphers, Doubles, &c. But the virtues of them, whereby they are to be preferred, are three: that they be not laborious to write and read; that they be impossible to decipher; and, in some cases, that they be without suspicion. The highest degree whereof is to write *omnia per omnia;* which is undoubtedly possible, with a proportion quintuple at most of the writing infolding to the writing infolded, and no other restraint whatsoever. This art of Ciphering hath for relative an art of Deciphering; by supposition unprofitable; but as things are, of great use. For suppose that Ciphers were well managed, there be multitudes of them that exclude the decipherer. But in regard of the rawness and unskilfulness of the hands through which they pass, the greatest matters are many times carried in the weakest Ciphers.

'In the enumeration of these private and retired arts, it may be thought I seek to make a great muster-roll of sciences; naming them for shew and ostentation, and to little other purpose. But let those which are skilfull in them judge whether I bring them in only for appearance, or whether in that which I speak of them (though in few marks) there be not some seed of proficience. And this must be remembered, that as there be many of great account in their countries and provinces, which when they come up to the Seat of the

Estate are but of mean rank and scarcely regarded; so these arts being here placed with the principle and supreme sciences, seem petty things; yet to such as have chosen them to spend their studies in them, they seem great matters.'

It must not be forgotten that our use of cipher codes to-day aims fully as often to enable us to say much in few words as to ensure secrecy in the message. I do not know to what extent merchants used ciphers in the sixteenth and seventeenth centuries. They could not often have had reason for expressing much in few words, but it is conceivable that they may have had need to express themselves secretly. As a class they were important agents of communication, as I have shown on another page. We know to-day that most tradesmen and merchants have an office-cipher with which prices and terms are recorded upon some corner of the merchandise. These mercantile ciphers are usually simple transpositions of figures or letters, examples of which may be seen in any of the old cipher-books. We also know that some great merchants, the Fuggers for example, acted as government agents on occasion; and it is to be taken for granted that many men of power and influence used ciphers in their correspondence, and so used them without danger so long as the correspondence was in the interest of their government, or at any rate not opposed to the party in power.

In Spedding's edition of the *De Augmentis Scientiarum*, page 447, translated into English, Bacon gives a full example of the cipher alluded to as 'omnia per omnia' in *The Advancement of Learning*, which I have just quoted. He also speaks of writing as it is 'performed either by the common alphabet (which is used by everybody) or by a secret and private one, agreed upon by particular persons; which they call *ciphers*.' He then gives an account of ciphers very like that which he gives in *The Advancement of Learning*, adding a careful description of the 'omnia per omnia' which he claims as his own invention. It may be said that his invention fails in two important qualities; for though simple in method, it is both laborious to construct and even more laborious to decipher. Laborious, I say, but not difficult; as any one will find who cares to practise it. It is by the misuse of this particular cipher that some recent writers have brought upon this interesting enquiry the rather frightened ridicule of the academic world, and of the ill-informed who are often to be found in that company.

Bacon closes his remarks on ciphers in the *De Augmentis* with several sentences on the art of deciphering, one of which is of importance to us here. He says that deciphering is 'a thing requiring both labour and ingenuity, and dedicated, as the other [ciphering] likewise is, to the secrets of princes.'

CHAPTER III

ANONYMITY AND PSEUDONYMITY

THE custom of unmistakably declaring one's self the author of literary works has become general only in very recent times. One might well say 'has become possible'; for before the invention of printing it was impossible, by means of what we may properly designate as a non-structural signature, to identify one's self permanently as the author of a given work. When no structural signature [1] was employed, nothing but strong internal evidence, such as we have, for instance, in the *Vita Nuova*, or contemporary allusions, or other trustworthy external evidence, could establish beyond all reasonable doubt the authorship of a writing or of any analogous production. Thus an author who had not taken the pains to sign his works internally

---

[1] Weit öfter sind die Hss. dagegen mit ähnlichen Zusätzen versehen, die uns ausdrücklich über die Entstehungszeit, über Namen, Stand und Herkunft des Textschreibers und Auftraggebers, über Benutzung gewisser Vorlagen, Ausführung etwaiger Verbesserungen u. a. m. unterrichten, nur ist es notwendig die Form und Fassung solcher Notizen peinlichst zu prüfen, denn es ist mannigfach vorgekommen, dass mechanische Abschreiber auch derartige Angaben aus ihren Vorlagen ohne Weiteres herübergenommen haben. Häufig erfährt man aus den meistens mit 'Explicit liber' anhebenden Schluss-Bemerkungen überhaupt erst den Namen des Werkes und seines Verfassers ; daneben fehlt es daselbst wieder an allerlei dem Charakter des Mittelalters eigenthümlichen Künsteleien und Kunststückchen nicht : da werden z. B. die Namen des Verfassers, oder des Schreibers, in einer Art Geheimschrift gegeben, müssen dieselben vielleicht von rückwärts gelesen werden oder die einzelnen dazu gehörigen Silben sind in eine Mehrzahl von Versen verstreut ; dazu treten dann weitere, nicht immer vollendete poetische Ergüsse, Danksagungen für die Hülfe übernatürlicher, göttlicher Kräfte bei der Schreibarbeit, Fürbitten für eigenes und fremdes Seelenheil, selbstbewusste Äusserungen über das Gelingen der gestellten Aufgabe oder demütige Entschuldigungen wegen etwaigen Misslingens derselben, sowie andere beiläufige Äusserungen, bald humoristisch übersprudelnden Inhalts, bald die Grenze der Decenz hart streifend oder überschreitend. Weniger sorgfältig sind hiergegen die Anfänge der Werke und Hss. behandelt. Seit dem 13. Jahrhundert findet man zwar fast ausnahmlos am oberen Rande der 1. Seite die Worte : 'Adsit principio sancta Maria meo' oder eine ähnliche Anrufung, dagegen unterbleibt seit dem 11. Jahrhundert nur zu oft die mit 'Incipit liber' einzuleitende Nennung des Titels, besonders gern aber lässt man den Namen des Verfassers ausser Acht und es gilt denselben anderweit, vielleicht aus dem Wortlaute des 1. Kapitels oder der Einleitung herauszuklügeln ; bei einzelnen Gedichten ist man so glücklich gewesen, den Namen des Werkes und des Verfassers aus den Anfangsbuchstaben der ersten Verse des Prologes oder des diesem erst folgenden Textes zuzammenzustellen. — Gustav Gröber, *Grundriss der Romanischen Philologie*, vol. i, edition 1888, p. 193. *Die schriftlichen Quellen*, § 9. *Anfangs- und Schlussbemerkungen*, von Wilhelm Schum.

(structurally), in such a way that his authorship could never be denied or forgotten, was in the power of his scribes, and often *became* anonymous despite himself; for even if a mere signature at the beginning or end of a manuscript could be regarded as a sure guarantee of its authorship, no such non-structural or inorganic signature could be expected invariably to survive the carelessness of copyists, the indifference of readers, or other vicissitudes. It may be that acrostics and other such devices were employed at first chiefly in order to escape involuntary anonymity. By multiplying identical copies of a work, the printing-press immensely lessened the danger that the work should suffer this fate;[1] but by preserving a name on a title-page, or, in some rare instances, at the end of a book, the printing-press was not necessarily preserving the name by which the author was known in every-day life.

But another kind of anonymity requires consideration. I mean that anonymity in which an author half-unconsciously acquiesces, or which is his destiny because he desires the praise or the pay that his contemporaries, his hearers, may bestow upon him, and is indifferent both to lasting fame and to oblivion. Though this kind of anonymity is rare nowadays, it was not rare in the literature of the Middle Ages. A notable proportion of the most beautiful literary works of that period cannot even be ascribed: their authors were impersonal; we have no evidence that it even occurred to them to mark as their own

---

[1] In mediæval MSS. the real or supposed name, or pseudonym, of the author commonly appears plainly at the beginning of the MS., but is often written over each work contained in a codex. It may also follow the *explicit*, or be embedded in the body of the work : innumerable examples might be cited. Printed books continued these various usages for a while; but gradually the title-page came to be the place for the insertion of non-structural authors' signatures. This last tradition had got a good start as early as 1500, roughly speaking, and by 1550 was firmly established. This development accompanied the decline of the habit of jumbling together various works in one volume. In other words, the custom of putting an author's name on the title-page, and there only, was due, in part at least, to the growth of the habit of printing each work by itself (specialisation).

As late as 1598 we have an example of the habit, so deceptive to the unwary historian, of printing several anonymous books under separate title-pages and binding them in one volume. The example which I have in mind is that of Barnfield's poems, to which I have alluded in *Part II*. Here we have *The Encomion of Lady Pecunia*, with a title-page containing the name of Richard Barnfield, followed by three books, each of which has a separate but anonymous title-page. The printer has placed (naturally enough) in the front of the group that volume which contained an author's name on its title-page. He may have believed that all four books were written by the same author. The arrangement of the fourth book may not have been his, but that of some patron who had the book thus printed. Who knows? And who knows that some of the poems in the fourth book are not Barnfield's?

what their minds had created. In this regard they do not differ from the painters, the architects, and other artists of their time.[1]

Anonymity is therefore either sought or not sought. With the cases in which it is not sought, in which it is often the natural result of an author's method, or of his indifference, we have dealt with extreme brevity; for it is with the cases in which anonymity is sought[2] that we are primarily concerned. If an author seeks anonymity, he does so to conceal his identity. His reason for so doing may be perfectly simple, or he may be actuated by a variety of motives, which we may, or may not, be able to ascertain. The desire to maintain a prestige which some kinds of writing might imperil or destroy, fear of official or private vengeance, a willingness to rest content with the praise of a few, aversion to becoming a 'familiar figure,' in other words, a dread of publicity, or the wish to enjoy fame unmolested, or (and this is a wholly different motive) the ambition to achieve some end which the open avowal of one's authorship would thwart, or finally, sheer delight in mystifying the public,— these are some of the many motives which in all times, and in every European country where literature has thriven, have led men to avail themselves of anonymity, i. e. of the privileges which anonymity affords. From no earlier than 1500 to no later than 1800 the number of anonymous writers is legion, and of these many could be shown to have employed deliberately the veil of anonymity.[3]

When the anonymous writer is bold enough to risk discovery, or wishes, on the contrary, to arouse no suspicion, or to send his pursuers[4] off on a false scent, he will often use a pseudonym. A pseudonym is merely a way of masking anonymity; it is anonymity in

[1] Of this type of anonymous writers something will be said later.

[2] All the important phases of anonymity are illustrated by innumerable examples in the special catalogues of anonymous works, such as the *Dictionnaire des ouvrages anonymes*, by Ant. Alex. Barbier, first published in 1825, and Halkett and Laing's *Dictionary of the Anonymous and Pseudonymous Literature of Great Britain;* it would be difficult to name any thoroughly scientific treatise on anonymity.

[3] 'On ne peut nier que de bons écrivains n'aient dédaigné de mettre leurs noms aux fruits de leurs veilles, et des savans distingués, que nous avons encore le bonheur de posséder, ont fait paraître presque tous leurs ouvrages sous le voile de l'anonyme; aussi, il me serait facile de prouver que dans toute bibliothèque composée d'ouvrages utiles il en existe un tiers sans indications d'auteurs, traducteurs ou éditeurs.' Barbier, in the 'Discours préliminaire' of his *Dictionnaire;* see the edition of 1882, vol. i, p. xxx. See also an excellent book *The Secrets of Our National Literature*, by William Prideaux Courtney. London, Constable & Co. Ltd., 1908.

[4] Among whom will be some biographers, though the eluding of biographers is usually incidental, and not a part of the anonymous writer's plan.

disguise, a trap for unwary biographers. For the anonymous writer himself it is a means, not always successful, of laying perpetual claim to the authorship of a given work. If he wishes to make assurance doubly sure, he may use not only the pseudonym, which he ordinarily causes to be put on the title-page, but he may contrive by the use of an acrostic, or some other device, to sign his work so securely that his signature can be removed or destroyed only by garbling his text. This may easily happen when new editions are printed, particularly when they are printed without the author's consent, or after his death. If, therefore, a scholar suspects any work to contain a hidden, i. e. a structural or organic signature, he should invariably search for it in the oldest editions; furthermore, he should try to ascertain whether it occurs in more than one edition; any change of typography made without the author's consent would be likely to destroy it. If it is still there, even though a slight change in typography, in a new edition, would have destroyed it, we have in this very fact the most convincing evidence that the author, or some one acting under his instructions, or knowing his will, so re-arranged the typography that the signature should remain undisturbed. If we discover a hidden signature, it behooves us to ascertain whether it occurs in all the editions printed before the death of the man whose name it may represent. A hidden signature is a structural signature; the passage in which it occurs is not unlike the corner-stone of a building, in which from time immemorial it has been customary for the architect to deposit his name, thus establishing for ever his claim to have been the man in whose brain the building was conceived. There is this essential difference, that the hidden signature of the author is an organic part of his work as he made it, whatever wrong may have been done him by scribes or printers, in new copies or in later editions.

As has been said, we may find both a hidden signature and another signature (ordinarily on the title-page), in one and the same book. Of these the hidden signature may have been known only to the author, or, at most, to the few whom he saw fit to trust. It may be revealed only when the motive for concealing it no longer exists; or it may never be revealed by the one, or by the few, to whom it was originally known; in which case only time and chance, or the patience of some one who suspects its existence, can bring it to light. One could enumerate various other fortunes which a hidden signature might incur. I cite examples later on to illustrate such cases. If, now, a name upon a title-page has long been regarded as the genuine, legal name of an author, the discovery of the hidden yet unmistakable signature of a different name in the same work must arouse the gravest suspicions as to the name on the title-page, particularly when nothing is positively known of any person for whom the name on the title-page might stand. If the two signatures are essentially different, of which would both the first impulse and mature reflexion cause us to say, ' *This* is a pseudonym, *this* is the true name of the author ' ? If a faith that we have long shared with other men still bids us affirm that the name on the title-page was the name of the author, and of his father before him, how shall we account for that other name, which stares us in the face, which will remain there for ever, as its bearer or deviser meant that it should, requiring a rational explanation ? What motive shall we attribute to an author who inserts, not in a manuscript, but in a printed book, the name of another man, still living, it may be, and perhaps powerful, when the act was done ? Did he do so, possibly, to pay a graceful tribute in return for some favour ? Or may he have wished, perhaps, to commemorate a kindred spirit, a boon companion, a friend who had shared in his intellectual life ? Or may it be that the two were really one ? Or can we suppose that the hidden signature, involving a change of typography and of text, was inserted without his leave ? However we would answer these questions, no upright man of good intelligence would identify what he could possibly suspect of being a pseudonym with the undeniable name of a known or real person, either in serious speech, or in a Life; and if a biographer persisted in identifying a possible pseudonym with the name of some person whom no trustworthy document unmistakably records as an author, his capacity as a historian might eventually be doubted and his authority as a writer of lives might be discredited.[1] No scientific mind will assume a sus-

---

[1] ' The Character of a believing Christian in paradoxes and seeming contradictions ' was inserted in 1648 in Bacon's *Remains*. Spedding doubted its origin, for various reasons, and assumed that it had been included in the *Remains* because (as he mistakenly assumed) it had appeared as a pamphlet in 1643 with Bacon's name on the title-page. I am interested in calling the reader's attention to Spedding's attitude towards a title-page in its aspect as evidence. He says, ' So far as I know, if the publisher of the edition of 1643 had not put Bacon's name upon the title-page, there would have been no reason at all for thinking that he had anything to do with it ; and as it is, the reason is so slight, that if the probabilities were otherwise balanced, it would hardly turn the scale. The name on the title-page of such a publication is enough to suggest and justify the enquiry *whether* there be any evidence, internal or

pected signature to be genuine, and not a pseudonym, until all the known evidences have been scrupulously examined and found to support such a contention beyond all reasonable doubt.

The slight evidential value accorded to title-pages by Spedding under some conditions has a warrant from Bacon's own words in his treatise *Of the Advancement of Learning* (Spedding, vol. iii, p. 281), where he says: 'Neither is the moral [customary] dedication of books and writings, as to patrons, to be commended: for that books (such as are worthy the name of books) ought to have no patrons but truth and reason; and the ancient custom was to dedicate them only to private and equal friends, or to entitle the books with their names; or if to kings and great persons, it was to some such as the argument of the book was fit and proper for. But these and the like courses may deserve rather reprehension than defence.' Bacon nevertheless dedicated his acknowledged works to King, patron, or friend; and the reader may be left to determine whether he entitled some of his books with other men's names.

I am in doubt as to the meaning to be given to Bacon's words, 'the ancient custom.' It is possible that he used it in the same sense as he used the phrase 'mine ancient friend.' He may refer to the ages which preceded his own by a few centuries, or again he may refer to the habits of Greek and Roman writers. I can cite no instance of such practice in the literature of the Greeks or the Romans; though Terence had to answer charges that he had taken a whole passage from Plautus's *Commorientes*, hashed up Greek plays in order to write his own, and, what concerns us here, that he had received assistance from great men who were constantly writing with him, and that he relied for success, not upon his own parts, but on the genius of his friends. (See *The Comedies of Publius Terentius Afer*, Latin and English, translated and privately printed for The Roman Society, 1900; 2 vols. 'The Adelphi,' Prologus, vv. 6–21; and 'Heauton Timoroumenos,' Prologus, vv. 14–26.)

It is also possible that 'our English Terence' was subjected to similar charges, though it is not certain that he was.

I have alluded to acrostics which are *known*, and which can be *seen* in many books of Shakespeare's day, and I hope that this book

external, to confirm the statement; but can scarcely be taken for evidence in itself, even in the absence of evidence the other way.' Lord Bacon's *Works*, vol. xiv, p. 289.

will be a spur to some patient scholar to reveal to us some acrostics which may now lie hidden in a simple transliteration. Tables for his guidance can be seen in the works of Trithemius, Della Porta, Selenus, Vigenère, and later writers.

Acrostics which are as yet *unknown*, because *unseen*, may contain information valuable alike to the student of literature and to the student of history. I infer that a man would be likely to hide (or to transliterate) matter which he wished to use merely as a mark of identification, or for the information of a few friends. Such matter is not necessarily to be found in verse alone. It is as easy to insert an acrostic or a structural signature in prose as in verse. I shall show several methods which were in use, both in verse and in prose.

It is a common and erroneous impression that an acrostic must of necessity interfere with the flow of composition. I shall show specimens which do interfere, and some which do not. The latter are the easiest of all kinds to make, and the most difficult to discover by one who has had no hint of their existence.

It must not be forgotten that, although acrostics can be produced by intention, and by exact methods which I shall exhibit, the same acrostics *may* be the result of chance. It will remain for the reader to determine how often the same rare accidents may be expected to recur with a remarkably definite frequency in the same book, and in corresponding places in that book. It is as if a log of wood were found in the way of an express train two miles out of Boston. This might be regarded as an accident. But a similar log found in a corresponding place two miles out of every important station between Boston and New York would, by many observers, be regarded as evidence of intention.

It is not likely that acrostics of the kind to which we shall ultimately confine our attention were made for any other purpose than that of identification, for in their essence such acrostics are private marks, of no significance to anybody whose notice they escape. They convey, and apparently are intended to convey, no message, unless the maker imparted a knowledge of his method to a few persons. It is possible that Bacon had taken John Davies of Hereford, for instance, into his confidence. Davies was the man to whom Bacon wrote in 1603, alluding to himself as a *concealed poet*. (Spedding, vol. iv, p. 65.) It is also possible that Thomas Freeman was in the secret when, in 1614, he printed an enigmatical sonnet to Shakespeare, beginning with these lines : —

> ' Shakespeare, that nimble Mercury thy brain
> Lulls many hundred Argus-eyes asleep.'

We have not hitherto regarded the actor or the playwright as a man who had anything to hide from the Argus-eyes of his contemporaries. Neither have his plays, nor his poems, lulled our Argus-eyes asleep. (I have slept at a performance of one of his plays, but the *play* was not the cause.) If Bacon, writing under the pseudonym Shakespeare or Shake-speare, with or without the consent, or to or not to the profit of the actor or some other William Shakespeare, purposely allowed the public to be confused thereby, then both these quotations become illuminating. But we have no direct evidence that he did so.

After a careful examination of the several attempts to saddle the plays of Shakespeare with infolded writings by means of Bacon's biliteral cipher and by word-ciphers, I found, as Mr. W. W. Greg found, that they will not stand a test of the simple method by the use of which they are said to be decipherable. I realised also that, if the author of the plays had desired anonymity, he would not have used methods which would have been as plain as daylight to many of his contemporaries familiar with the arts of the cipherer and the decipherer. Had he wished to put his name to his work so that it should escape detection, the only way to do so was by using a method which could be disclosed only by a guess, and which the author could say truthfully *might* be the result of chance. Such a method is that of writing a *hidden* acrostic in a series of corresponding places, like the beginning and ending of a play, poem, or block of prose. Such a method would be a plain variant of the simple acrostic which can be seen on page 55, and is an equally plain variant of the well-known cipher method to be seen on page 63. I have tested the truth of my supposition, with the results given in this book.

Let me illustrate what I mean by a hidden acrostic. Instead of making your acrostic so that it can be read down the initials of the first words of all the lines of a verse, as on page 55, let it be made so that the end letters only are visible, and let the interior letters of the acrostic run as they will through the verse. For instance, if you wish to write ' Frauncis Bacon' into a piece of prose or verse, you see to it that the initial letter of the first word of the first line is an F, and that the corresponding letter at the bottom of the page is an N. Then look over your composition and make sure that if after F you take the next initial R, and if after R you take the next initial A, and so on, reading the first line to the one hand and the next line to the other (in the manner of the primitive Greeks), the last letter of the name will fall on the N which you have placed at the end of your acrostic. (See examples on pp. 59 and 65.) Thus you will have allowed your name to wander where it will through the composition, as it were on a string, continuously, beginning and ending only in definite spots. This method is described in detail in my chapter on method; and it might account for another line in the sonnet by Freeman, quoted above: —

'Besides in plays thy wit winds like Meander.'

We have in these days so high a regard for the art of expression in writing, that the man who pursues it as a means of earning his living is honoured by his fellows, strangely enough, as a person of unusual intelligence. In antithesis, the Philosopher and the Poet, whose perfect work demands the highest intelligence, have been for centuries and are still deemed unlikely to be good judges of a simple business transaction. Many exceptions to this statement will spring to the mind of the reader, but in the main it will stand the test of reflexion.

In the days of Shakespeare, the scholar and the student were honoured in much the same way, but they made little money by the sale of their work because the trade of publishing was in its infancy. Poor students and scholars looked for a maintenance in the protection and rewards to be obtained from nobles and public men who were scholars themselves, or who liked to play the patron to merit in the arts and sciences.

A poet stood on another footing. If he chose to seek all men's suffrage, he had to face the fact that the great mass of printed verse, and indeed most verse that the philistine public knew anything about, was in the form of the popular song, or the ballad, often ribald, generally doggerel, and associated in the popular mind with the streets and alehouses. Poetry itself was regarded as a toy or amusement, a pastime for idle hours. It is easy to imagine the reason for this when we remember that skill in ditty-making, rhyming, and playing on stringed instruments, has been so common that at one time it was the practice for some barbers to keep musical instruments hanging in their shops, that their customers might amuse themselves while waiting their turn.

Those were days when most serious men gave much thought to religion and the problems which were forced upon them by the active political and religious intrigues of the Catholic and other sects. Life was almost hopelessly complicated by warring dogmas among the Protestants. Civil and religious government were so closely held in the same hands that religious opinion hostile to dogmas held by the Government was accounted treasonable. It is not difficult to imagine that, in such an atmosphere, the unimaginative and the godly Philistine in high office united in regarding poetry as the same class of people to-day regard a game of cards, or a visit to the theatre. Indeed, the suspicion that the theatre and cards are tools of the Devil is our direct inheritance from the active, self-searching, and litigious religious spirit of those days. It is still latent in the minds of many people who have not enjoyed a liberal education. The Philistine still holds in slight esteem all accomplishments whose bearing on our daily bread seems remote.

Among gentlemen in those days the flavour of the manuscript was not hurriedly exchanged for the smell of printer's ink. With many it argued a lack of dignity to hurry into print.[1] Any student can recall a score of instances where a writer allowed his work to remain in manuscript until after his death. Bacon voiced the feeling[2] when

[1] '"T is ridiculous for a Lord to Print Verses, 't is well enough to make them to please himself, but to make them publick, is foolish. If a man in his private Chamber twirls his Bandstrings, or plays with a Rush to please himself, 't is well enough, but if he should go into Fleetstreet, and sit upon a Stall, and twirl a Bandstring, or play with a Rush, then all the Boys in the Street would laugh at him.' (John Selden, *Table Talk*, reported by R. Milward. Arber's edition.) Selden was Bacon's junior by twenty-four years, but in what Tenison calls 'a transcript out of the Lord Bacon's last will, relating especially to his writings,' he [Tenison] gives the following passage : 'But towards that durable part of memory which consisteth in my writings, I require my servant, Henry Percy, to deliver to my brother Constable all my manuscript-compositions, and the fragments also of such as are not finished ; to the end that, if any of them be fit to be published, he may accordingly dispose of them. And herein I desire him to take the advice of Mr. Selden, and Mr. Herbert, of the Inner Temple, and to publish or suppress what shall be thought fit.' (*Baconiana*, p. 203. See Spedding, vol. xiv, p. 540.) Here we may see the type of man whose judgement of the world was respected by Bacon towards the close of his life. The passage is, however, not found in Bacon's will as it was published in Blackbourne's edition of Bacon's *Works*, vol. ii, p, 559 (Spedding).

[2] Letter to Lancelot Andrewes, Lord Bishop of Winchester, written in the summer of 1622. (Spedding, vol. xiv, pp. 370-71.)

he said that publication of a man's writings should take place after death, so that the immortal part of him should not make an untimely appearance. He published only three works over his name before his sixtieth year; [1] after that time he hurried forward the preparation of others. Even then years passed over his grave before some of his works were printed. A noble like Sir Philip Sidney might prefer to allow his work to pass around among his friends in manuscript, and to remain unprinted until years after his death. Fulke Greville's Life of Sir Philip was not printed until twenty-four years after its author's death. These are instances merely. The cultivated world was small then, and a work was often deemed to have fulfilled its author's purpose if his friends saw it only in manuscript. It was no uncommon thing for a man of means or position to keep scholarly servants employed in copying interesting manuscripts which passed through his hands in this way. Francis Bacon kept such men,[2] as is shown by his letters to his brother.

To men like Sidney or Bacon the opinion of the world was the opinion of the learned and of the *wits*. Their livelihood was assured in other ways, and they did not, so far as I know, try to make money by huckstering their scholarship or art directly over the counter as we do. I suspect that at that time scorn would have been a light word to express their feelings for such a method of money-making. Hedge-poets, and scribblers for the theatres, hired pamphleteers, the riff-raff of the pen and ink-pot, might write for a pittance, but they were another class.

In matters of wit or scholarship men in high place cared little for the opinion of the plain people. What they cared for was the opinion of the small group of their cultivated fellows and of the literati who came up through the universities of Oxford and Cambridge, and the Inns of Court. Among themselves they were careful of the reputation for authorship, as the habit of anonymity, and of writing under a mask, testifies. The writings of highly-placed men or men whose

---

[1] A noteworthy fact in view of the statement made by James Duport, of Trinity College, that Bacon 'showered the age with frequent volumes'; 'Imbuit et crebris saecla voluminibus.' (*Manes Verulamiani*: published by Wm. Rawley in 1626. Translated by E. K. Rand, and privately printed in 1903.) It is also worth remembering that Sir Frauncis Bacon, Knight, is included by Stowe and Howes (Edition 1614–15, p. 811) among 'Our moderne, and present excellent Poets which worthley florish in their owne workes, and all of them in my owne knowledge liued togeather in this Queenes raigne' [Elizabeth's].

[2] As one instance in proof, read Francis Bacon's letter to Anthony Bacon. (Spedding, vol. viii, p. 347.)

Our moderne, and present excellent Poets
10 which worthely florish in their owne workes,
and all of them in my owne knowledge lived
togeather in this Queéne's raigne, according
to their priorities as neére as I could, I have
orderly set downe (viz) George Gascoigne
Esquire, Thomas Church-yard Esquire, sir
Edward Dyer knight, Edmond Spencer Esquire, sir Philip Sidney Knight, Sir Iohn
Harrington knight, Sir Thomas Challoner
knight, Sir Frauncis Bacon knight, & Sir
20 Iohn Davie knight, Master Iohn Lillie gentleman, Master George Chapman gentleman
M. W. Warner gentleman, M. Willi. Shakespeare gentleman, Samuell Daniell Esquire,
Michaell Draiton Esquire, of the bath, M.
Christopher Marlo gen. M. Beniamine Iohnsō
gēleman, Iohn Marston Esqnier, M. Abraham
Frauncis gen. master Frauncis Meers gentle.
master Iosua Siluester gentle. master Thomas
Deckers gentleman, M. Iohn Flecher gentle.
30 M. Iohn Webster gentleman, M. Thomas
Heywood gentlemen, M. Thomas Middelton
gentleman, M. George Withers.
Thefe following were Latine Poets.
Master Gualter Hadon gentleman, Master
Nicholas Carr gentleman, M. Christopher Ot-
land gentle. Mathew Gwynn doctor of Phisicke
Thomas Lodge doctor of phisike, M. Tho.
Watson gentle. Thomas Campion doctor of
Phisicke, Richard Lateware doctor of diuinitie
40 M. Brunswerd gentleman, Master doctor Har-
uie, and master Willey gentleman.

Facsimile of part of page 811 in "*The Annales, or General Chronicle of England,*
begun first by maister John Stow, and after him continued and augmented with mat-
ters forreyne, and domestique, auncient and moderne, vnto the ende of this present yeere
1614 by Edmond Howes; gentleman." London. 1615.

birth warranted an aspiration to high place were so many hostages to fortune when printed, but were protected by courtesy while in manuscript, and passing among friends or acquaintance.

Even a man reputed to have been so humble in origin as Edmund Spenser is supposed to have written under a mask. Instance *The Shepherd's Calendar*, among the compositions of his first period, which was published anonymously, 1579–1580. Ostensibly it was not published by Spenser himself, though it was inscribed to Philip Sidney in a copy of verses signed with the masking name 'Immerito,' by most scholars supposed to be Spenser's, because the poem to which it was affixed ultimately appeared in a volume printed over Spenser's name. The reason for this anonymity (so R. W. Church surmises) was that the avowed responsibility for the poem might have been inconvenient for a young man pushing his fortune among the cross-currents of Elizabeth's Court. Mr. Church also says ('Spenser,' E.M.L. Series, p. 86) : 'A poet at this time still had to justify his employment by presenting himself in the character of a professed teacher of morality, with a purpose as definite and formal, though with a different method, as the preacher in the pulpit. Even with this profession he had to encounter many prejudices, and men of gravity and wisdom shook their heads at what they thought his idle trifling. But if he wished to be counted respectable and to separate himself from the crowd of foolish or licentious rhymers, he must intend distinctly, not merely to interest, but to instruct, by his new and deep conceits.'

Edmund Spenser and a man like Sidney were, however, at a great social distance from each other, and though Spenser might, perhaps, write anonymously to avoid shaking the confidence of those in authority, to whom he looked for advancement, Sidney would be as likely to pass his writings around among his friends without his name to them, from a feeling that among his social equals there was a lack of dignity in appearing concerned over authorship. Spenser might have been governed by both reasons. He is supposed to have been the son of a free journeyman cloth-worker of London.[1] Some have tried to fit him with a pedigree, but it hangs loosely from his shoulders. He had been a 'poor-scholar' both at school and at the University. In one important respect his case was like that of Francis Bacon: he was dependent on the favour of men in high place for a

[1] *Dictionary of National Biography.*

lucrative appointment, and such a man would then, as now, be likely to trim his sails to the prevailing wind, which at that time blew, from some quarters, a scorching blast on 'idle toys.' He would be likely to avoid, or hide,[1] any action that would be subject to 'interpreta- tion' by those on whom he depended — to use a phrase of Francis Bacon's when dealing with his own view of the problem in the dedication of the first edition of his *Essays* to his brother Anthony.

These *Essays* are a case in point. Their author found that a manu- script copy of them (so he leads us to infer) had fallen into the hands of a printer or bookseller, and that they were about to be published to the world at large without his permission. I reproduce this dedi- cation in facsimile because it will be of interest later.

The manifest inference to be drawn from this dedication is that these three little books (bound in one volume) had been circulating anonymously in copies, or in the original, among friends or acquaint- ances, in manuscript, as they had passed long ago from his pen, and had at last by some accident or breach of confidence come to the hands of the tradesman. We also have here the statement that Francis Bacon approved of anonymity in works ' of some nature,' and that he had reluctantly put his name to these.

Astonishment is often expressed that men of those days should wish their work to circulate anonymously. I have given some reasons for it, and I shall present others later. It is not difficult to imagine one good reason, when the writer of ' idle toys ' happened to be a man of high birth, poor for his station, with great philan- thropic aims, and with his way to make in the world of statecraft, the law, or arms, — almost the only lucrative professions which a

[1] My own experience affords an apt illustration here. It has its amusing as well as its serious aspect. My examination of the documents on which the biographies of Shakespeare are founded led me to follow the example of Mr. W. W. Greg, by making a careful scrutiny of the work of certain ingenious writers who have claimed to discover many curious cipher- writings by Bacon. The result of my scrutiny showed me that Mr. Greg's judgement was well founded. I was not satisfied, however, that I had exhausted the possible uses to which ciphers might have been put by a writer of Elizabethan times. My curiosity grew apace when my enquiries among professional literary friends drew from one of them the serious threat that my acquaintance would be dropped if I investigated the subject further; and from another the well-meant advice that if I would consult my best interests I should avoid a sub- ject connected in the professional mind with the work of charlatans; and from still another, that ' that is a matter on which the scholarly world has made up its mind.' My first question had been answered by my academic friends — as to Bacon's possible reason for anonymity. At the outset I had found that if I pursued a despised study my professional career might be endangered.

To M. Anthony Bacon
his deare Brother.

Louing and beloued Brother, I doe nowe like some that haue an Orcharde ill neighbored, that gather their fruit before it is ripe, to preuent stealing. These fragments of my conceites were going to print, To labour the staie of them had bin troublesome, and subiect to interpretation; to let them passe had beene to aduenture the wrong they mought receiue

A 3

Essayes.

Religious Meditations.

Places of perswasion and disswasion.

Seene and allowed.

AT LONDON,
Printed for Humfrey Hooper, and are to be sold at the blacke Beare in Chauncery Lane.
1597.

The Epistle

receiue by vntrue Coppies, or by some garnishment, which it mought please any that should set them forth to bestow vpon them. Therefore I helde it best discretion to publish them my selfe as they passed long agoe from my pen, without any further disgrace, then the weaknesse of the Author. And as I did euer hold, there mought be as great a vanitie in retiring and withdrawing mens conceites (except they bee of some nature) from the world, as in obtruding them : So in these particulars I haue played my selfe the Inquisitor, and find nothing to my vnderstanding in them contrarie or infectious to the state of Religion, or manners, but rather (as I suppose) medicinable. Only I disliked now to put them out because they will bee like the late new halfe-pence, which though the Siluer were good, yet the peeces were small.

Dedicatorie.

small. But since they would not stay with their Master, but would needes trauaile abroade, I haue preferred them to you that are next my selfe, Dedicating them, such as they are, to our loue, in the depth whereof (I assure you) I sometimes with your infirmities translated vppon my selfe, that her Maiestie mought naue the seruice of so actiue and able a mind, & I mought be with excuse confined to these contemplations & Studies for which I am fittest, so commend I you to the preseruation of the diuine Maiestie. From my Chamber at Graies Inne this 30. of Ianuarie. 1 5 9 7.

Your entire Louing brother.

Fran. Bacon.

young aristocrat could enter without loss of caste. I shall fortify my own imagination on this point with the good reasons given by a contemporary of Shakespeare, the author of *The Arte of English Poesie*.

This author was a courtier, on easy terms of speech with Elizabeth, as is shown by several sly remarks in his book, which are often addressed to her personally. As the writer of the dedication states, it seems 'by many express passages in the same at large, that it was by the Author intended to our Sovereign Lady the Queen, and for her recreation and service chiefly devised.' The writer of this dedication, by the way, bears the same initials as Richard Field, the printer of the book. We are led to suppose that it was this printer who wrote the dedication. In it he speaks of the manuscript as 'coming to my hands, with his bare title without any author's name or any other ordinary address,' — that is to say, anonymously. On reading this preface, which is given in facsimile on page 99, I at once suspected its authorship, for no printer in that day would have dared to print a manuscript which had, on its face, the evidence of having come from the privacy of Queen Elizabeth herself. Of this, later. At present, let us return to the subject of anonymity.

The supposedly unknown author of this book raises the Poet above all other artificers, scientific or mechanical, and indeed places his creations of the mind next in honour after those of God's divine imagination. He recites in a few pithy chapters how poets were the first priests, the first prophets, the first legislators and politicians in the world; how they were the first philosophers, astronomers, historiographers, orators, and musicians. He asks, 'If the art of poesie be but a skill appertaining to utterance, why may not the same be with us as with them [the Greeks and Latins], our language being no less copious, pithie, and significative than theirs, our conceipts the same, and our wits no less apt to devise and imitate than theirs were?' No writer before or since has placed the art of the poet on a higher plane. A man must be a poet to reveal the mysteries of God.

So much for the glory of the art. We will now hear him tell us how poets had become contemptible in the time of Elizabeth, and for what causes; and why many noblemen about the Court sought anonymity rather than fame. 'For the respects aforesaid in all former ages and in the most civil countries and common wealths, good Poets and Poesie were highly esteemed and much favoured of the greatest Princes.' Here he enumerates many notable instances and the rewards and dignities which the princes gave. 'Nor this reputation was given them in ancient times altogether in respect that Poesie was a delicate art, and the poets themselves cunning Prince pleasers, but for that also they were thought for their universal knowledge to be very sufficient men for the greatest charges in their common wealths, were it for counsel or for conduct, whereby no man need to doubt but that both skills may very well concur and be most excellent in one person.' Here again he gives several instances of poets who were at the same time great administrators, soldiers, and lawgivers. 'So as the Poets seemed to have skill not only in the subtleties of their art, but also to be meet for all manner of functions civil and martial, even as they found favour of the times they lived in, insomuch as their credit and estimation generally was not small. But in these days (although some learned princes may take delight in them) yet universally it is not so. For as well Poets as Poesie are despised, and the name become, of honourable infamous, subject to scorn and derision, and rather a reproach than a praise to any that useth it: for commonly whoso is studious in the Art or shows himself excellent in it, they call him in disdain a *Phantastical:* and a lightheaded or phantastical man (by conversion) they call a Poet. And this proceeds through the barbarous ignorance of the time, and pride of many Gentlemen, and others, whose gross heads not being brought up or acquainted with any excellent Art, nor able to contrive, or in any manner conceive any matter of subtlety in any business or science, they do deride and scorn it in all others as superfluous knowledges and vain sciences, and whatsoever device be of rare invention they term it *phantastical*, construing it to the worst side: and among men such as be modest and grave, and of little conversation, nor delighted in the busy life and vain ridiculous actions of the popular, they call him in scorn a *Philosopher* or *Poet*, as much to say as a phantastical man, very injuriously (God wot) and to the manifestation of their own ignorance, not making difference betwixt terms. For as the evil and vicious disposition of the brain hinders the sound judgement and discourse of man with busy and disordered phantasies, for which cause the Greeks call him φαντασικός, so is that part being well affected, not only nothing disorderly or confused with any monstrous imaginations or conceits, but very formal, and in his much multiformity *uniform*, that is well proportioned, and so passing clear, that by it as by a glass or mirror, are represented unto the soul all manner of beautiful visions, whereby the inventive part of the mind is so much holpen, as without it no man could devise any new or rare thing: and where it is not excellent in his kind, there could be no politic Captain nor any witty enginer or cunning artificer, nor yet any law maker or counsellor of deep discourse. . . .

' And this phantasy may be resembled to a glass as hath been said, whereof there be many tempers and manner of makings, as the *perspectives* do acknowledge, for some be false glasses and show things otherwise than they be in deed, and others right as they be in deed, neither fairer nor fouler, nor greater nor smaller. There be again of these glasses that show things exceeding fair and comely, others that show figures very monstrous and illfavoured. Even so is the phantastical part of man (if it be not disordered) a representer of the best, most comely and beautiful images or appearances of things to the soul and according to their very truth. If otherwise, then doth it breed Chimæras and monsters in man's imaginations, and not only in his imaginations, but also in all his ordinary actions and life which ensues. Wherefore such persons as be illuminated with the brightest irradiations of knowledge and of the verity and due proportion of things, they are called by the learned men not *phantastici* but *euphantasiote*, and of this sort of phantasy are all good Poets, notable Captains stratagematique, all cunning artificers and enginers, all Legislators, Politicians and Counsellors of estate, in whose exercises the inventive part is most employed and is to the sound and true judgement of man most needful. This diversity in the terms perchance every man hath not noted, and thus much be said in the Poet's honour, to the end no noble and generous mind be discomforted in the study thereof, the rather for that worthy and honourable memorial of that noble woman twice French Queen, Lady *Anne* of Britaine, wife first to King *Charles* the VIII, and after to *Lewis* the XII, who passing one day from her lodging towards the king's side, saw in a gallery *Master Allaine Chartier* the king's Secretary, an excellent maker or Poet leaning on a table's end asleep, and stooped down to kiss him, saying thus in all their hearings, " we may not of Princely courtesy pass by and not honour with our kiss the mouth from whence so many sweet ditties and golden poems have issued." But methinks at these words I hear some smilingly say, "I would be loath to lack living of my own till the Prince gave me a manor of new elm for my rhyming."[1] And another to say, "I have read that the Lady *Cynthia* came once down out of her sky to kiss the fair young lad *Endymion* as he lay asleep: and many noble Queens that have bestowed kisses upon their Princes paramours, but never upon any Poets." The third methinks shruggingly saith, "I kept not to sit sleeping with my Poesy till a Queen came and kissed me." But what of all this? Princes may give a good Poet such convenient countenance and also benefit as are due to an excellent artificer, though they neither kiss nor coax them, and the discreet Poet looks for no such extraordinary favours, and as well doth he honour by his pen the just, liberal, or magnanimous Prince, as the valiant, amiable or beautiful, though they be every one of them the good gifts of God.

'So it seems not altogether the scorn and ordinary disgrace offered unto Poets at these days is cause why very few Gentlemen do delight in the Art, but for that liberality is come to fail in Princes, who for their largesse were wont to be accounted the only patrons of learning, and first founders of all excellent artificers. Besides it is not perceived that Princes themselves do take any pleasure in this science, by whose example the subject is commonly led, and allured to all delights and exercises be they good or bad, according to the grave saying of the historian, "*Rex multitudinem religione implevit, quae semper regenti similis est*"; And peradventure in this iron and malicious age of ours, Princes are less delighted in it, being over earnestly bent and affected to the affairs of Empire and ambition, whereby they are, as it were, enforced to endeavour themselves to arms and practices of hostility, or to entend to the right pollicing of their states, and have not one hour to bestow upon any other civil or delectable Art of natural or moral doctrine: nor scarce any leisure to think one good thought in perfect and godly contemplation, whereby their troubled minds might be moderated and brought into tranquillity. So as, it is hard to find in these days of noblemen or gentlemen any good *Mathematician*, or excellent *Musician*, or notable *Philosopher*, or else a cunning Poet: because we find few great Princes

[1] The author, on a preceding page, had alluded to the gift to Chaucer, by Richard II, of the manor of New Holme in Oxfordshire. These sarcasms on Elizabeth's parsimony are rather cheeky in print, but would have passed well enough if they were read to her with the right kind of a smile. My quotations are chiefly from chapter viii, Arber.

much delighted in the same studies. Now also of such among the Nobility or gentry as be very well seen in any laudable sciences, and especially in making or Poesie, it is so come to pass that they have no courage to write, and if they have, yet are they loath to be knowen of their skill. So as I know very many notable Gentlemen in the Court that have written commendably and suppressed it again, or else suffered it to be published without their own names to it: as if it were a discredit for a gentleman to seem learned, and to show himself amorous of any good Art.'

He ends this chapter with an exhortation: 'Since therefore so many noble Emperors, Kings and Princes have been studious of Poesie and other civil arts, and not ashamed to bewray their skills in the same, let none other meaner person despise learning, nor (whether it be in prose or in Poesie, if they themselves be able to write, or have written anything well or of rare invention) be any whit squeamish to let it be published under their names, for reason serves it, and modesty doth not repugn.'

Brave advice! And there must have been some very powerful reason to prevent him from putting his own name publicly to so brilliant a book!

There are ways, however, of putting one's name to a manuscript privately, for identification by one's self and possibly by a few close friends: methods some of which were open to men who were accustomed to the use of ciphers, and cipherers' tricks. I shall show how this was done in the books (*The Arte of English Poesie* among them) to which I directed attention on the first page.

The most careless reader knows that pen-names and pseudonyms have been used by writers in this and previous centuries. The habit may be the outcome of prudence, self-interest, modesty, fright, or intellectual or social pride. It depends on the purpose of the book, in conjunction with the worldly or unworldly aims of the writer. Upon these motives I have dwelt at length. There lies before us a large field for precise research, and for speculation.[1]

[1] See Appendix for further remarks on the conventional uses of false names, mere pen-names, and on the survival of writings which seem to contain no name (that is, of anonymous or supposedly anonymous works).

CHAPTER IV

METHOD

UNLESS all the acrostic signatures in this book are accidents, we must regard them as the means by which Francis Bacon, his brother, or his confidential servants placed an identifying mark upon works for which their author wished not to appear to be responsible before the world at large. The same remarks must hold for Ben Jonson, John Milton, and the rest. This supposition I use as a working hypothesis.

Where an acrostic occurs in a complimentary verse, I leave it to the common sense of the reader to determine to whom and by whom the verse was written.

The device is simply that of a hidden acrostic, the end letters of which are visible and prominent in their position, but the inner letters of which are hidden and follow one another in their proper sequence from one visible end to the other visible end of the acrostic.

The word 'sequence' is here used by me for the sake of convenience. The mathematician will not justify the use of the word 'series,' for the component figures of a mathematical series must bear a definite relation to one another. In this method of Bacon's, the letters of the string, between the first and last of which is placed an acrostic, need bear no definite mathematical relation to one another. Chance may govern their position. Evidence that design has been exercised is seen in the fact that by placing your pencil on the first letter of the string you can predict the position of the final letter of the acrostic.

The features of this scheme, or trick, are as follows: —

(1) Having surveyed what you have written, you choose a prominent or an appropriate place to begin, and an equally prominent or appropriate place to end your acrostic.

(2) Your choice of places for beginning and ending will, as a rule, be determined by the ease with which the acrostic can be adapted to the words at the corners of the stanza, poem, column, page, or series of pages.

(3) It is often easy to change a word at the corner, or in the text, in order to fit the acrostic to the place chosen.

(4) The places naturally chosen for a signature are : the dedication, the preface, the so-called printer's preface or address to a patron or the reader; the first page or the last page; or, if convenience or prudence dictates, the second page or the last page but one. Sometimes there is a signature both at the beginning and at the ending of a piece. Sometimes also, and this is very often the case, one half of the acrostic will run from one corner of the text and the other half from an opposite corner, and they will be made to meet in the midst of the text, on the same letter, thus, we may say, *keying* the cipher to the same letter.

(5) You will not read your acrostic into the text following its meaning as we now do, from left to right; but you will read alternately from left to right, then right to left, to the one hand on the first line, to the other hand on the next line, and so on, until you have completed your name. This affords you the facility that comes of treating your text as if it were a continuous *string* of letters. (See examples on pp. 49, 51.) Hence I shall always allude to this method as a 'string' cipher.

(6) You may apply this string cipher to (*a*) initials; (*b*) terminals, i. e. letters beginning and ending a word; (*c*) terminals of all whole words and part-words, i. e. parts divided by a hyphen; (*d*) all letters in the text; (*e*) outside letters of a page or side of a page; (*f*) initials outside of words of a page, or side of a page; (*g*) capitals.

(7) Whichever letters you choose to employ—initials, terminals, all letters, capitals, outside letters or initials, the method of employing them is the same. It is this:—

Having settled upon your visible ends, you follow your acrostic in the lines of the text, in alternate directions as if the letters were on a string, until it ends on the letter on which you have decided as the visible end of your acrostic.

If you are dealing with the *outside* letters or initials only, of a page, you naturally read in one direction only. But if you are dealing with the lines of the text, and, say, with the *initials* of the words,—having the point of departure, you follow the lines in alternate directions as if the letters were on a string (ignoring all letters but initials). Suppose you wish to insert the name *Frauncis Bacon:* you begin your acrostic with an *F* prominent as the initial of a corner-word, and then seek the next initial *R*, then the next initial *A*, and so on until you have come to the end of your name, *which must be the letter N pre-*

arranged as the visible end of your acrostic. If it will not so fall, then, if you are the cipherer, you must use your skill as an editor and so change a word here or there as to force the end of your name to fall on the letter that you have prearranged to be the visible end of your acrostic. You will be able to do this in many cases by changing the position of your *R*, or your *O*, or any one or two of the words the initials of which you find in your way.

(8) A very little practice will enable you to see with how much ease this can be done with no loss of beauty, or change of metre, or sense, in your composition.

(9) Often in making a cipher you will find it easy to begin independently from opposite ends of the acrostic and force your cipher to key itself on a given letter which may be found standing handy in the midst of the composition. For instance the Latin ablative *Francisco*, if spelled from one visible end, and the word *Bacono*, if spelled from the other, can be readily made to meet on the same letter *O*.

(10) I have considered an acrostic as 'keyed,' not only when arranged as just described, but also when it begins at a monogram or letter at one corner of a block of type, stanza, page, column, etc., and ends at a monogram or letter at the other end or opposite corner; but it must be so considered also when it runs from the first letter of the first word to the first letter of the last word, or to the first letter of the first word of the last line.

(11) When dealing solely with capital letters of one font, I have considered the acrostic as 'keyed' when it runs from end to end of the side of a page: also, when it runs from the initial of the last word of a book to the initial of the first word of the same book, as is the case with the book entitled *Of the Coulers of good and euill, a fragment.* Also, when it runs around the outside of a page and meets on two adjoining letters. Also, when two different acrostics lead to the same letter.

(12) You will find that some of the signatures in this book have been found where some seemingly accidental *double entente* in the text made the place chosen by the cipherer peculiarly appropriate. For instance, signatures will be found to key from opposite ends of a column, on the initial *N* of the word *Name* or on the *O* in *owner.* Or, immediately under the line, 'There to all Eternity it lives.' Or, on the line next to 'My hand is ready to perform the Deed.'

In some of these cases it seems as if a line might easily have been written with the purpose of giving the name a half humorously chosen place, depending on the *double entente* of the text.

(13) Another ingenious and very simple method, to which we have already alluded, is that of using the outside letters of a page. Still another, a variant of the foregoing, is that of using the initials of all the outside words of a page, or of a poem. A good example of this trick is seen in Ben Jonson's poem, *To the memory of my beloved The Author*, in the First Folio of Shakespeare's Plays, a facsimile of which is shown on page 324. A remarkable example of this trick is seen in Heming and Condell's dedication of the same Folio, and also in the address *To the Great Variety of Readers*, facsimiles of both of which are given on pages 312 and 321.

(14) As a working hypothesis I shall suppose that the cipherer has been governed in his choice of a place in which to insert his name (or on which to make his acrostic meet from opposite corners) by any of the following circumstances: (*a*) That the page is either at or near the beginning or end of the work to be signed; (*b*) that the accidental fall of the letters is auspicious, or can be easily made so; (*c*) that the word or lines carry a *double entente* which can be turned to account.

I shall also suppose that when the cipherer has taken advantage of an auspicious fall of the text in other than the usual places for a signature, he has marked the place by a wrong pagination or by some other such easy way to enable him to put his hand on it.

(15) Although this method might be discovered to, or by, a contemporary like Jonson, Hall,[1] or Marston, it is of such a nature that no direct charge of authorship could be made on the strength of it. The satirists might write epigrams of caustic moral or literary criticism, but they could not name their man without laying themselves open to a prosecution for libel, if the man they satirised by innuendo was powerful, and held that the reputation for the authorship of the satirised works would have injured him in his career. For the defendant to have proved that the complainant signed his name in this acrostic fashion would have necessitated some such laborious work as this of mine.

Acrostics in poetry, so we learn in the encyclopædias, are a kind of

[1] See *Part II.*

composition the lines whereof are disposed in such a manner that the initial letters make up some person's name, title, motto, or the like. The word is derived from the Greek ἄκρος, at one of the extremes (Latin, 'summus,' or 'extremus'), and στίχος, a line of writing, or a verse.

There are also acrostics where the name or title is made up by the initial letters of inner words, or the last letters of the final ones; and other acrostics which go backwards, beginning with the first letter of the last verse and proceeding upwards.

In these costermonger times we have come to regard ourselves and our learned leaders as very serious persons, and to be shocked when we catch a Pundit gambolling along the bypaths of intellectual recreation. The truth is that many of us, *malgré nous*, are prigs, and walk through life with our heads in the clouds, stooping sometimes to earth to get a little food and to attend to some practical duty. We who have this habit of mind are wont to look askance and to cough when we find a fellow Olympian winking to himself over something that has amused him below the level of his nose.

Many of the modern encyclopædias class this clever and, in its day, useful art of acrostics, among the puerilities and the literary triflings of men who should have been employed more profitably. At some future time similar critics in similar encyclopædias may regret the time wasted by ourselves over the game of bridge, or in writing verses in difficult rimes.[1] What we are prone to regard as puerilities, because we do not always understand the purposes which they served in bygone times, have fared like many activities once identified in the imagination of the Puritan with the vices of the courtly life of his time.

The use and exercise of this skill in acrostics is of great antiquity. Cicero tells us[2] that the Sibylline oracles were written in a kind of

---

[1] '. . . Rime being no necessary adjunct or true ornament of poem or good verse, in longer works especially, but the invention of a barbarous age, to set off wretched matter and lame metre; graced indeed since by the use of some famous modern poets, carried away by custom, but much to their own vexation, hindrance, and constraint to express many things otherwise, and for the most part worse, than else they would have expressed them.' (Milton in his preface on the verse in *Paradise Lost*. Edited by Masson, 1882.)

[2] 'Non esse autem illud carmen furentis, cum ipsum poema declarat, (est enim magis artis et diligentiae, quam incitationis et motus), tum vero ea quae ἀκροστιχὶς dicitur, cum deinceps ex primis versus literis aliquid connectitur, ut in quibusdam Ennianis, [quae Ennius fecit]. Id certe magis est attenti animi, quam furentis. Atque in Sibyllinis ex primo versu cujusque sententiae primis litteris illius sententiae carmen omne praetexitur. Hoc scriptoris est, non furentis; adhibentis diligentiam, non insani.' (*De Divinatione*, lib. II, § liv.)

acrostics. The Greeks cultivated the art, and so did their intellectual successors, the Latins. The arguments of the comedies of Plautus contain acrostics on the names of the respective plays (*Encyclopædia Britannica*), and Ben Jonson himself has used the same device in the versified argument which precedes his own play, *Volpone*.[1]

A rude form of acrostic is to be found in the Holy Scriptures, for instance in twelve of the Psalms, hence called the Abecedarian Psalms, — the most notable being Psalm cxix. This is composed of twenty-two divisions or stanzas, corresponding to the twenty-two letters of the Hebrew alphabet. (Walsh, *Literary Curiosities*.)

We learn from the *Dictionnaire Universel* (Larousse) that 'L'acrostiche passa avec l'usage de la langue latine chez les écrivains des premiers siècles de l'ère chrétienne. Il fleurit au moyen âge dans les cloîtres; il occupa l'esprit des poètes de la Renaissance, qui en augmentèrent à l'envi les difficultés. Aujourd'hui l'acrostiche est à peu près abandonné et l'on traite volontiers de laborieuses niaiseries, *nugae* difficiles, tout ce qui ressemble à ce jeu d'esprit.'

La Grande Encyclopédie also says that 'On appelle acrostiche une poésie faite de telle sorte que les premières ou les dernières lettres de chaque vers forment, par leur réunion, un ou plusieurs mots — généralement des noms propres. Les premières ou dernières lettres, composant le mot ou les mots qu'on a pris pour sujet, sont disposées verticalement, de telle façon que le nom mis en acrostiche se lise du premier coup d'œil.

'Mais les acrostiches sont parfois plus compliqués: certains poètes ont augmenté la difficulté en faisant répétér à la fois aux premières et aux dernières lettres des vers le mot proposé. D'autres sont allés plus loin et ont fait des acrostiches triples, quadruples, quintuples, reproduisant le mot un nombre quelconque de fois, souvent de la façon la plus bizarre, verticalement, horizontalement, en diagonale, en forme de croix, etc. . . . . Nos poètes du moyen âge et de la Renaissance ont laissé de nombreux acrostiches latins et français: ce sont eux surtout qui se sont évertués à faire, en ce genre infiniment secondaire, des tours de force d'une ridicule bizarrerie. A cette époque, il arriva très souvent aux poètes de se servir de l'acrostiche pour cacher leur propre nom, ou bien encore le nom de quelque maîtresse à laquelle ils addressaient leurs vers.'

[1] See page 3.

U and V: I and J: I and Y.

V. In Middle-English, *v* is commonly written *u* in the MSS., though many editors needlessly falsify the spellings of the originals to suit a supposed popular taste. Conversely, *u* sometimes appears as *v*, most often at the beginnings of words, especially in the words *vs*, *vse*, *vp*, *vn-to*, *vnder*, and *vn-* used as a prefix. The use of *v* for *u*, and conversely, is also found in early printed books, and occurs occasionally down to rather a late date. Cotgrave ranges all F. words (i. e. French words) beginning with *v* and *u* under the common symbol *V*. We may also note that a very large proportion of the words which begin with *v* are of French or Latin origin; only *vane*, *vat*, *vinewed*, *vixen*, are English. (*An Etymological Dictionary of the English Language*, by the Rev. Walter W. Skeat, Litt.D.)

The distinction now made by typographers and writers between *U* and *V*, *I* and *J*, was not firmly established until after Bacon's day, either in capitals or in the lower-case. The capital *V* was often used for the capital *U* at that time, but the use of a capital *U* for a capital *V* was not common. The same usages of course applied to the contemporary manuscripts.

The letter *y* at that time, and for some time afterwards, was occasionally used in the place of the letter *i* in such words as tyme = time; ayre = air; lyon = lion, and in many others.

For our purpose it is not necessary to call the reader's attention to other peculiarities of sixteenth and seventeenth century typography. Those which I have mentioned are those which concern our work.

The letter U or V in the name ffrauncis.

Wherever *V* or *U*, *v* or *u*, fall between the *a* and the *n* in the acrostic figure of *Frauncis* or *ffrauncis*, I have included them in the spelling. They may sometimes be passed over without spoiling the spelling of *Francis*, or *ffrancis*, as the name was sometimes spelled.

The treatment of words not regularly set.

I have found that for acrostic purposes a line of type is treated as a line of letters, and that it is sometimes the case in verse that a word or two has been carried up to the line above, or to the line below, as for instance in the following lines: —

Ant. Favours? By Ioue that thunders. What art thou,
      Thid. One that but performes   (Fellow?

The word which is carried over belongs to the line on which it stands typographically; and in reading for the acrostic it must be read with that line.

The treatment of abbreviated names of characters, and stage-directions.

I have found that for acrostic purposes the abbreviated names of characters are not used in the acrostic spelling, except in very few well-defined instances to which I have called attention in their places.

I have found that for acrostic purposes the stage-directions are not used[1] in the acrostic spelling; but, *and this is important,* the lines of stage-directions are to be followed in their proper order, although their letters do not count in the acrostic.

A line of type to be regarded as a row of letters.

In reading acrostics we must remember that a line of type is to be regarded as a row of letters, regardless of their meaning. If the acrostic is to be read on the initials, the spacing of the words will give you the initials. If the acrostic is to be read on the terminals, the same convenience is derived from the spacing of the words. If the acrostic is to be read on the capitals, it would not matter if there were no spacing of words, and the same is the case if the acrostic is to be read on all the letters of all the words. If the acrostic is to be read on the first letters of the several lines, it does not matter if there is but one letter to a line. Typographically speaking, a single letter between an upper and a lower line of type is *ipso facto* a line of type in itself.

Throughout this book I shall take it for granted that each reader has taken the trouble to master thoroughly the foregoing features of the method. If in the following pages I have unwittingly been obscure, it will be easy to refer to this chapter.

Those who follow me with the books themselves should use the first known editions, especially in prose. In verse it is sometimes possible to read the acrostic as well in a modern as in a first edition. As a rule, however, the habit of modernising the spelling, or of carrying over a line to fit a narrow column, will prevent the reader from following the acrostic. Another reason for using first editions is that in them it was customary to use capital letters of extraordinary size

[1] With the few exceptions noted in their places.

in prominent places in a verse or a page. These large capitals are often used by the cipherer as marks or pointers to draw the attention of the *illuminati* to the hidden name of the author. Acrostic-makers called them *Leaders*. (See page 88.)

In one or two cases I have been unable to obtain photographs of first editions; for instance I have used Haslewood's edition (1811) of the *Partheniades*, which were not printed until their appearance (1788) in the second volume of the *Progresses*, from the Cotton MSS. I have also been obliged to content myself with Begley's transcripts of A. B.'s sonnet in *England's Helicon*, and of F. B.'s dedication in *Palladis Palatium*.

It must be borne in mind that when the cipherer's main object is the *insertion* of a cipher, the matter containing the cipher is of secondary importance. In that case the obvious meaning of a passage containing a cipher is, or may be, chosen or designed to allay suspicion; so that when the text has no apparent indication to suggest a cipher, the absence of suggestion by no means indicates the absence of a cipher. The cipherer relies safely on the fact that the reader will fix his attention on the *obvious* meaning of the written matter, and that he will therefore not suspect the *hidden*, or secondary, meaning of the arrangement of the types of which the matter is composed. The more obvious the meaning, the more easy it is to insert a cipher without arousing suspicion.

The ciphers or acrostics which I have discovered reverse the order of intention described above. In each case the acrostic is of secondary importance, and was put into the composition after it was written, and, so far as we can judge, for the purposes of identification, or for a personal satisfaction. Thus the writing was done free from all restraint and with little thought of the name that was to be inserted after its completion, or when it came to be printed.

Surprise will be expressed that a poet should take so much *time* to put his name to his work in such a manner. The reply to this implication is to suggest that the reader practise with his own name on a column of the first magazine which comes to his hand. He will find that it takes but three or four minutes to insert his name from one corner to another, and to modify the words without interfering with the meaning of the text. In other words it will take about as much time as it takes to write out a cheque and sign it. He can key his cipher to the centre if he choose, by arranging it so that it runs from opposite corners to a letter in the middle of the column. This takes very little more time.

There is no need to suppose that the poet himself inserted all the signatures. Any one of several competent servants could have done it for him.

CHAPTER V

PRACTICAL SPECIMENS OF ACROSTICS AND STRUCTURAL SIGNATURES

Most of the devices which now follow are acrostics, which may be plainly visible, like the specimen on page 55; or hidden, like the specimen on page 59. They may be partly hidden and partly visible, with enough of the acrostic in sight to spur the suspicious or conversant to find out the method by which the gaps may be filled in. The structural signatures in *Part II* are acrostics of this latter kind.

At the risk of repetition let us give the steps again.

Instead of exposing the whole name, as in the Walsingham specimen on page 54, suppose that the first and last initial letters are exposed, respectively on the upper and lower right- or left-hand corners of a stanza or distinct block of prose, the rest of the letters of the name being allowed to run through the stanza and to fall on the initial letters of any word they will. Then all that a cipherer has to do is to see that the name begins, for instance, on the top left-hand corner initial of the text, and ends on the initial of the word at the left-hand corner at the bottom; he can change any intermediate word, and ensure the result by the use of the ' string ' cipher method.

Bear in mind that when you are dealing with *initials*, you deal with no other letters but initials. The rest are *nulls*, for the nonce.

Note. — In a few places I have deemed it necessary to frame the text with a set of short pointers to alternate lines, so that the reader may follow my hand with the least possible trouble. In some cases also, for the same reason, I have underlined the words or letters involved in the ciphers. It is my wish that each reader shall satisfy himself that each signature is to be found where I say that it stands ; so I have not made marks on most of the facsimiles. Each reader may do this for himself.

When I use ' graphic ' figures, I treat as *straight* lines all signatures which run from opposite point to point. Their actual direction is, of course, often zig-zag, but I have deemed it best to show the ' line of least resistance.' The same rule holds good when the acrostic starts out from a corner and ' keys ' itself back again to the nearest letter on the same corner of the text from whence it set out. Here the zig-zag line of the circular figure will be ' graphically ' shown as a plain circle from point to point.

Bear in mind that when you are dealing with *all* letters, you are not dealing with initials only. So also in the use of terminals and capitals.

A little care will soon develop facility.

Let us now look at a few ciphers of which ours is a simple variant. For instance: The hidden letters of a name may be made to fall in the text in a definite mathematical sequence, as in the prose example from Selenus, shown on page 63. This method is difficult, and not suitable for a signature such as we have in mind, because it controls the composition even more than does the Walsingham example on page 54. It would take a long stretch of text to enable the writer to make a signature with ease.

The most skilful signature that I have seen, based on this method of the early cipherers, is that of Poe, shown on page 69, in which he puts the name of Frances Sargent Osgood.

The method of inserting a message into a non-significant text, by a system of mathematical sequence, was common, and as many changes can be rung upon it as the cipherer chooses. They all can be easily detected, however, by a competent decipherer.

As Francis and Anthony Bacon were familiar with ciphers, they might easily have discerned the ease and the secrecy which would come by discarding the mathematical sequence in favour of a sequence with limitations imposed only by the length of the text itself. As thus: —

BACON

BCADCPOHN

BRCAKDCNPOSHN

BARCAKDCBNPOSHN

BBAAARCAKDBCBNOPOSHN

Here it is evident that if you seek the next letter in the name in its proper sequence, you will spell 'Bacon' in each of the above lines. Now imagine each of these letters to be an initial of a word and see the result when the method is applied to a piece of my own composition on page 59.

Now note what happens when a letter is allowed to stand in the wrong position: —

BBAAARCAKDBCBNOPOSHN ⎱
B A   C   O   N ⎰ In correct position.

BBAAARCAKODBCBNOPOSHN ⎱
B A   C   O   N ⎰ In wrong position.

By allowing the O to follow the K we have spoiled the cipher: that is, we have prevented it from running from the visible end B to the visible end N.

Now note what happens when we remove the first C: —

BBAAARAKODBCBNOPOSHN
B A   C   O   N

The cipher runs out correctly again: but it could have been rectified as easily by removing the obstructing O.

Note also that it by no means follows that the acrostic will read both forwards and backwards. To make it read both ways, forwards and backwards, it must be designed so to read.

The reader will readily see that the name could be thrown on an entirely new set of letters by the removal of the A; and that the change of a single letter might easily obliterate the name or cipher.

Here we have the letters in a string. Suppose that each letter is the initial letter of a word; then in order to keep them in a string all that was necessary was to fall back on the zig-zag method of writing used by the early Greeks (already alluded to), and described by William Blair in the article on Ciphers in *Rees's Encyclopædia*, the simplest and most meaty article on the subject that I have yet seen. The Chinese to-day write in the same way, but up and down; and Cicero, in a metonymical sense, uses the word *Exarare*, meaning to write on a tablet; i. e. to plough back and forth over the field.

This string or zig-zag order will give an acrostic on initials, terminals, capitals, or all letters in the text, and running alternately with and against the *sense* of the text or composition, and absolutely independent of its meaning.

The following strings of letters show how a string of initials, etc., may read forwards; backwards; forwards and backwards; forwards but not backwards; backwards but not forwards; at the will of the cipherer.

(a) Forwards (to right) and backwards (to left). Spelling NOCAB.

```
NABCDEFGHIJKLMOPQRSTUVWXYZCAGFEDNB
N---------------O-------- - ---CA-----B
N---------------O-------- - ---CA-----B
```

(b) Forwards but not backwards. Spelling NOCAB.

```
NABCDEFGHIJKLMNOPQRSTVWXYZCAGFEDHB
N--------------O------ - ---CA-----B
--------------NO------ - ---CA-----B
```

(c) Backwards but not forwards. Spelling NOCAB.

```
NABODEFGCHIJKLMPORSTUVWXYZABCDEFGB
N--O----C-------------- - ----A-----B
N--O----C-------------- - ---AB------
```

(aa) Forwards and backwards. Spelling BACON.

```
BCDEADCDEFGHIKLMNOPRSTUVWXYABCDOFN
B---A-C---- --- ---O------ - --------N
B----------------------- ----- - --A-C-O-N
```

(bb) Forwards but not backwards. Spelling BACON.

```
BCDBFEGHIKLMNOPQRSTUWABCEFGHILMNON
B------------------ - A-C-------ON
---B-------------- - A-C--------ON
```

(cc) Backwards but not forwards. Spelling BACON.

```
BCDEFGHIKLMNOPRSTUVWABCEFONHIKLMPN
B----------------- - A-C--O-------N
B----------------- - A-C--ON-------
```

'Graphic' Example of Bacon's Method

The letters are shown as if they were strung on a string, and keyed from and at different points.

1. Left to right.   → F · R · A · U · N · C · I · S ·   B · A · C · O · N →

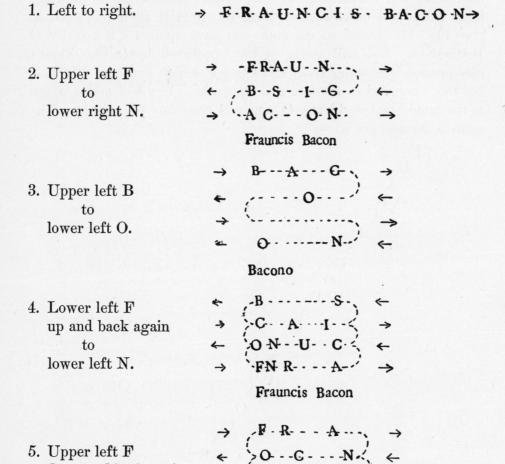

2. Upper left F
       to
    lower right N.

Frauncis Bacon

3. Upper left B
       to
    lower left O.

Bacono

4. Lower left F
    up and back again
       to
    lower left N.

Frauncis Bacon

5. Upper left F
    down and back again
       to
    upper left O.

Francisco Bacono

The reader will observe that it does not matter how many letters may fall between the letters of the name, so long as they are not allowed to interfere with the spelling of the name itself, from point to point.

Another Example of the String Acrostic

On the opposite page is a string of 723 letters. Begin to read from the letter F which begins the first line, to the right on the first line, to the left on the second line, to the right again on the third line, and so on, downwards, taking the next R, then the next A, then the next N, and so on, until you have spelled FRANCISCO BACONO. You will arrive at the bracketed letter O. Repeat this process beginning from the letter F which ends the last line, but this time read to the left, and upwards. You will arrive again at the same bracketed letter O, and will thus key the cipher. The acrostic figure here is: —

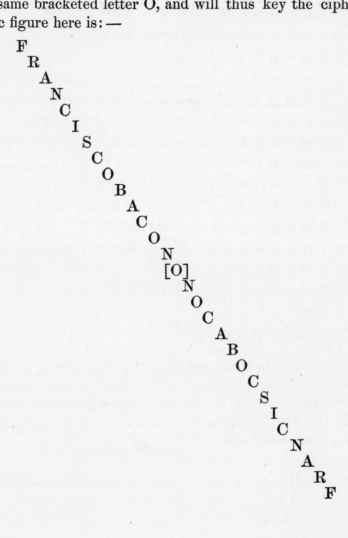

```
F M P T S P A B T D O D E W A A M N P S O M I A M P T I O
B L T R T G W W T M O W C D Y O O R T F S T E A D W O L L
T W S R H S H E A P F O T L I I A M T S F T T S C A V D B
A F E A B A I M N T A N T T O A T S O A S T B B I H I S S
M S A A S B A I A S B D H E O B T T C H G C T T D D L B M
T A C T D M H A V A C T S V A T H R H R T A P T Q T V A T
L B T Y T M C W Y W A D S E T W L E W M W S S I B T C H N
E V G M S T I T A H T C N H B I E T C T C W F A W T D F T
M T W M W T T Y W W B N N B V O L M G S M W V I I S W I B
P B W H I L I I O W I B B H O N H M B A V A W H B F M W A
V I O M D F M T E T A H G C O G A R L S M O E K F M D F W
S A H M P F H F M B W T P P T B H S A A F V O M S N W A M
A S A W I W B S B L B N S H T A I M O T G S O T L S O T S
B M T B A D W W M A T V H A I T S I N B B D B N C A A W W
A S O T F T P W E P S M A T V B A B I M W N M P [O] P M N W
B T A W D S W H E F L A V I A A T S W C A R H O F M D M M
G A T I O O H H M R N W D L B F W O L T H D G M F O V C B
B F W S S M C W M O W I T Y W T M S W G H I D I O W D A D
W A P P O T P B F T W I F F M T F M T S D F T A M N W M O
L T F C M W M A L T S T S R T V B O B S F S S T A T I W F
B M S S A V H F H S A S M P F S B W T O T O O H T W I H B
O S A E E T M F W C O W O E O F T C T D M W A I O T O H L
F A F S O T T S T W A C T C W A L T S G V T E V O T V T D
O C T O E T V T A M F F S T T S W C A W D L W H O B T B A
B E T C O L M S N M B W T B S T G N F O M D N B O S F
```

The above string is composed of the initials of the words of the text of a Folio page given in another part of this volume. The initials are here printed in the order in which they appear, as strings, in the first Folio page of *The Comedie of Errors*. The strings run from either end to the centre letter [O].

It must be remembered that the string cipher-method (as I call it for convenience), which Bacon used, is not less definite in its aspect as a series of letters than is the method of the cipherer who uses such a series as, say, the initial of every second word, or the initial of every fifth word. In Bacon's method, we find that he uses, say, the first F of the first line, then the *next* R, then the *next* A; and so on. The *next* is, mathematically, precisely as definite in sequence as the *second*. Bacon does *not* use *any following* R, and then *any following* A; but he uses always the *next* R and the *next* A, etc. The result is then as certain as a stated mathematical sequence, when you remember that the sequence begins and ends on two fixed points.

It is also worth remembering that a mathematical series is no less subject to chance than the limited alphabetical sequence used by Bacon, though at first sight it seems to be so. The one is as susceptible of being produced by design as the other. For instance; it is possible that if you were to empty on the floor a bag containing a million figures, they might *by chance* so remain on the floor that they would exhibit a regularly formed multiplication-table up to 5 times 10. But it is not within the bounds of imagination that the same figures again thrown down, with the same lack of design, would yield the same or even nearly the same results. There is a *chance* that they would, however.

The curious in such matters of chance may be interested to know that William Blair, in his article on Ciphers in *Rees's Encyclopædia*, gives a table which was prepared by the British Admiralty to show how many transpositions may be made of an alphabet of 36 letters for signals. (Mentioned on page 47.) I reproduce here four rows of figures showing, respectively, how many times 10, 16, 24, 36, letters may be transposed.

    10. 3,628,800.
    16. 20,922,789,888,000.
    24. 620,448,401,733,239,439,360,000.
    36. 371,993,326,789,901,217,467,999,448,150,835,200,000,000.

The mind refuses to grasp these figures, and a mathematician alone could tell us how many chances there are against two identical transpositions turning up when no design has been exercised.

To return to our specimens, let me say that I have prepared a few mathematical and other acrostic ciphers to show that a mere tyro at the work can make them in a few minutes. I have also wished to show the reader how easy it is to force even that most delicate of all common poetic forms, the Sonnet, to receive one of Bacon's acrostics twenty odd years after the poem had been written, with no forethought of such treatment. Let me again remind the reader that the specimens of acrostics and structural signatures in this chapter have been given to enable him to form an idea of the long period during which such literary devices have been used. The specimens will also enable the reader to practise his hand and eye in several acrostic methods before he begins to read *Part II*, containing the signatures of Francis Bacon, and others, which it is the purpose of this book to set forth for the first time.

We will set out with the definition of an acrostic as it is given in Murray's *A New English Dictionary:* 'A short poem (or other composition) in which the initial letters of the line, taken in order, spell a word, phrase, or sentence. Sometimes the last or middle letters of the lines, or all of them, are similarly arranged to spell words, etc., whence a distinction of *single*, *double*, or *triple* acrostics.'

This definition is correct except in saying that an acrostic is a *short* poem. Witness Boccaccio's *l'Amorosa Visione*, which is a very long example.

Explanation of Specimen A.

This specimen shows an ordinary 'visible' acrostic in its simplest form.

It is to be read on the initial of the first word of each line, beginning at the initial of the first word of the first line and ending on the initial of the first word of the last line.

The acrostic is SIR FRANCIS WALSINGHAM.

Note how this method cramps the author's construction.

Note also, that the matter is here of equal importance with the acrostic; because the intention is to pay a visible compliment and not to fix an identifying mark of authorship.

The acrostic figure here is: —

Shall, etc.
I
R
F
R
A
N
C
I
S
W
A
L
S
I
N
G
H
A
Make, etc.

When describing the burial of Sir Francis Walsingham, Stow says that 'these verses called Acrostickes are also hanged up.' (*Survey of London*, 4th edition, 1617, p. 1632, as quoted by John Nichols.)

Specimen A.

Shall Honour, Fame, and Titles of Renowne,
In Clods of Clay be thus inclosed still?
Rather will I, though wiser Wits may frowne,
For to inlarge his Fame extend my Skill.
Right, gentle Reader, be it knowne to thee,
A famous Knight doth here interred lye,
Noble by Birth, renowned for Policie,
Confounding Foes, which wrought our Jeopardy.
In Forraine Countries their Intents he knew,
Such was his zeal to do his Country good,
When Dangers would by Enemies ensue,
As well as they themselves, he understood.
Launch forth ye Muses into Streams of Praise,
Sing, and sound forth Praise-worthy Harmony;
In *England* Death cut off his dismall Dayes,
Not wronged by Death, but by false Trechery.
Grudge not at this imperfect Epitaph;
Herein I have exprest my simple Skill,
As the First-fruits proceding from a Graffe:
Make then a better whosoever will.

    Disce quid es, quid eris;
    Memor esto quod morieris.   E. W.

Explanation of Specimen B.

This acrostic, or structural signature, by Villon is here produced to show that the printer's habit of using a capital for the first letter of every line, in verse, has made obvious an open vertical acrostic which might be readily overlooked by the careless reader of the manuscript on the opposite page.

Villon A S'Amye.[1]

Faulse beaulté,[2] qui tant me couste chier,
Rude en effect, ypocrite doulceur;
Amour dure, plus que fer, à mascher;
Nommer que puis de ma desfaçon Seur,
Cherme felon, la mort d vng poure cuer,
Orgueil mussé, qui gens met au mourir;
Yeulx sans pitié. ne veult droicte rigeur,
Sans empirer, vng poure secourir?

Mieulx m'eust valu auoir esté sercher
Ailleurs secours, c'eust esté mon onneur.
Riens ne m'eust sceu hors de ce fait hasier;
Trotter m'en fault en fuyte, à deshonneur.
Haro, haro, le grant & le mineur!
Et, qu'est-ce cy? mourray, sans coup ferir,
Ou pitié veult, selon ceste teneur,
Sans empirer, vng poure secourir.

Vng temps viendra, qui fera dessecher,
Iaunir, flestrir, vostre espanye fleur:
Ie[3] m'en risse, s'enfant peusse marcher,
Lors—mais nennil—ce seroit donc foleur.
Las, viel seray; vous, laide, sans couleur.
Or, beuuez fort, tant que ru peut courir.
Ne donnez pas à tous ceste douleur,
Sans empirer, vng poure secourir.

Envoi.

Prince amoureux, des amans le greigneur,
Vostre mal gré ne vouldroye encourir;
Mais tout franc cuer doit, pour Nostre Seigneur,
Sans empirer, vng poure secourir.

[1] *Grant Testament*, p. 60. *Œuvres Complètes de François Villon.* Publiées d'après les manuscrits et les plus anciennes éditions, par Auguste Longnon: Paris, 1892.

[2] The Stockholm MS. reads *amour*, and shows a few other slight variations.

[3] In most of his acrostic signatures Villon uses one *i* in his name; in this the first *i* is vocalic, and *l mouillé* is represented with an *il* (as in the word mouillé itself). Observe that the acrostic in the third stanza does not include the initial letter of the first word of the refrain.

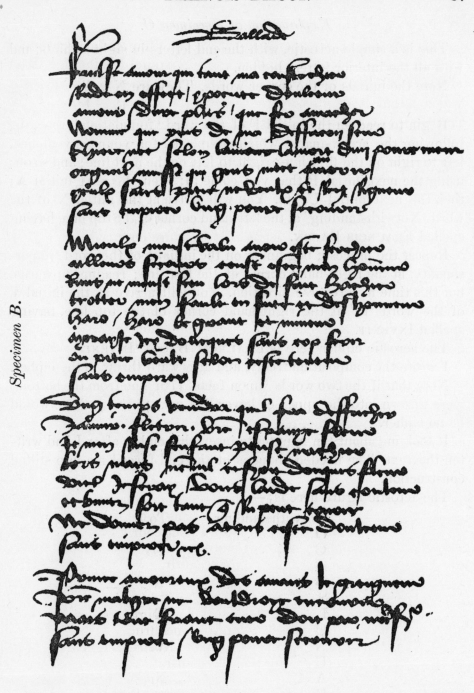

Specimen B.

Ballade. Reproduced from page 51 recto, *Le Petit et Le Grant Testament de François Villon*, etc. Reproduction facsimile du manuscrit (about 1470) de Stockholm, avec une introduction de Marcel Schwob. Paris, 1905. (Harvard.)

Explanation of Specimen C.

This is a simple acrostic, with the end letters in sight as hints, and with all the interior letters hidden.

Note the initials of the corner words. They are N . T

F . I

Begin to read on the initial F of the word 'foundation,' upwards, following the arrow-marks which are placed for your convenience, left to right on the first line; right to left on the next line; and so on; using the next initial R that you come to; then the next initial A; then the next initial U, etc. You will arrive at the initial N of the word 'Notwithstanding' at the left-hand corner of the top line, having spelled FRAUNCIS BACON.

Repeat the process; beginning on the initial I of the word 'impersonality, at the right-hand corner of the last line; reading upwards, but this time in a reverse direction. You will arrive at the initial T of the word 'to' at the right-hand corner of the top line, having spelled INVENIT.

The acrostic cipher here is FRAUNCIS BACON INVENIT.

I wrote the composition freely, and afterward threw in the cipher.

Note that if the two words 'upon facts' (7th line from the bottom) were thrown into the upper or lower line next to them, there would be no cipher.

It took me about ten minutes to insert this cipher after I had written the text. The needed changes at the end forced me into stilted construction.

The acrostic figure here is: —

Notwithstanding	To
O	
C	I
A	
B	N
S	
I	E
C	
N	V
U	
A	N
R	
Foundation	Impersonality.

The next example (Specimen D) is a good example of this method.

Specimen C.

A pair of parallel acrostics, running from lower to upper corners (a) FRAUNCIS BACON. (b) INVENIT. Illustrating Bacon's method.

N OTWITHSTANDING the vested interests to ←
→ which protection is given by reactionary pol-
icies in religious government, there has been ←
→ a steady growth of scientific training which
has taught men to pay more attention to facts ←
→ than to plausible inferences or attractive theories.

To-day men care little whether Moses wrote the ←
→ Pentateuch; but they care much about the practical effect of his teaching. The belief held ←
→ by many educated persons until a very recent date,
that the world as we know it was made by the ←
→ Creator in six working days, is now regarded
with amusement. So literary and historical ←
→ beliefs, so far as they are not based on facts,
have no inherent force for good, and must go down ←
→ before a scientific investigation. These remarks
apply alike to the whole range of science, whether ←
→ of chemistry, religion, mathematics, or to the
history of literature. The *odium litterarium* springs ←
→ from the same source as the *odium theologicum,*
namely from a mind befogged by inferences not based ←
→ upon facts.

The bane of modern literary history is a habit ←
→ of reading between the lines. A reputation in
scholarship built on this basis is jeopardised ←
→ by every honest search among documents. It is a
habit opposed to that openmindedness the obvious ←
→ foundation of which is impersonality.

Explanation of Specimen D.

The method of this example is similar to that used in Specimen C.

Begin to read on the initial F of the word 'free,' which is the last word of the last line; to the left; on the initials; upwards; to the initial O of the word 'ore-throwne,' which is the last word of the top line; having spelled FRANCISCO.

Again, begin on the initial B of the word 'be' at the end of the last line but one; to the right; upwards; to the same initial O of the word 'ore-throwne' at the same right-hand corner of the top line; having spelled BACONO.

The acrostic cipher here is FRANCISCO BACONO: i. e. BY FRANCIS BACON.

This specimen is a facsimile (except as to size) of the 'Epilogue' to *The Tempest* as it appears in the first Folio of *The Plays of Mr. William Shakespeare*. It is a specially interesting example, as scholars have hitherto regarded *The Tempest* as the last play that the poet wrote. If this surmise is right, this Epilogue is the playwright's last word to his audience, and the place where he would be very likely to sign his name in cipher if writing either under a pseudonym or anonymously.

The acrostic figure here is:—

Ore-throwne,	Ore-throwne,
C	N
S	O
I	C
C	A
N	Be
A	
R	
Free	

That is, FRANCISCO BACONO,[1] — BY FRANCIS BACON.

---

[1] I leave it to others to discuss the correctness of the cipherer's Latin. As a working hypothesis, I shall treat the name Francisco Bacono as if it were the ablative case of Franciscus Baconus. It is possible that both Francisco Bacono and Antonio Bacono were Italianate pet-names used by the two brothers and their intimates.

EPILOGVE,
ſpoken by *Proſpero*.

→ Now my *Charmes* are all oro-throwne,
  And what ſtrength I haue's mine owne. ←
→ Which is moſt faint: now 'tis true
  I muſt be heere confinde by you, ←
→ Or ſent to Naples, Let me not
  Since I haue my Dukedome got, ←
→ And pardon'd the deceiuer, dwell
  Inthis bare Iſland, by your Spell, ←
→ But releaſe me from my bands
  with the helpe of your good hands: ←
→ Gentle breath of yours, my Sailes
  Muſt fill, or elſe my proiect failes, ←
→ which was to pleaſe: Now I want
  Spirits to enforce: Art to inchant, ←
→ And my ending is deſpaire,
  Vnleſſe I be relieu'd by praier ←
→ Which pierces ſo, that it aſſaults
  Mercy it ſelfe, and frees all faults. ←
→   As you from crimes would pardon'd be,
  Let your Indulgence ſet me free. ← Exit.

Specimen D.

'The Epilogue' to *The Tempest*, showing acrostics described on the previous page. The pointers and underlinings will show the reader how to read in alternate directions, and will thus carry him to the words the initials of which make the acrostic.

Explanation of Specimen F.

This specimen was invented by me to show that the method exemplified by Specimen E may be used to enable a writer to write around a cipher, and at the same time say what is in his mind about any subject, with reasonable freedom in his composition.

The initial of the first word here is significant, and the initials of the following thirteen words are nulls, or non-significant. This order or series of significant initials and non-significant initials must be read from left to right and is repeated throughout the page, and will yield on examination the sentence: —

WILLIAM STONE BOOTH INVENIT.

The reader will find that, if he follows my directions, he will extract the following words from the page: —

While . it . link . literature . in . always . matter . spirit . The . offered . never . entitled . Barrister . of . of . the . has into . napping . various . Elizabeth . not . it . the.

It will be seen that the initials of these words yield the sentence, if put down in consecutive order.

As many changes can be rung on this mathematical method of ciphering as there are combinations of numbers. Sometimes a cipherer would begin with a number of nulls, and make his significant initials fall on an uneven series like, say, the following fifth, sixth, seventeenth, and thirtieth initials. It is merely a matter of agreement as to the understanding which he has with his correspondent. A skilful cipherer could write two ciphers into the same page of composition, — the one in an easy series, intended to be found out and to mislead, — the other to convey the true message.

Specimen F.

While this book is addressed to students of History, there is little doubt that it will also interest the open-minded students of English Literature. Present methods of teaching link the two subjects too closely together. The ability to distinguish good from bad literature is guided at present by the same set of men as are engaged in teaching the History of Literature. The two functions must be related and should always be interdependent, but they differ essentially from each other. The one is a matter of literary beauty; the other, of evidence. The one brings into play the spirit of the literary artist, the other the mental equipment of the trained cross-examiner. The same man is rarely trained in the two abilities, though both gifts are offered by Nature to the man who will cultivate them. Their marked difference has never been so well exposed as in a recent book by Mr. G. G. Greenwood, entitled *The Shakespeare Problem Restated.* Mr. Greenwood is an accomplished and reliable scholar, a Barrister, and a Member of Parliament, and his able work proves to the satisfaction of the man whose vision is not befogged by inference, that in the minds of his educated contemporaries William Shakespeare the Actor was not identified with William Shakespeare the Poet. This is a very important step in an interesting historical discussion which has been, unfortunately, allowed by the most respected of our academic leaders to drift into the hands of the layman. In plain words our leaders have been caught napping. They have not taken into account the bare possibility that any one of various good reasons may have determined a great genius and ambitious young favourite of Elizabeth to publish poetry under a pseudonym. They have overlooked the possibility that this not only might be done easily, but might be done with such skill that it would completely hoodwink all but a very few contemporaries. They have apparently forgotten the letters of Junius, and appear to have ignored the methods of Francesco Colonna.

Specimen G.[1]

If the reader wish to try his hand at this easy cipher let him decide on his series, and rule his paper into as many divisions as there are numbers in his series. He will then write his message down the column on which fall the significant numbers of his series, and will fill in the other columns with the non-significant words.

For instance, if he wish to say 'Lord Burghley is opposed to your plan,' in a series of 1 and 7, he will rule 8 columns thus: —

L	Let	your	actions	be	governed	by	a	policy
O	of	amity	between	the	king's	minister	and	our
R	royal	mistress.	At	the	time	of	the	lamented
D	death	of	our	late	Chancellor,	this	business	was
B	brought	to	a	head.	His	Lo'ship	now	rests
U	upon	the	terms	of	the	treaty,	and	the
R	reasons	which	led	to	its	adoption.	Her	Matie
G	gives	her	entire	consent,	and	my	Lo	Burghley
H	has	withdrawn	all	opposition	to	the	course	now
L	left	open	by	the	death	of	the	prince.
E	Every	article	in	this	treaty	must	be	by
Y	your	Excell^cy	carefully	maintained	in	its	original	draft,
I	in	as	much	as	her	most	gracious	and
S	sacred	Matie	desires	nothing	so	much	as	friendly
	etc.	etc.						

Here we have a message which now looks like an acrostic, but which when re-written with, for example, nine words to the line, will not show evidence of design. To a person having the key to the series, the despatch contains a message which negatives its ostensible meaning. The despatch might be shown to the prince to whom the receiver was accredited, without arousing in him suspicion as to the writer's actual policy.

---

[1] This specimen is given in further illustration of the device employed in the ciphers used in Specimens E and F.

Specimen H.

By spelling from the initial B of the word 'By,' with which this paragraph begins, and then taking the next initial A, and then the next initial C, and so on, to the right on the first line, to the left on the second line, to the right on the third line, and so on; the reader will not fail to arrive at this capital O when he has spelled the word BACONO. Now continue the experiment by spelling from the initial F of the first word of the last line; to the right on the last line, to the left on the last line but one, and so on upwards; taking the next initial R, then the next initial A, then the next initial N, etc., completing the spelling of FRANCISCO; you will arrive at the last letter of the acrostic surname, and finish reading at the capital O which is the node of the acrostic.

The acrostic figure here is: —

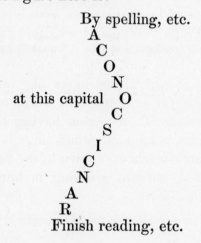

By spelling, etc.

B
A
C
O
N
at this capital O
C
S
I
C
N
A
R

Finish reading, etc.

The above specimen tells its own story. I have invented it in order that the reader may see how simple it is to throw one of the 'string cipher' signatures into a passage describing the making of the signature which is to be found in that passage. *Part II* contains several signatures made in this way.

Explanation of Specimen I.

The valentine on the opposite page was written by Edgar Allan Poe to his friend Frances Sargent Osgood.[1] It contains an acrostic which I have exposed for the reader's convenience.

In order to decipher this acrostic as he printed it you would have had to discover that you must read the first letter of the first line, then the second letter of the second line, then the third letter of the third line, and so on, until you have spelled the name of FRANCES SARGENT OSGOOD.

Note that this acrostic is read from left to right on every line; but that each line is treated by itself as a string of letters.

Note the close resemblance to the Bacon method if there had been a natural sequence instead of the mathematical sequence which is so easily exposed; and if the lines had been read as on a continuous string instead of as a series of broken strings from left to right.

Bacon's method is child's play compared with this method of Poe, because its sequence of letters is not a forced and definitely mathematical series, though equally definite in its results.

[1] *The Works of Edgar Allan Poe.* Edited by J. H. Ingram, 1899, vol. iii, p. 23.

Specimen I.

A Valentine.

1. F   For her this rhyme is penned, whose luminous eyes,
2. R   Brightly expressive as the twins of Leda,
3. A   Shall find her own sweet name, that nestling lies
4. N   Upon the page, enwrapped from every reader.
5. C   Search narrowly the lines! — they hold a treasure
6. E   Divine — a talisman — an amulet
7. S   That must be worn at heart. Search well the measure —
8. S   The words — the syllables! Do not forget
9. A   The trivialest point, or you may lose your labor!
10. R   And yet there is in this no Gordian knot
11. G   Which one might not undo without a sabre,
12. E   If one could merely comprehend the plot.
13. N   Enwritten upon the leaf where now are peering
14. T   Eyes scintillating soul, there lie perdus
15. O   Three eloquent words oft uttered in the hearing
16. S   Of poets, by poets — as the name is a poet's too.
17. G   Its letters although naturally lying
18. O   Like the knight Pinto — Mendez Ferdinando —
19. O   Still form a synonym for Truth. — Cease trying!
20. D   You will not read the riddle, though you do the best you can do.

Specimen J.

Am folgenden Tage wurde von Jerusalem auf=
gebrochen Und der Weg nach der syrischen Küste zu
Pferde gemacht. Tiefste Trauer, tiefstes Mitleid mit
Arbogasts Schicksal im Herzen, Ohne jedoch ein Wort
über ihn zu sprechen, Ritt die Prinzessin nach dem
Einschiffungsplatze dahin.

    Holdseliger Engel, Ermanne Dich! Da läßt
sich Nichts mehr ändern, Redete sie der Graf unter
Liebkosungen in Jaffa an. Ich weiß es, erwiderte
die Prinzessin aufseufzend.

The above specimen is a passage from the eighteenth chapter
(page 183) of the *Prinzessin von Portugal,* which passed as the work
of Alfred Meiszner, but which was the work of Franz Hedrich. You
will see the words 'AUTOR HEDRICH' by abstracting in their proper
order the types with a heavier face than is seen in the other types
of the text. (See *Alfred Meiszner — Franz Hedrich,* von Franz
Hedrich: Berlin, 1890, pp. 132–3.)

Specimen K.

This example is given, because it helps to illustrate the kind of learned ingenuity which was at the base of this kind of once common intellectual amusement, and method of structural signature.

It is verse written by some one in the olden time, and to speak technically it is at once acrostic, mesostic, and telestic; and in addition to these qualities you will see that the name JESUS appears in the middle of the verse in the form of a cross.

I	Inter cuncta micans	I		gniti sidera coelI	I
E	Expellit tenebras	E	toto Phoebus ut robE	E
S	Sic caecas removit	IESUS	caliginis umbraS	S
V	Vivificansque simul	U	ero praecordia motU	U
S	Solem justitiae	S	ese probat esse beatiS	S

Explanation of Specimen L.

This specimen is a sonnet of my own, which I use here to show how easily an acrostic may be inserted in it.

Note that in order to insert the cipher signature (the Latin ablative), *Francisco Bacono,* in a circular figure, that is to say, from the initial of the first word of the last line throughout the sonnet and back to the initial of the first word of the last line but one, the only changes needed are one word in the fourth line and four words in the last three lines.

The change does not make the sonnet worse than it was before. I have taken liberties with this sonnet, as my regard for it is of the same nature as that of Touchstone for Audrey; and for much the same reasons. 'Tis a poor sonnet, sir, an ill-favoured thing, sir, but mine own. It was written in 1889.

Note that it took but a few moments to make the necessary changes.

A poet might have been even more expeditious.

Begin to read on the initial F of the word 'Fate' (first word on the last line); upwards; to the right, or to the left; on the initials; throughout the sonnet, and back again, having spelled FRANCISCO BACONO; you will arrive at the exclamation 'O!' (first word on the last line but one).

The acrostic figure here is:—

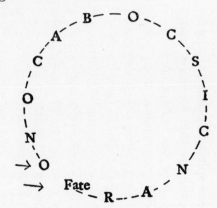

Specimen L.

A SONNET.

Before the insertion of the cipher.

Thou deathless spirit of primæval morn,
Embodied in the life that we must lead,
Which dying ever yet is ever born;
For all our suffering whence must come our meed?
In thy relentless progress dost thou need
Our bitter pangs of death, our throes of birth,
That by each change some little thou art freed
To bend the forces of opposing earth?
Dost thou by change our life make better worth,
Or art thou but a life within a life:
A being that feels not sorrow, no, nor mirth,
Yet is with all our joys and sorrows rife?
If thou couldst speak, wouldst thou thy answer give,
'Thy need is love: love thou, and loving live'?

THE SAME SONNET.

After the insertion of the cipher.

Thou deathless spirit of primæval morn,
Embodied in the life that we must lead,
Which dying ever yet is ever born;
For all our suffering whence shall come our meed?
In thy relentless progress dost thou need
Our bitter pangs of death, our throes of birth,
That by each change some little thou art freed
To bend the forces of opposing earth?
Dost thou by change our life make better worth,
Or art thou but a life within a life:
A being that feels not sorrow, no, nor mirth,
Yet is with earthly joys and sorrows rife?
O! couldst thou speak, wouldst thou thy answer give,
'Fate bids thee love. Love thou, and loving live'?

Specimen N.

An acrostic compliment from Ben Jonson to Tom Coryat. See the first edition of *Coryat's Crudities* (1611).

> To the Right Noble, *Tom Tell-Troth,* of
>   *his trauailes, the* Coryate *of Odcombe,*
>   and   his   *Booke*   now   going   to
>   *trauell.*

T rie and trust *Roger,* was the word, but now
H onest *Tom Tell-Troth* puts downe *Roger, How*?
O f trauell he discourseth so at large,
M arry he sets it out at his owne charge;
A nd therein (which is worth his valour too)
S hewes he dares more then *Paules Church-yard* durst do.

C ome forth thou bonnie bouncing booke then, daughter
O f *Tom* of *Odcombe* that *odde* Jouiall Author,
R ather his sonne I should haue cal'd thee, why?
Y es thou wert borne out of his trauelling thigh
A s well as from his braines, and claimest thereby
T o be his *Bacchus* as his *Pallas:* bee
E uer his thighes *Male* then, and his braines *Shee.*

Ben. Jonson.

Specimen O.

The Argument to *Volpone*. — An acrostic down the initials of the front.

V   Volpone, childless, rich, feigns sick, despairs,
O   Offers his state to hopes of several heirs,
L   Lies languishing: his parasite receives
P   Presents of all, assures, deludes; then weaves
O   Other cross plots, which ope themselves, are told.
N   New tricks for safety are sought; they thrive: when bold,
E   Each tempts the other again, and all are sold.

This acrostic is to be seen in any good edition of the *Works* of Ben Jonson. He made others, but this may serve to show that a man so contemptuous of ' puerilities ' used this form of intellectual exercise, or amusement, in his own plays.

Another illustration of the method employed in ' Specimens C, D, H.'

One can perform a simple experiment to illustrate the mechanical principle which underlies Bacon's method of using the types.

Let us say that there are twelve letters in the name FRANCIS BACON.

Chalk two lines any number of feet apart, on the floor. Place the toe of your left foot on one line and step out towards the other. Take twelve steps so that at your twelfth step your right toe shall exactly touch the line in front of you. If your eyes are open you can do this as often as you like; but with your eyes closed (and therefore by chance) you will be very unlikely to do it at all.

Bacon starts out from the first letter of a definite string of types, say from a letter F. He steps over all intervening letters until he reaches an R, then he steps over all letters until he reaches an A, and so on, until he has spelled his name. He takes his twelve steps so that the last letter of his name shall be the last letter in the definite string of types with which he is working.

This may be done easily with the eyes open, but with the eyes shut (that is to say, *by chance*) so rarely can it be done that mathematicians tell me the facts as to its rarity are so patent as not to be worth the calculation.

Observe that I have arranged the lines and words of the above illustration so that you can read (by following the method there described) ONOCAB OCSICNARF, that is, FRANCISCO BACONO spelled backwards, beginning at the initial O of the first word of the first line and ending on the initial F of the first word of the last line.

Specimen Q.

L'AMOROSA VISIONE.

By Boccaccio.

For this specimen the reader is referred to any well equipped library. I must be pardoned for omitting a facsimile. The poem is in fifty chapters, occupies over two hundred pages, and describes a dream in which the poet, guided by a lady, sees heroes and lovers of ancient and mediæval times. The work is remarkable because the whole poem of fifty chapters is an acrostic on a gigantic scale, perhaps the most astounding instance in literature.[1]

Adolf Gaspary, in his *Geschichte der Italienischen Literatur*,[2] follows his remarks upon the *Ameto* by saying: 'Aber wie in Boccaccio's Geiste sich die ernsten moralischen Gedanken der voraufgegangenen Literatur umformten, sieht man noch besser in einem anderen allegorischen Werke, der *Amorosa Visione*, welche offenbar Dante's Comödie nachgeahmt ist. Dieses Poem, geschrieben sehr bald nach dem *Ameto* [1341 oder 1342] besteht aus 50 kurzen Gesängen in Terzinen, und der Verfasser hat sich dabei die ungeheure Schwierigkeit auferlegt, aus dem ganzen langen Gedichte ein Acrostichon zu bilden; die Anfangsbuchstaben der sämmtlichen ersten Verse der Terzinen ergeben zusammengesetzt zwei *sonetti codati* und ein *sonetto doppio codato*, welche die Widmung des Werkes an Maria Fiametta enthalten.'

The *Amorosa Visione*, like the *Divina Commedia*, is written in terza rima, and the initial letters of all the triplets throughout the work compose three poems of considerable length, in the first of which the whole is dedicated to Boccaccio's lady-love, under her name Maria. In addition to this, the initial letters of the first, third, fifth, seventh, and ninth lines of the dedicatory poem form the name of Maria; so that we have here an acrostic in the second degree.

---

[1] Girolamo Claricio, imolese, nel 1521, fu il primo ad iscoprire che *L'Amorosa visione* del Boccaccio era un poema acrostico, rilevando due sonetti ed una canzonetta dalle iniziali de' terzetti. *Nuova Enciclopedia Italiana*, p. 419.

[2] Berlin, 1888, vol. ii, p. 20, et seqq.; or, Italian translation, by V. Rossi, vol. ii. Turin, 1891, p. 18.

Explanation of Specimen R.

This is a fair specimen of an acrostic doubled and crossed. Only by special type-setting has this acrostic been made obvious.

In the eyes of such Presbyterian and Puritan historians as Arthur Wilson and Sir Symonds D'Ewes, this clever literary love-knot would perhaps have been classed with 'lascivious toys'; in much the same way that each of them interpreted, from hearsay, the platonism and scientific theories of Francis Bacon in the obscure light of their own imaginations. (See Walter Begley, *Bacon's Nova Resuscitatio*, vol. iii, pp. 100 to 142.) An interesting comment is made on this subject (presumably) by Bacon himself,[1] in one of his notes to *The Shepherd's Calender*, when explaining what may seem to Spenser's readers to be a reference to *disorderly love.* No man's attitude towards this subject could be more clearly expressed. This unpuritanical frankness itself may well have given cause for all sorts of foul accusations by prurient gossips, and by historians who neither knew Bacon nor understood his lofty culture.

I have hung this serious comment to a trivial occasion; but it will serve as a hint for those who wish to follow up the subject, and to whom a nod is as good as a wink. (See also *New Atlantis:* Spedding, vol. iii, pp. 152–153.)

To return to our acrostic. Read on the initials from the upper left to the lower right-hand corner for the Lover's name: and from the lower left to the upper right-hand corner for the name of his Lass.

The Lady who caused this woe was Mary Brandon; the Lover was Thomas Rivers.

---

[1] Presumably by Bacon himself, inasmuch as his name is signed by means of a string cipher in the Epistle to Gabriel Harvey, and in the General Argument to the whole Book. These acrostic signatures are shown in their proper place in *Part II*. We learn from the writer of these two introductory documents to *The Shepherd's Calender* that he also wrote the notes to that poem.

Specimen R.

Though crost in our affections, still the flames
Of Honour shall secure our noble Names
Nor shall Our fate divorce our faith, Or cause
The least Mislike of love's Diviner lawes.
Crosses sometimes Are cures, Now let us prove
That no strength Shall Abate the power of love:
Honour, wit, beauty, Riches, wise men call
Frail fortune's Badges, In true love lies all.
Therefor to him we Yield, our Vowes shall be
Paid Read, and written in Eternity
That All may know when men grant no Redress,
Much love can sweeten the unhappinesS.

Specimen S.

A Runic monogrammatic cipher, used as a structural signature by Cynewulf, about A. D. 800. (*Christ*, lines 797–807.)

> Þonne ᛣ cwacað,　　gehȳreð Cyning mæðlan,
> rodera Ryhtend,　　sprecan rēþe word
> þām þe him ǣr in worulde　　wāce hȳrdon,
> þendan ᚼ ond ᚾ　　ȳþast meahtan
> frōfre findan.　　Þǣr sceal forht monig
> on þām wongstede　　wērig bīdān
> hwæt him æfter dǣdum　　dēman wille
> wrāþra wīta.　　Biþ se ᚹ scæcen
> eorþan frætwa.　　ᚢ wæs longe
> ᛚ flōdum bilocen,　　lifwynna dæl,
> ᚠ on foldan.

LETTERS.	NAMES.	KEMBLE'S DEFINITIONS.
ᛣ	cēn	torch
ᚣ	ȳr	bow
ᚾ	nēd	need
[M]	eoh	horse
ᚹ	wēn (wynn)	[hope]
ᚢ	ūr	bull
ᛚ	lagu	water, sea
ᚠ	feoh	money

The Runes in the above verses not only serve as words with which the learned might complete the sense of the lines in which they fall, but being letters in themselves, they also spell the name of the poet. (See *The Christ of Cynewulf*, edited with introduction, notes, and glossary, by Albert S. Cook, Boston: Ginn & Company, 1900, pp. 30, 31, 151–157.)

Specimen T.

Oba íh thero búacho gúati   hiar íauuiht missikérti,
　gikrúmpti thera rédino,   thero quít ther euangéliO:
Thuruh krístes kruzi   bimíde ih hiar thaz uuízi,
　thuruh sína gibúrt;   es íst mir, drúhtin, thanne thúrfT.
Firdílo hiar thio dáti,   ioh, drúhtin, mih giléiti,
　thaz ih ni mángolo thes dróf   in hímilriches fríthoF.
Rihti pédi mine,   thar sin thie drúta thine,
　ioh minaz múat gifréuui mir   in euuon, drúhtin, mit thíR.
In hímilriches scóni   dúa mir thaz gizámi,
　ioh mih íó thárauuisi,   thoh ih es uuírdig ni sI.
Drúhtin, dúaz thuruh thíh,   firdanan uuéiz ih filu míh,
　thin gibót ih ofto méid,   bi thiu thúlta ih thráto mánag leiD.
Vuéiz ih thaz giuuísso,   thaz íh thes uuírthig uuas ouh só,
　thiu uuérk firdilo mínu   gináda, druhtin, thínU
Saríó nú giuuaro   thaz ih thir thíono zioro
　ellu iár innan thés   ioh dága mines líbeS.
Vuanta unser líb scal uuesan tház,   uuir thíonost duen íó thínaz,
　thaz húggen thera uuúnnu   mit krístes selbes mínnV
Vuóla sies íó ginúzzun,   thie uuíllen sines flízzun,
　ioh sínt sie nu mit rédinu   in hímilriches fréuuidV,
In hímiles gikámare   mit míhilemo gámane,
　mit míhileru líubi,   thes uuórtes mir gilóubI
Zi héllu sint gifíarit   ioh thie ándere gikérit,
　thar thultent béh filu héiz,   so ih iz álles uuio ni uuéiZ.
Alla uuórolt zeli du ál,   so man in búachon scál,
　thiz fíndistu ana duála,   thaz ságen ih thir in uuárA.
Nim góuma in álathrati,   uuio abél dati,
　uuior húgu rihta sinan   in selb drúhtinaN.
　　etc.　　　etc.　　　etc.

This example shows an acrostic on the terminal letters of alternate
lines of type. That is to say, on the initial letter of the first line, and
on the end letter of the second line, and so on. The complete reading of the acrostic, which is the same at both ends of the lines
runs : —

OTFRIDUS UUIZANBURGENSIS MONACHUS HARTMUATE ET
UUERINBERTO SANCTI GALLI MONASTERII MONACHIS

The poem in which it appears is *Ad Monachos St. Galli,* and is to
be seen in Otfrid's *Evangelienbuch* (about A. D. 868). See *Otfrids
von Weissenburg Evangelienbuch:* Text und Einleitung, von Dr
Johann Kelle. Regensburg, 1856; or later editions.
　I have given enough of the verse to show the form of the acrostic,
and the structural signature.

Specimen U.

Showing the structural signature of Ormin, or Orrm.

Ormulum:[1] *Dedication*, lines 322–325. (Twelfth Century.)

Icc þatt tis Ennglissh hafe sett
Englisshe menn to lare,
Icc wass þaer þaer I crisstnedd wass
Orrmin bi name nemmnedd

Ormulum, lines 1 and 2.

Þiss boc iss nemmnedd Orrmulum
Forrþi þatt Orrm itt wrohhte,

Specimen V.

Showing the structural signature of Crestien de Troyes.

Yvain,[2] the last paragraph. (Twelfth Century.)

Del chevalier au lion fine
Crestiiens son romanz einsi ;
Ou'onques plus conter n'an oï,
Ne ja plus n'an orroiz conter,
S'an n'i viaut mançonge ajoster.

Specimen W.

Showing the structural signature of Marie de France.

Guigemar:[3] the prologue. (Twelfth Century.)

Ki de bone matire traite,
mult li peise, se bien n'est faite.
Oëz, seignur, que dit Marie,
ki en sun tens pas ne s'oblie.

[1] *The Ormulum.* (Jun. MS. I. Bodleian Lib.) : edited by R. M. White, 2 vols., Oxford, 1852.

[2] Kristian von Troyes : *Yvain* (written about 1175). See edition by Wendelin Foerster : Halle, 1902.

[3] See Prologue to *Guigemar*, in *Die Lais der Marie de France*, edited by Karl Warnke, 2d edition, Halle, 1900, p. 5.

SUNDRY ANALOGOUS SPECIMENS.

There are a few other analogous forms of this use of letters which may be of interest as showing the antiquity and the prevalence of it. The Greeks composed lipogrammatic works, in which one letter of the alphabet is omitted. A lipogrammatist is a letter-dropper. In this manner Tryphiodorus wrote his *Odyssey*. He had not an ' a ' in his first book, nor ' b ' in his second; and so on with the subsequent letters, one after another. This Odyssey was in imitation of the lipogrammatic *Iliad* of Nestor. Athenæus mentions an Ode by Pindar, in which he had purposely omitted the letter ' s.' There is in Latin a prose work by Fulgentius, which is divided by him into twenty-three chapters, according to the order of the letters of the alphabet (Latin). From 'a' to 'o' are still remaining. The first chapter is without 'a'; the second without 'b'; the third without 'c'; and so on with the rest. There are five prose novels that have sometimes been attributed to Lope de Vega: the first without 'a,' the second without 'e,' the third without 'i,' and so on through the list of vowels.[1]

In the *Ecloga de Calvis*, by Hugbald the monk, every word begins with a 'c.' In the *Pugna Porcorum* all the words begin with a 'p'; and in the *Canum cum cattis certamen*, printed in the same work (*Nugae Venales*), all the words begin with a 'c.' Gregorio Leti presented a discourse to the Academy of the Humourists at Rome, throughout which he had purposely omitted the letter 'r.'

Lord North, in the Court of James I, wrote a set of sonnets, each of which begins with a successive letter of the alphabet. The Earl of Rivers, in the reign of Edward IV, translated the *Moral Proverbs* of Cristina of Pisa, a poem of about two hundred lines, most of which he contrived to conclude with the letter 'e.'

Other wits, the author of *The Arte of English Poesie* among them, composed verses in the form of pillars, roundels, hearts, wings, altars, and true-love knots. Tom Nash ridiculed Gabriel Harvey for this practice, and Ben Jonson satirically described their grotesque shapes as : —

'A pair of scissors and a comb in verse.'

[1] I am indebted to my friend Professor F. De Haan for the following title : — *Varios efectos de amor en cinco novelas exemplares y nuevo artificio de escriuir prosas, y versos, sin una de las cinco letras Vocales, excluyendo Vocal differente en cada Nouela. Autor Alonso de Alcala y Herrera. En Lisboa, Manuel de Sylva, 1641* [from Salvá, Catálogo de la Biblioteca de Salvá, Valencia, 1872, 2 vols ; vol. ii, No. 2015].

A different conceit regulated Chronograms, which were used to show dates. The numeral letters, in whatever part of the word they stood, were distinguished from other letters by being written in capitals. In the following chronogram: —

> . . . feriam sidera vertice,

by the elevation of capitals this line is made to give the year of our Lord thus: —

> . . . feriaM siDera VertIce;
> *i. e.* M   D   V   I

The initial letters of Acrostics are thus alluded to by Richard Owen Cambridge, in *The Scribleriad:* —

> Firm and compact, in three fair columns wove,
> O'er the smooth plain, the bold *acrostics* move;
> High o'er the rest the TOWERING LEADERS rise
> With *limbs gigantic*, and *superior size*.

A feat more difficult than that of inventing acrostics is that of *reciprocal verses*, which give the same words whether backwards or forwards. The following lines are attributed to Sidonius Apollinaris: —

> Signa te signa temere me tangis et angis.
> Roma tibi subito motibus ibit amor.[1]

---

[1] This example and those on the previous page I have culled from Disraeli's *Curiosities of Literature*, and from Walsh's *Handy-Book of Literary Curiosities*.

Specimen X.

I have reserved to the last this specimen which is peculiarly suggestive to us.

The Hypnerotomachia Poliphili was published anonymously in 1499, in Venice. It professes to relate its author's love for Polia, a nun, his search after her, and their union, at the close of sundry trials and adventures, in the realm of Venus. The story is a dream or reverie, and represents the epoch of transition from the Middle Age to the Renaissance, in its fourfold intellectual craving after the beauty of antiquity, the treasures of erudition, the multiplied delights of art, and the liberty of nature.[1]

Long after the publication of the book its author's name was discovered. It had been hidden by the very simple device of using the initial letter of each chapter throughout the book, so that when the initials were written down consecutively, they disclosed the sentence *Poliam frater Franciscus Columna peramavit* — Brother Francesco Colonna passionately loved Polia. Colonna was a Dominican monk and the last words of the first edition of his work show that it was written at Treviso in 1467. It is not difficult to surmise his reason for concealing his name.

This device of Colonna's is important to us, for it contains the principle which underlies the formation of a string cipher, and at the same time illustrates the use of a string of letters as a means of identification.

[1] See *Renaissance in Italy*, by J. A. Symonds, vol. iv, pp. 189–206; 1904.

Note. — The facsimiles are reproduced approximately the same size as the originals, except in the case of the Folios, where a considerable reduction in size was necessary.

A comparison of the facsimiles with the originals from which they were taken will in a few cases show that the white background has been cleaned, and that one or two blots have been removed, so that the reader unaccustomed to old books and old typography may be able to see the letters without unnecessary obstruction. Where a letter has been so broken as to be doubtful, I have allowed it to stand, and have referred to another edition where it may be seen in good condition.

Where the original was too faded to be reproduced by photography, I have either strengthened the negative, or darkened the original. When the latter action has been necessary I have done it myself.

THE ARTE
OF ENGLISH
POESIE.

Contriued into three Bookes: The firſt of Poets
and Poeſie, the ſecond of Proportion,
the third of Ornament.

AT LONDON
Printed by Richard Field, dwelling in the
black-Friers, neere Ludgate.
1589.

A colei

Che se steſſa raſſomiglia
& non altrui.

(*The Arte of English Poesie — Its Frontispiece*)

CHAPTER VI

THE ARTE OF ENGLISH POESIE — THE PARTHENIADES

Signature 1 (The Arte of English Poesie).

THIS is a particularly interesting example, because of its bearing on the authorship of a famous book, *The Arte of English Poesie*, which was published anonymously in 1589. A few comments about the book will be found on page 120.

Note that the dedication opens with a signature R. F. in the third person, and closes with the same signature R. F. in the first person. These initials ostensibly stand for those of the printer, Richard Field; but they are also made to serve another purpose. (See pp. 99–100.)

I frame the facsimiles from *The Arte of English Poesie*, to direct the reader with arrow-heads. In the rest of the book the reader will be left to his own skill in following my directions. I advise each reader to mark his own copy when he checks my work.

Begin to read on the initial F in the first initial-signature ' R. F.'; to the left; downwards; taking the next initial R; then the next initial A; then the next initial U (or V); and so on; on the initials of the words; spelling FRAVNCIS BACON, you will have arrived at the initial N of the word 'not,' which is followed by the word 'scypher' and then by the words 'her Maiesties honour.' The cipherer has thus approached ' *her Majesty's honour.*' He then makes his exit backwards, in the fashion of the courtier: so you will continue to read from the initial N of the word ' not,' where we left off, and *spell backwards:* to the left on the initials as before; downwards; until you have come to the initial F of the last initial-signature ' R. F.,' having spelled NOCAB SICNVARFF, ' a device of some novelty.'

The acrostic figure here is:—

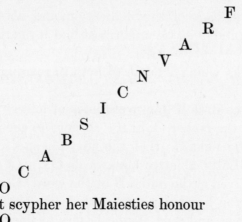

Not scypher her Maiesties honour

From the Black-friers, etc.
F   (R. F.)

Note that the name is spelled *Fravncis* down to the 'not,' and *ffravncis* as it runs out.

Signature 2 (The Arte of English Poesie).

Now, again turn to the first page of this dedication, and note the cipher, or, if you like, the capital O in the uppermost line at the right-hand corner of the page. (See pp. 99–100.)

Disregard the arrow-marks which I made to help in reading the previous name.

Treat the lines of words, now, as if they were lines of letters on a string. Begin to read from the cipher O, in the corner; to the left; taking the next N; then the next O; then the next C; and so on, until you have spelled the Latin ablative backwards ONOCAB (i. e. BACONO). You will have arrived at the initial B of the word 'Booke.' This signature is keyed if you begin again from the same cipher O at the upper right-hand corner, and read all the letters to the right, but skipping the bracketed words '(right Honorable).' You will arrive at the same initial B of the same word 'Booke.'

The acrostic figure here is:—

$$\text{Right Hon}O$$
$$N$$
$$O$$
$$C$$
$$A$$
$$\text{T}\text{His Booke}$$

To wit: THIS BOOKE BY BACON.

I regard this as a weak signature, since, in order to key it, we had to leave out the two bracketed words '(right Honorable).' But it is sufficiently remarkable to warrant its inclusion.

TO THE RIGHT HONO
RABLE SIR VVILLIAM CECILL
KNIGHT, LORD OF BVRGHLEY, LORD
HIGH TREASVRER OF ENGLAND, R.F.
Printer wisheth health and prosperitie, with
the commandement and yse of his
continuall seruice.

THis Booke (right Honorable) comming
to my handes, with his bare title without any
Authours name or any other ordinarie addresse, I doubted how well it might become me
to make you a present thereof, seeming by many expresse passages in the same at large, that
it was by the Authour intended to our Soueraigne Lady the Queene, and for her recrea-
tion and seruice chiefly deuised, in which case to make any other person
her highnes partener in the honour of his guift it could not stãd with my
dutie, nor be without some preiudice to her Maiesties interest and his
merrite. Perceyuing besides the title to purport so slender a subiect,
as nothing almost could be more discrepant from the grauitie of your
yeeres and Honorable function, whose contemplations are euery houre
more seriously employed vpon the publicke administration and seruices:
I thought it no condigne gratification, nor scarce any good satisfaction
for such a person as you. Yet when I considered, that bestowyng vpon
your Lordship the first vewe of this mine impression (a feat of mine
owne simple facultie) it could not scypher her Maiesties honour or
prerogatiue in the guift, nor yet the Authour of his thanks: and seeing the thing it selfe to be a deuice of some noueltie (which commonly
A B iij

(*The Arte of English Poesie — The Dedication*)

26323

THE EPISTLE DEDICATORIE.

→ *giueth euery good thing a speciall grace) and a noueltie so highly ten-* ←
ding to the most worthy prayses of her Maiesties most excellent name
→ *(deerer to you I dare conceiue them any worldly thing besides) mee* ←
thought I could not deuise to haue presented your Lordship any gift ←
→ *more agreeable to your appetite, or fitter for my vocation and abilitie* ←
to bestow, your Lordship beyng learned and a louer of learning, my pre- ←
→ *sent a Booke and my selfe a printer alwaies ready and desirous to* ←
be at your Honourable commaundement . And thus I ←
→ *humbly take my leaue from the Black-friers, this* ←
xxviij. of May. 1 5 8 9.

→ Your Honours most humble
at commaundement, ←

→ R. F.

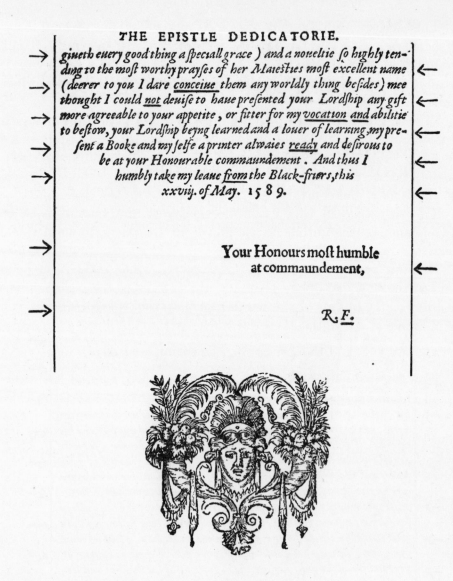

(*The Arte of English Poesie — Dedication continued*)

Signature 3 (The Arte of English Poesie).

This acrostic is found on pages 81 and 82 of *The Arte of English Poesie*. (See also in Arber's Edition, pp. 111 and 112.) It is a roundell, a geometrical figure, doggerel because it is necessary to cramp the composition into the figure, which the author describes thus:—

' This figure hath three principal partes in his nature and vse much considerable: the circle, the beame, and the center. The circle is his largest compasse or circumference: the center is his middle and indiuisible point: the beame is a line stretching directly from the circle to the center, and contrariwise from the center to the circle.'

The signature in this example runs from the end of each of two beams, on the initials of the words of the poem, to an identical centre. (See pp. 103–04.)

Begin to read on the initial O of the word ' one,' at the right-hand end of the first line of the poem; to the left or to the right; downwards; on the initials of the words; spelling backwards ONOCAB, you will arrive at the initial B of the word ' be ' in the line:—

' And though he be, still turnde and tost.'

Now begin again on the initial O of the word ' one' at the right-hand end of the last line of the poem; and read to the left; upwards; on the initials of the words; spelling ONOCAB, you will again arrive at the initial B of the same word ' be ' as before: thus keying the cipher, from ends to centre.

The acrostic figure here is:—

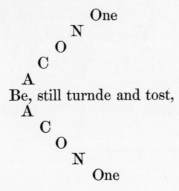

```
                    One
                 N
               O
             C
           A
Be, still turnde and tost,
           A
             C
               O
                 N
                    One
```

BACONO, i. e. ' By Bacon.'

Signature 4 (The Arte of English Poesie).

This acrostic also is found in *The Arte of English Poesie*, on pages 82 and 83 (Arber's Edition, pp. 112 and 113). It is another specimen of the roundell, and the signature runs from the end of each beam until it reaches a common letter in the centre.

Note that the initial of the first word of the first line is F, and that the initial of the first word of the last line is B. (See pages 104–5.)

Begin to read from the initial F of the first word of the first line; to the right; on the terminals of the words; downwards; spelling FRANCISCO, you will arrive at the terminal O of the word 'to' (5th line, p. 83).

Begin to read from the initial B of the first word of the last line of the poem; to the right; upwards; on the terminals; spelling BACONO, you will again arrive at the same terminal O of the word 'to' (5th line, p. 83).

The acrostic figure here is: —

<pre>
            First her authoritie regall
          R
           A
            N
             C
              I
               S
                C
            tO himselfe.

              N

             O

            C

          A
        Beame, circle, centre of all my round.
</pre>

OF PROPORTION LIB. II.   8r

The Roundell or Spheare.

The moſt excellent of all the figures Geometrical is the round
for his many perfections. Firſt becauſe he is euen & ſmooth, without any angle, or interruption, moſt voluble and apt to turne, and
to continue motion, which is the author of life: he conteyneth in
him the commodious deſcription of euery other figure, & for his
ample capacitie doth reſemble the world or vniuers, & for his in-
definiteneſſe hauing no ſpeciall place of beginning nor end, bea-
reth a ſimilitude with God and eternitie. This figure bath three
principall partes in his nature and vſe much conſiderable : the circle, the beame, and the center. The circle is his largeſt compaſſe or
circumference: the center is his middle and indiuiſible point : the
beame is a line ſtretching directly from the circle to the center, &
contrariwiſe from the center to the circle . By this deſcription our
maker may faſhion his meetre in Roundel, either with the circumference, and that is circlewiſe, or from the circuference, that is, like
a beame, or by the circumference, and that is ouerthwart and dya-
metrally from one ſide of the circle to the other.

*A generall reſemblance of the Roundell to God, the world
and the Queene.*

All and whole, and euer, and <u>one</u>,
Single, ſimple, eche where, alone,
Theſe be counted as Clerkes can tell,
True properties, of the Roundell.
His ſtill turning by conſequence
And change, doe breede both life and ſence.
Time, meaſure of ſtirre and reſt,
Is alſo by his courſe expreſt.
How ſwift the circle ſtirre aboue,
His center point doeth <u>neuer</u> moue :
All thiugs that euer were <u>or</u> be,
Are <u>cloſde</u> in his concauitie.
And though he <u>be</u>, ſtill turnde <u>and</u> toſt,
No roome there wants nor none is loſt.
The Roundell hath no bonch or <u>angle</u>,
Which may his <u>courſe</u> ſtay or entangle.
The furtheſt part of all his ſpheare,

N ſij

(The Arte of English Poesie)

8₂ OF PROPORTION. LIB. II.

Is equally both farre and neare. ←
→ So doth none *other* figure fare
Where natures chattels closed are: ←
→ And beyond his wide compasse,
There is no body nor no place, ←
→ *Nor* any wit that comprehends,
Where it begins, or where it ends: ←
→ And therefore all men doe agree,
That it purports eternitie: ←
→ God aboue the heauens so hie
Is this Roundell, in world the skie, ←
→ Vpon earth she, who beares the bell
Of maydes and Queenes, is this Roundell: ←
→ All and whole and euer alone,
Single, sans peere, simple, and *one*. ←

A speciall and particular resemblance of her Maiestie
to the Roundell.

→ FIrst her authoritie regall
Is the circle compassing all: ←
→ The dominion great and large
Which God hath geuen to her charge: ←
→ Within which most spatious bound
She enuirons her people round, ←
→ Retaining them by oth and liegeance.
Within the pale of true obeysance: ←
→ Holding imparked as it were,
Her people like to heards of deere. ←
→ Sitting among them in the middes
Where she allowes and bannes and bids ←
→ In what fashion she list and when,
The seruices of all her men. ←
→ Out of her breast as from an eye,
Issue the rayes incessantly ←
→ Of her iustice, bountie and might
Spreading abroad their beames so bright, ←
→ And reflect not, till they attaine

The

(*The Arte of English Poesie*)

OF PROPORTION LIB. II.

The fardest part of her domaine.
And makes eche subiect clearely see,
What he is bounden for to be
To God his Prince and common wealth,
His neighbour, kinred and to himselfe.
The same centre and middle pricke,
Whereto our deedes are drest so thicke,
From all the parts and outmost side
Of her Monarchie large and wide,
Also fro whence reflect these rayes,
Twentie hundred maner of wayes
Where her will is them to conuey
Within the circle of her suruey.
So is the Queene of Briton ground,
Beame, circle, center of all my round.

Of the square or quadrangle equilater.

The square is of all other accompted the figure of most sollidi-
tie and stedfastnesse, and for his owne stay and firmitie requireth
none other base then himselfe, and therefore as the roundell or
Spheare is appropriat to the heauens, the Spire to the element of
the fire : the Triangle to the ayre, and the Lozange to the water:
so is the square for his inconcussable steadinesse likened to the
earth, which perchaunce might be the reason that the Prince of
Philosophers in his first booke of the *Ethicks*, termeth a constant
minded man, euen egal and direct on all sides, and not easily ouerthrowne by euery litle aduersitie, *hominem quadratū,* a square man.
Into this figure may ye reduce your ditties by vsing no moe verses
then your verse is of sillables, which will make him fall out
square, if ye go aboue it wil grow into the figure *Trapezion,* which
is some portion longer then square. I neede not giue you any example, bycause in good arte all your ditties, Odes & Epigrammes
should keepe & not exceede the nomber of twelue verses, and the
longest verse to be of twelue sillables & not aboue, but vnder that
number as much as ye will.

The figure Ouall.

This figure taketh his name of an egge, and also as it is thought

(*The Arte of English Poesie*)

Signature 7.

It is worth noting that if you begin to read from the initial O of the word ' of ' at the beginning of the last line of ' The Conclusion ' of *The Arte of English Poesie;* to the right; upwards; on the terminals of all the words; spelling ONOCAB OCSICNARF (Francisco Bacono), you will again arrive at the same terminal F of the word ' of ' in the 8th line from the top of the last page. (See pp. 111–12.)

The acrostic figure here is: —

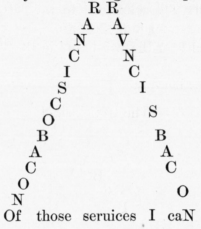

fit for any seruice oF greater importance

Of   those   seruices   I   caN

It is interesting to compare this pyramidal form of acrostic with the similar form of that found in the Sonnets. (1, 2, and 3.)

Signature 8.

It has been pointed out to me by my friend W. L. Stoddard that

if the large initial A at the beginning of the first line of 'The Conclusion' of *The Arte of English Poesie* be treated as a blind, and

if you begin to read on the capital N which follows that large A; to the right; downwards; on the terminals of all the words; spelling NOCAB SICNVARF, you will arrive at the terminal F of the word 'of' (8th line from top of the last page). (See pp. 111–12.)

The acrostic figure will be:—

fit for any seruice oF

Four of these acrostics may be shown in one figure, thus:—

ANd with this . . . I make aN

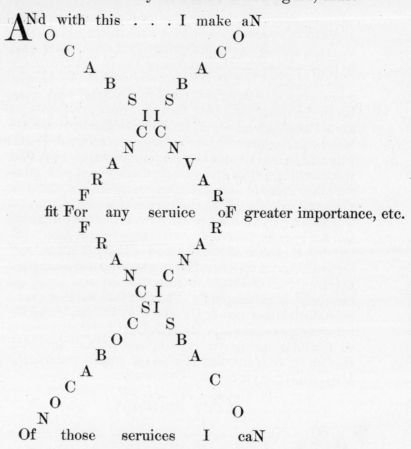

fit For   any   seruice   oF greater importance, etc.

Of   those   seruices   I   caN

(See 'The Conclusion' to *The Arte of English Poesie* on the opposite page)

which the Poet speakes or reports of another mans tale or doings, as *Homer* of *Priamus* or *Vlisses*, he is as the painter or keruer that worke by imitation and representation in a forrein subiect, in that he speakes figuratiuely, or argues subtillie, or perswades copiously and vehemently, he doth as the cunning gardiner that vsing nature as a coadiutor, furders her conclusions & many times makes her effectes more absolute and straunge. But for that in our maker or Poet, which restes onely in deuise and issues from an excellent sharpe and quick inuention, holpen by a cleare and bright phantasie and imagination, he is not as the painter to counterfaite the naturall by the like effects and not the same, nor as the gardiner aiding nature to worke both the same and the like, nor as the Carpenter to worke effectes vtterly vnlike, but euen as nature her selfe working by her owne peculiar vertue and proper instinct and not by example or meditation or exercise as all other artificers do, is then most admired when he is most naturall and least artificiall. And in the feates of his language and vtterance, because they hold aswell of nature to be suggested and vttered as by arte to be polished and reformed. Therefore shall our Poet receaue prayse for both, but more by knowing of his arte then by vnseasonable vsing it, and be more commended for his naturall eloquence then for his artificiall, and more for his artificiall well desembled, then for the same ouermuch affected and grossely or vndiscretly bewrayed, as many makers and Oratours do.

The Conclusion.

ANd with this (my most gratious soueraigne Lady)I make an end, humbly beseeching your pardon, in that I haue presumed to hold your eares so long annoyed with a tedious trifle, so as vnlesse it proceede more of your owne Princely and naturall mansuetude then of my merite, I feare greatly least you may thinck of me as the Philosopher Plato did of *Aniceris* an inhabitant of the Citie *Cirene*, who being in troth a very actiue and artificiall man in driuing of a Princes Charriot or Coche(as your Maiestie might be)and knowing it himselfe well enough, comming one day into Platos schoole, and hauing heard him largely dispute in matters

(*The Arte of English Poesie — The Conclusion*)

25   **OF ORNAMENT. LIB. III.**

Philofophicall, I pray you (quoth he) geue me leaue alfo to fay fomewhat of myne arte, and in deede fhewed fo many trickes of his cunning how to lanche forth and ftay, and chaunge pace, and turne and winde his Coche, this way and that way, vphill downe hill, and alfo in euen or rough ground, that he made the whole affemblie wonder at him. Quoth Plato being a graue perfonage, verely in myne opinion this man fhould be vtterly vnfit for any feruice of greater importance then to driue a Coche. It is great pitie that fo prettie a fellow, had not occupied his braynes in ftudies of more confequence. Now I pray God it be not thought fo of me in defcribing the toyes of this our vulgar art. But when I confider how euery thing hath his eftimation by oportunitie, and that it was but the ftudie of my yonger yeares in which vanitie raigned. Alfo that I write to the pleafure of a Lady and a moft gratious Queene, and neither to Prieftes nor to Prophetes or Philofophers. Befides finding by experience, that many times idleneffe is leffe harmefull then vnprofitable occupation, dayly feeing how thefe great afpiring mynds and ambitious heads of the world ferioufly fearching to deale in matters of ftate, be often times fo bufie and earneft that they were better be vnoccupied, and peraduenture altogether idle, I prefume fo much vpon your Maiefties moft milde and gracious iudgement howfoeuer you conceiue of myne abilitie to any better or greater feruice, that yet in this attempt ye wil allow of my loyall and good intent always endeuouring to do your Maieftie the beft and greateft of thofe feruices I can.

Note

The Partheniades which follow this page are reprinted from the edition of them which is printed by Haslewood with *The Arte of English Poesie* (1811). So far as I know, there is no earlier printed edition than that given in the second volume of the *Progresses* (1788). Haslewood says that he collated his edition with the Cotton MS.

Signature 9 (The Partheniades).

This acrostic is to be found in the opening verse of *The Parthen-iades.* The author quotes some of these poems in *The Arte of Eng-lish Poesie,* and there alludes to the seventh as his own.[1]

The last two lines of this Partheniade contain an amusingly open hint to the decipherer.

We frame the verse with arrow-marks, and regard the initials of the last word of the last line, and the last line but one, as afford-ing us the clue for which we are looking (N and B of the words 'name' and 'blame').

Begin to read on the initial B of the word 'blame'; to the left; up-wards; on the initials of the words of the poem; to the top of the poem and back; having spelled BACON, you will find yourself at the initial N of the word 'name,' thus keying the cipher from the initial of the last word of the last line but one to the initial of the last word of the last line.

Note that there is but one initial N in this whole poem.

The acrostic figure here is: —

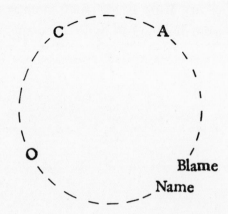

[1] *The Arte of English Poesie,* Arber's Edition, p. 251.

The Partheniades.

The Principall Addresse in nature of a New Yeares Gifte; seem-
inge therebye the Author intended not to have his Name
knowne.

Parthe; I. Thaleia.

Gracious Princesse, where Princes are in place, ←

→   To geue you gold, and plate, and perles of price

It seemeth this day, saue your royall advice   ←

→ Paper presentes should haue but little grace;

But sithe the tyme so aptly serues the case,   ←

→ And as some thinke, youre Highnes takes delighte

Oft to peruse the styles of other men,   ←

→   And oft youre self, wth Ladye Sapphoe's pen,

In sweet measures of poesye t'endite   ←

→ The rare affectes of your hevenly sprighte;

Well hopes my Muse to skape all manner blame, ←

→ Vttringe your honours to hyde her owner's name

Signature 10 (*The Partheniades*).

This acrostic is found in the 12th *Partheniade* (*Urania*).

Note the arrangement of the initials of the overhanging words

of the last two stanzas,

B
F
F
B

Begin to read on the initial N of the first word of the first verse; to the right; downwards; on the initials of the words; spelling NOCAB (i. e. BACON backwards), you will arrive at the initial B of the word ' But.'

Begin again to read on the initial N of the last word of the last stanza; to the left; upwards; spelling NOCAB, you will arrive at the initial B of the word ' By,' thus giving us a figure running through the whole poem, and joining on the monogram of capitals at the side of the 3d stanza.

The acrostic figure here is: —

Not youre   [1st word, 1st verse.]
O
C
A
But to possesse
Fortune
For
    By all consents.
        A
          C
            O
              None   [Last word, last verse.]

FRANCIS BACON 117

Signature 11.

Now note the initial N of the first word of the 3d stanza, and the initials $\frac{F}{B}$ heading the *last two* lines of the same stanza.

Begin to read on the initial B of the first word of the last line of this stanza; to the right; upwards; spelling BACON, you will arrive at the initial N of the word ' Not,' the first word of the first line of the stanza; giving us a vertical figure, thus: —

<pre>
Not any one.   [1st word, 3rd stanza.]
O
C
A
By all consents
    A
        C
            O
                None.   [Last word, last stanza.]
</pre>

NOTE. — I have combined this acrostic with that of the last signature.

The Partheniades

PURPOSE.

Howe twoo principall Exploytes of her Ma[tie] since shee came to the Crowne, to weete, Establishment of Religion and Peace, doe assuredly promise her in this life a most prosperous raigne; and, after her death, a woorthye and longe lastinge name.

What Causes mooved so many Forreinge Princes to bee Sutours
to her Ma[tie.] for Mariage; and what, by Coniecture,
hath hitherto mooved her to refuse them all.

Parthe: 12. Vrania.

Not youre bewty, most gratious Soveraigne,
  Nor maydenly lookes, mayntaynde w[th.] maiestye,
    Your stately porte, w[ch.] dothe not matche but stayne,
    For your Pallas, your presence, and your trayne;
  All Princes courtes, myne eye coulde ever see,
Not your quicke witts, your sober governance,
  Your cleer forsighte, your faytfull memory,
So sweete features, in soe stayed countenance,
Nor languages, w[th.] plenteous vtterance,
So able to discourse and entertayne.

Not noble race, farre beyonde Cesar's raigne,
  Runne in right line, and bloode of noynted kinges;
Not large empire, armyes, treasures domayne,
  Lustye liu'ries of Fortune's deerst derlings;
Not all the skills fitt for a princely dame,
  Your lerned Muse w[th.] youth and studye bringes;

Not true honoure, ne that imortall fame
    Of mayden raigne, your onely owne renowne;
And noe Queene's ells, yet suche as yeeldes youre name,
    Greater glorye than dooth your treble crowne.

Not any one of all these honourde partes,
    Youre princely happs and habites that doe move;
Or as yt were en?cell all the hartes
    Of Christen Kinges to quarrell for your love.
☞ But to possesse at once, and all the goode
    Arte and engyn, and every starre above,
☞ Fortune or kinde, coolde farce in fleshe and bloode
    Was force ynoughe to make so many strive
☞ For your person, who in our worlde stoode,
    By all consents, the mignonst mayde to wiue.

☞ But now, (saye they), what crueltye coold dryue
    By such repulse, your harte harder then stone,
So many hopes of Princes to depriue;
    Forsoothe, what guyftes God from his regall throne
Was woont to deale, by righte distributyue
    Share meale to eche, not all to any one,
O peerles yow, or ells no one alive;
    Your pride serves you to seize them all alone.
        Not pride, Madame, but prayse of your lyon;
        To conquer all, and be conquer'd by none.

NOTE.—This Partheniade is quoted in *The Arte of English Poesie* (on page 224 of Arber's Reprint). The hands were not in the original.

A note on the authorship of 'The Arte of English Poesie.'

Speculation about the authorship of this book has run wild on account of the pseudonymous and, as we now know, the purposely misleading dedication: and also because of the inability of some literary historians to say frankly that they do not know, when what they do know is that they have no facts on which to base a statement that shall be final.

We owe Mr. Edward Arber hearty thanks for his careful reprint of the original text; but like his predecessor Haslewood he befogs himself by an attempt to use some passages in the book to afford him a basis for the date of its composition and for the age of the supposed author.

The book affords no direct evidence for an exact settlement of either of these questions, as it might have been a juvenile work revised at the date of printing, without a revision of anachronisms. We know that the author of Shakespeare's work took good material where he found it, and is supposed to have been blamed for it by his contemporaries. We also are told by William Rawley that Francis Bacon always improved another man's work when he reproduced it. We also know from Spedding that Bacon collected copies of other men's manuscripts when they were worth preserving. As we know these literary habits, it is conceivable that in order to make a complete work on the ' Arte of English Poesie,' Bacon gathered useful material from all directions. It is also possible that he did not straighten out chronological references which aided him in preserving that reticence which appears to have been his confirmed habit or *policy* in all matters relating to poetry, except in his glowing references to it in the *De Augmentis Scientiarum*. (Spedding, vol. iv, pages 314 seqq., and 336.)

Mr. Arber, like other men who have written about this book, is led astray by the ascription of the work to one Master Puttenham in the second edition of Camden's *Remaines*. He has felt obliged to find a Puttenham who would fit the case, and has accepted a George Puttenham as a likely candidate, chiefly on account of his name and his age. He sums up his very inconclusive researches into the history of this man by asking the question, ' *Can he* [the author of the book] *be George Puttenham of whose existence there can be no doubt, but whose name is first possibly* (note that slippery phrase) *associated in print with this work so late as 1614?'*

Now observe the method of writing literary history which has enmeshed us in this muddle over a pseudonym.

Having asked the question, 'Can he be George Puttenham?' Mr. Arber prints the name of George Puttenham (in red ink) on the title-page of his edition, as if George Puttenham were the undisputed author whose title was proved, instead of being based on the wildest and *unanswered* guess.

I am not now writing history, so I shall refer every one, for all the *facts* which we *know*, to a full and very clear statement of them by the Rev. Walter Begley, in the first volume of his work entitled *Bacon's Nova Resuscitatio* (London: Gay & Bird, 1905).

I must, however, mention one fact which we get from Begley (vol. i, p. 102).

It refers to Richard Carew's manuscript of *The Excellencie of the English Tongue*, the matter of which was inserted in the second edition of Camden's *Remaines*, in 1614, and contains the much quoted passage: 'And in a word, to close up these proofs of our copiousness, looke into our Imitations of all sorts of verses affoorded by any other language, and you shall find that Sir Philip Sydney, Master Puttenham, Master Stanihurst and divers more have made use how farre wee are within compasse of a fare imagined possibilitie in that behalfe.'

I quote Begley's own words (*ubi supra*): 'Quite by chance, I happened to hear that Richard Carew's original manuscript was in the British Museum, and on making inquiries I found it among other papers of Camden's which at his death in 1623 came into the Cottonian collection of manuscripts, and had been arranged and bound together in large folio volumes. I took a printed copy of Camden's *Remaines* (1614), containing the first notice of Puttenham by Carew, and began to collate the manuscript and the book word for word. I found that the printer had copied the manuscript very accurately, and had even reproduced from it the curious reading, "Shakespheare and Barlowe's fragment," which has always been supposed to be an early reference to Shakespeare and Marlowe, muddled by the printer. But I found Carew's manuscript had it so most legibly ; in fact, the manuscript and the book agreed word for word, except in one instance, where a later hand in blacker ink had crossed out "couler" and written "colored" above it, and the printed text had "coloured."

'And now came the great surprise. When I came to the Puttenham passage, Maister Puttenham was not there, and never had been, for there was no room for him in the manuscript; for, while the printed *Remaines* read, "Sir Philip Sidney, Maister Puttenham, and Maister Stanihurst," the manuscript had most plainly, without blot or erasure, "Sir Philip Sydney, Mr. Stanihurst."

'So it became pretty plain that "Maister Puttenham" had been foisted in between Sidney and Stanihurst, since Carew's manuscript had been received by Camden — for it is clear that Camden *did* receive this very manuscript, for it owes its salvation to being amongst his papers left to Cotton.'

In the last paragraph even Begley shows the signs of his academic training in vicious historical methods of handling evidence; for he takes it for granted that the manuscript left by Camden to Cotton was the identical manuscript from which the passage in the *Remaines* was printed. It is probable enough that the manuscript was that copy, and it is also possible enough that it was the original manuscript; but after all why not stick to the evidence, which is remarkable enough as it is?

Here we have what looks like an insertion of the words 'Maister Puttenham' into the text of Carew's article while it was passing through the hands of the printers. Here, again, the author Richard Carew himself might have read the proof of his particular article. I do not know what agreement there was between Carew and Camden that Carew should see the proof before it finally went to the press.

We do know, and the knowledge at this point is subject for reflexion, that Camden (and Cotton) thought well enough of Francis Bacon's judgement and knowledge to submit the manuscript of the *Annales* to Bacon, and that Bacon made many interpolations in it which Camden embodied in the printed work. These evidences of Bacon's relations with Camden, as interpolator, can be seen in Spedding's edition of Bacon's *Works*. (Vol. vi, pp. 350–364.)

The 'Dedication' to the book is suspect on its face. They had an unpleasant way of slitting a man's ears or his nose in those days. Ben Jonson and Chapman had a narrow escape from this punishment for printing something which was thought by a powerful man to be derogatory to the Scots. Here we have the case of a printer who is *supposed* to say that he prints a book 'intended to our soveraigne Lady the Queene, and for her recreation and service chiefly devised.' I should surmise that for doing such a thing without good warrant a printer would lay himself open to punishment. The 'Dedication' mentions nothing about permission.

CHAPTER VII

VENUS AND ADONIS— LUCRECE— SHAKESPEARE'S SONNETS — THE PASSIONATE PILGRIME— A LOVER'S COMPLAINT— POEMS WRITTEN BY WIL. SHAKE-SPEARE, GENT. — THE PHŒNIX AND THE TURTLE

Signature 12.

THIS acrostic is found written from the letter at the upper right-hand corner to the letter at the lower left-hand corner of William Shakespeare's dedication of the first edition of *Venus and Adonis* to the Earl of Southampton. Follow the same method of alphabetical sequence as heretofore, but use the terminals—first and last letters of all words, and of all visible divisions of words.

Begin to read on the terminal N of the word 'in,' at the upper right-hand corner of the 'Dedication'; to the left; downwards; to the left-hand terminal F of the part-word 'full' at the lower left-hand corner of the 'Dedication'; having spelled NOCAB SICNVARF, i. e. Frauncis Bacon, spelled backwards.

The acrostic figure here is: —

For the convenience of readers I print the 'Dedication' to show the terminals of words and part-words in a larger type, so that they may be followed the more easily. The facsimile is on an ensuing page.

NOTE. — The facsimiles are reproduced approximately the same size as the originals. The first five are photographed from the facsimiles edited by Mr. Sidney Lee for the Clarendon Press.

ighT HonourablE, I KnoW NoT HoW I ShalL OffenD IN
DedicatinG MY VnpolishT LineS TO YouR LordshiP, NoR
HoW ThE WorldE VvilL CensurE MeE FoR ChoosinG SO
StronG A ProppE TO SupporT SO VveakE A BurtheN,
OnelyE IF YouR HonouR SeemE BuT PleaseD, I AC-
CounT MY SelfE HighlY PraiseD, AnD VowE TO TakE AduantagE OF AlL
IdlE HoureS, TilL I HauE HonoureD YoU VvitH SomE GraueR LabouR. BuT
IF ThE FirsT HeirE OF MY InuentioN ProuE DeformeD, I ShalL BE SoriE IT
HaD SO NoblE A GoD-FatheR : AnD NeueR AfteR EarE SO BarreN A LanD,
FoR FearE IT YeelD ME StilL SO BaD A HaruesT, I LeauE IT TO YouR HonoU-
RablE SurueY, AnD YouR HonoR TO YouR HeartS ContenT, VvicH I WisH
MaY AlvvaieS AnsvverE YouR OvvnE VvisH, AnD ThE VvorldS HopE-
FulL ExpectatioN.

The 'Dedication' of *Venus and Adonis*, showing in large type the terminals of
the words and part-words.

My friend Mr. G. H. Parker has shown me another remarkable reading in this 'Dedication,' which is in its own way as convincing as an acrostic.[1]

Read the 'Dedication' down to the word 'mee,' and continue in the order used in our common reading, from left to right, but using only the terminals and spelling FRAUNCIS BACON, you will arrive at the terminal N of the word 'expectation'—the last terminal in the 'Dedication.'

The reading will thus appear:—

> Right Honourable, I know not how I shall offend in
> dedicating my vnpolisht lines to your Lordship, nor
> how the world vvill censure mee FRAUNCIS BACON.

The terminals will be seen to fall on the following words and part-words:—

how the world vvill censure mee FoR
                                 A
                              Vveake
                 burtheN
                        aC-count
                          Idle
              houreS
                        But
                        A
                        Content
                        Ovvne
              expectatioN

It looks as if we have here the explanation of the much discussed phrase, 'the first heire of my invention.' By the time the reader has read this book through, he will have begun to realise the extent to which Francis Bacon fathered his writings on other men. Spedding gives numerous examples, and the Northumberland manuscript contains others, in which the 'father' is the Earl of Essex, Arundel, Sussex, etc. Here the 'father' is William Shakespeare, Bacon's invention,

---

[1] This is a trick similar to that shown by Begley in *Is It Shakespeare?* page 355. The unknown discoverer of that device came close to a discovery of the trick of reading the types as if they were threaded on a string. His discovery was an important step in my own search for a possible method of hiding an acrostic in such a way that it would not interfere with the heat of composition.

to which *Venus and Adonis* is the first heir. This is, so far as we know, the first time that a poem had been fathered on that handsome pseudonym — often spelled *Shake-speare*, and suggestive of Pallas ' *the Spear-shaker*,' who, so Bacon tells us in his *De Sapientia Veterum*, was born *in armour*, fully equipped, out of Jove's head. (See Begley, *Is It Shakespeare?* pp. 284–287.)

That any one could regard so sophisticated a poem as *Venus and Adonis* as a first poem of a rustic and inexperienced young man, has long made me feel that literary history and criticism rested on insecure foundations. It has seemed impossible to believe that the gossamer biography of Shakespeare, spun upon 'scholarly inference,' which is all that we have yet had from our academic leaders, would not be blown away by a cool breeze from the land of documents and common sense.

VENVS
AND ADONIS

Vilia miretur vulgus: mibi flauus Apollo
Pocula Castalia plena ministret aqua.

LONDON
Imprinted by Richard Field, and are to be sold at
the signe of the white Greyhound in
Paules Church-yard.
1593.

TO THE RIGHT HONORABLE
Henrie VVriothesley, Earle of Southampton,
and Baron of Titchfield.

 *Ight Honourable, I know not how I shall offend in
dedicating my vnpolisht lines to your Lordship, nor
how the worlde vvill censure mee for choosing so
strong a proppe to support so vveake a burthen,
onelye if your Honour seeme but pleased, I ac-
count my selfe highly praised, and vowe to take aduantage of all
idle houres till I haue honoured you vvith some grauer labour. But
if the first heire of my inuention proue deformed, I shall be sorie it
had so noble a god-father: and neuer after eare so barren a land,
for feare it yeeld me still so bad a haruest, I leaue it to your Honourable suruey, and your Honor to your hearts content, vvhich I wish
may alvvaies ansvvere your ovvne vvish, and the vvorlds hopefull expectation.*

Your Honors in all dutie,

William Shakespeare.

(The 'Dedication' of *Venus and Adonis*)

Signature 13 (Venus and Adonis).

We find still another acrostic in this poem. This time it is in the last stanza.

Frame the stanza and begin to read on the terminal N of the last word, 'seen,' in the stanza, using all the letters in the verse as if they were strung on a string; to the right *or* to the left; upwards throughout the stanza and back; spelling NOCAB SICNUARFF (i. e. ffrauncis Bacon, spelled backwards), you will, after reading in either direction, find yourself on the letter F of the word 'Finis.'

The acrostic figure here is: —

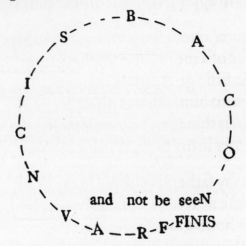

VENVS AND ADONIS.

She bowes her head,the new-ſprong floure to ſmel,
Comparing it to her Adonis breath,
And ſaies within her boſome it ſhall dwell,
Since he himſelfe is reſt from her by death;
    She crop's the ſtalke, and in the breach appeares,
    Green-dropping ſap,which ſhe cōpares to teares.

Poore floure(quoth ſhe)this was thy fathers guiſe,
Sweet iſſue of a more ſweet ſmelling ſire,
For euerie little griefe to wet his eies,
To grow vnto himſelfe was his deſire;
    And ſo tis thine,but know it is as good,
    To wither in my breſt,as in his blood.

Here was thy fathers bed, here in my breſt,
Thou art the next of blood,and tis thy right.
Lo in this hollow cradle take thy reſt,
My throbbing hart ſhall rock thee day and night;
    There ſhall not be one minute in an houre,
    VVherein I wil not kiſſe my ſweet loues floure.

Thus weary of the world, away ſhe hies,
And yokes her ſiluer doues,by whoſe ſwift aide,
Their miſtreſſe mounted through the emptie skies,
In her light chariot,quickly is conuaide,
  Holding their courſe to Paphos,where their queen,
  Meanes to immure her ſelfe, and not be ſeen.
FINIS

LVCRECE.

LONDON.
Printed by Richard Field, for Iohn Harrifon, and are
to be fold at the figne of the white Greyhound
in Paules Churh yard.   1 5 9 4.

TO THE RIGHT
HONOVRABLE, HENRY
VVriothesley, Earle of Southhampton,
and Baron of Titchfield.

HE loue I dedicate to your
Lordship is without end:wher-
of this Pamphlet without be
ginning is but a superfluous
Moity. The warrant I haue of
your Honourable disposition,
not the worth of my vntutord
Lines makes it assured of acceptance. VVhat I haue
done is yours, what I haue to doe is yours, being
part in all I haue, deuoted yours . VVere my worth
greater, my duety would shew greater, meane time,
as it is, it is bound to your Lordship; To whom I wish
long life still lengthned with all happinesse.

Your Lordships in all duety.

William Shakespeare.

A 2

Signature 14.

This acrostic is found in the first page of the text of the first known edition of *Lucrece*, published in 1594. (See page 137.)

The phrase in the dedication to Southampton, 'whereof this Pamphlet without beginning,' is suggestive to a man on the look-out for a cipher.

The eye is at once caught by the big monogram F^R_B at the head of the first stanza of the poem.

Begin to read on the large F of the monogram; on the initials of the words; in the usual zig-zag string fashion; to the right; downwards; spelling FRAN, you will find yourself at the initial N of the word 'name' in the first line of the second stanza.

Begin again to read on the initial B of the monogram; to the right, or to the left; on the initials; downwards; spelling BACON, you will again arrive at the initial N of the word 'name' in the first line of the second stanza.

Begin to read on the letter B used as the printer's 'signature' at the foot of the page; to the right, or to the left; upwards; on the initials of the words; spelling BACON, you will again arrive at the initial N of the word 'name.'

Here we have the signature keyed from point to point, and spelling in its entirety FRAN BACON, which is the form of signature used by him in the dedication to his brother Anthony of the first edition of the *Essays*, a facsimile of which is given on page 28.

The acrostic figure here is:—

F   F B
  R   A
         C
    A O
      Name of, etc.
       O
       C
       A
       B   [The printer's 'signature.']

Signature 15.

A hint from my friend Mr. Walter Arensberg called my attention to another acrostic, which I had overlooked, on the first page of *The Rape of Lucrece.*

Begin to read from the capital B (the printer's 'signature') at the foot of the page; to the right; upwards; on the terminals; spelling BACONO, you will arrive at the initial terminal O of the word ' of ' in the line: —

        ' Hap'ly that name of chast, vnhap'ly set.'

Begin to read from the initial O of the word ' of '; to the left; upwards; still on the terminals; spelling OCSICNARF (Francisco, backwards), you will arrive at the terminal F of the word ' OF ' at the end of the string of type on the page (THE RAPE OF).

The acrostic figure here is: —

```
        THE RAPE OF
                 R
                 A
                 N
                 C
                 I
                 S
                 C
Hap'ly that name Of chast, unhap'ly set
                 N
                 O
                 C
                 A
                 B   [The printer's 'signature' at the
                        foot of the page.]
```

THE RAPE OF
LVCRECE.

FRom the befieged Ardea all in poſt,
Borne by the truſtleſſe wings of falſe deſire,
  Luſt-breathed TARQVIN, leaues the Roman hoſt,
And to Colatium beares the lightleſſe fire,
VVhich in pale embers hid, lurkes to aſpire,
  And girdle with embracing flames, the waſt
  Of COLATINES fair loue, LVCRECE the chaſt.

Hap'ly that name of chaſt, vnhap'ly ſet
This bateleſſe edge on his keene appetite:
VVhen COLATINE vnwiſely did not let,
To praiſe the cleare vnmatched red and white,
VVhich triumpht in that skie of his delight:
  VVhere mortal ſtars as bright as heauēs Beauties,
  VVith pure aſpects did him peculiar dueties.

B

The acrostic figure here is: —

For he the night before in Tarquins Tent,

R
 A
  N
   C
    I
     S
      C
       O
      B
       A
        C
         O
          N

Oh happinesse enjoyed but of a few,

         N
        O
        C
       A
      B
      O
     C
    I
   C
  N
 A
R

From theeuish eares because it is his owne ?

THE RAPE OF LVCRECE.

For he the night before in Tarquins Tent,
Vnlockt the treasure of his happie state:
VVhat priselesse wealth the heauens had him lent,
In the possession of his beauteous mate.
Reckning his fortune at such high proud rate,
    That Kings might be espowsed to more fame,
    But King nor Peere to such a peerelesse dame.

O happinesse enioy'd but of a few,
And if possest as soone decayed and done:
As is the morning siluer melting dew,
Against the golden splendour of the Sunne.
An expir'd date canceld ere well begunne.
    Honour and Beautie in the owners armes,
    Are weakelie fortrest from a world of harmes.

Beautie it selfe doth of it selfe perswade,
The eies of men without an Orator,
VVhat needeth then Appologie be made
To set forth that which is so singuler?
Or why is Colatine the publisher
    Of that rich iewell he should keepe vnknown,
    From theeuish eares because it is his owne?

                                        Perchance

Signature 17.

As we found that the last stanza of *Venus and Adonis* had been turned to account, so we now find that a similar trick has been used in the last stanza of *Lucrece*.

Note that the big capital N, used by the printer to denote the folding of the paper into what the printing craft term *signatures*, has been put up out of its proper place at the bottom of the page to a position above the word 'Finis.' This is hint enough for another signature which might be expected to be at the end of the poem.

Begin to read from this capital N; upwards; to the right; on terminals; throughout the whole stanza and back again; spelling NOCAB NARF (FRAN BACON), you will arrive at the initial F of FINIS.

Begin to read from the F of FINIS; upwards; to the right, or to the left; on terminals; throughout the whole stanza and back again, or throughout the whole page and back again; spelling FRAN BACON, you will arrive at the printer's " signature " N, each time.

The acrostic figure here is:—

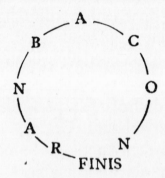

Signature 18.

Observe that this last page of *Lucrece* is so planned that by reading from the initial F of the word FINIS; on initials only; upwards; to the right (or to the left); to the top of the last stanza and back again, or to the top of the page and back again; you will arrive at the capital N (the printer's " signature ") after having spelled F. BACON, in each case.

THE RAPE OF LVCRECE.

This fayd, he ſtrooke his hand vpon his breaſt,
And kiſt the fatall knife to end his vow:
And to his proteſtation vrg'd the reſt,
VVho wondring at him, did his words allow.
Then ioyntlie to the ground their knees they bow,
    And that deepe vow which Brvtvs made before,
    He doth againe repeat, and that they ſwore.

VVhen they had ſworne to this aduiſed doome,
They did conclude to beare dead Lvcrece thence,
To ſhew her bleeding bodie thorough Roome,
And ſo to publiſh Tarqvins fowle offence;
VVhich being done, with ſpeedie diligence,
    The Romaines plauſibly did giue conſent,
    To Tarqvins euerlaſting baniſhment.

N

FINIS.

Signature 19.

This acrostic is found in the first three of *Shake-speare's Sonnets*, as they appear in the first known edition, published in 1609.

My reason for taking these three sonnets is, in the first place, that they virtually form a 42-line poem composed of three sonnets. The fourth sonnet begins on the same subject, but with a fresh treatment of it, as if it might have been the first of a second batch sent to the same person on another occasion. On *a priori* grounds we may reasonably suppose that the sonnets were sent or written in this way, and also because we find this group of them so printed in the *Poems by Wil. Shake-speare. Gent.*, published in 1640, a strong indication that that was the way they were seen in a manuscript used in the preparation of that edition of poems. I give a facsimile of the three sonnets as they appeared in the edition of 1640, where they are treated as one poem, and are entitled 'Love's Crueltie.'

This signature is hidden with unusual care; although, to be sure, the hint of its existence is in full sight. (See pp. 150–51.)

Note the monogram formed by the initials at the head of the first sonnet $\mathbf{F}^{R}_{B}$ and the words $\mathbf{L}^{Ooke}_{Now}$ at the head of the third.

Note also the initial of each end word of the *inner* indented lines (i. e. the 2d line and 13th line). They are N   O

                                       B   B

As a working hypothesis I shall pay attention to the large cipher O in the monogram $\mathbf{L}^{O}_{N}$; for to a man playing with the appearances of words as well as their meaning, it is possible that the words $\mathbf{L}^{Ooke}_{Now}$ may have been chosen to mean ' Looke ON Now'; also ' Lo!'

Begin to read from the large cipher O of the monogram (third sonnet); to the right; downwards, on the initials of the words; spelling backwards ONOCAB, you will arrive at the initial B of the word ' But,' at the *beginning* of the 13th line.

Begin again to read from the same large cipher O of the monogram; to the left; downwards, on the initials of the words; spelling backwards ONOCAB, you will arrive at initial B of the word 'be,' at the *end* of the 13th line.

Here we have the initials B of the first and last words of the 13th line as bases or butts from which to work. The acrostic figure at this stage being: —

L O
   N
   O   O
   C   C
   A   A
   But   Be

Now let us see what happens when we read from the large N of the monogram.

Begin to read on the initial N of the word 'Now' at the beginning of the 2d indented line; on the initials of the words; to the right; downwards; spelling NOCAB (Bacon spelled backwards), you will arrive at the initial B of the word 'be,' at the end of the inner indented line next the bottom of the sonnet, i. e. at the *end* of the 13th line.

Now, again, begin to read from the same initial N of the word 'Now,' at the beginning of the 2d indented line; to the left; downwards; on the initials of the words; spelling backwards, NOCAB, you will find yourself at the initial B of the word 'But,' at the *beginning* of the inner indented line next the bottom of the sonnet, i. e. at the *beginning* of the 13th line.

Now begin to read from the initial B of the word 'But,' at the beginning of the 13th line; to the right; on the initials of the words; upwards; spelling BACONO, you will arrive at the initial O of the word 'other,' at the end of the second line.

Now begin to read from the initial B of the same word 'But,' at the beginning of the 13th line; to the left; on the initials of the words; upwards; spelling BACONO, you will again arrive at the capital O in the word 'other.'

Now begin to read from the initial B of the word 'be,' at the *end* of the 13th line; to the left; upwards; spelling BACONO, you will arrive at the initial O of the word 'other,' at the *end* of the 2d line.

Now, again, begin to read from the same initial B of the word 'be,' at the *end* of the 13th line; to the right; upwards; spelling BACONO, you will arrive at the initial O of the word 'other,' again.

Here we seem to have the two letters O of the word LOoke and of the word 'other' to guide us as a start.

Now begin to read from the initial O of the word 'other' at the *end* of the second line of the third sonnet; on the initials of the words;

O   L^{Ooke}

to the left; using the capitals N in the monogram L^{Ooke}_{Now}; upwards; spelling backwards ONOCAB OCSICNARF, i. e. 'Francisco Bacono,' you will find yourself at the large F of the monogram at the head of the first sonnet.

The acrostic figure here is: —

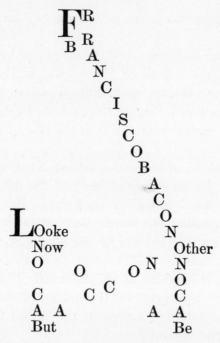

Now begin to read from the large N of the monogram L^O_N; to the right; upwards; on the initials of the words; spelling backwards NOCAB SICNARFF, i. e. 'ffrancis Bacon,' you will again arrive at the large F of the monogram at the head of the first sonnet.

Repeat the same reading, but to the left, and spelling NOCAB SICNARF, you will still arrive at the large F at the head of the first sonnet.

The figure in its entirety is a pyramid upon a firm base, thus:—

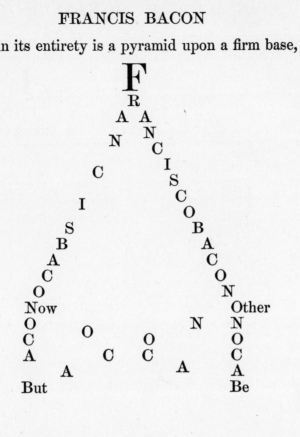

SHAKE-SPEARES

SONNETS.

Neuer before Imprinted.

AT LONDON
By *G. Eld* for *T. T.* and are
to be folde by *william Aspley.*
1609. Q 4

SHAKE-SPEARES,
SONNETS.

FRom faireſt creatures we deſire increaſe,
   That thereby beauties *Roſe* might neuer die,
But as the riper ſhould by time deceaſe,
His tender heire might beare his memory:
But thou contracted to thine owne bright eyes,
Feed'ſt thy lights flame with ſelfe ſubſtantiall ſewell,
Making a famine where aboundance lies,
Thy ſelfe thy foe,to thy ſweet ſelfe too cruell:
Thou that art now the worlds freſh ornament,
And only herauld to the gaudy ſpring,
Within thine owne bud burieſt thy content,
And tender chorle makſt waſt in niggarding:
   Pitty the world,or elſe this glutton be,
   To eate the worlds due,by the graue and thee.

2

VVHen fortie Winters ſhall beſeige thy brow,
   And digge deep trenches in thy beauties field,
Thy youthes proud liuery ſo gaz'd on now,
Wil be a totter'd weed of ſmal worth held:
Then being askt,where all thy beautie lies,
Where all the treaſure of thy luſty daies;
To ſay within thine owne deepe ſunken eyes,
Were an all-eating ſhame,and thriftleſſe praiſe.
How much more praiſe deſeru'd thy beauties vſe,
If thou couldſt anſwere this faire child of mine
Shall ſum my count,and make my old excuſe
Proouing his beautie by ſucceſſion thine.
              B   This

SHAKE-SPEARES

This were to be new made when thou art ould,
And see thy blood warme when thou feel'st it could,

3

Looke in thy glasse and tell the face thou vewest,
Now is the time that face should forme an other,
Whose fresh repaire if now thou not renewest,
Thou doo'st beguile the world, vnblesse some mother.
For where is she so faire whose vn-eard wombe
Disdaines the tillage of thy husbandry?
Or who is he so fond will be the tombe,
Of his selfe loue to stop posterity?
Thou art thy mothers glasse and she in thee
Calls backe the louely Aprill of her prime,
So thou through windowes of thine age shalt see,
Dispight of wrinkles this thy goulden time.
  But if thou liue remembred not to be,
  Die single and thine Image dies with thee.

4

VNthrifty louelinesse why dost thou spend,
Vpon thy selfe thy beauties legacy?
Natures bequest giues nothing but doth lend,
And being franck she lends to those are free:
Then beautious nigard why doost thou abuse,
The bountious largesse giuen thee to giue?
Profitles vserer why doost thou vse
So great a summe of summes yet can'st not liue?
For hauing traffike with thy selfe alone,
Thou of thy selfe thy sweet selfe dost deceaue,
Then how when nature calls thee to be gone,
What acceptable *Audit* can'st thou leaue?
  Thy vnus'd beauty must be tomb'd with thee,
  Which vsed liues th'executor to be.

5

THose howers that with gentle worke did frame,
The louely gaze where euery eye doth dwell
Will play the tirants to the very same,

And

Poëmes:

Loves crueltie:

FRom faireſt creatures we deſire increaſe,
  That thereby beauties *Roſe* might never die,
But as the riper ſhould by time deceaſe,
His tender heire might beare his memory :
But thou contracted to thine owne bright eyes,
Feedſt thy lights flame with ſelfe ſubſtantiall fevvell,
Making a famine where aboundance lies,
Thy ſelfe thy foe,to thy ſweet ſelfe too cruell:
Thou that art novv the worlds freſh ornament,
And only herauld to the gaudy ſpring,
Within thine owne bud burieſt thy content,
And tender chorle makſt waſt in niggarding :
  Pitty the world,or elſe this glutton be,
  To eate the worlds due,by the grave and thee.
When fortie Winters ſhall beſeige thy brow,
And digge deep trenches in thy beauties field,
Thy youthes proud livery ſo gaz'd on novv,
Will be a totter'd weed of ſmall worth held :
Then being askt,where all thy beautie lies,
Where all the treaſure of thy luſty dayes ;
To ſay within thine owne deepe ſunken eyes,
Were an all-eating ſhame,and thriftleſſe praiſe.
How much more praiſe deſerv'd thy beauties uſe,
If thou couldſt anſwere this faire child of mine
Shall ſum my count,and make my old excuſe,
Prooving his beautie by ſucceſſion thine.
  This were to be new made when thou art old,
  And ſee thy blood warme when thou feel'ſt it cold.
                                             Looke

Shakespeare's first three sonnets as they appear in the collection of his poems
published in 1640, and entitled, *Poems Written by Wil. Shake-speare. Gent.*

Poëms.

Looke in thy glaffe and tell the face thou veweſt,
Now is the time that face fhould forme an other,
Whoſe freſh repaine if novv thou not reneweſt,
Thou doo'ſt beguile the world, unbleſſe ſome mother.
For where is ſhe ſo faire whoſe un-eard wombe
Diſdaines the tillage of thy husbandry ?
Or who is he ſo fond will be the tombe,
Of his ſelfe love to ſtop poſteritie ?
Thou art thy mothers glaſſe and ſhe in thee
Calls backe the lovely Aprill of her prime,
So thou through windowes of thine age ſhalt ſee,
Diſpight of vvrinkles this thy goulded time.
     But if thou live remember not to be,
     Die ſingle and thine Image dies vvith thee.

Youthfull glory.

OThat you were your ſelfe, but love you are
     No longer yours, then you your ſelfe here live,
Againſt this comming end you ſhould prepare,
And your ſvveet ſemblance to ſome other give.
So ſhould that beauty which you hold in leaſe
Find no determination, then you were
Your ſelfe again after your ſelfes deceaſe,
When your ſweet iſſue your ſvveete forme ſhould beare.
Who lets ſo faire a houſe fall to decay,
Which husbandry in honour might uphold,
Againſt the ſtormy guſts of winters day
And barren rage of deaths eternall cold ?

Signature 21.

The ignoring of the big initial of a sonnet is exemplified also in the 142d Sonnet. Here, however, we find that the outer letters of the indents have been used as the terminals of the acrostic. Let us look at the plan of the indent. (See p. 159).

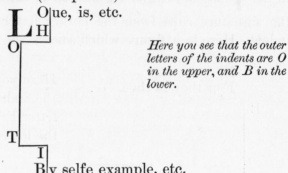

Here you see that the outer letters of the indents are O in the upper, and B in the lower.

The O in the upper indent is used as it was used in the 3d Sonnet.

Begin to read from the initial B of the word 'By'; to the right; upwards; on all the *terminals* of all the words; spelling Bacono, you will arrive at the initial O at the top of the upper indent.

The acrostic figure here is:—

L Oue is my sinne, etc.
  N
  O
  C
  A
By selfe example, etc.

Signature 22.

While we are dealing with these pages of *Shake-speare's Sonnets*, we may as well note the acrostic which is to be seen in the 140th Sonnet.

Observe that the cipherer has here found it convenient to use the initial of the first word of the first line, and that of the first word of the last line as the visible ends of his signature.

Begin to read from the initial B of the word 'Beare,' which is the initial of the first word of the last line; to the right; upwards; on all the letters of all the words; spelling Bacono, you will arrive at the letter O in the word 'nOt' (6th line from top). Then continue to read from the letter O of the word 'nOt'; to the right; upwards; on all the letters of all the words; spelling Onocab, you will arrive at the large initial B of the word B^E which is the first word of the first line of the sonnet.

The acrostic figure here is:—

Be wise as thou art cruell, etc.
A
C
O
N
Though nOt to loue, etc.
N
O
C
A
Beare thine eyes straight, etc.

Signature 23.

This acrostic is found in the 52d Sonnet by Shakespeare.

Begin to read from the initial B of the word ' Being,' which is the first word of the last line; to the right; upwards; on the initials of the words; spelling BACONO, you will arrive at the capital O of the corresponding indent of the first line.

Note the plan of the indents: —

The outer letter of the upper indent is O, and the outer letter in the lower indent is B, with which we began the acrostic.

The acrostic figure here is: —

O

N

O

C

A

B

SHAKE-SPEARES.

More sharpe to me then spurring to his side,
For that same grone doth put this in my mind,
My greefe lies onward and my ioy behind.

51

THus can my loue excuse the slow offence,
Of my dull bearer, when from thee I speed,
From where thou art, why shoulld I hast me thence,
Till I returne of posting is noe need.
O what excuse will my poore beast then find,
When swift extremity can seeme but slow,
Then should I spurre though mounted on the wind,
In winged speed no motion sha'l I know,
Then can no horse with my desire keepe pace,
Therefore desire (of perfects loue being made)
Shall naigh noe dull flesh in his fiery race,
But loue, tor loue, thus shall excuse my iade,
    Since from thee going, he went wilfull slow,
    Towards thee ile run, and giue him leaue to goe.

52

SO am I as the rich whose blessed key,
Can bring him to his sweet vp-locked treasure,
The which he will not eu'ry hower suruay,
For blunting the fine point of seldome pleasure.
Therefore are feasts so sollemne and so rare,
Since sildom comming in the long yeare set,
Like stones of worth they thinly placed are,
Or captaine Iewells in the carconet.
So is the time that keepes you as my chest,
Or as the ward-robe which the robe doth hide,
To make some speciall instant speciall blest,
By new vnfoulding his imprison'd pride.
    Blessed are you whose worthinesse giues skope,
    Being had to tryumph, being lackt to hope.

53

VVHat is your substance, whereof are you made,
That millions of strange shaddowes on you tend?
                                    Since

Signature 24.

This acrostic is found in the 71st Sonnet by Shakespeare. (p. 165).

Begin to read from the initial N of the first word of the first line; to the right; downwards; on all the letters of all the words; spelling Nocab Einohtna (= 'Anthonie Bacon,') you will arrive at the initial A of the first word of the last line.

The acrostic figure here is: —

Noe Longer mourne, etc.

O
C
A
B
E
I
N
O
H
T
N

And mocke you, etc.

Signature 25.

This acrostic also is found in the 71st Sonnet. (p. 165).

Note the plan of the indents: —

Begin to read from the capital O of the upper indent; to the right; downwards on all the letters of all the words; spelling Onocab Oinotna (= 'Antonio Bacono'), you will arrive at the capital A of the outer, lower indent.

The acrostic figure here is: —

N Oe Longer mourne, etc.
  N
  O
  C
  A
  B
  O
  I
  N
  O
  T
  N
And mocke you, etc.

Signature 26.

There is still another acrostic in this 71st Sonnet.

Note that there is but one letter F in the top line of the sonnet, and that the last letter of the last line is the N of the word ' gon.'

Begin to read from the only F in the top line; to the left; downwards; on all the letters of all the words; spelling FFRAUNCIS BACON, you will arrive at the letter N of the word ' gon,' which is the last letter of the last line.

The acrostic figure here is: —

N Oe Longer mourne For
               F
               R
               A
               U
               N
               C
               I
               S
               B
               A
               C
               O
             goN.

Signature 27.

There is still another acrostic in this 71st Sonnet.

Begin to read from the initial N of the first word of the first line; to the right; downwards; either on the initials, the terminals, or on all the letters of all the words; spelling Nocab (= 'Bacon '), you will arrive each time at the initial B of the word 'But,' which is the first word of the 12th line (i. e. the lower overhanging initial).

The acrostic figure here is: —

N
O
C
A
But let your loue, etc.

Begin to read from the initial N of the first word of the first line; to the right; downwards; on all the letters of all the words; spelling Nocab, you will (as we have already seen) arrive at the initial B of the word 'But' (12th line).

Begin again to read from the letter N of the word 'gon,' which is the last letter of the last line; to the left; upwards; on all the letters of all the words; spelling Nocab, you will again find yourself at the initial B of the word 'But,' thus keying the signature from both ends of the string of letters to a common point.

The acrostic figure here is: —

N
O
C
A
But let your love, etc.
     A
       C
         O
           goN.

The reader will judge for himself whether this sonnet is addressed to Anthonie Bacon by his brother ffrauncis Bacon, or is written by Anthonie Bacon and addressed to ffrauncis. We know that Francis Bacon was threatened with assassination during the rebellion of Essex (letter to Sir Robert Cecil: Spedding, vol. ix, p. 162); and it is worth observing that in the 74th Sonnet the writer says: —

'my body being dead,
The coward conquest of a wretches knife.'

SHAKE-SPEARES

70

THat thou are blam'd shall not be thy defect,
For slanders marke was euer yet the faire,
The ornament of beauty is suspect,
A Crow that flies in heauens sweetest ayre.
So thou be good, slander doth but approue,
Their worth the greater beeing woo'd of time,
For Canker vice the sweetest buds doth loue,
And thou present'st a pure vnstayined prime.
Thou hast past by the ambush of young daies,
Either not assayld, or victor beeing charg'd,
Yet this thy praise cannot be soe thy praise,
To tye vp enuy, euermore inlarged,
    If some suspect of ill maskt not thy show,
    Then thou alone kingdomes of hearts shouldst owe.

71

NOe Longer mourne for me when I am dead,
Then you shall heare the surly sullen bell
Giue warning to the world that I am fled
From this vile world with vildest wormes to dwell:
Nay if you read this line, remember not,
The hand that writ it, for I loue you so,
That I in your sweet thoughts would be forgot,
If thinking on me then should make you woe.
O if (I say) you looke vpon this verse,
When I (perhaps) compounded am with clay,
Do not so much as my poore name reherse;
But let your loue euen with my life decay.
    Least the wise world should looke into your mone,
    And mocke you with me after I am gon.

72

O Least the world should taske you to recite,
What merit liu'd in me that you should loue
After my death (deare loue) forget me quite,
For you in me can nothing worthy proue.
Valesse you would deuise some vertuous lye,

To

Signature 28.

This acrostic is found in the 111th Sonnet by Shakespeare.

Note the large **O**, or cipher at the beginning of the sonnet.

Begin to read from the initial F of the word ' For,' which follows the large **O**; to the right; downwards; on all the letters of all the words; spelling FRAUNCIS BACON, you will arrive at the initial N of the word 'name.'

Continue to read from the N of ' name '; to the right, or to the left; still on all the letters of all the words; downwards; spelling NOCAB SICNUARF, you will arrive at the last letter F in the sonnet. The signature is thus keyed from the first and the last letter F in the sonnet, to the common centre N of the word ' name.'

The acrostic figure here is : —

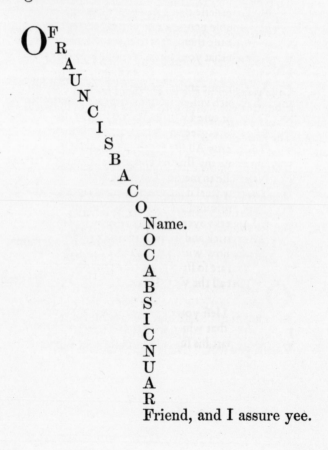

Friend, and I assure yee.

SONNETS.

Then giue me welcome,next my heauen the best,
Euen to thy pure and most most louing brest.

111

O For my sake doe you wish fortune chide,
The guiltie goddesse of my harmfull deeds,
That did not better for my life prouide,
Then publick meanes which publick manners breeds.
Thence comes it that my name receiues a brand,
And almost thence my nature is subdu'd
To what it workes in,like the Dyers hand,
Pitty me then,and wish I were renu'de,
Whilst like a willing pacient I will drinke,
Potions of Eysell gainst my strong infection,
No bitternesse that I will bitter thinke,
Nor double pennance to correct correction.
    Pittie me then deare friend,and I assure yee,
    Euen that your pittie is enough to cure mee.

112

YOur loue and pittie doth th'impression fill,
Which vulgar scandall stampt vpon my brow,
For what care I who calles me well or ill,
So you ore-greene my bad,my good alow?
You are my All the world,and I must striue,
To know my shames and praises from your tounge,
None else to me,nor I to none aliue,
That my steel'd sence or changes right or wrong,
In so proscund *Abisme* I throw all care
Of others voyces,that my Adders sence,
To cryttick and to flatterer stopped are:
Marke how with my neglect I doe dispence.
    You are so strongly in my purpose bred,
    That all the world besides me thinkes y'are dead.

113

SInce I left you,mine eye is in my minde,
And that which gouernes me to goe about,
Doth part his function,and is partly blind,

Seemes

Signature 29.

This acrostic is found in the 152d Sonnet by Shakespeare.
Note the plan of the indents: — N|
                                    B|‾
                                  I|
                                  ‾|
                                    |
                                    |
                                    |
                              O|
                               ‾F|
                                 T|

Begin to read from the capital N of the upper indent; to the right;
downwards; on all the letters of the words; spelling NOCAB, you
will arrive at the initial B of the word 'But,' which begins the next
line. The acrostic figure here is: —

                    N
                    O
                    C
                    A
                    But thou art twice, etc.

Signature 30.

The following acrostic is also found in this 152d Sonnet.

Begin to read from the initial F of the word 'For' in the lower
indent; to the right; upwards; on all the letters of all the words;
spelling FRANCISCONOCAB, you will arrive at the initial B of the
word 'But' in the corresponding place in the upper indent.

The acrostic figure here is: — But thou art, etc.
                    A
                    C
                    O
                    N
                    dOe I accuse thee,
                    C
                    S
                    I
                    C
                    N
                    A
                    R
                    For I haue sworn, etc.

Shake-speares

But ryfing at thy name doth point out thee,
As his triumphant prize,proud of this pride,
He is contented thy poore drudge to be
To ftand in thy affaires,fall by thy fide.
   No want of confcience hold it that I call,
   Her loue,for whofe deare loue I rife and fall.

152

IN louing thee thou know'ft I am forfworne,
But thou art twice forfworne to me loue fwearing,
In act thy bed-vow broake and new faith torne,
In vowing new hate after new loue bearing:
But why of two othes breach doe I accufe thee,
When I breake twenty:I am periur'd moft,
For all my vowes are othes but to mifufe thee:
And all my honeft faith in thee is loft.
For I haue fworne deepe othes of thy deepe kindneffe:
Othes of thy loue,thy truth,thy conftancie,
And to inlighten thee gaue eyes to blindneffe,
Or made them fwere againft the thing they fee.
   For I haue fworne thee faire,more periurde eye,
   To fwere againft the truth fo foule a lie.

153

CVpid laid by his brand and fell a fleepe,
A maide of *Dyans* this aduantage found,
And his loue-kindling fire did quickly fteepe
In a could vallie-fountaine of that ground:
Which borrowd from this holie fire of loue,
A datelesse liuely heat ftill to indure,
And grew a feething bath which yet men proue,
Againft ftrang malladies a foueraigne cure:
But at my miftres eie loues brand new fired,
The boy for triall needes would touch my breft,
I fick withall the helpe of bath defired,
And thether hied a fad diftemperd gueft.
   But found no cure,the bath for my helpe lies,
   Where *Cupid* got new fire;my miftres eye.

154

A pleasant conceited Comedie:

Enter Iaquenetta and the Clowne.

Iaquenetta. God giue you good morrow M.Perſon.

Nath. Maiſter Perſon, *quaſi* Perſon? And if one ſhoulde
be perſt, Which is the one?   (head.

Clo. Marrie M.Scholemaſter, he that is likleſt to a hoggs-

Nath. Of perſing a Hogshead, a good luſter of conceit
in a turph of Earth, Fier enough for a Flint, Pearle enough
for a Swine : tis prettie, it is well.

Iaque. Good M. Parſon be ſo good as read me this letter,
it was geuen me by *Coſtard,* and ſent me from *Don Armatho:*
I beſeech you read it.

*Nath. Facile precor gellida, quando pecas omnià ſub vmbra ru-
minat,* and ſo foorth. Ah good olde *Mantuan,* I may ſpeake
of thee as the traueiler doth of *Uenice, vemchie, vencha, que non
te vnde, que non te perreche.* Olde *Mantuan,* olde *Mantuan,*
Who vnderſtandeth thee not, loues thee not, *vt re ſol la mi fa:*
Vnder pardon ſir, What are the contentes? or rather as *Hor-
race* ſayes in his, What my ſoule verſes.

Holo. I ſir, and very learned.

Nath. Let me heare a ſtaffe, a ſtauze, a verſe, *Lege dominte:*
If Loue make me forſworne, how ſhall I ſweare to loue?
Ah neuer ſayth could hold, yf not to beautie vowed.
Though to my ſelfe forſworne, to thee Ile faythfull proue,
Thoſe thoughts to me were Okes, to thee like Oſiers bowed
Studie his by a s leaues, and makes his booke thine eyes.
Where all thoſe pleaſures liue, that Art would comprehend.
If knowledge be the marke, to know thee ſhall ſuffiſe.
Well learned is that tongue, that well can thee commend,
All ignorant that ſoule, that ſees thee without wonder.
Which is to mee ſome prayſe, that I thy partes admire,
Thy eie *Ioues* lightning beares, thy voyce his dreadful thûder
Which not to anger bent, is muſique, and ſweete fier.
Celeſtiall as thou art, Oh pardon loue this woug,
That ſinges heauens prayſe, with ſuch an earthly tong.

Pedan. You finde not the apoſtraphas, and ſo miſſe the
accent. Let me ſuperuiſe the cangenet.

Nath. Here are onely numbers ratefied, but for the ele-

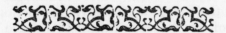

IF Loue make me forſworn, how ſhal I ſwere to loue?
O, neuer faith could hold, if not to beauty vowed :
Though to my ſelfe forſworn, to thee Ile conſtant proue,
thoſe thoghts to me like Okes, to thee like Oſiers bowed.
Studdy his byas leaues, and makes his booke thine eies,
where all thoſe pleaſures liue, that Art can comprehend:
If knowledge be the marke, to know thee ſhall ſuffice :
Wel learned is that toung that well can thee commend,
All ignorant that ſoule, that ſees thee without wonder,
Which is to me ſome praiſe, that I thy parts admyre :
Thine eye Ioues lightning ſeems, thy voice his dreadfull
which (not to anger bent) is muſick & ſweet fire (thunder
    Celeſtiall as thou art, O, do not loue that wrong :
    To ſing heauens praiſe, with ſuch an earthly toung.

Signature 33 (A Louer's Complaint).

This acrostic is found in the first stanza of *A Louer's Complaint,* which was appended to the *Sonnets* in the edition of 1609, and is there printed over the signature of William Shake-speare.

Treat the whole of the first stanza as if it were a continuous string of letters. Note the monogram at the head of the first verse, F$^{R}_{A}$

Note that at the front end of the string will be the initial F of the monogram, and that the letter at the other end of the string will be the letter N of the word 'raine.' *Ignore the silent letter 'e.'*

Begin to read on the letter N in the word 'raine'; to the left; upwards; spelling backwards NOCAB SICNARF, you will arrive at the initial F of the monogram F$^{R}_{A}$, and at the beginning of the string of letters composing the stanza, with the exception of the silent 'e,' which is seemingly used here as a blind.

The acrostic figure here is: —

F$^{Rom}_{A}$
       N
         C
           I
             S
               B
                 A
                   C
                     O
                      raiNe.

This is to be classed as a 'weak' acrostic, as it ignores the final 'e' and begins on the second letter from the end. Compare it with the acrostic by Villon, given on page 55, in which Villon ignores the refrain, and does not object to an extra *i* in his name.

This poem contains forty-seven stanzas. Turn to the edition which was printed with the *Sonnets* in 1609, and from which the above stanza is reproduced. Begin to read from the initial F of the first word of the first line; to the right; down through the poem; treating all lines as a string of letters, in the usual way; using the capital letters only; spelling FRAVNCIS BACON, you will arrive at the initial N of the first word of the first line of the twenty-fourth stanza.

Begin to read from the initial A of the first word of the last line of the last stanza in the poem; to the right; up through the poem; on the capital letters; spelling ANTHONIE BACON, you will again arrive at the initial N of the first word of the first line of the twenty-fourth stanza.

A Louers complaint.

BY

WILLIAM SHAKE-SPEARE.

FRom off a hill whose concaue wombe reworded,
A plaintfull story from a sistring vale
My spirrits t'attend this doble voyce accorded,
And downe I laid to list the sad tun'd tale,
Ere long espied a sickle maid full pale
Tearing of papers breaking rings a twaine,
Storming her world with sorrowes, wind and raine.

Vpon her head a plattid hiue of straw,
Which fortified her visage from the Sunne,
Whereon the thought might thinke sometime it saw
The carkas of a beauty spent and donne,
Time had not sithed all that youth begun,
Nor youth all quit, but spight of heauens fell rage,
Some beauty peept, through lettice of sear'd age.

Oft did she heaue her Napkin to her eyne,
Which on it had conceited charecters:
Laundring the silken figures in the brine,
That seasoned woe had pelleted in teares,
And often reading what contents it beares:
As often shriking vndistinguisht wo,
In clamours of all size both high and low.

Some-times her leueld eyes their carriage ride,
As they did battry to the spheres intend:
Sometime diuerted their poore balls are tide,
To th'orbed earth ;sometimes they do extend,
Their view right on, anon their gases lend,

Te

Signature 34.

This is another acrostic from the edition of poems published in 1640, and entitled *Poems written by Wil. Shake-speare. Gent.*

Note the monogram at the head of the first stanza and the initial B of the first word of the last line of the poem. They are:— F B

Begin to read from the initial F of the first word of the first line; to the right; downwards; using all the letters of all the words; spelling FRANCISCO, you will arrive at the letter O of the word 'How,' at the beginning of the 9th line of the poem.

Now reverse the order. Begin to read from the same letter O of the word 'How' at the beginning of the 9th line of the poem; to the left; in the reverse direction; still downwards; using all letters of all words; spelling backwards ONOCAB, you will arrive at the initial B of the word 'Bad,' thus keying the signature FRANCISCONOCAB, i. e. 'FRANCISCO BACONO,' from the first letter F of the first line to the first letter B of the last line.

The acrostic figure here is:—

F
R
A
N
C
I
S
C
HOw many tales, etc.
N
O
C
A
Bad in the best, etc.

Poëms.

He fpying her, bounſt in (whereas he ſtood)
Oh *Ioue* (quoth ſhe) vvhy was not I a flood?

The unconſtant Louer.

FAire is my love, but not fo faire as fickle,
Milde as a Dove, but neither true nor truſtie,
Brighter then glàſſe, and yet as glaſſe is brittle,
Softer then wax, and yet as Iron ruſty ;
  A lilly pale, vvith damaske die to grace her,
  None fairer, nor none falſer to deface her.

Her lips to mine how often hath ſhe joyned,
Betweene each kiſſe her oathes of true love ſwearing :
How many tales to pleaſe me hath ſhe coyned,
Dreading my love, the loſſe thereof ſtill fearing.
  Yet in the midſt of all her pure proteſtings,
  Her faith, her oathes, her teares, and all were jeaſtings.

She burnt vvith love, as ſtraw with fire flameth,
She burnt out love, as ſoone as ſtraw out burneth;
She fram'd the love, and yet ſhe foyld the framing,
She bad love laſt, and yet ſhe fell a turning.
  Was this a lover, or a Letcher whether ?
  Bad in the beſt, though excellent in neither.

(*The Unconstant Lover*)

Signature 35.

This acrostic is found in the 'Threnos' of *The Phœnix and the Turtle*, which appeared over the signature of William Shake-speare, in a book by one Robert Chester, published in 1601, under the following title (see p. 182):

Love's Martyr; or Rosalyn's Complaint. Allegorically shadowing the truth of Love, in the constant Fate of the Phœnix and Turtle. A Poem enterlaced with much Varietie and Raretie; now first translated out of the venerable Italian Torquato Caeliano, by Robert Chester. With the true legend of the famous King Arthur, the last of the nine Worthies, being the first essay of a new British poet; collected out of divers authentical Records. To these are added some new compositions, of several modern writers whose names are subscribed to their several works, upon the first subject: viz, the Phœnix and Turtle.

Among the authors of the added compositions are Marston, Chapman, Ben Jonson, and 'Ignoto.' This part of the book is introduced with a separate title-page which runs:—

Hereafter follow diverse poeticall Essaies on the former subject, viz, The turtle and Phœnix. Done by the best and chiefest of our modern writers, with their names subscribed to their particular works; never before extant: And now first consecrated by them all generally to the love and merit of the true-noble Knight Sir John Salisburie. Dignum laude virum Musa vetat mori. MDCI.

Shakespeare's share in this book has given rise to much theory among some scholars, but as they have been unable to produce documentary evidence to give validity to their inferences, we must be content to accept the work on the strength of its own title-pages, which, by the way, are plain enough in their meaning, so far as they go.

Shakespeare's 'Threnos' to *The Phœnix and Turtle* is printed on a page by itself, in the edition prepared for *The New Shakespeare Society's Publications*, by Grosart. As I have been unable to see the original I have been obliged to use Grosart's edition, which is said to be an exact reproduction of the spelling of the original.

Note that the initial of the first word of the first line of the 'Threnos' is B, and that the initial of the first word of the last line is F.

Here we have the initials B. F. to guide us. (See p. 182.)

Begin to read from the initial F of the word 'For,' at the beginning of the last line of the poem; to the right; on *all* the letters of *all* the words; upwards; spelling Francisco, you will arrive at the letter O of the word 'not,' in the middle line of the poem.

Now reverse the order. Begin to read from the same letter O of the same word 'not,' in the middle line of the poem; to the right; that is to say, in the reverse direction; still upwards, however; and spelling backwards Onocab, you will find yourself at the initial B of the first word of the first line of the 'Threnos.'

Here we have the signature 'Francisco Bacono,' written consecutively as an acrostic, but to be read as a signature from the initial of the first word of the last line, and from the initial of the first word of the first line, and meeting in the middle of the poem on the same letter O.

The acrostic figure here is: —

```
        B Eautie, Truth, and Raritie,
        A
        C
        O
        N
   Twas nOt
        C
        S
        I
        C
        N
        A
        R
   For these dead Birds, etc.
```

Threnos

BEautie, Truth, and Raritie,
    Grace in all simplicitie,
Here enclosde, in cinders lie.

Death is now the *Phœnix* nest,
And the Turtles loyall brest,
To eternitie doth rest.

Leauing no posteritie,
Twas not their infirmitie,
It was married Chastitie.

Truth may seeme, but cannot be,
Beautie bragge, but tis not she,
Truth and Beautie buried be.

To this vrne let those repaire,
That are either true or faire,
For these dead Birds, sigh a prayer.

                    William Shake-speare.

This copy of the poem I have collated with the text of a reprint as it appears in the edition by Grosart in *The New Shakespeare Society's Publications.* I have been unable to see a copy of the original.

CHAPTER VIII

'DOUBTFUL' PLAYS — *PERICLES, PRINCE OF TYRE; TWO NOBLE KINSMEN*

Note. — The facsimiles are approximately of the same size as the originals.

Signature 36.

This signature is found on the last line of the first page of *The Late and much admired Play, Called Pericles, Prince of Tyre,* as it appears in the first known quarto edition, published in 1609.

The last line runs: —

' Bad child, worse father, to entice his owne.'

Begin to read on the initial B of the first word of the line; to the right; on all the letters of all the words; spelling Bacono, you will arrive at the initial O of the word 'owne.' (See p. 187.)

The cipher thus runs from the initial of the first word to the initial of the last word, thus : —

BAd Child, wOrse father, to eNtice his Owne.
BA . C.... . O... .... .N........ O . . . — Bacono.

Compare this signature with that in the *Hamlet* Quarto.

Signature 37.

This acrostic is also found on the first page of *The Play of Pericles, Prince of Tyre.* (See p. 187.)

Begin to read from the terminal F of the word ' of,' in the title, which is above the text of the play; to the left; downwards; on the terminals of all the words on the page; spelling FRAUNCIS BACON, you will arrive at the terminal N of the word ' owne' (the silent ' e' is ignored, as in other cases).

The acrostic figure here is: —

The Play oF Pericles
R
A
U
N
C
I
S
B
A
C
O
his owNe.

THE LATE,

And much admired Play,

Called

Pericles, Prince of Tyre.

With the true Relation of the whole Hiſtorie,
aduentures,and fortunes of the ſaid Prince :
As alſo,
The no leſſe ſtrange,and worthy accidents,.
in the Birth and Life,of his Daughter
MARIANA.

As it hath been diuers and ſundry times acted by.
his Maieſties Seruants,at the Globe on.
George the Banck-ſide. *Steevens.*

By VVilliam Shakeſpeare.

Imprinted at London for *Henry Goſſon,* and are
to be ſold at the ſigne of the Sunne in
Pater-noſter row, &c.
1 6 0 9.

The Play of Pericles
Prince of Tyre. &c.

Enter Gower.

TO sing a Song that old was sung,
From ashes, auntient *Gower* is come,
Assuming mans infirmities,
To glad your eare, and please your eyes:
It hath been sung at Feastiuals,
On Ember eues, and Holydayes:
And Lords and Ladyes in their liues,
Haue red it for restoratiues :
The purchase is to make men glorious,
Et bonum quo Antiquius eo melius :
If you, borne in those latter times,
When Witts more ripe, accept my rimes;
And that to heare an old man sing,
May to your Wishes pleasure bring :
I life would wish, and that I might
Waste it for you, like Taper light.
This *Antioch*, then *Antiochus* the great,
Buylt vp this Citie, for his chiefest Seat;
The fayrest in all *Syria.*
I tell you what mine Authors saye:
This King vnto him tooke a Peere,
Who dyed, and left a female heyre,
So bucksome, blith, and full of face,
As heauen had lent her all his grace :
With whom the Father liking tooke,
And her to Incest did prouoke :
Bad child, worse father, to intice his owne
A 2.

Signature 38.

This acrostic is found in the 'Epilogue' of the same edition of the same play, *Pericles, Prince of Tyre.* (See p. 193.)

Note the words Fame / Name which end the lines of the second *indent.* The initials of these words are F and N.

Begin to read from the initial F of the word 'Fame'; to the right; on the initials of the words; upwards; *throughout the entire epilogue and back;* spelling FRAVNCIS BACON, you will find yourself at the initial N of the word 'name,' having keyed the cipher.

The cipher can be keyed also by reading from the same initial F; spelling FRAVNCIS BACON, in the same way, but *to the left,* throughout the whole epilogue in the contrary direction, you will still arrive at the initial N of the same word 'name.'

The trick has been made easy here by keeping all words with an initial N *below* the word 'Fame.' A very simple thing to do in such doggerel verse, as we often see in prologues and epilogues.

The acrostic figure here is :—

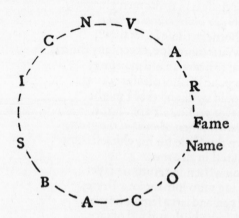

Signature 39.

This 'Epilogue' contains a still more ingenious but very easily made acrostic. (See p. 193.)

You will note that there are two words 'Finis' on the page: one before the 'Epilogue' and one after it.

Let us take the upper 'Finis' first.

Begin to read from the initial F of the word 'Finis'; to the right; downwards; on all letters of *all* words below 'Finis'; spelling FRAVNCIS BACON, you will arrive at the letter N of the word 'In.' Then begin from the same letter N of the word 'In'; without changing the direction, but spelling backwards, NOCAB SICNVARF, you will arrive at the initial F of the last word 'Finis.'

The acrostic figure here is:—

Reading down through the verse.

FINIS.
F
R
A
V
N
C
I
S
B
A
C
O
IN Helycanus may you well descrie,
O
C
A
B
S
I
C
N
V
A
R
FINIS.

Frauncis Bacon.

Signature 40.

Now let us begin again to read from the initial F of the upper word 'Finis'; to the right; downwards; on all the letters of all the words; spelling FRANCISCO BACONO, you will arrive at the letter O in the word 'yOu.' Then begin from the same letter O in the word 'yOu'; without changing the direction, but spelling backwards ONOCAB OCSICNARF, you will arrive at the initial F of the word 'Finis,' at the bottom of the page. (See p. 193.)

The acrostic figure here is : —

Reading down through the verse.

FINIS.
R
A
N
C
I
S
C
O
B
A
C
O
N

In Helycanus may yOu well descrie,

N
O
C
A
B
O
C
S
I
C
N
A
R
FINIS.

Francisco Bacono.

Signature 41.

Begin now to read from the initial F of the lower 'Finis'; to the right; upwards; on all the letters of all the words; spelling FRAVN-CIS BACON, you will arrive at the letter N in the word 'turNe.' Then begin from the same letter N of the word 'turNe,' without changing the direction, but spelling backwards NOCAB SICNVARFF, you will arrive at the initial F of the word 'Finis,' from which we began to read the last signature. (See p. 193.)

The acrostic figure here is: —

Reading up through the verse.

FINIS.
F
R
A
V
N
C
I
S
B
A
C
O
turNe,
O
C
A
B
S
I
C
N
V
A
R
FINIS.

ffrauncis Bacon.

Signature 42.

Finally, begin to read from the initial F of the lower 'Finis'; to the right; upwards; on all the letters of all the words; spelling Francisco Bacono, you will arrive at the letter O of the word 'honOr'd.' Then begin from the same letter O in the word 'honOr'd'; without changing the direction, but spelling backwards Onocab Ocsicnarff, you will arrive at the initial F of the upper word 'Finis.'

The acrostic figure here is: —

Reading up through the verse.

```
                    FINIS.
                    F
                    R
                    A
                    N
                    C
                    I
                    S
                    C
                    O
                    B
                    A
                    C
                    O
                    N
           honOr'd name
                    N
                    O
                    C
                    A
                    B
                    O
                    C
                    S
                    I
                    C
                    N
                    A
                    R
Francisco Bacono.   FINIS.
```

This is the first time that I have found the name Francisco spelled with a double "ff." I give it for what it is worth.

Pericles Prince of Tyre.

Per. Heauens make a Starre of him, yet there my
Queene, wee'le celebrate their Nuptialls, and our selues
will in that kingdome spend our following daies, our sonne
and daughter shall in *Tyrus* raigne.

Lord *Cerimon* wee doe our longing stay,
To heare the rest vntolde, Sir lead's the way.

FINIS.

Gower.

In *Antiochus* and his daughter you haue heard
Of monstrous lust, the due and iust reward:
In *Pericles* his Queene and Daughter seene,
Although assayl'de with *Fortune* fierce and keene.
  Vertue preferd from fell destructions blast,
  Lead on by heauen, and crown'd with ioy at last.
In *Helycanus* may you well descrie,
A figure of trueth, of faith, of loyaltie:
In reuerend *Cerimon* there well appeares,
The worth that learned charitie aye weares.
  For wicked *Cleon* and his wife, when Fame
  Had spred his cursed deede, the honor'd name
Of *Pericles*, to rage the Cittie turne,
That him and his they in his Pallace burne:
The gods for murder seemde so content,
To punish, although not done, but meant.
  So on your Patience euermore attending,
  New ioy wayte on you, heere our play has ending.

FINIS.

Signature 43.

This acrostic is found in the 'Prologue' to the first known edition of *The Two Noble Kinsmen*, published in Quarto, in 1634 — the time that Bacon's manuscripts were being prepared for the press by Rawley and others. (See p. 197.)

Here we have a cipher planned and keyed with what seems to be unusual care. It was discovered for me by my friend Mr. John Macy.

Note that there is a *Florish* of trumpets at the top of the page, and a *Florish* also at the bottom. Our attention is therefore attracted to each end.

Begin to read on the initial F of the word 'Florish' at the top of the page; to the right; downwards; on the initials of the words; throughout the whole prologue and back; spelling FRAVNCIS BACON, you will arrive at the initial N of the word 'Noblenesse' in the middle of the page (15th line from top).

Begin to read from the initial F of the word 'Florish' at the *bottom* of the page; to the left; upwards; throughout the whole prologue and back; spelling FRAVNCIS BACON, you will again arrive at the initial N of the word 'Noblenesse,' and thus keying the cipher.

The acrostic figure here is: —

```
Florish                              B
   R                          A      S
   A                                 I
   V                          C      C
   N                     O           N
   C                                 V
   I              Noblenesse         A
   S           O                     R
   B        A C                   Florish
```

Signature 44.

Begin again to read from the initial F of the word 'Florish' at the top of the page of this prologue; to the right; downwards; on the initials of the words; spelling FRA BACON, you will arrive at the initial N of the word 'Noblenesse.'

Begin again to read from the initial F of the word 'Florish' at the bottom of the page; upwards; to the right; on the initials of the words; spelling FRA BACON, you will arrive at the initial N of the word 'Noblenesse,' having keyed the cipher.

The acrostic figure here is: —

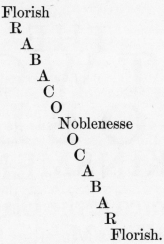

Florish
R
  A
    B
     A
      C
       O
         Noblenesse
       O
        C
         A
          B
           A
            R
             Florish.

Note that the initial of the first word of the first line of this prologue is N: and that the initial of the first word of the last line
is O.

Begin to read from the initial N of the word 'New,' beginning the
first line of the 'Prologue'; to the right; downwards; on the initials
of the words; spelling Noᴄᴀʙ, i. e. Bacon, backwards, you will arrive at the initial B of the word 'be' in the line : —

    'And the first sound this child heare, be a hisse.'

Begin now to read from the initial B of this same word 'be,' continuing on this line to the left as you left off; downwards; spelling
Bᴀᴄᴏɴᴏ, you will arrive at the initial O of the word 'Our' at the
beginning of the last line.

The acrostic thus runs from the initial of the first word of the *first*
line to the initial of the first word of the *last* line.

The acrostic figure here is: —

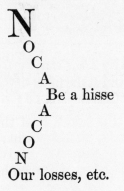

N
  O
    C
     A
       Be a hisse
     A
    C
  O
  N
Our losses, etc.

THE
TWO
NOBLE
KINSMEN:
Prefented at the Blackfriers
by the Kings Maiefties fervants,
with great applaufe:

Written by the memorable Worthies
of their time;
{ Mr. *John Fletcher*, and } Gent.
{ Mr. *William Shakfpeare*. }

Printed at *London* by *Tho.Cotes*, for *Iohn Waterfon:*
andare to be fold at the figne of the *Crowne*
in *Pauls* Church-yard. 1 6 3 4.

PROLOGVE.

Florish.

NEw Playes, and *Maydenheads*, are neare a kin,
Much follow'd both, for both much mony g'yn,
If they stand sound, and well : And a good Play
(Whose modest Sceanes blush on his marriage day,
And shake to loose his honour) is like hir
That after holy Tye, and first nights stir
Yet still is Modestie, and still retaines
More of the maid to sight, than Husbands paines ;
We pray our Play may be so ; For I am sure
It has a noble Breeder, and a pure,
A learned, and a Poët never went
More famous yet twixt Po and silver Trent.
Chaucer (of all admir'd) the Story gives,
There constant to Eternity it lives ;
If we let fall the Noblenesse of this,
And the first sound this child heare, be a hisse,
How will it shake the bones of that good man,
And make him cry from under ground, O fan
From me the witles chaffe of such a wrighter (lighter
That blastes my Bayes, and my fam'd workes makes
Then Robin Hood ? This is the feare we bring;
For to say Truth, it were an endlesse thing,
And too ambitious to aspire to him ;
Weake as we are, and almost breathlesse swim
In this deepe water. Do but you hold out
Your helping hands, and we shall take about,
And something doe to save us : You shall heare
Sceanes though below his Art, may yet appeare
Worth two houres trdvell. To his bones sweet sleepe :
Content to you. If this play doe not keepe,
A little dull time from us, we perceave
Our losses fall so thicke, we must needs leave.

Florish.

Signature 45.

This acrostic is found in the 'Epilogue' to the *Two Noble Kinsmen*, in the Quarto edition of 1634.

Note the last word of the 'Epilogue,' and the word which follows it: they are: $\begin{matrix} \text{night.} \\ \text{Florish.} \end{matrix}$ the initials of which are $\begin{matrix} \text{N} \\ \text{F} \end{matrix}$

Begin to read from the initial N of the word 'night'; to the left; upwards and throughout the whole epilogue and back; on the initials; spelling NOCAB SICNUARF, i. e. FRAUNCIS BACON, backwards, you will arrive at the initial F of the word 'Florish,' having keyed the cipher.

The acrostic figure here is: —

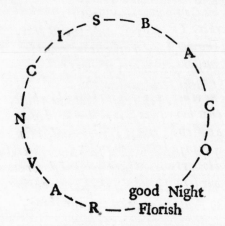

EPILOGVE.

I Would now aske ye how ye like the Play,
But as it is with Schoole Boyes, cannot say,
I am cruell fearefull: pray yet stay a while,
And let me looke upon ye: No man smile?
Then it goes hard I see; He that has
Lov'd a yong hansome wench then, show his face:
Tis strange if none be heere, and if he will
Against his Conscience let him hisse, and kill
Our Market: Tis in vaine, I see to stay yee,
Haue at the worst can come, then; Now what say ye?
And yet mistake me not: I am not bold
We haue no such cause. If the tale we haue told
(For tis no other) any way content ye)
(For to that honest purpose it was ment ye)
We haue our end; and ye shall haue ere long
I dare say many a better, to prolong
Your old loues to us: we, and all our might,
Rest at your service, Gentlemen, good night.

Florish.

FINIS.

CHAPTER IX

PLAYS WHICH HAVE APPEARED ANONYMOUSLY, OR OVER THE NAME OF CHRISTOPHER MARLOWE

TAMBURLAINE THE GREATE—THE FAMOUS TRAGEDY OF THE RICH JEW OF MALTA

Signature 46.

THIS acrostic is found in the Quarto edition of *Tamburlaine the Greate*, published in 1605. (See p. 206.)

The method of hiding the cipher is peculiarly 'foxy,' for all words beginning with an initial N have been excluded from the text of the first page, thus driving the decipherer over to the next page for the point where the names key. At the same time the monograms are in full view on the first page.

We will treat the first page on its own account first; and then the first two pages as one block of type.

Note the monograms on the front page. They are:—

Begin to read from the initial O of the word 'Of' at the beginning of the last line of the first page; to the right; on the *terminals* (first and last letters of every word of the text); upwards; spelling backwards ONOCAB, you will arrive at the large monogram **B**Rother, etc.

The acrostic figure here is:—

B
A
C
O
N

Of Europe, etc.

F
R
A
—
—
B
F
—
—
O

NOTE.—The facsimiles are approximately the same size as the originals.

Signature 47.

Now begin to read from the monogram F at the beginning of the text on the first page; to the right; downwards; on the initials of the words of the text; spelling FRAN, you will arrive at the initial N of the word 'Now' at the beginning of the second line of the second page.

Now begin to read from the monogram B on the first page; to the right; downwards; on the initials of the words of the *text;* spelling BACON, you will arrive at the initial N, again, of the same word 'Now' at the beginning of the second line of the second page.

The acrostic figure here is: —

F

    R

B A
  A
   C
    O

Now to be ruld and governed by a man.

Signature 48.

We are now over on the second page. (See p. 207.)

Note that the initials of the first word on the first line, and of the first word on the second line are $\frac{F}{N}$ of the words $\frac{For}{Now}$

Begin to read from the initial F of the word 'For'; to the right; downwards; on the initials of the words of the text; throughout the whole of page 2 and back, upwards, over on to page 1, throughout the whole of page 1 and back; spelling FRAUNCIS BACON, you will arrive again at the initial N of the word 'Now,' to which we keyed the previous signature.

The acrostic figure here is : —

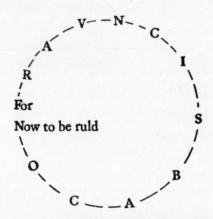

Observe that there is no initial N on the text of the first page. There is no initial O in the first sixteen lines of the second page. There is no initial N in the last twenty-one lines of the second page. The first initial U in the text of the second page is of the word 'uppon' in the 22d line.

This plan of excluding obstructive initials, or of placing necessary initials where they are needed, is very simple, but it enables a cipherer to construct what is, in appearance only, a difficult signature or acrostic.

We have here, then, two signatures keyed to the same initial N, at the beginning of the second line of the second page.

Tamburlaine the Greate.

*VVho, from the state of a Shepheard
in Scythia , by his rare and
wonderfull Conquests, became
a most puissant and mighty
Monarque.*

LONDON
Printed for Edward White, and are to be solde
at the little North doore of Saint Paules-
Church, at the signe of the Gunne.
1 6 0 5.

This title-page is printed that the reader may see that the play was published
anonymously in its first known edition, 1605.

To the Gentlemen Readers and others,
that take pleaſure in reading
Hiſtories.

Entlemen, and curteous Readers who-
ſoeuer: I haue heere publiſhed in Print
for your ſakes, this tragicall diſcourſe
of the Scythian Shepheard, Tamberlaine, that became ſo great a Con-
querour, and ſo mighty a Monarque: My hope is, that
it will bee now no leſſe acceptable vnto you to
reade after your ſerious affaires and ſtudies, then it
hath bene (lately) delightfull for manye of you to
ſee, when the ſame was ſhewed in London vpon Sta-
ges: I haue (purpoſely) omitted and left out ſome
fond and friuolous ieſtures, digreſſing (and in my
poore opinion) farre vnmeete for the matter, which I
thought, might ſeeme more tedious vnto the wiſe, then
any way elſe to be regarded, though (happilye) they
haue bene of ſome vaine cōceited fondlings greatly ga-
ped at, what times they were ſhewed vppon the
Stage in their graced deformities: neuertheleſſe now,
to bee mingled in print with ſuch matter of worth,
it would prooue a great diſgrace to ſo honorable and
ſtately a Hiſtory: Great follye were it in me, to commend vnto your wiſdomes, eyther the eloquēce of the
Authour that writte it, or the worthineſſe of the
A 2   matter

In view of the prominence given to the word 'Brother,' on the first page of the
text of this play (see p. 206), it is worth observing that if you begin to read from
the initial A of the word 'Authour,' which is the first word of the last line of the
above page, to the right; upwards; on the terminals; spelling ANTONIO BACONO,
you will arrive at the terminal 'O' of the word 'who,' at the opposite upper
corner of the page; having traversed the entire page.

To the Reader.

matter it felfe: I therefore leaue it vnto your learned
cenfures, & my felfe the poore Printer thereof vnto
your mofte curteous and fauourable protections,
which if you vouchfafe to doe, you fhall euer
more binde me to imploy what trauell
and feruice I can to the aduaun-
cing and pleafuring of
your excellent
degree.

Yours mofte at com-
mandement.

R. I. Printer.

Signature 49.

This acrostic is found on the last page of the play. (See p. 210.)

Here we again have the same initials F N, of the words 'For now,' but this time at the beginning of the first line of the text on the page.

Begin to read from the initial F of the word 'For' at the beginning of the first line of the page; to the right; on the initials of the words of the *text;* downwards; throughout the whole page and back continuously; spelling FRAVNCIS BACON, you will arrive at the initial N of the word 'now,' next to the word 'For,' from which we started; and thus key the cipher.

Now note that the last line of the page preceding this page runs: —

'My hand is ready to perform the deed.'

The acrostic figure here is: —

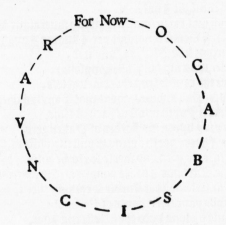

Signature 50.

Observe how Signature 49 has been keyed.

Begin to read from the initial F of the word ' Finis ' ; to the right; upwards; on the initials of the words of the text; spelling FRAVNCIS BACON, you will again arrive at the initial N of the word 'now,' on which the Signature 49 ended.

The acrostic figure here is:—

For Now, etc.

Reading upwards.

O
C
A
B
S
I
C
N
V
A
R
FINIS.

Two things are to be noted here. The one, that this page has been used by the cipherer in the same manner that he used the first two pages of the text of the play; the other, that the cipherer seems to have taken advantage of the *double entente* of the last line of the preceding page.

the Scythian Shepheard.

For now her marriage time shall worke vs rest,
  Vsum.and heer's the crowne my Lord,helpe set it on.
  Tam.Then sit thou downe(diuine Zenocrate)
And heere we crowne thee Queene of Persia,
And all the kingdomes and Dominions
That late the power of Tamburlaine subdude,
As Iuno when the Gyants were supprest,
That darted mountaines at her Brother Ioue,
So lookes my loue,shaddowing in her browes,
Triumphes and Trophées for my victories :
Or as Latonas daughter bent te armes,
Adding more courage to my conquering minde,
To gratifie the sweete Zenocrate,
Egiptians,Moores,and men of Asia,
From Barbarie vnto the Westerne Indie,
Shall pay a yearely tribute to thy Sire,
And from the bounds of Affricke to the bankes
Of Ganges,shall his mightie arme extend.
and now my Lords and louing followers,
That purchas'd Kingdomes by your martiall deedes,
Cast off your armour,put on Scarlet robes,
Mount vp your royall places of estate,
Enuironed with troopes of noble men,
and there make lawes to rule your prouinces.
Hang vp your weapons on Alcides poste,
For Tamburlaine takes truce with all the world.
Thy first betrothed Loue Arabia
Shal we with honor(as beseemes)entombe
With this greate Turke,and his faire Emperesse,
Then after all these solemne Exequies,
We will our celebrated rites of marriage solemnize.

F I N I S.

Signature 51.

This acrostic is found in the first known edition of *The Famous Tragedy of The Rich Jew of Malta*, published in 1633; i. e. forty years after the death of Marlowe! William Rawley was at this time preparing the acknowledged works of Francis Bacon for the press, or for publication, and Bacon's executors were about to place in Gruter's hands those which he edited and had published later in Holland. Thomas Heywood furnishes a dedication, in which he alludes to the play 'As I ushered it unto the Court, and presented it to the Cock-pit, with these Prologues and Epilogues here inserted.'

I can think of two reasons for this special mention of the prologues and epilogues: one, that Heywood may have written them; the other, that their position crowded together on two pages at the front of the book is to be brought to our attention thereby. There may be other reasons; we do not know.

We do know, however, that on the last line of the last epilogue the two words '(by me)' are bracketed together. Bracketed words are common enough, but these two attract our attention; in connexion with the initial of the word 'mind,' which is directly over them, thus, $\frac{\text{mind}}{\text{(by me)}}$. The initials of this group of words are $\frac{\text{M}}{\text{(B M)}}$ (See pp. 218–19.)

Treat both pages as one for our purpose. (See pp. 218–19.)

Begin to read on the initial B of the word 'by' in the brackets; to the right; upwards; on the initials of the words; throughout the text of both pages and back continuously; spelling BACON BARON VER-ULAM, you will arrive at the initial M of the word 'me' bracketed with the word 'by' from which we started out.

The acrostic figure here is: —

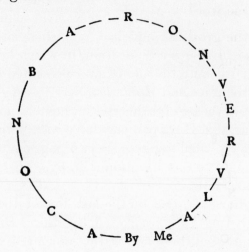

Signature 52.

Begin to read from the initial B of the word 'by' in the brackets; to *the left ;* upwards; on the initials of the words; throughout the text of both pages and back continuously; spelling B<small>ACON</small> B<small>ARON</small> V<small>ERULAM</small>, you will arrive at the initial M of the word 'mind' immediately over the word 'by.' The signature is thus keyed in both directions from the group of initials $\frac{M}{(B\ M)}$ (See p. 219.)

The acrostic figure here is:—

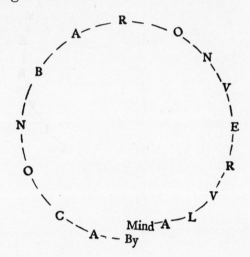

The questions suggested here are: What relation did Heywood bear to William Rawley or to Bacon's literary executors, in the publication of this play, so long kept out of print? Who had been holding the manuscript for so long a time? Was it excluded from the Shakespeare volume because Marlowe had long been recognised as its father? Who wrote *Hero and Leander,* which is mentioned in the 'Prologue' to *The Stage at the Cocke-pit ;* and in which 'one' is there said to have gained *a lasting memorie?*

There is, indeed, room for much interpretation in the possible answers to these questions.

Signature 53.

This acrostic is found in Tho. Heywood's 'Dedication' of *The Rich Jew* to his worthy friend Mr. Thomas Hammon. (See pp. 216–17.)

Begin to read on the initial T of the word '*Tuisimus*'; to the right; upwards; on the terminals of the words; spelling TINEVNI NOCAB SICNUARF, you will arrive at the terminal F of the word 'OF' which immediately precedes the words GRAYES INNE.

The acrostic figure here is:—

OF GRAYES INNE, &c.
R
A
U
N
C
I
S
B
A
C
O
N
I
N
V
E
N
I
Tuisimus:

The Famous
TRAGEDY
OF
THE RICH IEVV
OF *MALTA.*

AS IT WAS PLAYD
BEFORE THE KING AND
Qveene, IN HIS MAJESTIES
Theatre at *White-Hall*, by her Majesties
Servants at the *Cock-pit*.

Written by CHRISTOPHER MARLO.

LONDON;
Printed by *I. B.* for *Nicholas Vavasour*, and are to be sold
at his Shop in the Inner-Temple, neere the
Church. 1 6 3 3.

TO
MY VVORTHY
FRIEND, M.ʳ T H O M A S,
HAMMON, OF G R A Y E S
INNE, &c.

His **Play**, compoſed by ſo worthy an Authour as Mr. *Marlo*; and the part of the Jew preſented by ſo vnimitable an Actor as Mr. *Allin*, being in this later Age commended to the Stage: As I vſher'd it unto the Court, and preſented it to the Cock-pit, with theſe Prologues and Epilogues here inſerted, ſo now being newly brought to the Preſſe, I was loath it ſhould be publiſhed without the ornament of an Epiſtle ; making choyce of you vnto whom to deuote it ; then whom (of all thoſe Gentlemen and acquaintance, within the compaſſe of my long knowledge) there is none more able to taxe

A 3   Ignorance

The Epiſtle Dedicatory:

Ignorance, or attribute right to merit. Sir, you haue bin
pleaſed to grace ſome of mine owne workes with your
curteous patronage ; I hope this will not be the worſe
accepted, becauſe commended by mee ; ouer whom,
none can clayme more power or priuilege than your
ſelfe. I had no better a New-yeares gift to preſent you
with ; receiue it therefore as a continuance of that in-
uiolable obliegement, by which, he reſts ſtill ingaged ;
who as he euer hath, ſhall alwayes remaine,

Tuißimus :

THO. HEYVVOOD.

The

The Prologue ſpoken at Court.

Gracious and Great, that we ſo boldly dare,
('Mongſt other Playes that now in faſhion are)
To preſent this ; writ many yeares agone,
And in that Age, thought ſecond vnto none ;
We humbly craue your pardon : we purſue
Toe ſtory of a rich and famous Jew
Who liu'd in Malta : you ſhall find him ſtill,
In all his proiects, a ſound Macheuill ;
And that's his Character : He that hath paſt
So many Cenſures, is now come at laſt
To haue your princely Eares, grace you him ; then
You crowne the Action, and renowne the pen.

Epilogue.

IT is our feare (dread Soueraigne) we haue bin
Too tedious ; neither can't be leſſe than ſinne
To wrong your Princely patience : If we haue ;
(Thus low deiected) we your pardon craue :
And if ought here offend your eare or ſight,
We onely Act, and Speake, what others write.

The

(*The Famous Tragedy of The Rich Jew of Malta*)

Prologues and Epilogues. 1.

The Prologue to the Stage, at
the Cocke-pit.

* Marlo.

* Allin.

WE know not how our Play may paſſe this Stage,
But by the beſt of * Poets in that age
The Malta Jew had being, and was made;
And He, thenby the beſt of * Actors play'd:
In Hero and Leander, one did gaine
A laſting memorie: in Tamberlaine,
This Jew, with others many: th' other wan
The Attribute of peereleſſe, being a man
Whom we may ranke with (doing no one wrong)
Proteus for ſhapes, and Roſcius for a tongue,
So could he ſpeake, ſo vary; nor is't hate

* Perkins.

To merit: in * him who doth perſonate
Our Jew this day, nor is it his ambition
To exceed, or equall, being of condition
More modeſt; this is all that he intends,
(And that too, at the vrgence of ſome friends)
To proue his beſt, and if none here gaine-ſay it,
The part he hath ſtudied, and intends to play it.

Epilogue.

IN Graving, with Pigmalion to contend;
Or Painting, with Apelles; doubtleſſe the end
Muſt be diſgrace: our Actor did not ſo,
He onely aym'd to goe, but not out-goe.
Nor thinke that this day any prize was plaid,
Here were no betts at all, no wagers laid;
All the ambition that his mind doth ſwell,
Is but to heare from you, (by me) 'twas well.

(*The Famous Tragedy of The Rich Jew of Malta*)

Prologues and Epilogues. 2.

Signature 54.

This acrostic is found on the last page of the play *The Famous Tragedy of The Rich Jew of Malta,* and in the same edition.

Note the words beginning the first four lines at the top of the

Nay

page. They are: We   The initial of the first is N; and the ini-

Besides

For

tials of the last two are B
                           F

Treat all four lines as a string of letters. (See p. 222.)

Begin to read on the initial N of the word 'Nay'; to the right; downwards; on all the letters of all the words; spelling Nocab Sicnuarf, you will arrive at the initial F of the word 'For.'

Begin to read on the initial F of the word 'For'; to the right; *upwards;* on all the letters of all the words; spelling Frauncis Bacon, you will arrive at the initial N of the word 'Nay'; thus keying the cipher forwards and backwards, from the same letters.

The acrostic figure here is:—

Nay
O
C
A
Besides
S
I
C
N
U
A
R
For with thy, etc.

Signature 55.

There is still another acrostic signature in this last page of *The Famous Tragedy of The Rich Jew of Malta.* (See p. 222.)

Observe that the initial of the first word of the first line is N, and that the initial of the first word of the last line is also an N.

Begin to read from the initial N of the first word of the first line; to the right; downwards; on the terminals of the words of the text; spelling Nocab Narff (=ffran Bacon), you will end your spelling on the F of the word ' fall ' and the F of the word ' father.'

Begin to read from the initial N of the first word of the last line; to the right; upwards; on the terminals of the words of the text; spelling Nocab Narff (=ffran Bacon), you will end your spelling on the F of the word ' father ' and the F of the word ' fall.'

The acrostic figure here is: —

Nay, Selim, etc.
O
C
A
By this.
N
A
R
Fall
Father
R
A
N
Be freed
A
C
O
Neither to Fate, etc.

The Iew of Malta.

Gov. Nay, *Selim*, ftay, for fince we haue thee here,
We will not let thee part fo fnddenly :
Befides, if we fhould let thee goe, all's one,
For with thy Gallyes couldft thou nor get hence,
Without fresh men to rigge and furnish them.
    Caly. Tush, Gouernor, take thou no care for that,
My men are all aboord,
And doe attend my comming there by this.
    Gov. Why hardft thou not the trumpet found a charge?
    Caly. Yes, what of that ?
    Gov. Why then the houfe was fir'd,
Blowne vp and all thy fouldiers maffacred.
    Caly. Oh monftrous treafon !
    Gov. A Iewes curtefie :
For he that did by treafon worke our fall,
By treafon hath deliuered thee to vs :
Know therefore, till thy father hath made good
The ruines done to *Malta* and to vs,
Thou canft not part : for *Malta* shall be freed,
Or *Selim* ne're returne to *Ottamen.*
    Caly. Nay rather, Chriftians, let me goe to Turkey
In perfon there to meditate your peace ;
To keepe me here will nought aduantage you.
    Gov. Content thee, *Calymath*, here thou muft ftay,
And liue in *Malta* prifoner ; for come call the world
To refcue thee, fo will we guard vs now,
As fooner shall they drinke the Ocean dry,
Then conquer *Malta*, or endanger vs.
So march away, and let due praife be giuen
Neither to Fate nor Fottune, but to Heauen.

FINIS.

CHAPTER X

ENGLAND'S HELICON—PALLADIS PALATIUM

[Literary collections which have been connected with the name of John
Bodenham, or which have appeared anonymously.]

Signature 56.

THIS acrostic is to be found in the laudatory sonnet initialled A. B.
and placed in the vestibule of *England's Helicon,* a book attributed
to a John Bodenham, and published in 1600. Reference to *The Dictionary of National Biography* yields us a very shadowy personal-
ity for this name. Next to nothing is known about it. I shall refer
the curious reader to Walter Begley's *Bacon's Nova Resuscitatio*
for fuller information on this and other books of a similar nature
with which Master John Bodenham's name has been definitely
connected. Begley's eighth chapter of his first volume is entitled
' Who was John Bodenham?' In that chapter he gives some interesting reasons of the inferential kind for regarding the initials A. B.,
with which the sonnet is signed, as those of Anthony Bacon; and
also for *believing* that the person to whom, under the name of John
Bodenham, the sonnet is addressed, is Anthony's own brother Francis
Bacon. (See p. 226.)

If the acrostic signatures which I find in this sonnet are evidence,
Walter Begley must be regarded as having made a brilliantly correct
surmise.

Note that the initials of the words beginning the last two lines of
the sonnet (they are indented) are $\begin{smallmatrix}T\\A\end{smallmatrix}$ of the words $\begin{smallmatrix}\text{Take}\\\text{And}\end{smallmatrix}$

Note also that we shall at first deal solely with the sestett, which
is separate from the rest of the sonnet.

Begin to read from the initial T of the word ' Take '; to the right;
upwards; throughout the whole of the sestett; using *all* the letters of
all the words; and back again; spelling TINEVNI NOCAB EINOHTNA,
i. e. Anthonie Bacon Invenit, you will arrive at the initial A of the
word ' And '; thus keying the signature.

The acrostic figure here is: —

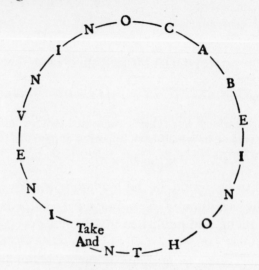

We have here the interesting suggestion that Anthony Bacon was conversant with this method of making an invisible signature, and that he was expressing his sympathy with his brother Francis in the latter's design to preserve for posterity some poems which might otherwise have been lost to us.

Signature 57.

Now note the address:—

'To his Loving Kinde Friend Maister John Bodenham'; and compare it with the tone and the words of Francis's dedication of the first edition of his *Essayes* to his brother Anthony; a usual form at that time. (See p. 226.)

Now begin to read on the initial F of the word 'Friend'; to the right; downwards; on all the letters of the words; until you shall have spelled FRANCIS BACON, you will arrive at the letter N of the word 'count.'

Now begin to read from the initial A of the initial signature A. B.; to the right; upwards; on all the letters of the words; until you shall have spelled ANTHONIE BACON, you will arrive again at the letter N in the word 'count,' thus keying the two signatures, and exposing the sentence, ' *To his Loving Kinde Friend Francis Bacon, Anthonie Bacon.*'   The acrostic figure here is:—

```
To his Loving Kinde F
                     R
                      A
                       N
                        C
                         I
                          S
                           B
                            A
                             C
                              O
By both of which, I cannot couNt
                                O
                                 C
                                  A
                                   B
                                    E
                                     I
                                      N
                                       O
                                        H
                                         T
                                          N
                                           A
```

Note that at the reading of each name the name *Bacon* begins upon the letter B of the word 'By' in the line printed above.

England's Helicon.

To his Loving Kinde Friend Maister John Bodenham.

Wits Common-wealth, the first-fruites of thy paines,
　　Drew on *Wits Theater* thy second Sonne:
By both of which, I cannot count the gaines,
　　And wondrous profit that the world hath wonne.
Next, in the *Muses Garden*, gathering flowers,
　　Thou mad'st a Nosegay, as was never sweeter:
Whose sent will savour to Times latest howres,
　　And for the greatest Prince no Poesie meeter.

Now comes thy *Helicon* to make compleate
　　And furnish up thy last impos'd designe:
My paines heerin I cannot terme it great,
　　But what-so-ere, my love (and all) is thine.
　　　Take love, take paines, take all remaines in me:
　　　And where thou art, my hart still lives with thee.

A. B.

As I have not had access to the original copy, I have been obliged to content myself with the reprint of this sonnet given by Begley in volume I of his *Bacon's Nova Resuscitatio*, page 111.

Signature 58.

This acrostic is found in the 'Dedication' of the first known edition (1604) of the *Palladis Palatium;* of which, so Begley says, but one copy is known to exist, in a private library (Britwell). (See p. 228.)

Here again I shall refer the reader for the history of the book to the admirable account (though marred by some inferences) by Begley, in *Bacon's Nova Resuscitatio,* volume ɪ, cap. xii. There he lists it with the little group of books, connected directly or indirectly with the names of John Bodenham, and in one instance (*Palladis Tamia*) of Francis Meres.

Note the initials F. B., supposed to be those of the printer Francis Burton. They are placed (as in the case of *The Arte of English Poesie*) both at the entrance of the 'Dedication,' and at its exit, or foot.

We will begin to read from the F of the supposed Burton initials, at the beginning of the 'Dedication' (sixth line); to the right; downwards; on the initials of the words; spelling F. Bacono, you will arrive at the initial O of the word 'of' (32d line).

Now begin to read from the initial F of the supposed Burton initials, at the *end* of the 'Dedication'; to the right; upwards; on the initials of the words; spelling F. Bacono, you will again arrive at the initial O at the same word 'of'; thus keying the signature.

The acrostic figure here is: —

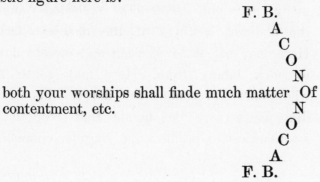

both your worships shall finde much matter Of
contentment, etc.

Palladis Palatium.

To the right worshipfull Stephen Smalman, of Wildertop in the Countie of Salop
Esquire, and one of his Majesties Justices of
peace in the same countie: and unto the
right vertuous Gentlewoman Mistris Jane
Smalman his beloved wife, F. B. wisheth
encrease of all godlines in this life, and in
the life to come eternall happinesse.

THe happy successe which this authors
former booke hath gayned under the shaddow of
your worships winges, and also the kinde acceptance of so slender a dedication as proceeded from
my unpollished pen, have embouldened me again
to present your worships with an other parcell of
the same mans labours, in hope that you both
will (as formerly you have done) yeald a favour-
able allowance unto this worke, and also a kinde
construction of my rude though well meaning
Epistle.

The booke for argument containeth varietie of
many excelent sentences collected out of
the choicest writings of the auncient fathers.
Here may wit finde pleasant and sweete flowers
to suck hunny from. Here may youth finde
wholesome precepts to derect his future
life. Here may the minde that readeth with
an intention to profit, reape singular commoditie.

Here may the wearied and defatigate spirit, recreate itself with variable delightes. Here may most (good) dispositions light upon some thinges to fitte their desires. And here I doubt not but both your worships shall finde much matter of contentment, when your leasures will affoorde you time to peruse it. I trust that I need not frame any Apologie in the defence or excuse of the booke it selfe, for vertue is to be loved for it owne sake, and therefore I hope that the matter it selfe, will winne favour unto it selfe. If not yet I know that, *Virescit vulnere virtus:* Vertue if she be wounded can heale it selfe, and will appeare by so much more glorious, by how much more eagerly vice endevoureth to dimme the brightnesse thereof.

Wherfore in ful perswatiō that it shall gaine your worships good liking, I commend you both unto the fruition of the best joyes that eyther of you can wish unto your owne selves, and rest a devoted wel-willer unto both your worships.

F. B.

CHAPTER XI

SOME POEMS WHICH HAVE APPEARED UNDER THE NAME OF
EDMUND SPENSER: AND SOME PROSE WHICH HAS BEEN
ATTRIBUTED TO EDWARD KIRKE

Ruines of Rome : printed in *Complaints.*

Virgil's Gnat : printed in *Complaints.*

The Visions of Petrarch : printed in *Complaints.*

E. K.'s Epistle to Gabriel Harvey: printed with *The
Shepheardes Calender.*

The Generall Argument: The Shepheardes Calender.

Immeritô to his Booke.

Daphnaïda.

An Hymne in honour of Love.

An Hymne of Heauenly Love.

An Hymne of Heavenly Beautie.

NOTE.— The facsimiles are approximately the size of the originals, except
where they have been reduced from a folio size to that of my page.

This title-page is printed in order that the reader may see how the name of the supposed author is printed. The cut is a composite of two pages. A clear part was obtained from each. The border from one: the centre from the other.

The Printer to the
Gentle Reader.

INCE my late setting
foorth of the *Faerie
Queene*, finding that it
hath found a fauoura-
ble paffage amongft.
you; I haue fithence
endeuoured by all good meanes (for
the better encreafe and accomplifhment
of your delights, to get into my handes
fuch fmale Poemes of the fame Authors;
as I heard were difperft abroad in fundrie
hands, and not eafie to bee come by, by
himfelfe; fome of them hauing bene di-
uerflie imbeziled and purloyned from
him, fince his departure ouer Sea. Of the
which I haue by good meanes gathered
togeather thefe fewe parcels prefent,
which I haue caufed to bee imprinted al-

A 2   to-

To the Reader.

togeather, for that they al feeme to containe like matter of argument in them:
being all complaints and meditations of
the worlds vanitie; verie graue and profitable. To which effect I vnderftand that
he befides wrote fundrie others, namelie
Ecclefiaftes, & *Canticum canticorum* tranf-
lated, *A fenights flumber*, *The hell of louers*,
his Purgatorie, being all dedicated to Ladies; fo as it may feeme he ment them all
to one volume. Befides fome other Pam-
phlets loofelie fcattered abroad: as *The
dying Pellican*, *The howers of the Lord*, *The
facrifice of a finner*, *The feuen Pfalmes*, &c.
which when I can either by himfelfe, or
otherwife attaine too, I meane likewife
for your fauour fake to fet foorth. In the
meane time praying you gentlie to accept of thefe, & gracioullie to entertaine
the new Poet.   *I take leaue.*

Signature 59.

This acrostic is found in the last stanza ('L'Envoy') of *The Ruines of Rome*, which was printed in *Complaints* and published in 1591. The facsimiles are from that edition.

Begin to read from the initial B of the word 'Bellay' at the beginning of the first line; to the right; downwards; on the initials (*or* the terminals) of the words; spelling BACON, you will arrive at the initial N of the word 'name.'

The acrostic figure here is: —

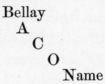

Signature 60.

Now note that the initials of the last word of the last line and the last word of the last line but one are $\frac{N}{F}$ of the words $\frac{name}{fame}$.

Begin to read from the initial F of the word 'fame'; to the left; upwards; throughout the whole stanza and back; on the initials of the words; spelling FRAN BACON, you will find yourself at the initial N of the word 'name' again.

The acrostic figure here is: —

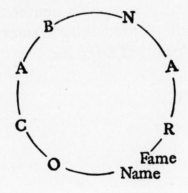

Signature 61.

Begin to read from the initial F of the word 'fame'; to the left; upwards; and back again; throughout the whole stanza; on the *terminals*, i. e. the first and last letters of each word; spelling Francis Bacon, you will find yourself back again at the initial N of the word 'name,' thus keying the cipher.

The acrostic figure here is: —

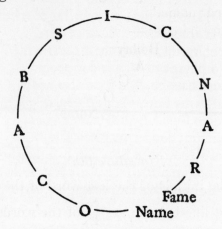

Ruines of Rome.

32

Hope ye my yerſes that poſteritie
Of age enſuing ſhall you euer read ?
Hope ye that euer immortalitie
So meane Harpes worke may chalenge for her meed?
    If vnder heauen anie endurance were,
Theſe moniments,which not in paper writ,
But in Porphyre and Marble doo appeare,
Might well haue hop'd to haue obtained it.
    Nath'les my Lute,whom *Phœbus* deignd to giue,
Ceaſe not to ſound theſe olde antiquities :
For if that time doo let thy glorie liue,
Well maiſt thou boaſt,how euer baſe thou bee,
    That thou art firſt,which of thy Nation ſong
    Th'olde honour of the people gowned long.

L'Envoy.

*Bellay,*firſt garland of free Poëſie   (wits,
That *France* brought forth, though fruitfull of braue
Well worthie thou of immortalitie,
That long haſt traueld by thy learned writs,
    Olde *Rome* out of her aſhes to reuiue,
And giue a ſecond life to dead decayes :
Needes muſt he all eternitie ſuruiue,
That can to other giue eternall dayes.
    Thy dayes therefore are endles,and thy prayſe
Excelling all,that euer went before;
And after thee,gins *Bartas* hie to rayſe
His heauenly Muſe,th'Almightie to adore.
    Liue happie ſpirits,th'honour of your name,
    And fill the world with neuer dying fame.
                FINIS.

Signature 62.

This acrostic is found in the prefatory poem to *Virgil's Gnat,* as the poem is printed in the *Complaints.*

Begin to read from the initial F of the word 'For' beginning the 11th line; to the right; upwards; on the initials of the words; to the top of the stanza and back; spelling Frauncis Bacon, you will arrive at the initial N of the word 'Ne' beginning the line immediately above the F from which we started.

Now again begin to read from the same initial F of the same word 'For'; to the right; downwards; throughout the whole stanza and back; spelling Frauncis Bacon, you will arrive, as before, at the same initial N of the same word 'Ne' which begins the line: —

'Ne further seeke to glose vpon the text:'

The acrostic figure in each case is: —

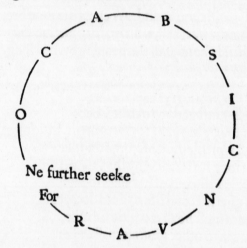

Virgils Gnat.
Long since dedicated

To the most noble and excellent Lord,
the Earle of Leicester, late
deceased.

WRong'd, yet not daring to expresse my paine,
To you (great Lord) the causer of my care,
In clowdie teares my cause I thus complaine
Vnto your selfe, that onely priuie are:
    But if that any Oedipus vnware
Shall chaunce, through power of some diuining spright,
To reade the secrete of this riddle rare,
And know the purporte of my euill plight,
    Let him rest pleased with his owne insight,
Ne further seeke to glose vpon the text:
For griefe enough it is to grieued wight
To feele his fault, and not be further vext.
    But what so by my selfe may not be showen,
May by this Gnatts complaint be easily knowen.

H   **VVe**

Observe that *your selfe*, and *my selfe*, are separate words in each instance.

Signature 63.

This acrostic is found in the first verse of *The Visions of Petrarch*, as that poem appears in *Complaints*.

Begin to read from the initial **B** of the word 'Being,' which begins the first line; to the right; downwards; on the initials of the words; spelling BACONO, i. e. By Bacon, you will arrive at the initial O of the word 'Oft,' which begins the last line. This acrostic thus runs through the whole stanza on the initials, and is keyed from the first letter of the first word of the first line to the first letter of the first word of the last line of the poem.

The acrostic figure here is: Being
A
C
O
N
Oft

Signature 64.

There is still another acrostic in this first page of *The Visions of Petrarch*.

Begin to read from the initial B of the word 'Being' (1st word, 1st line); to the right; downwards; on the terminals; spelling BACONO, you will arrive at the terminal O of the word 'so' (8th line, 1st stanza).

Begin to read from the initial F of the word 'found' (last word, last line, 2d stanza); to the left; upwards; on the terminals; spelling FRANCISCO, you will again arrive at the terminal O of the word 'so' (8th line, 1st stanza); thus keying the cipher from the initials of the words at the opposite ends of the string to a common centre.

The acrostic figure here is:—

Being one day, etc.
A
C
O
N
sO in their cruel race
C
S
I
C
N
A
R
cannot be Found.

The Visions of Petrarch
formerly translated.

1

BEing one day at my window all alone,
So manie strange things happened me to see,
   As much it grieueth me to thinke thereon.
At my right hand a Hynde appear'd to mee,
   So faire as mote the greatest God delite;
Two eager dogs did her pursue in chace,
Of which the one was blacke, the other white:
With deadly force so in their cruell race
   They pincht the haunches of that gentle beast,
That at the last, and in short time I spide,
Vnder a Rocke where she alas opprest,
Fell to the ground, and there vntimely dide.
   Cruell death vanquishing so noble beautie,
   Oft makes me wayle so hard a destenie.

2

   After at sea a tall ship did appeare,
Made all of Heben and white Yuorie,
The sailes of golde, of silke the tackle were,
Milde was the winde, calme seem'd the sea to bee,
   The skie eachwhere did show full bright and faire;
With rich treasures this gay ship fraighted was:
But sudden storme did so turmoyle the aire,
And tumbled vp the sea, that she (alas)
   Strake on a rock, that vnder water lay,
And perished past all recouerie.
O how great ruth and sorrowfull assay,
Doth vex my spirite with perplexitie,
   Thus in a monent to see lost and drown'd,
   So great riches, as like cannot be found.

Z 2   The

Signature 65.

This acrostic is found in the ' Epistle ' to Gabriel Harvey, which prefaces the ' Generall Argument ' of *The Shepheardes Calender*. The facsimiles are from the first known and anonymous edition of 1579.

Much ingenious surmise, based upon other ingenious surmises, has led some scholars to attribute the initials E. K., by which the ' Epistle ' is signed, to one Edward Kirke. The initials may be his, but we are not here concerned with that discussion. (See p. 245.)

Note the large initial **N** which begins the ' Post-script ' and which is followed by a capital O or cipher.

Begin to read from the large initial **N** ; on the terminals of all words in the ' Post-script '; to the right; downwards; spelling NOCAB SICNARFF, you will arrive at the initial F of the word 'from,' which begins the last sentence, ' from my lodging at London thys 10. of Aprill. 1579.'

Begin again to read, this time from the initial F of the word 'from ' on which we have found the signature to end; on the terminals of all the words; to the left; upwards; spelling FFRANCIS or

FFRAVNCIS BACON, you will arrive at the large initial **N** with which the ' Post-script ' begins.

The acrostic figure here is: —

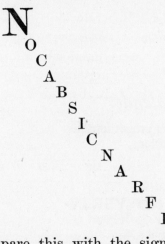

From my lodging at London, etc.

Compare this with the signature of *Venus and Adonis*. Also compare it with the signatures which are found in *The Shepheardes Calender* after it had been reset in the Folio edition of 1611, thirty-two years later. The above signatures are destroyed by the resetting, and new signatures are provided.

T H E
Shepheardes Calender
Conteyning tvvelue Æglogues proportionable
to the twelve monethes.

Entitled
TO THE NOBLE AND VERTV-
eus Gentleman most worthy of all titles
both of learning and cheualrie M.
Philip Sidney.
(∵)

AT LONDON.
Printed by Hugh Singleton, dwelling in
Creede Lane neère vnto Ludgate at the
figne of the gplden Tunne, and
are there to be folde.
1579.

Epiſtle.

payne; the thinges though vvorthy of many, yet being knowen to few. Theſe my preſent paynes if to any they be pleaſurable or profitable, be you iudge, mine ovvn good Maiſter Haruey, to vvhom I haue both in reſpect of your vvorthineſſe generally, and othervvyſe vpon ſome particular & ſpecial conſiderations voued this my labour, and the mayden-head of this our commen frends Poetrie, himſelſe hauing already in the beginning dedi-cated it to the Noble and vvorthy Gentleman, the right worſhipfull Ma. Phi. Sidney, a ſpecial ſauourer & maintainer of all kind of learning.) VVhoſe cauſe I pray you Sir, yf Enuie ſhall ſtur vp any wrongful accuſaſion, defend vvith your mighty Rhetorick & other your rare gifts of learning, as you can, & ſhield with your good vvil, as you ought, againſt the malice and outrage of ſo many enemies, as I knovv vvilbe ſet on fire with the ſparks of his kindled glory. And thus recōmending the Author vnto you, as vnto his moſt ſpe-cial good frend, and my ſelſe vnto you both, as one making ſinguler account of tvvo ſo very good and ſo choiſe frends, I bid you both moſt hartely farvvel, and commit you & your moſt commendable ſtudies to the tuicion of the greateſt.

Your ówne aſſuredly tò
be commaunded E. K.

Poſt ſcr

NOvv I truſt M. Haruey, that vpon ſight of your ſpeciall frends and fellow Poets doings, or els for enuie of ſo many vnworthy Quidams, vvhich catch at the gar-lond, vvhich to you alone is devve, you vvill be perſvvaded to pluck out of the hateful darkneſſe, thoſe ſo many excellent Engliſh poemes of yours, vvhich lye hid, and bring thē forth to eternall light. Truſt me you doe both them great wrong, in depriuing them of the deſired ſonne, and alſo your ſelſe, in ſmoothering your deſerued prayſes, and all men generally, in withholding from them ſo diuine pleaſures, which they might conceiue of your gallant Engliſh verſes, as they haue already doēn of your Latine Poemes, which in my opinion both for inuention and Elocution are very delicate, and ſuperexcellent. And thus againe, I take my leaue of my good Mayſter Haruey. from my lodging at Londōn thys 10. of Aprill. 1579.

Signature 66.

This acrostic is found in the ' Epistle' to Gabriel Harvey which prefaces the ' Generall Argument' of *The Shepheardes Calender*, as it appears in the Folio edition of Spenser's works, published in 1611.

Note the initial B of the word ' But,' which begins the last line of the first page of this ' Epistle.' Read up on the outside letters of the left-hand side of the page (ignoring the large ornamental letter V); spelling BACON, you will arrive at the capital N at the top of the page in the word ' uncouth.' (See pp. 249-53.)

The acrostic figure here is: —

N
O
V C
A
B

Note that this acrostic may be read downwards and backwards also.

Signature 67.

Now we shall deal solely with the *capital letters* throughout the whole five pages of this address.

Begin to read from the capital N at the top of the first page, and on which we have found Signature 66 to end; on capital letters alone; through the text; spelling NOCAB SICNARF (i. e. Francis Bacon, backwards), you will arrive at the capital F of the word ' From' in the last line of the last page of the ' Epistle.'

The acrostic figure here is: —

NOCABSICNAR From my lodging at London, the tenth of Aprill, 1579.

Signature 68.

Note the large letter N of the word 'Now' with which the 'Post-script' begins. (See p. 253.)

Begin to read from the initial F of the word 'From' in the last line of the 'Post-script,' which ended Signature 67; to the right; on the initials of the words; upwards; spelling F. BACON, you will arrive at the initial N of the word 'Now' with which the 'Post-script' begins.

The acrostic figure here is:—

N
  O
    C
      A
        B

From my lodging at London, etc.

Combining Signatures 66, 67, 68, we have:—

'Francis Bacon. From my lodging at London,
the tenth of April, 1579,'

running throughout the whole Epistle, on the capitals, and keyed at the beginning and the end in this way:—

V N O C A B S I C N A R N O C A B

From my lodging at London, etc.

Compare these signatures with those in the first edition of *The Shepheardes Calender*, which was published anonymously in 1579, and of which I show facsimiles on pages 245, 255. Compare them also with the signature to the *Essayes. Of The Coulers of Good and Euil.*

THE
FAERIE QVEEN:
THE
Shepheards Calendar:

Together
WITH THE OTHER
Works of England's Arch-Poët,
EDM. SPENSER:

¶ Collected into one Volume, and
carefully corrected.

Printed by H. L. for Mathew Lownes.
Anno Dom. 1611.

TO THE MOST EXCELLENT

and learned, both Oratour and Poet, maſter
*Gabriel Haruey,*his verie ſpeciall and ſingular good friend, *E. K.*
commendeth the good liking of this his good labour, and the
patronage of the new Poët.

Ncouth, *vnkiſt*, ſaide the old famous Poet *Chaucer:* whom for his excellencie and wonderfull skill in ma-king, his ſcholler *Lidgate,* a woorthy ſcholler of ſo ex-cellent a maſter, calleth the loadſtarre of our language: and whom our *Colin Clout* in his Eglogue calleth *Ty-tirus,* the God of Shepheards; comparing him to the worthineſs of the Roman *Tytirus, Virgil.* VVhich pro-uerbe, mine owne good friend M. *Haruey,* as in that good old poet, it ſerued well *Pindarus* purpoſe, for the bolſtering of his bawdie brocage, ſo very wel taketh place in this our new Poet, who for that he is vncouth (as ſaid *Chau-cer*) is vnkiſt; and vnknown to moſt men, is regarded but of a fewe. But I doubt not, ſo ſoone as his name ſhall come into the knowledge of men, and his worthineſſe be ſounded in the trumpe of Fame, but that he ſhall be not onely kiſt, but alſo beloued of all, embraced of the moſt, and wondred at of the beſt. No leſſe, I thinke, deſerueth his wittineſſe in deuiſing, his pithineſſe in vttering, his complaint of loue ſo louely, his diſcourſes of pleaſure ſo plea-ſantly, his paſtorall rudeneſſe, his morall wiſeneſſe, his due obſeruing of *De-corum* euerie where, in perſonages, in ſeaſons, in matter, in ſpeech, and ge-nerally, in all ſeemelie ſimplicitie of handling his matters, and framing his words: the which of many things that in him be ſtrange, I know will ſeeme the ſtrangeſt; the wordes themſelues beeing ſo ancient, the knitting of them ſo ſhort and intricate, and the whole period and compaſſe of his ſpeech ſo delightſome for the roundneſſe, and ſo graue for the ſtrangeneſſe. And firſt of the words to ſpeake, I grant they be ſomething hard, and of moſt men vn-vſed, yet both Engliſh, and alſo vſed of moſt excellent Authours, and moſt famous poets. In whom, when as this our poet hath beene much trauailed and throughly read, how could it be (as that worthy Oratour ſaid) but that walking in the Sunne, although for other cauſe hee walked, yet needes hee muſt be ſunne-burnt; and hauing the ſound of thoſe ancient poets ſtill ring-ing in his eares, hee mought needs in ſinging, hit out ſome of their tunes. But whether hee vſeth them by ſuch caſualtie and cuſtome, or of ſet purpoſe

A 2.   and

NPC
L
CCET
GS
RTVW
MH
P
PC
B I
F
NI
D
I
A
I
EA
I
O
S
B

THE EPISTLE.

and choiſe, as thinking thē fitteſt for ſuch ruſticall rudeneſſe of Shepheards; either for that their rough ſound would make his rimes more ragged and ruſticall: or elſe becauſe ſuch old and obſolete words are moſt vſed of Country folke; ſure I thinke, and thinke I thinke not amiſſe, that they bring great grace, and as one would ſay, authoritie to the verſe. For albe, amongſt many other faults, it ſpecially be obiected of *Valla*, againſt *Liuie*, and of other againſt *Saluſt*, that with ouer-much ſtudie they affect antiquitie, as couering thereby credence, and honour of elder yeeres; yet I am of opinion, and eke the beſt learned are of the like, that thoſe ancient ſolemne words, are a great ornament, both in the one, and in the other: the one labouring to ſet foorth in his worke an eternall image of antiquitie, and the other carefully diſcourſing matters of grauitie and importance. For, if my opinion faile not, *Tuli* in that booke, wherein he endeuoureth to ſet forth the patterne of a perfect Orator, ſaith, that oft-times an ancient word maketh the ſtile ſeeme graue, and as it were reuerend, no otherwiſe then we honour and reuerence gray haires, for a certaine religious regard, which we haue of old age. Yet neither euery where muſt old wordes be ſtuffed in, nor the common Dialect, & maner of ſpeaking ſo corrupted thereby, that as in old buildings, it ſeeme diſorderlie and ruinous. But as in moſt exquiſite pictures, they vſe to blaze and portrait, not onely the daintie lineaments or beautie, but alſo round about it to ſhadow the rude thickets and craggie clifts, that by the baſeneſſe of ſuch parts, more excellencie may accrew to the principall (for oftentimes wee finde our ſelues, I know not how, ſingularly delighted with the ſhew of ſuch naturall rudeneſſe, and take great pleaſure in that diſorderly order): euen ſo doe thoſe rough and harſh tearmes, enlumine and make more cleerely to appeare the brightneſſe of braue and glorious words. So, oftentimes, a diſcord in muſicke maketh a comely concordance: ſo great delight tooke the worthie poet *Alceus*, to behold a blemiſh in the ioynt of a well-ſhaped bodie. But if any will raſhly blame ſuch his purpoſe in choice of old & vnwonted words, him may I more iuſtly blame and condemne, either of witleſſe headineſſe in iudging, or of heedleſſe hardineſſe in condemning: for not marking the compaſſe of his bent, he will iudge of the length of his caſt. For in my opinion, it is one eſpeciall praiſe of many, which are due to this poet, that he hath laboured to reſtore as to their rightfull heritage, ſuch good and naturall Engliſh words, as haue been long time out of vſe, and almoſt cleane diſherited. Which is the onely cauſe, that our mother tongue, which trulie of it ſelfe is both full enough for proſe, & ſtately enough for verſe, hath long time been counted moſt bare and barren of both. Which defaut, when as ſome endeuoured to ſalue and recure, they patched vp the holes with peeces and ragges of other languages; borrowing heere of the French, there of the Italian, euery where of the Latine; not weighing how ill thoſe tongues accord with themſelues, but much worſe with ours: So now they haue made our Engliſh tongue a gallimaufrey, or hodgepodge of all other ſpeeches.

Other

Marginal letters
S
C
I L
F
V L
S
I
F T
O
Y
D
B
I
S
A
B
I
F
E
W
W
F
I L
S
E

THE EPISTLE.

Other-some, not so well seene in the English tongue, as perhaps in other languages, if they happen to heare an old word, albeit very naturall and significant, cry out straight way, that we speake no English, but gibberish, or rather, such as in old time *Euanders* mother spake: whose first shame is, that they are not ashamed, in their owne mother tongue, to bee counted strangers, and aliens. The second shame no lesse then the first, that what they vnderstand not, they straightway deeme to be senselesse, & not at all to be vnderstood: Much like to the Mole in *Aesops* fable, that beeing blind herselfe, would in no wise be perswaded that any beast could see. The last, more shamefull then both, that of their owne country and naturall speech (which together with their Nurses milke they sucked) they haue so base and bastard iudgement, that they will not onely theselues not labour to garnish & beautifie it, but also repine, that of other it should be embellished; Like to the dog in the maunger, that himselfe can eate no hay, & yet barketh at the hungrie bullock, that so faine would feed: whose currish kinde, though it cannot bee kept frō barking, yet I conne them thank that they refraine from byting.

Now, for the knitting of sentences, which they call the ioynts & members thereof, & for all the compasse of the speech, it is round without roughnesse, and learned without hardnesse, such indeed as may be perceiued of the least, vnderstood of the most, but iudged onely of the learned. For what in most English writers vseth to be loose, and as it were vnright, in this Author is well grounded, finely framed, and stronglie trussed vp together. In regard whereof, I scorne and spew out the rakehelly rout of our ragged rymers (for so themselues vse to hunt the letter) which without learning boast, without iudgement iangle, without reason rage and fome, as if some instinct of poeticall spirit had newly rauished them aboue the meannesse of common capacitie. And beeing in the midst of all their brauerie, suddenly, either for want of matter, or rime, or hauing forgotten their former conceit, they seeme to be so pained & trauailed in their remembrance, as it were a woman in childbirth, or as that same Pythia, when the traunce came vpon her: *Os rabidum fera corda domans, &c.*

Neuerthelesse, let them a Gods name feed on their owne folly, so they seeke not to darken the beames of others glorie. As for *Colin*, vnder whose person the Authors selfe is shadowed, how farre he is from such vaunted titles, and glorious shewes, both himselfe sheweth, where he saith:

Of Muses Hobbinoll, I conne no skill.   And

Enough is me to paint out my vnrest, &c.

And also appeareth by the basenesse of the name, wherein it seemeth hee chose rather to vnfold great matter of argument couertly, then professing it, not suffice thereto accordingly. Which moued him rather in Aeglogues thē otherwise to write; doubting perhaps his ability, which he little needed; or minding to furnish our tongue with this kind, wherein it faulteth; or following one example of the best & most ancient poets, which deuised this kinde

A 3.

OE
E
E
T
MMA
T
N
L
I
N
F
EA
I
I
A
PO
NG
AC
A
OMHIA
E
A
WA

THE EPISTLE.

of writing, beeing both so base for the matter, and homely for the maner, at
the first to trie their habilities : like as young birds, that be newlie crept out
of the nest, by little and little first prooue their tender wings, before they
make a greater flight. So flew *Theocritus*, as you may perceiue hee was al- **S T**
readie full fledged. So flew *Virgil*, as not yet well feeling his wings. So flew **S V S**
Mantuane, as not beeing full somd. So *Petrarque.* So *Boccace.* So *Marot*, **MSPSBSM**
Sanazarus, and also diuerse other excellent both Italian and French poets, **SIF**
whose footing this Authour euery where followeth : yet so as few, but they **A**
be well sented, can trace him out. So finally flieth this our new Poet, as a **SP**
bird whose principals be scarce growne out, but yet as one that in time shall
be able to keepe wing with the best.

   Now, as touching the generall drift and purpose of his Aeglogues, I mind **NAI**
not to say much, himselfe labouring to coceale it. Onely this appeareth, that **O**
his vnstaied youth had long wandered in the common Labyrinth of Loue, **LL**
in which time, to mitigate & allay the heate of his pasion, or else to warne
(as hee saith) the young shepheards [his equals and companions] of his vn-
fortunate folly, he compiled these twelue Aeglogues; which for that they be **A**
proportioned to the state of the twelue Moneths, he tearmeth it the *Shep-* **MS**
heards Calender, applying an old name to a new worke. Heerevnto haue I **CHI**
added a certaine Glosse or scholion, for the exposition of old wordes, & **G**
harder phrases ; which manner of glosing and commenting, well I wote, **I**
will seeme strange and rare in our tongue : yet, for so much as I knew, many **I**
excellent and proper deuises, both in words and matter, would passe in the
speedie course of reading, either as vnknowne, or as not marked ; & that in
this kind, as in other wee might be equall to the learned of other nations, I **I**
thought good to take the paines vpon me, the rather for that by meanes of
some familiar acquaintance I was made priuie to his counsaile & secret mea- **I**
ning in the, as also in sundry other works of his. Which albeit I knowe hee **WI**
nothing so much hateth, as to promulgate, yet thus much haue I aduentu- **I**
red vpon his friendship, himselfe being for long time far estranged, hoping
that this will the rather occasion him, to put foorth diuerse other excellent
works of his, which sleep in silence, as his Dreams, his Legends, his Court **DLC**
of *Cupid*, & sundry others, whose comendation to set out, were very vaine, **C**
the things though worthy of many, yet beeing knowne to few. These my **T**
present paines, if to any they be pleasurable, or profitable, be you iudge,
mine owne maister *Haruey*, to whom I haue both in respect of your worthi- **HI**
nesse generally, & otherwise vpon some particular & speciall considerations,
vowed this my labour, & the maidenhead of this our common friends poetrie, himselfe hauing already in the beginning dedicated it to the Noble and **N**
worthy Gentleman, the right worshipfull maister *Philip Sidney*, a speciall **GPS**
fauourer & maintainer of all kinde of learning. Whose cause, I pray you **WI**
sir, if enuie shall stirre vp any wrongfull accusation, defend with your mighty Rhetoricke, and other your rath gifts of learning, as you can, and shield **R**
                                                  with

THE EPISTLE.

with your good will, as you ought, against the malice & outrage of so many
enemies, as I know will be set on fire with the sparks of his kindled glorie.
And thus recommending the Authour vnto you, as vnto his most speciall
good friend, and my selfe vnto you both, as one making singular account of
two so very good & so choise friends, I bid you both most hartily farewell,
& commit you & your commendable studies to the tuition of the greatest.

Your owne assuredly to be
commaunded, E. K.

Post scr.

NOw I trust, M. *Haruey*, that vpon sight of your speciall friends and
fellow poets dooings, or else for enuie of so many worthy Quidams,
which catch at the garland which to you alone is due, you will be perswaded to pluck out of the hateful darkness, those so many excellent English poems of yours, which lie hid, and bring them foorth to eternall light. Trust
me, you doe them great wrong, in depriuing them of the desired sunne, and
also your selfe, in smothering your deserued praises, and all men generally,
in with-holding from them so diuine pleasures, which they might conceiue
of your gallant English verses, as they haue already done of your Latine poems, which in my opinion, both for inuention and elocution, are very delicate and superexcellent. And thus againe, I take my leaue of my good M.
Haruey. From my lodging at London, the tenth of Aprill. 1579,

I
AA
I
Y
EK
P
NOIMH
Q
E
T
EL
AIM
HFLA

Signature 69.

This acrostic is found in the last paragraph of ' The generall Argument of the whole Booke' as it is printed in the first known edition of *The Shepheardes Calender*, which was published anonymously in 1579. This general argument follows the 'Epistle,' in the Folio edition of Spenser's *Works* published in 1611.

Begin to read from the last letter 't,' which is the last terminal letter in the paragraph; on the terminals of all words in the paragraph; to the left; upwards; spelling TINEVNI NOCAB, you will arrive at the capital B of the word ' But ' which is the first terminal of the paragraph.

The acrostic figure here is: —

<pre>
          But our Author, etc.
            A
             C
              O
               N
                I
                 N
                  V
                   E
                    N
                     I
       _____ throughoutT
</pre>

This acrostic was destroyed by the resetting of the matter in the Folio edition of the *Works* in 1611. It is interesting to compare the acrostics which appear in the two editions, and also to compare the above acrostic with that found in the ' Dedication ' of *Venus and Adonis*.

special iudgemẽt. For albeit that in elder times, vvhen as yet the coũmpt of the yere was not perfected, as aftervvarde it was by Iulius Cæsar, they began to tel the monethes from Marches begianing, and according to the same God (as is sayd in Scripture) comaunded the people of the Ievves to count the moneth Abil, that vvhich vve çall March, for the first moneth, in remembraunce that in that moneth he brought them out of the land of Ægipt: yet according to tradition of latter times it hath bene othervvise obserued both in gouernment of of the church, and rule of Mightiest Realmes. For from Iulius Cæsar vvho first obserued the leape yeere vvhich he called Bissextilem Annum, and brought in to a more certain course the odde vvandring dayes vvhich of the Greekes vvere called ῥθμεῖνομοι. of the Romans intercalares (for in such matter of learning I am forced to vse the termes of the learned) the monethes haue bene nombred xij. vvhich in the first ordinaunce of Romulus vvere but tenne, countinp but CCCiiij. dayes in euery yeare, and beginning with March. But Numa Pompilius, vvho vvas the father of al the Romain ceremonies and religion`, seeing that reckoning to agree neither vvith the course of the sonne, nor of the Moone, therevnto added tvvo monethes, Ianuary and February: wherin it seemeth, that vvise king minded vpon good reason to begin the yeare at Ianuarie, of him therefore so called tanquam Ianua anni the gate and entraunce of the yere, or of the name of the god Ianus , to which god for that the old Paynims attributed the byrth & beginning of all creatures nevv comming into the vvorlde, it seemeth that he therfore to him assigned the beginning and first enrraunce of the yeare . vvhich account for the most part hath hetherto continued. Notvvithstanding that the Ægiptians beginne theyr yeare at September, for that according to the opinion of the best Rabbins, and very purpose of the scripture selse ; God made the vvorlde in that Moneth, that is called of them Tisti And therefore he commaunded them, to keepe the feast of Pauilions in the end of the yeare, in the xv. day of the seuenth moneth, vvhich before that time was the first.

But our Authour respecting nether the subtiltie of thone parte, nor the antiquitie of thother, thinketh it fittest according to the simplicitie of commen vnderstanding, to begin vvith Ianuarie, wening it perhaps no decorũ, that Sepheard should be seene in matter of so deepe insight, or canuase a case of so doubtful iudgment. So therefore beginneth he, & so continueth he throughout.

Signature 70.

This acrostic is found in 'The generall Argument of the whole Booke' (*The Shepheardes Calender*), which follows the address to Gabriel Harvey with which we have just dealt. The facsimile is from the Folio edition of Spenser's *Works* published in 1611. (See pp. 258–60.)

Note that the last two paragraphs of this 'Argument' begin with the initial F and B, of the words 'For' and But.' Here we have a hint.

Begin to read from the initial F of the word 'For,' which begins the first of the last two paragraphs of the 'Argument'; to the right; downwards; on the initials of the words of the text; spelling FRAUNCIS BACON, you will arrive at the initial N of the word 'Notwithstanding' at the lower right-hand corner of the page.

Signature 71.

Now begin to read from the initial B of the word 'But,' which begins the last paragraph; to the right; on the initials of the words; upwards; spelling BACON, you will arrive again at the initial N of the word 'Notwithstanding.'

Signature 72.

Now begin to read again from the initial B of the word 'But'; *to the left;* on the initials of the outside words of the paragraph; spelling BACONO, i. e. By Bacon, you will arrive at the initial O of the word 'our.' This cipher can be repeated backwards from the initial O of the word 'our'; spelling ONOCAB, you will arrive at the initial B of the word 'But.' Thus the signature is not only keyed both ways itself, but is planned to be a base from which we can key the two previous acrostics.

The complete acrostic figure here is: —

For albeit, etc.

```
   R
    A
     V
      N
       C
        I
Sig. 70.      S
               B
                A
                 C
                  O
                     Notwithstanding
Sig. 71.             O
                     C
                     A
                     But our Authour      neither      of     |
                     Antiquitie                              com-
Sig. 72.             |
                     |
                     |
                     |                                         |
                     |                                         case
                  of |_____|
```

Note that by beginning the last paragraph with an initial B, the cipherer afforded himself the opportunity to give himself a base or butt for his signature.

The generall Argument of the whole Booke.

*L*ittle, I hope, needeth me at large to diſcourſe the firſt o-
riginall of Aeglogues, hauing alreadie touched the ſame.
But, for the word Aeglogues, I knowe is vnknowne to
moſt, and alſo miſtaken of ſome the beſt learned (as they
thinke) I will ſay ſomewhat thereof, beeing not at all im-
pertinent to my preſent purpoſe.

They were firſt of the Greekes, the inuentours of
them, called Aeglogas, as it were, Aegon, or Aeginomon logi, that is Gate-
heards tales. For although in Virgil and others, the ſpeakers be more Shepheards, then Goatheards, yet Theocritus, in whom is more ground of authoritie then in Virgil, this ſpecially from that deriuing, as from the firſt head &
vvell-ſpring the whole inuention of theſe Aeglogues, maketh Goatheards
the perſons and Authors of his tales. This beeing, who ſeeth not the groſneſſe
of ſuch as by colour of learning would make vs beleeue, that they are more
rightly tearmed Eclogai, as they would ſay, extraordinarie diſcourſes of vn-
neceſſarie matter : which definition, albe in ſubſtance and meaning it agree
with the nature of the thing, yet no whit anſwereth with the Analyſis & interpretation of the word. For they be not tearmed Eglogæ, Aeglogues : which
ſentence this Authour verie well obſeruing, vpon good iudgement, though
indeede fewe Goatheards haue to doe herein, neuertheleſſe doubteth not to call
them by the vſed and beſt knowne name. Other curious diſcourſes heereof I
reſerue to greater occaſion.

Theſe twelue Aeglogues euery where anſwering to the ſeaſons of the twelue
Moneths, may be well diuided into three formes or rankes. For either they be
Plaintiue, as the firſt, the ſixt, the eleuenth, and the twelfth : or Recreatiue,
ſuch as all thoſe be, which containe matter of loue, or commendation of ſpeciall
perſonages : or Morall, which for the moſt part be mixed with ſome Satyri-
call bitterneſſe ; namely, the ſecond of reuerence due to old age, the fift of coloured deceit, the ſeauenth and ninth of diſſolute Shepheards and Paſtors, the
tenth of contempt of Poetrie and pleaſant wits. And to this diuiſion may euerie thing heerein be reaſonably applied : a few onely except, whoſe ſpecial purpoſe and meaning I am not priuie to. And thus much generally of theſe twelue
Aeglogues.

Aeglogues. Now will we speake particularly of all, and first of the first, which he calieth by the first Monethes name, Ianuarie: wherein to some he may seeme fowly to haue faulted, in that he erroniously beginneth with that Moneth, which beginneth not the yeere. For it is well knowne, and stoutly maintained with strong reasons of the learned, that the yeere beginneth in March: for then the sunne renueth his finished course, and the seasonable Spring refresheth the earth, and the pleasaunce thereof beeing buried in the sadnesse of the dead Winter, now worne away, reuiueth.

This opinion maintaine the old Astrologers and Philosophers, namelie, the reuerend Andalo, *and* Macrobius, *in his holy daies of* Saturne: *which account also was generally obserued, both of Grecians & Romans. But sauing the leaue of such learned heads, we maintaine a custome of counting the seasons from the Moneth Ianuary, vpon a more speciall cause then the heathen Philosophers euer could conceiue: that is, for the incarnation of our mightie Sauiour, & eternall Redeemer the Lord Christ, who as the renewing the state of the decaied World, and returning the compasse of expired yeeres, to their former date, and first commencement, left to vs his Heires a memoriall of his byrth, in the end of the last yeere and beginning of the next. Which reckoning, beside that eternall Monument of our saluation, leaneth also vpon good proofe of speciall iudgement.*

For albeit that in elder times, when as yet the count of the yeere was not perfected, as afterward it was by Iulius Cæsar, *they beganne to tell the Moneths from Marches beginning; and according to the same, God (as is said in Scripture) cōmaunded the people of the Iewes to count the Moneth* Abib, *that which we call March, for the first Moneth, in remembrance that in that Moneth hee brought them out of the Land of Aegypt: yet, according to tradition of latter times it hath beene otherwise obserued, both in gouernment of the Church, and rule of mightiest Realmes. For from Iulius* Cæsar, *who first obserued the leape yeere, which he called* Bissextilem Annum, *and brought into a more certaine course the odde wandring daies, which of the Greekes were called* Hyperbainontes, *of the Romanes* Intercalares *(for in such matter of learning I am forsed to vse the tearmes of the learned) the Moneths haue beene numbred twelue, which in the first ordinance of* Romulus *were but tenne, counting but 3c4 daies in euery yeere, and beginning with March. But* Numa Pompilius, *who was the father of all the Romane Ceremonies, and Religion, seeing that reckoning to agree neither with the course of the Sunne, nor the Moone, therevnto added two Moneths, Ianuarie and Februarie: wherein it seemeth, that wise king minded vpon good reason to beginne the yeere at Ianuarie, of him therefore so called* tanquam Ianua anni, *the gate & enterance of the yeere, or of the name of the god* Ianus: *to which god, for that the old Paynims attributed the birth and beginning of all creatures new cōming into the world, it seemeth that he therefore to him assigned, the beginning and first entrance of the yeere. Which account for the most part hath hitherto continued. Notwithstanding,*

THE ARGVMENT.

ding, that the Egyptians beginne their yeere at September, for that according to the opinion of the best Rabbines, and very purpose of the Scripture it selfe, God made the world in that Moneth, that is called of them Tiſri. And therefore he cõmaunded them to keepe the feast of Pauilions, in the end of the yeere, in the xv. day of the ſeuenth Moneth, which before that time was the firſt.

But our Authour, reſpecting neither the ſubtiltie of the one part, nor the antiquitie of the other, thinketh it fitteſt, according to the ſimplicitie of common vnderſtanding, to beginne with Ianuarie; weening it perhaps no decorum that ſhepheards ſhould be ſeene in matter of ſo deepe in-ſight, or canuaſe a caſe of ſo doubtfull iudgement. So therefore beginneth hee, and ſo continueth hee throughout.

Signature 73.

This acrostic is found in the poem ' To His Booke,' signed with the masking name ' Immeritô,' and introducing *The Shepheardes Calender*.

The facsimile is reproduced from the first known and anonymous edition of *The Shepheardes Calender*, published in 1579. It is a curious fact that this page is closely similar in type and in setting with the page as it appeared in the Folio edition of the *Works* of Edmund Spenser in 1611; thirty-two years later.

Note the words which mark the indents:—

> Goe
> Under.
> But

As a working hypothesis we shall go under the word ' But' by beginning to read from the initial B of that word; to the right; on the initials of the words; down through the poem and back; spelling BACON, you will arrive at the initial N of the word ' name' at the other end of the same line.

Now note the initials of the front words of the three lines: —

B	' But if that any aske thy name,
Say	Say thou wert base begot with blame:
F	For thy thereof thou takest shame.

Having read from the initial B of the word ' But' *downwards*, let us read from the initial F of the word ' For'; on the initials of the words; *upwards* (*or* downwards) and back, continuously, throughout the poem until you have spelled FRAUNCIS BACON; you will arrive again at the initial N of the word ' name.'

Now begin to read from the initial B of the word ' blame'; to the left; on the initials of the words; down and back again; spelling BACON, you will arrive at the initial N of the word ' name.'

Now begin to read from the initial N of the word ' name' upwards; on the initials of the outside words of the poem; entirely round the poem; spelling NOCAB, i. e. Bacon, backwards, you will arrive at the initial B of the word ' blame.'

Now again begin to read from the initial B of the word ' blame'; downwards; on the initials of the outside words of the poem; entirely around the poem; spelling BACON, you will arrive again at the initial N of the word ' name.'

Begin to read from the initial B of the word 'But'; to the right; downwards; on all the letters of all the words; spelling BACONO, you will arrive at the terminal ô of the masking name 'Immeritô.'

The acrostic figure here is: —

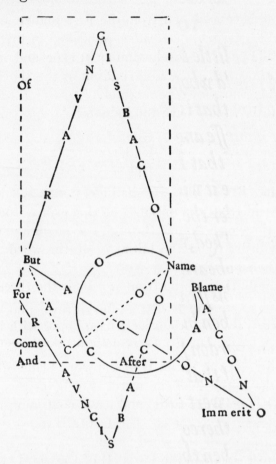

TO HIS BOOKE.

Goe little booke: thy selfe present,
As child whose parent is vnkent:
To him that is the president
Of noblesse and of cheualree,
And if that Enuie barke at thee,
As sure it will, for succoure flee
    Vnder the shadow of his wing,
And asked, who thee forth did bring,
A shepheards swaine saye did thee sing,
All as his straying flocke he fedde:
And when his honor has thee redde,
Craue pardon for my hardyhedde.
    But if that any aske thy name,
Say thou wert base begot with blame:
For thy thereof thou takest shame.
And when thou art past ieopardee,
Come tell me, what was sayd of mee:
And J will send more after thee.

                        Jmmeritô.

Signature 74.

This acrostic is found in the second stanza of *Daphnaïda*, as it is printed in the first known edition of 1591. (See p. 267.)

Note the initials of the first word of each line in the stanza; they are:—

B
O
L
N
T
F
B

Begin to read from the initial B of the word 'But,' which is the first word of the first line of the stanza; to the right; downwards; on the initials of the words; throughout the stanza and back again continuously; spelling BACONO, you will arrive at the initial O of the word 'Or,' which is the first word of the second line of the stanza.

The acrostic figure here is:—

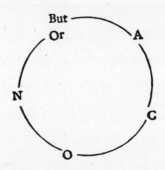

Now note the initials $\frac{F}{B}$, with which the first two words of the last two lines begin.

Begin to read from the initial F of the word 'For,' which is the first word of the last line but one; to the right; upwards; on all letters of all words; spelling FRANCISCONOCAB, you will arrive at the initial B, which begins the first word of the first line of the stanza.

Begin to read from the initial B of the word 'But,' which is the first word of the first line; to the right; downwards; on all the letters of all the words; spelling BACONOCSICNARF, you will arrive at the initial F of the word 'For,' which is the first word of the last line but one of the stanza.

The acrostic figure here is: —

But

        A
           C
              O
                    N
                  I S C   frOm hence:
                C
          N
       A
    R
F

But here no tunes, etc.

Signature 75.

This acrostic is found in the last three stanzas of *Daphnaïda*, as they appear in the first known edition of 1591. (See pp. 271–72.)

Note the initials of the first word of each of the first three lines of
the third stanza from the end. They are $\begin{matrix} B \\ N \\ B \end{matrix}$. Note the same initials
in the corresponding positions of the last stanza.

Our attention is drawn to the last three stanzas by these N. B.'s.

Begin to read from the initial B of the word 'But,' which begins the first line of the third stanza from the end; to the right; downwards; on the initials of the words; spelling BACONO, you will arrive at the initial O of the word 'ouercast.'

Begin to read from the initial B of the first word of the last line of the last stanza; to the right; upwards; on the initials of the words; spelling BACONO, you will arrive again at the initial O of the same word 'ouercast,' and thus key the cipher.

The acrostic figure here is : —

<pre>
        But he no waie, etc.
          A
            C
              O
                N
                  Ouercast,
                N
              O
            C
          A
        But what of him, etc.
</pre>

Signature 76.

This acrostic is found in the last stanza of *Daphnaïda,* as it appears in the first known edition of 1591. (See p. 272.)

Begin to read from the initial B of the word 'But,' which is the first word of the first line of the stanza; to the right on all the letters of all words; spelling BACONO, you will arrive at the letter 'O' of the word 'thereto,' which is the last word on that line.

Now note again the initials of the first word of each of the first three lines of this stanza. They are

B
N
B

We have accounted for one B in this group.

Begin to read from the initial B of the word 'But,' which is the first word of the third line of this stanza; to the right; upwards; on all the letters of all words; spelling BACONO, you will again arrive at the letter 'O' of the word 'thereto,' which is the last word of the first line.

Now see how these two signatures are keyed to the same point.

Begin to read from the initial F of the word 'FINIS'; to the left; upwards; on all the letters of all the words; spelling FRANCISCO BACONO, you will again arrive at the letter 'O' of the word 'thereto,' which is the last word of the first line of the stanza.

The acrostic figure here is: —

```
B A C O N O
N     A  C  O  N    N
B        A    C    O    N      O
                              C
                              A
                              B
                              O
                          C
                          S
                      I
                      C
                  N
              A
              R
          FINIS
```

Daphnaida.
As one difpofed wilfullie to die,
That I fore grieu'd to fee his wretched cafe.

Tho when the pang was fomewhat ouerpaft,
And the outragious pafsion nigh appeafed,
I him defirde,fith daie was ouercaft,
And darke night faft approched,to be pleafed
To turne afide vnto my Cabinet,
And ftaie with me,till he were better eafed
Of that ftrong ftownd,which him fo fore befet.

But by no meanes I could him win thereto,
Ne longer him intreate with me to ftaie,
But without taking leaue,he foorth did goe.
With ftaggring pace and difmall lookes difmay,
As if that death he in the face had feene,
Or hellifh hags had met vpon the way :
But what of him became I cannot weene.

FINIS.

DAPHNAIDA.

When ye doe heare my sorrowfull annoy,
Yet pitty me in your empassiond spright,
And thinke that such mishap, as chaunst to me,
May happen vnto the most happiest wight;
For all mens states alike vnstedfast be.

And ye my fellow Shepheards, which do feed
Your carelesse flocks on hils and open plaines,
With better fortune, then did me succeed;
Remember yet my vndeserued paines:
And when ye heare, that I am dead or slaine,
Lament my lot, and tell your fellow swaines;
That sad A L C Y O N dyde in lifes disdaine.

And ye faire Damsels, Shepheards deare delights,
That with your loues doe their rude harts possesse,
When as my hearse shall happen to your sights,
Vouchsafe to deck the same with Cyparesse;
And euer sprinkle brackish teares among,
In pitty of my vndeseru'd distresse,
The which I wretch endured haue thus long.

And ye poore Pilgrims, that with restlesse toyle
Wearie your selues in wandring desert wayes,
Till that you come, where ye your vowes assoyle,
When passing by, ye read these wofull layes,
On my graue written, rue my D A P H N E S wrong,
And mourne for me that languish out my dayes:
Cease Shepheard, cease, and end thy vndersong.

THus when he ended had his heauie plaint,
The heauiest plaint that euer I heard sound,

His cheekes wext pale, and sprights began to faint,
As if againe he would haue fallen to'ground;
Which when I saw, I (stepping to him light)
Amooued him out of his stonie swound,
And gan him to recomfort as I might.

But he no way recomforted would be,
Nor suffer solace to approach him nie,
But casting vp a sdeignfull eye at me,
That in his traunce I would not let him lie,
Did rend his haire, and beate his blubbred face,
As one disposed wilfully to die,
That I sore grieu'd to see his wretched case.

Tho when the pang was somewhat ouer-past,
And the outrageous passion nigh appeased,
I him desirde, sith day was ouer-cast,
And darke night fast approached, to be pleased
To turne aside vnto my Cabinet,
An stay with me, till he were better eased
Of that strong stownd, which him so sore beset.

But by no meanes I could him win thereto,
Ne longer him intreat with me to stay;
But without taking leaue he forth did goe
With staggring pase and dismall lookes dismay,
As if that death he in the face had seene,
Or hellish hags had met vpon the way:
But what of him became, I cannot weene.

FINIS.

COM-

This page is printed so that the reader may see the signature as it was printed
in the Folio edition of Edmund Spenser's *Works* published in 1611.

Signature 78.

This acrostic is found in the first verse of 'An Hymne in Honour of Love,' as it is printed in the volume entitled *Fowre Hymnes Made by Edm. Spenser*, and published in 1596. (See p. 277.)

Note the first two capitals in the first word of the first stanza, they

are L^O This I take as a hint to look over the page. The first thing to strike me is the fall of the initials of the first word of each line in the first stanza. They are:—

L^O
_P
A
D
F
B
O

Begin to read from the capital O which follows the large L; to the right; on all the letters of all the words; downwards; spelling OCSICNARF, you will arrive at the initial F of the word 'Faine.'

Now begin to read from the initial O of the word 'Or' which is the first word of the last line; to the right; upwards; on all the letters of all words; spelling ONOCAB, you will arrive at the initial B of the word 'By.'

The acrostic figure here is:—

L Ove, that long since hath, etc.
C
S
I
C
N
A
R
Faine would I seeke, etc.
By any seruice, etc.
A
C
O
N
Or ought that else, etc.

Here we find the initials $\frac{F}{B}$ to be the centre of an acrostic which reads outwards to the cipher or capital O at the top and the bottom of the figure. Note that these two capital O's are the only two ciphers in the first stanza.

While we are on this page we may observe that if you begin to spell from the initial B of the word 'But,' which is the first word of the last line of the page; to the right (*or* to the left); upwards; on the initials of the words; spelling BACON, you will arrive at the initial N of the word 'name.'

The acrostic figure here is: —

Name

O

C

A

But if thou wouldst, etc.

Note that on the front page of each of the other three 'Hymnes' in the book there are three full stanzas. The last stanza on this page has been cut so that the first letter of the last line of the page is the initial B of the word 'But.' The two remaining lines of the stanza are printed on the next page.

Fovvre Hymnes,

MADE BY
EDM. SPENSER.

LONDON,
Printed for VVilliam Ponſonby.
1596.

AN HYMNE IN
HONOVR OF
LOVE.

LOue, that long since haft to thy mighty powre,
Perforce fubdude my poore captiued hart,
And raging now therein with reftleffe ftowre,
Doeft tyrannize in euerie weaker part;
Faine would I feeke to eafe my bitter fmart,
By any feruice I might do to thee,
Or ought that elfe might to thee pleafing bee.

And now t'affwage the force of this new flame,
And make thee more propitious in my need,
I meane to fing the praifes of thy name,
And thy victorious conquefts to areed;
By which thou madeft many harts to bleed
Of mighty Victors, with wyde wounds embrewed,
And by thy cruell darts to thee fubdewed.

Onely I feare my wits enfeebled late,   (bred,
Through the fharpe forrowes, which thou haft me
Should faint, and words fhould faile me, to relate
The wondrous triumphs of thy great godhed.
But if thou wouldft vouchfafe to ouerfpred
                    A iij

Signature 79.

This acrostic is found in the first page of 'An Hymne in Honour of Love,' as it is printed in the Folio edition of the *Works* of Edmund Spenser, and published by Mathew Lownes, in 1611.

Note the initials of the last three lines of the first stanza; they

F   Faine
are   B, of the words By, which we have already used in dealing
O   Or

with the Quarto *Fowre Hymnes* of 1596.

Here we have the initials F, B, and O, or a cipher, to guide us.

Begin to read from this O; downwards; on the *outside* letters of the page of *text;* spelling backwards Onocab, you will arrive at the initial B of the word 'By': having completely circled the page.

The acrostic figure here is: —

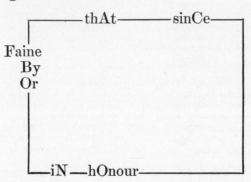

AN HYMNE, IN
honour of Loue.

Loᴠᴇ, that long since haſt to thy mightie powre
Perforce ſubdude my poore captiued hart,
And raging now therein with reſtleſſe ſtowre,
Dooſt tyrannize in euery weaker part;
Faine would I ſeeke to eaſe my bitter ſmart,
  By any ſeruice I might do to thee,
  Or ought that elſe might to thee pleaſing bee.

And now t'aſſwage the force of this new flame,
And make thee more propitious in my need,
I meane to ſing the prayſes of thy name,
And thy victorious conqueſts ro areed;
By which thou madeſt many harts to bleed
  Of mighty Victors, with wide wounds embrew'd,
  And by thy cruell darts to thee ſubdew'd.

Onely I feare my wits enfeebled late,
Through the ſharpe ſorrowes, which thou haſt me bred,
Should faint, and words ſhould faile me to relate
The wondrous triumphs of thy great god-hed.
But if thou wouldſt vouchſafe to ouer-ſpred
  Me with the ſhadow of thy gentle wing,
  I ſhould enabled be thy acts to ſing.

Come then, ô come, thou mighty God of loue,
Out of thy ſiluer bowres and ſecret bliſſe,
Where thou dooſt ſit in Vᴇɴᴠs lap aboue,
Bathing thy wings in her Ambroſiall kiſſe,
That ſweeter farre then any Nectar is;
  Come ſoftly, and my feeble breaſt inſpire
  With gentle furie, kindled of thy fire.

And ye ſweet Muſes, which haue often prou'd
The piercing points of his auengefull darts;
And ye faire Nimphs, which oftentimes haue lou'd
The cruell worker of your kindly ſmarts,
Prepare your ſelues, and open wide your harts,
  For to receiue the triumph of your glory,
  That made you merry oft, when ye were ſorie.

And yee faire bloſſomes of youths wanton breed,
Which in the conqueſts of your beautie boſt,
Wherewith your louers feeble eyes you feed,
But ſterue their harts, that needeth nurture moſt,
Prepare your ſelues, to march amongſt his hoſt,
  And all the way this ſacred Hymne doe ſing,
  Made in the honour of your Soueraigne King.

Gʀeat god of might, that reigneſt in the mind,
And all the bodie to thy heſt dooſt frame,
Victor of gods, ſubduer of mankind,
That dooſt the Lions and fell Tygers tame,
Making their cruell rage thy ſcornfull game,
  And in their roring taking great delight;
  Who can expreſſe the glory of thy might?

Or who aliue can perfectly declare
The wondrous cradle of thine infancie?
When thy great mother Vᴇɴᴠs firſt thee bare,
Begot of Plentie and of Penurie,
Though elder then thine owne natiuitie;
  And yet a child, renewing ſtill thy yeares:
  And yet the eldeſt of the heauenly Peares.

For ere this worlds ſtill mouing mightie maſſe,
Out of great Chaos vgly priſon crept,
In which his goodly face long hidden was
From heauens view, and in deepe darkneſſe kept;
Loᴠᴇ, that had now long time ſecurely ſlept
  In Vᴇɴᴠs lap, vnarmed then and naked,
  Gan reare his head, by Cʟoᴛʜo beeing waked.

And taking to him wings of his owne heat,
Kindled at firſt from heauens life-giuing fire,
He gan to moue out of his idle ſeat,
Weakely at tirſt, but after with deſire
Lifted aloft, he gan to mount vp hier,
  And like freſh Eagle, made his hardie flight
  Through all that great wide waſte, yet wanting light.

Yet wanting light to guide his wandring way,
His owne faire mother, for all creatures ſake,
Did lend him light from her owne goodly ray:
Then through the world his way he gan to take,
The world that was not, till be did it make;
  Whoſe ſundry parts he from themſelues did ſeuer,
  The which before had lyen confuſed euer.

The earth, the ayre, the water, and the fire,
Then gan to range themſelues in huge array,
And with contrary forces to conſpire
Each againſt other, by all meanes they may,
Threatning their owne confuſion and decay:
  Ayre hated earth, and water hated fire,
  Till Loᴠᴇ relented their rebellious ire.

Signature 80.

This acrostic is found in the first stanza of 'An Hymne of Heavenly Love,' as it is printed in the volume entitled *Fowre Hymnes,* published in 1596.

As in previous cases our attention is attracted by the first two capitals of the first word in the stanza. They are L^o and they prompt us to scrutinise the stanza.

Begin to read from the capital O, or cipher, which follows the large L; to the right; downwards; on all the letters of the words; throughout the whole stanza and back again continuously; spelling Onocab Ocsicnarf, you will arrive at the initial F of the word 'From,' which is the first word of the second line of the stanza.

The acrostic figure here is:—

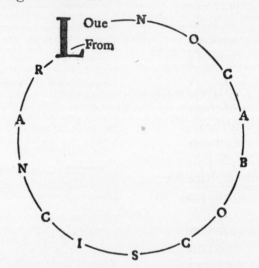

The first three pages of this poem are reproduced in facsimile in order that the reader may compare them with the corresponding stanzas, as they are printed in the Folio edition of Spenser's *Works* published in 1611, in which there is to be found another acrostic.

While going to press I see that there is still another acrostic on this facsimile (see p. 281). Begin to read from the terminal F of the word 'OF' (AN HYMNE OF); to the left; downwards; on terminals; spelling Fran, you will arrive at the terminal N of the word 'In' (2d stanza, 2d line). Begin to read from the initial B of the word 'Before,' at the foot of the page; to the right; upwards; on the terminals; spelling Bacon, you will again arrive at the terminal N of the word 'In' (2d stanza, 2d line), and thus key the cipher from opposite ends of the string to a common centre.

24

AN HYMNE OF
HEAVENLY
LOVE.

LOue, lift me vp vpon thy golden wings,
From this bafe world vnto thy heauens hight,
Where I may fee thofe admirable things,
Which there thou workeft by thy foueraine might,
Farre aboue feeble reach of earthly fight,
That I thereof an heauenly Hymne may fing
Vnto the god of Loue, high heauens king.

Many lewd layes (ah woe is me the more)
In praife of that mad fit, which fooles call loue,
I haue in th'heat of youth made heretofore,
That in light wits did loofe affection moue.
But all thofe follies now I do reproue,
And turned haue the tenor of my ftring,
The heauenly prayfes of true loue to fing.

And ye that wont with greedy vaine defire
To reade my fault, and wondring at my flame,
To warme your felues at my wide fparckling fire,
Sith now that heat is quenched, quench my blame,
And in her afhes fhrowd my dying fhame :
For who my paffed follies now purfewes,
Beginnes his owne, and my old fault renewes.

                                        Before

HEAVENLY LOVE.   25

BEfore this worlds great frame, in which al things
  Are now containd, found any being place,
Ere flitting Time could wag his eyas wings
About that mightie bound, which doth embrace
The rolling Spheres, & parts their houres by space,
That high eternall powre, which now doth moue
In all these things, mou'd in it selfe by loue.

It lou'd it selfe, because it selfe was faire; ·
(For faire is lou'd;) and of it selfe begot
Like to it selfe his eldest sonne and heire,
Eternall, pure, and voide of sinfull blot,
The firstling of his ioy, in whom no iot
Of loues dislike, or pride was to be found,
Whom he therefore with equall honour crownd.

With him he raignd, before all time prescribed,
In endlesse glorie and immortall might,
Together with that third from them deriued,
Most wise, most holy, most almightie Spright,
Whose kingdomes throne no thought of earthly
Can cōprehēd, much lesse my trebling verse (wight
With equall words can hope it to reherse.

Yet o most blessed Spirit, pure lampe of light,
Eternall spring of grace and wisedome trew,
Vouchsafe to shed into my barren spright,
Some little drop of thy celestiall dew,
That may my rymes with sweet infuse embrew,
And giue me words equall vnto my thought,
To tell the marueiles by thy mercie wrought.

                D iij

26   AN HYMNE OF

Yet being pregnant ſtill with powrefull grace,
And full of fruitfull loue, that loues to get
Things like himſelfe, and to enlarge his race,
His ſecond brood though not in powre ſo great,
Yet full of beautie, next he did beget
An infinite increaſe of Angels bright,
All gliſtring glorious in their Makers light.

To them the heauens illimitable hight,
Not this round heauē, which we frō hence behold,
Adornd with thouſand lamps of burning light,
And with ten thouſand gemmes of ſhyning gold,
He gaue as their inheritance to hold,
That they might ſerue him in eternall blis,
And be partakers of thoſe ioyes of his.

There they in their trinall triplicities
About him wait, and on his will depend,
Either with nimble wings to cut the skies,
When he them on his meſſages doth ſend,
Or on his owne dread preſence to attend,
Where they behold the glorie of his light,
And caroll Hymnes of loue both day and night.

Both day and night is vnto them all one,
For he his beames doth ſtill to them extend,
That darkneſſe there appeareth neuer none,
Ne hath their day, ne hath their bliſſe an end,
But there their termeleſſe time in pleaſure ſpend,
Ne euer ſhould their happineſſe decay,
Had not they dar'd their Lord to diſobay.

                                        But

Signature 81.

This acrostic is found on the first page of 'An Hymne of heauenly Loue,' as it is printed in the Folio edition of the *Works* of Edmund Spenser, published by Mathew Lownes, in 1611. (See p. 286.)

Our attention is attracted by the initials $\frac{F}{B}$ of the words $\frac{For}{Beginnes,}$

which begin the last two lines of the 'Prologue'; and by the $\mathbf{B}$ which begins the first line after the ruled line.

Our attention is also attracted by the initials $\frac{B}{F}$ of the words $\frac{Both}{For}$ at the beginning of the last two lines of the page. These two lines seem to be crowded into the page, but that may have been the printer's idea of typesetting. $\mathbf{B}$

Begin to read from the big $\mathbf{B}$ below the ruled line; to the right; downwards; on the initials of the words; spelling BACONO, you will arrive at the initial O of the word 'of.'

Begin again to read from the initial F of the first word of the last line of the page; to the right; upwards; on the initials of the words; spelling FRANCISCO BACONO, you will arrive at the initial O of the same word 'of,' again; and thus keying the cipher.

The acrostic figure here is:—

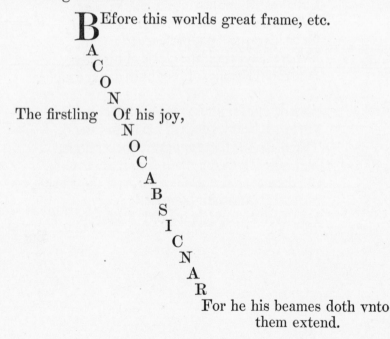

BEfore this worlds great frame, etc.

A
 C
  O
   N

The firstling   O f his joy,

   N
    O
    C
     A
     B
      S
      I
       C
       N
       A
        R

For he his beames doth vnto
them extend.

Signature 82.

Begin again to read from the big initial **B**; to the right; upwards; on the initials of the words; spelling BACON, you will arrive at the initial N of the word 'name' at the end of the first line of the column.

The acrostic figure here is: —

<pre>
              Name
            O
          C
        A
      B efore this worlds great frame, etc.
</pre>

Signature 83.

There is still another acrostic to be seen on this facsimile (see p. 286). The last verses of *An Hymn in Honour of Beauty* are to be seen at the top of the page.

Begin to read from the initial F of the word 'FINIS'; to the right; upwards; through the lines of the poem to which it is the completing word; on the initials; spelling FRA BACON, you will arrive at the initial N of the word 'name.'

The acrostic figure here is: —

<pre>
    Name
    O
    C
    A
    B
    A
    R
    FINIS.
</pre>

of Heauenly Loue.

Singing this Hymne in honour of thy name,
Compyld by me, which thy poore liegeman am,

In lieu whereof, grant, ô great Soueraigne,
That she whose conquering beautie doth captiue
My trembling hart in her eternall chaine,
One drop of grace at length will to me giue,
That I her bounden thrall by her may liue :
    And this same life, which first from me she reaued,
    May owe to her, of whom I it receaued.

And you faire V E N V s dearling, my deare dread,
Fresh flowre of grace, great Goddesse of my life,
When your faire eyes these fearefull lines shall read,
Deigne to let fall one drop of due reliefe,
That may recure my harts long pyning griefe,
    And shew what wondrous powre your beauty hath,
    That can restore a damned wight from death.

FINIS.

AN HYMNE, OF
heauenly Loue.

L Ov E, lift me vp vpon thy golden wings,
   From this base world vnto thy heauens hight,
Where I may see those admirable things,
Which there thou workest by thy soueraine might,
Farre aboue feeble reach of earthly sight,
    That I thereof an heauenly Hymne may sing
    Vnto the god of L o v E, high heauens King.

Many lewd layes (ah woe is me the more)
In praise of that mad fit, which fooles call loue,
I haue in th'heat of youth made heretofore,
That in light wits did loose affection moue.
But all those follies now I doe reproue,
    And turned haue the tenor of my string,
    The heauenly praises of true loue to sing.

And ye that wont with greedy vaine desire,
To read my fault, and wondring at my flame,
To warme your selues at my wide sparkling fire,
Sith now that heat is quenched, quench my blame,
And in her ashes shrowd my dying shame,
    For who my passed follies now pursewes,
    Beginnes his owne, and my old fault renewes.

B Efore this worlds great frame, in which all things
   Are now contain'd, found any beeing place,
Ere flitting Time could wag his eyas wings
About that mighty bound, which doth embrace
The rolling Sphere, & parts their houres by space,
    That high Eternall powre, which now doth moue
    In all these things, mou'd in it selfe by loue.

It lou'd it selfe, because it selfe was faire;
(For faire is lou'd;) and of it selfe begot
Like to it selfe his eldest sonne and heire,
Eternall, pure, and void of sinfull blot,
The firstling of his ioy, in whom no iot
    Of loues dislike, or pride was to be found,
    Whom he therefore with equall honor crownd.

With him he raignd, before all time prescribed,
In endlesse glorie and immortall might,
Together with that third from them deriued,
Most wise, most holy, most almightie Spright,
Whose kingdoms throne, no thoughts of earthly wight
    Can comprehend, much lesse my trembling verse,
    With equall words can hope it to reherse.

Yet ô most blessed Spirit, pure lampe of light,
Eternall spring of grace and wisedome true,
Vouchsafe to shed into my barren spright,
Some little drop of thy celestiall dew,
That may my rimes with sweet infuse embrew,
    And giue me words equall vnto my thought,
    To tell the marueiles by thy mercy wrought.

Yet beeing pregnant still with powrefull grace,
And full of fruitfull loue, that loues to get
Things like himselfe, and to enlarge his race,
His second brood, though not of powre so great,
Yet full of beautie, next he did beget
    An infinite increase of Angels bright,
    All glistring glorious in their Makers light.

To them the heauens illimitable hight
(Not this round heauen, which wee from hence behold,
Adornd with thousand lamps of burning light,
And with ten thousand gemmes of shining gold)
He gaue, as their inheritance to hold,
    That they might serue him in eternall blis,
    And be partakers of those ioyes of his.

There they in their trinall triplicities
About him wait, and on his will depend,
Either with nimble wings to cut the skies,
When he them on his messages doth send,
Or on his owne drad presence to attend,
    Where they behold the glory of his light,
    And caroll Hymnes of loue both day and night.

Both day and night is vnto them all one,
For he his beames doth vnto them extend,

F 2.   That

Signature 84.

This acrostic is found on the page facing the last page of 'An Hymne of Heavenly Beavtie,' as it is printed in the volume entitled *Fowre Hymnes*, published in 1596.

Begin to read from the initial F of the word 'For,' which is the first word of the first line of the page; to the right; downwards; on the initials of the words; spelling FRANCISCONOCAB, you will arrive at the initial B of the word 'bee,' which is the last word of the last stanza.

The acrostic figure here is:—

          For she out of her secret threasury,
       R
        A
         N
          C
           I
            S
             C
              Of Gods high praise, etc.
              Ne from thenceforth doth any, etc.
            O
             C
              A

All other sights but fayned shadowes Bee

Note that the acrostic 'BACON' runs through the last stanza from the initial N of the word 'Ne,' which is the first word of the first line of the stanza, to the initial B of the word 'bee,' which is the last word of the last line of the stanza.

44   **AN HYMNE OF**

For ſhe out of her ſecret threaſury,
Plentie of riches forth on him will powre,
Euen heauenly riches, which there hidden ly
Within the cloſet of her chaſteſt bowre,
Th'eternall portion of her precious dowre,
Which mighty God hath giuen to her free,
And to all thoſe which thereof worthy bee.

None thereof worthy be, but thoſe whom ſhee
Vouchſaſeth to her preſence to receaue,
And letteth them her louely face to ſee,
Wherof ſuch wondrous pleaſures they conceaue,
And ſweete contentment, that it doth bereaue
Their ſoule of ſenſe, through infinite delight,
And them tranſport from fleſh into the ſpright.

In which they ſee ſuch admirable things,
As carries them into an extaſy,
And heare ſuch heauenly notes, and carolings
Of Gods high praiſe, that filles the braſen sky,
And feele ſuch ioy and pleaſure inwardly,
That maketh them all worldly cares forget,
And onely thinke on that before them ſet.

Ne from thenceforth doth any fleſhly ſenſe,
Or idle thought of earthly things remaine,
But all that earſt ſeemd ſweet, ſeemes now offenſe,
And all that pleaſed earſt, now ſeemes to paine,
Their ioy, their comfort, their deſire, their gaine,
Is fixed all on that which now they ſee,
All other ſights but fayned ſhadowes bee.

                                        And

HEAVENLY BEAVTIE. 45

And that faire lampe, which vseth to enflame
The hearts of men with selfe consuming fyre,
Thenceforth seemes fowle, & full of sinfull blame;
And all that pompe, to which proud minds aspyre
By name of honor, and so much desyre,
Seemes to them basenesse, and all riches drosse,
And all mirth sadnesse, and all lucre losse.

So full their eyes are of that glorious sight,
And senses fraught with such satietie,
That in nought else on earth they can delight,
But in th'aspect of that felicitie,
Which they haue written in their inward ey;
On which they feed, and in their fastened mynd
All happie ioy and full contentment synd.

Ah then my hungry soule, which long hast fed
On idle fancies of thy foolish thought,
And with false beauties flattring bait misled,
Hast after vaine deceiptfull shadowes sought,
Which all are fled, and now haue left thee nought,
But late repentance through thy follies prief;
Ah cesse to gaze no matter of thy grief.

And looke at last vp to that soueraine light,
From whose pure beams al perfect beauty springs,
That kindleth loue in euery godly spright,
Euen the loue of God, which loathing brings
Of this vile world, and these gay seeming things;
With whose sweete pleasures being so possest,
Thy straying thoughts henceforth for euer rest.

G

CHAPTER XII

MR. WILLIAM SHAKESPEARE'S COMEDIES, HISTORIES, AND TRAG-
EDIES, WHICH HAVE BEEN ASSIGNED TO THE ACTOR WILLIAM
SHAKSPERE

SIGNATURES 85–94 are found in the lines signed with the initials
B. I. facing the portrait in the first Folio.

Signature 85.

Begin to read from the initial B of the word 'But'; on the initials
of the outside words of the stanza; upwards and all the way round
the stanza; spelling BACON, you will arrive at the initial N of the
word 'Not,' thus keying the signature. See diagrams A, B, C, E
(pp. 297–301).

The acrostic figure here is: —

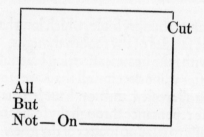

NOTE. — Excepting *Diagram A*, which is taken from Halliwell-Phillips' facsimile, all the other facsimiles in this chapter are taken from the first Folio of
1623, as it appears in the reproduction made by the Clarendon Press under the
supervision of Mr. Sidney Lee. They have been reduced to the size of my page.
I am indebted to the never-failing courtesy of the Oxford University Press for
permission to make the reproductions.

Signature 86.

Begin to read from the initial N of the word 'Not'; on the initials of the outside words of the stanza; to the right and upwards and around; spelling backwards NOCAB, you will arrive at the initial B of the word 'But,' thus keying the signature. See diagrams A, B, C, E (pp. 297–301).

The acrostic figure here is:—

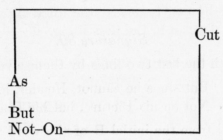

Signature 87.

Begin to read from the initial B of the word 'But'; on the *outside letters* of the stanza; upwards and all around the stanza; spelling BACON, you will arrive at the initial N of the word 'Not,' thus keying the signature. See diagrams A, B, C, F (pp. 297–301).

The acrostic figure here is:—

```
THISFIGURETHATTHOUHERESEESTPUT
I                                  T
W                                  E
W                                  E
O                                  T
A                                  T
H                                  E
A                                  E
But                                E
NOT ONHIS PICTURE BUTHIS BOOKE
```

Signature 92.

Begin to read from the initial B of the word 'But'; to the right, and upwards; on the initials of the words; throughout the stanza and back; spelling BEN IONSON, you will arrive at the initial N of the word 'Not,' thus keying the signature. See diagrams A, B, C (pp. 297–99).

The acrostic figure here is: —

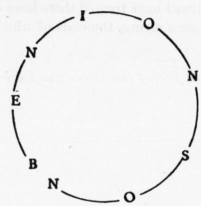

Signature 93.

Now turn to diagrams A and D (pp. 297–300).

Omit the words which overhang at the front of the stanza, and deal solely with the terminals of the other words (i. e. the first and last letters).

Begin to read from the initial F of the word 'Figure'; to the right; downwards; on the terminals of the words; spelling FRANCIS or FFRANCIS BACON, you will arrive at the initial N of the word 'Not,' thus keying the signature from the initial at the one end of the string to the initial at the other. See diagrams A, D (pp. 297 and 300).

The acrostic figure here is: —

Figure
R
A
N
C
I
S
B
A
C
O
Not

Signature 94.

Begin again to read from the initial F of the word 'Figure'; to the right; on the initials of the words, and of the signature; downwards and throughout the verse *continuously* without a break; until you have spelled FRANCIS BACON VISCT ST ALBAN SON OF SIR NICHOLAS BACON BEN IONSON INVENIT, you will arrive again at the initial T of the word 'This,' with which the verse commences.

This acrostic may be represented in a circular graphic, thus:—

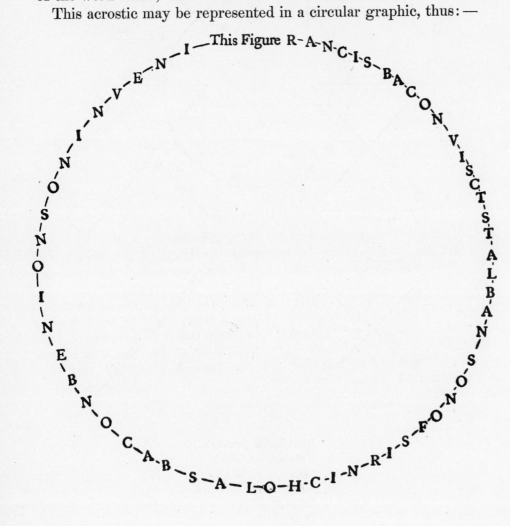

It may also be represented by a series of definite acrostic figures, as thus: —

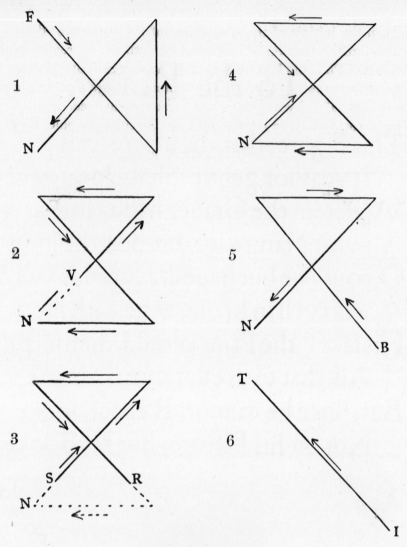

1. FRANCIS BACON
2. VISct St. ALBAN
3. SON OF SIR (N)
4. NICHOLAS BACON
5. BEN IONSON
6. INVENIT

These six acrostics give a consecutive reading from the initial F of the word 'Figure' to the initial T of the word 'This.'

This Figure, etc.

Diagram A.

To the Reader.

This Figure, that thou here feeſt put,
   It was for gentle Shakeſpeare cut,
Wherein the Grauer had a ſtrife
   with Nature, to out-doo the life :
O, could he but haue dravvne his wit
   As well in braſſe, as he hath hit
His face , the Print vvould then ſurpaſſe
   All, that vvas euer vvrit in braſſe.
But, ſince he cannot, Reader, looke
   Not on his Picture, but his Booke.

B. I.

Stanza, or Lines, facing the Droeshout Portrait.

Diagram B.

To the Reader.

T F   t   t   h   ſ   p
  I w ſ g   S   c
W   t G   h   aſ
  w N   t o   t l
O c   h b h   d   h w
  A w i b   a h h   h
H ſ   t P   w   t ſ
  A t vv e   vv i b
B ſ   h c   R   l
N o h P   b h B

                              B. I.

Stanza facing the Droeshout Portrait, from which all letters except the initials of the words have been erased.

Diagram C.

To the Reader: —

T F t t h s p
I w f g S c
W t G h a s
w N t o t l
O c h b h d h w
A w i b a h h h
H f t P w t s
A t v e v i b
B s h c R l
N o h P b h B

B. I.

Stanza facing the Droeshout Portrait, showing the initials of the words in their exact relations to one another.

Diagram D.

To the Reader:—

```
T s | F e t t u h e s t p t
    | I t w s f r g e S e c t
W n | t e G r h d a s e
    | w h N e t o o o t e l e
O   | c d h e b t h e d e h s w t
    | A s w l i n b e a s h e h h h t
H s | f e t e P t w d t n s e
    | A l t t v s e r v t i n b e
B t | s e h e c t R r l e
    | N t o n h s P e b t h s B e
```

B. I.

Stanza facing the Droeshout Portrait, showing the *terminals* of the words in their exact relations to one another. The line marks off those words which overhang.

Diagram E.

This Figure That Thou Here Seest Put	
It	Cut
Wherein	Strife
With	Life
O	Wit
As	Hit
His	Surpasse
All	Brasse
But	Looke
Not On His Picture But His Booke	

Stanza facing the Droeshout Portrait, showing the initials of the outside words of the verse.

Diagram F.

```
THISFIGURETHATTHOUHERESEESTPUT
I                                         T
W                                         E
W                                         E
O                                         T
A                                         T
H                                         E
A                                         E
B                                         E
NOT ON HISPICTURE BUTHIS BOOKE
```

Stanza facing the Droeshout Portrait, showing the outside letters of the stanza.

Signature 98.

Begin to read from the same initial F of the same word 'for'; to the left; downwards; on the initials of the words; spelling FRA BACON, you will arrive at the initial N of the word 'name.' (See pp. 312–313.)

The acrostic figure here is: —

For
R
A
B
A
C
O
Name

Signature 99.

Begin to read from the same initial F of the same word 'for'; to the right; upwards throughout the whole page and back again; on the initials of the words; spelling FRANCIS BACON, you will arrive at the initial N of the same word 'name.' (See pp. 312–313.)

The acrostic figure here is: —

Signature 100.

Now turn to the second page and note that the initials of the last words of the first two lines are $^{B}_{F}$ of the words $^{Booke}_{For.}$ (See p. 313.)

Begin to read from the initial F of the word 'for,' at the end of the second line of the second page; to the left; upwards; back through the whole of the first page; on the initials of the words; spelling FRA BACON, you will arrive at the initial N of the word 'Noble,' as before.

The acrostic figure is:—

Noble
O
C
A
B
A
R
For

Signature 101.

Begin to read from the same initial F of the same word 'for,' at the end of the second line of the second page; to the left; upwards; back through the whole of the first page and back again; on the initials of the words; spelling FRAVNCIS BACON, you will arrive at the initial N of the word 'name' on the first page again. (See pp. 312–313.)

The acrostic figure is:—

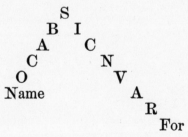

Signature 102.

Begin to read from the initial N of the word 'name'; to the left; downwards and over the page; on the initials of the words; spelling backwards NOCAB F, you will arrive at the initial F of the word 'for' at the end of the second line of the second page. (See pp. 312–313.)

The acrostic figure is: —

Name
O
C
A
B
For

Signature 103.

Begin to read from the initial N of the word 'name'; to the right; downwards and over the page; on the initials of the words; spelling backwards NOCAB F, you will again arrive at the initial F of the word 'for' at the end of the second line of the second page. (See pp. 312–313.)

The acrostic figure is: —

Náme
O
C
A
B
For

Signature 104.

We are now fairly on the second page, with the initials B $\overset{B}{F}$ of the words $\underset{\text{'both'}}{\text{'}}\overset{\text{'Booke'}}{\underset{\text{'for'}}{}}$ to guide us. (See pp. 312–313.)

Begin to read from the initial F of the word 'for' at the end of the second line; to the left; downwards; on the initials of the words; throughout the whole of the page and back; spelling FRAUNCIS BACON, you will arrive at the initial N of the word 'name' (in the fifth line from the bottom of the text).

The acrostic figure is:—

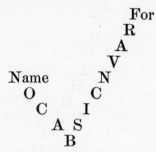

Signature 105.

Begin to read from the initial B of the word 'bounden' (above the names of the players); upwards; to the right, *or to the left;* on the initials of the words; spelling BACON, you will find yourself at the initial N of the same word 'name.' (See pp. 312–313.)

The acrostic figure is:—

Name
O
C
A
Bounden

Signature 106.

Now turn to the first page again.   (See pp. 312–313.)

Begin to read from the initial F of the word 'for,' at the end of the first line of the address; to the right; downwards, and over to the second page; on the initials of the words; spelling FRAUNCIS BACON, you will arrive at the initial N of the word 'noble' (ninth line from top, second page).

The acrostic figure is: —

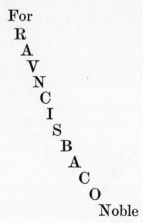

```
          For
        R
         A
         V
         N
          C
           I
            S
             B
              A
               C
                O
                 Noble
```

Signature 107.

Begin to read from the initial B of the word 'Booke,' at the end of the first line of the second page; to the right, *or to the left;* downwards; on the initials of the words; spelling BACON, you will arrive at the same initial N of the same word 'noble.'   (See pp. 312–313.)

The acrostic figure is: —

```
        Booke
       A
       C
       O
     Noble
```

Signature 108.

Observe the initials of the words $\begin{smallmatrix}\text{`Booke'}\\\text{`for,'}\end{smallmatrix}$ at the end of the first two lines of the second page of this 'Dedication.' (See pp. 312–313.)

Begin to read from the initial F of the word 'for'; to the right, *or to the left;* downwards; on the initials of the words; throughout the whole page and back; spelling FFRAUNCIS BACON, you will, in each case, arrive at the initial N of the word 'name' (eighth line from bottom of page), which is thus keyed in two directions.

The acrostic figure is:—

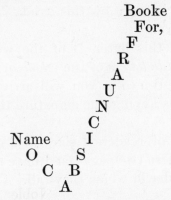

We have thus found the words 'Noble,' 'name,' 'Booke,' 'bounden,' keyed together in many directions.

Signature 109.

Now having found our attention attracted by several ciphers directed to the word ' Noble ' at the end of the top line of the first page, let us look at it carefully. (See pp. 312–313.)

Let us suppose, as a working hypothesis, that the cipherer had noticed the possibilities of the ornamental head-piece, and had drawn a straight line from each arrow, through the first line of the wording as can be done in the illustration. You will observe that the lines will cut out the words ' To,' and ' Noble.'

Let us again suppose that our attention is drawn to this word ' Noble ' in some special way by this trick. The letter B is the centre letter of the word.

Begin to read from this letter B of the word ' Noble '; to the right; around the *outside letters* of the *whole of the two pages* of the ' Dedication '; spelling BACONO, you will arrive at the letter O of the word ' Noble '; thus keying the signature through 132 letters.

For the convenience of readers I show in a diagram (see p. 311) the outside letters of these two pages, and have marked the letters of the signature in the order in which they fall.

The outside letters of the two pages of ' Dedication' to the Earls of Pembroke and Montgomery.

→ →

T O T H E M O S T N O B L E

Left column (reading down): T A I O W E K A P E B O L R W

Right column (reading down): E D E N M E Y D P S R D S E R L E E D H O E R O G T I E E R N O E I Y M S H O E D S Y I H H D O T N O S N E L

Left column (lower, reading down): F S T D L F W H T V C S T B D T A B W A A P M R N N T M T Y W H S Y I H

↑ ↑ ↑ ↓ ↓ ↓

H E N R Y C O N D E L L

←

TO THE MOST NOBLE
AND
INCOMPARABLE PAIRE
OF BRETHREN.

WILLIAM
Earle of Pembroke, &c. Lord Chamberlaine to the
Kings most Excellent Maiesty.

AND

PHILIP
Earle of Montgomery, &c. Gentleman of his Maiesties
Bed-Chamber. Both Knights of the most Noble Order
of the Garter, and our singular good
LORDS.

Right Honourable,

*Hilst we studie to be thankful in our particular, for
the many fauors we haue receiued from your L.L
we are falne vpon the ill fortune, to mingle
two the most diuerse things that can bee, feare,
and rashnesse; rashnesse in the enterprize, and
feare of the successe. For, when we valew the places your H.H.
sustaine, we cannot but know their dignity greater, then to descend to
the reading of these trifles: and, vvhile we name them trifles, we haue
depriu'd our selues of the defence of our Dedication. But since your
L.L. haue beene pleas'd to thinke these trifles some-thing, heereto-
fore; and haue prosequuted both them, and their Authour liuing,
vvith so much fauour: we hope, that (they out-liuing him, and he not
hauing the fate, common with some, to be exequutor to his owne writings) you will vse the like indulgence toward them, you haue done*

A 2   vnto

vnto their parent. There is a great difference, whether any Booke choose his Patrones, or finde them : This hath done both. For, ſo much were your L L. likings of the ſeuerall parts, when they were acted, as before they were publiſhed, the Volume ask'd to be yours. We haue but collected them, and done an office to the dead, to procure his Orphanes, Guardians; without ambition either of ſelfe-profit, or fame: onely to keepe the memory of ſo worthy a Friend, & Fellow aliue, as was our SHAKESPEARE, *by humble offer of his playes, to your moſt noble patronage. Wherein, as we haue iuſtly obſerued, no man to come neere your L.L. but with a kind of religious addreſſe; it hath bin the height of our care, who are the Preſenters, to make the preſent worthy of your H.H. by the perfection. But, there we muſt alſo craue our abilities to be conſiderd, my Lords. We cannot go beyond our owne powers. Country hands reach foorth milke, creame, fruites, or what they haue: and many* Nations *(we haue heard) that had not gummes & incenſe, obtained their requeſts with a leauened Cake. It was no fault to approch their Gods, by what meanes they could: And the moſt, though meaneſt, of things are made more precious, when they are dedicated to Temples. In that name therefore, we moſt humbly conſecrate to your H.H. theſe remaines of your ſeruant* Shakeſpeare; *that what delight is in them, may be euer your L.L. the reputation his, & the faults ours, if any be committed, by a payre ſo carefull to ſhew their gratitude both to the liuing, and the dead, as is*

Your Lordſhippes moſt bounden,

IOHN HEMINGE.
HENRY CONDELL.

Signature 110.

This acrostic is found in the address *To the great Variety of Readers*, which follows the 'Dedication' to the Earls of Pembroke and Montgomery. (See p. 321.)

To prepare the reader's mind let me transliterate Bacon's name. The name contains this alphabet A. B. C. O. N. Here it is transliterated on each letter.

B	N	C	A	O	B	N	C	A	O
A		B		C		O		N	
C	O	O	N	N	A	A	B	B	C

This is a simple transliteration as it was known to the cipherers of the Elizabethan times. (See Selenus, *Cryptomenytices*, pp. 82, 174, 175, 262.)

Note the large monogram

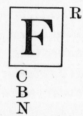

and the letters which adjoin it.

Now use your knowledge of the transliteration table given above, and complete the transliteration of the letters which depend from the monogram. You will immediately get

F^R

C
A B O
N

that is to say you will have Fᴿ Bᴀᴄᴏɴ, staring you in the face.

Now begin to read from the initial B of the word 'braines,' the second word below the monogram; upwards; on the initials of the outside words of the page of text; round the page; spelling Bᴀᴄᴏɴ, you will arrive at the initial N of the word 'not,' which is immediately below the word 'braines,' from which we started.

I give this diagram to show how the signature is keyed around the page on the initials of the outside words, to the full name.

Rom the most able, to him that can but spell: There

weighd
up-
alone
you
read,
best
your
spare
shil-
wel-
Trade
sit
dailie,
Ap-
Court,
commendation.
that
° owne
de-
office
to
diuerse
frauds
those,
all
was
mind
that
papers.
them
to
hold
him
him,
so
your
others.
him.

commend
° braines
° not
lings
come
or
on
know
peales
then
It
the
writings
parted
of
haue
stolne
and
are
the
a
and
easinesse
But
you
your
you
therefore
surely
we
guides
And   such   Readers   we   wish

The letters involved in the signature are marked by a circle.

Signature 111.

Now begin to read from the monogram [F] to the right; downwards; on the initials of the words; spelling FRAVN-CIS BACON, you will arrive at the initial N of the word 'not' again, and thus keying the cipher. (See p. 321.)

The acrostic figure here is: —

[F]Rom

F
R
A
V
N
C
I
S
B
A
C
O
Not

This signature will also run if spelled backwards. Begin to read from the initial N of the word 'not'; to the right; upwards; on the initials of the words; spelling NOCAB SICNVARF, you will arrive at the large initial F, and key the former signature between the same points.

This signature will also run forwards or backwards on the terminals — that is to say, on the first and last letters of every word, if it is spelled between the same end letters.

Signature 112.

This page is like the 'Dedication' to the Earls of Pembroke and Montgomery in that the signature is arranged to read on the outside letters also. (See p. 321.)

Begin to read from the initial B of the word 'braines,' on which we began the last cipher but one (No. 110); upwards; on the outside letters of the page; including the title and including or excluding the *Henrie Condell;* spelling BACON, you will find that in order to spell it you will be again obliged to arrive at the initial N of the word 'not,' having completely encircled the page.

On the next page I give the outside letters of the page with those letters marked which are involved in this cipher.

The last line is given with both the last line of the text and the name *Henrie Condell*, so that the reader may take both and see for himself that the result will be the same whichever he uses.

Diagram.

```
  T O T H E G R E A T V A R I E T Y O F R E A D E R S
-   F .......................................................... E
      ... A(are) ................... R(rather) ................ D -
-       ...................................................V(vp) P
      ... C(capacities) .................. N(not) ........... E -
-       ................................ I(It) ............... U
      .S(stand) ................................................ D -
-       .......................... B(but) ..................... T
      C(commend) . A(a) .......................................... R -
-   Braines ........... O(or) .................................... E -
*   N(not) ........................................................ L -
    L                                                             L
    C                                                             E
    O                                                             T
    O                                                             E
    K                                                             P
    P                                                             T
    T                                                             N
    I                                                             T
    T                                                             E
    W                                                             E
    P                                                             E
    O                                                             O
    H                                                             E
    S                                                             S
    A                                                             E
    A                                                             L
    T                                                             S
    A                                                             D
    A                                                             T
    E                                                             S
    B                                                             M
    Y                                                             O
    Y                                                             D
    Y                                                             M
    T                                                             M
    S                                                             O
    W                                                             R
    G                                                             S
    A N D S U C H R E A D E R S W E W I S H H I ...... M
    I ................................................ E
    H E N R I E C O N D E L .................... L
```

Diagram showing the signatures of Fravncis Bacon from the large F to the initial N of the word 'not'; and the way the signature is keyed by reading from the initial B of the word 'braines'; upwards; around the whole page; on the *outside letters* of the page; spelling Bacon, and ending again on the initial N of the word 'not.'

Signature 113.

This acrostic is also found in the address *To the great Variety of Readers.* (See p. 321.)

Begin to read from the large initial F, to the right; downwards; on the terminals of all the words of the address; spelling FFRAVN-CIS BARON VERULAM OF VERULAM, you will arrive at the terminal M of the word 'him,' which is the last word of the address.

The reader must remember that in this acrostic the V in Verulam is a V in the facsimile, but that the U of Fravncis *and* Verulam may be U or V in the facsimile. The acrostic will not be found unless this is kept in mind.

The acrostic figure here is:—

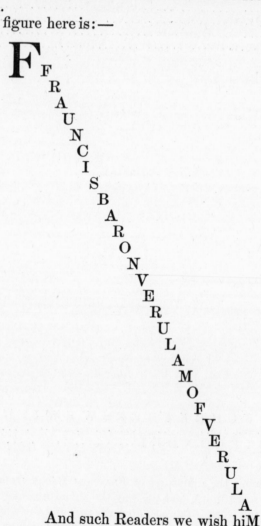

And such Readers we wish hiM

Compare this signature with that in *Venus and Adonis.*

To the great Variety of Readers.

Diagram of the typography showing the terminals in large type.

 roM ThE MosT AblE, TO HiM ThaT CaN BuT SpelL : TherE
YoU ArE Number'D. WE HaD RatheR YoU WerE WeighD.
EspeciallY, WheN ThE FatE OF AlL BookeS DependS VP-
ON YouR CapacitieS : AnD NoT OF YouR HeadS AlonE,
BuT OF YouR PurseS. WelL ! IT IS NoW PubliquE, & YoU
WiL StanD FoR YouR PriuiledgeS WeE KnoW : TO ReaD,
AnD CensurE. DO SO, BuT BuY IT FirsT. ThaT DotH BesT
CommenD A BookE, ThE StationerR SaieS. TheN, HoW OddE SoeueR YouR
BraineS BE, OR YouR WisdomeS, MakE Your LicencE ThE SamE, AnD SparE
NoT. IudgE YouR Sixe-Pen'ortH, YouR ShillingS WortH, YouR FiuE ShiL-
LingS WortH AT A TimE, OR HigheR, SO YoU RisE TO ThE IusT RateS, AnD WeL-
ComE. BuT, WhaT EueR YoU DO, BuY. CensurE WilL NoT DriuE A TradE,
OR MakE ThE IackE GO. AnD ThougH YoU BE A MagistratE OF WiT, AnD SiT
ON ThE StagE AT Black-FrierS, OR ThE CocK–PiT, TO ArraignE PlayeS DailiE,
KnowE, ThesE PlayeS HauE HaD TheiR TrialL AlreadiE, AnD StooD OuT AlL AP-
PealeS ; AnD DO NoW ComE FortH QuitteD RatheR BY A DecreE OF CourT,
ThaN AnY Purchas'D LetterS OF CommendatioN.

IT HaD BenE A ThinG, WE ConfessE, WorthiE TO HauE BenE WisheD, ThaT
ThE AuthoR HimselfE HaD Liu'D TO HauE SeT FortH, AnD OuerseeN HiS OwnE
WritingS ; BuT SincE IT HatH BiN Ordain'D OtherwisE, AnD HE BY DeatH DE-
ParteD FroM ThaT RighT, WE PraY YoU DO NoT EnviE HiS FriendS, ThE OfficE
OF TheiR CarE, And PainE, TO HauE CollecteD & Publish'D TheM ; AnD SO TO
HauE Publish'D TheM, AS WherE (BeforE) YoU WerE Abus'D WitH DiuersE
StolnE, AnD SurreptitiouS CopieS, MaimeD, AnD DeformeD BY ThE FraudS
AnD StealtheS OF IniuriouS ImpostorS, ThaT Expose'D TheM : EueN ThosE,
ArE NoW Offer'd TO YouR VieW Cur'D, AnD PerfecT OF TheiR LimbeS ; And AlL
ThE ResT, AbsolutE IN TheiR NumberS, AS HE ConceiueD ThĒ, WhO, AS HE WaS
A HappiE ImitatoR OF NaturE, WaS A MosT GentlE ExpresseR OF IT. HiS MinD
AnD HanD WenT TogetheR : AnD WhaT HE ThoughT, HE VttereD WitH ThaT
EasinessE, ThaT WE HauE ScarcE ReceiueD FroM HiM A BloT IN HiS PaperS.
BuT IT IS NoT OuR ProuincE, WhO OnelY GatherR HiS WorkS, AnD GiuE TheM
YoU, TO PraisE HiM. IT IS YourS ThaT ReadE HiM. AnD TherE WE HopE, TO
YouR DiuerS CapacitieS, YoU WilL FindE EnougH, BotH TO DraW, AnD HolD
YoU : FoR HiS WiT CaN NO MorE LiE HiD, TheN IT CoulD BE LosT. ReadE HiM,
ThereforE ; AnD AgainE, AnD AgainE : AnD IF TheN YoU DoE NoT LikE HiM,
SurelY YoU ArE IN SomE ManifesT DangeR, NoT TO VnderstanD HiM. AnD SO
WE LeaueE YoU TO OtherR OF HiS FriendS, WhoM IF YoU NeeD, CaN BeE YouR
GuideS : IF YoU NeeD TheM NoT, YoU CaN LeadE YouR SelueS, AnD OtherS.
AnD SucH ReaderS WE WisH HiM.

                    A3   *Iohn Heminge.*
                                                       Henrie Condell.

To the great Variety of Readers.

Rom the most able, to him that can but spell: There
you are number'd. We had rather you were weighd.
Especially, when the fate of all Bookes depends vpon your capacities : and not of your heads alone,
but of your purses. Well ! It is now publique, & you
wil stand for your priuiledges wee know : to read,
and censure. Do so, but buy it first. That doth best
commend a Booke, the Stationer saies. Then, how odde soeuer your
braines be, or your wisedomes, make your licence the same, and spare
not. Iudge your sixe-pen'orth, your shillings worth, your fiue shillings worth at a time, or higher, so you rise to the iust rates, and welcome. But, what euer you do, Buy. Censure will not driue a Trade,
or make the Iacke go. And though you be a Magistrate of wit, and sit
on the Stage at *Black-Friers*, or the *Cock-pit*, to arraigne Playes dailie,
know, these Playes haue had their triall alreadie, and stood out all Ap-
peales; and do now come forth quitted rather by a Decree of Court,
then any purchas'd Letters of commendation.

    It had bene a thing, we confesse, worthie to haue bene wished, that
the Author himselfe had liu'd to haue set forth, and ouerseen his owne
writings; But since it hath bin ordain'd otherwise, and he by death departed from that right, we pray you do not enuie his Friends, the office
of their care, and paine, to haue collected & publish'd them; and so to
haue publish'd them, as where (before) you were abus'd with diuerse
stolne, and surreptitious copies, maimed, and deformed by the frauds
and stealthes of iniurious impostors, that expos'd them : euen those,
are now offer'd to your view cur'd, and perfect of their limbes; and all
the rest, absolute in their numbers, as he conceiued thē. Who, as he was
a happie imitator of Nature, was a most gentle expresser of it. His mind
and hand went together : And what he thought, he vttered with that
easinesse, that wee haue scarse receiued from him a blot in his papers.
But it is not our prouince, who onely gather his works; and giue them
you, to praise him. It is yours that reade him. And there we hope, to
your diuers capacities, you will finde enough, both to draw, and hold
you : for his wit can no more lie hid, then it could be lost. Reade him,
therefore; and againe, and againe : And if then you doe not like him,
surely you are in some manifest danger, not to vnderstand him. And so
we leaue you to other of his Friends, whom if you need, can bee your
guides : if you neede them not, you can leade your selues, and others.
And such Readers we wish him.

                    A 3   *Iohn Heminge.*
                                      Henrie Condell.

Signature 114.

This acrostic is found in the poem signed by Ben Jonson, and addressed *To the memory of my beloued, The AVTHOR Mr. VVilliam Shakespeare: And what he hath left vs.* (See pp. 324, 325.)

The first thing to be noted here is that the word 'AVTHOR' is printed in capitals.

The second thing to be noticed is that the initials of the last word of the first and the second lines of the poem are $\frac{N}{F}$ of the words 'name' 'Fame', which are the first and the last letters of the name 'Francis Bacon.'

I have marked off the *outside words* of the whole poem. There are 172 words in all.

Begin to read from the initial N of the word 'name'; to the left; on the initials of the outside words of the poem; spelling backwards the name Nocab Sicnarf, i. e. Francis Bacon, you will arrive at the initial F of the word 'Fame,' having keyed the signature completely around the poem, on the initials.

The acrostic figure here would be a circular graphic, but I have thought best to show the actual diagram of the words.

Diagram showing the initials of the outside words of Ben Jonson's complimentary poem.

	*
To Draw No Enuy (Shakespeare) On Thy	Name
Am	* Fame
While	Such
As	Much
Tis	Wayes
Were	Praise
For	Light
Which	* Right
Or	* Aduance
The	Chance
Or	Praise
And	Raise
These	Whore
Should	More
But	Indeed
Above	* Need
I	Age
The	Stage
My	By
* Chaucer	Lye
* A	Roome
Thou	Tombe
And	Liue
And	Giue
That	Excuses
I	Muses
For	Yeeres
I	Peeres
And	Out-shine
Or	Line
And	Greeke
From	Seeke
For	Aeschilus
Euripides	Us
Paccuuius	Dead
To	Tread
And	On
Leaue	Comparison
Of	Rome
Sent	Come
Triumph	Showe
To	Owe
He	Time
And	Prime
When	Warme
Our	* Charme
Nature	Designes
And	Lines
Which	Fit
As	Wit
The	Aristophanes
Neat	Please
* But	Lye
As	Family
Yet	Art
My	Part
For	Be
His	He
Who	Sweat
* Such	Heat
Upon	Same
And	Frame
Or	Scorne
For	Borne
And	Face
Liues	Race
Of	Shines
* In	Lines
In	Lance
As	Ignorance
Sweet	Were
To	Appeare
And	Thames
That	Iames
But	Hemisphere
Aduanc'd	There
Shine	Rage
Or	Stage
Which	Night
And Despaires Day. But For Thy Volumes	Light

To the memory of my beloued,
The AVTHOR
MR. WILLIAM SHAKESPEARE: 8
AND
what he hath left vs.

O draw no enuy (Shakespeare) on thy name,
  Am I thus ample to thy Booke, and Fame:
While I confesse thy writings to be such,
As neither Man, nor Muse, can praise too much.
'Tis true, and all mens suffrage. But these wayes
Were not the paths I meant vnto thy praise:
For seeliest Ignorance on these may light,
  Which, when it sounds at best, but eccho's right;
Or blinde Affection, which doth ne're aduance
  The truth, but gropes, and vrgeth all by chance;
Or crafty Malice, might pretend this praise,
  And thinke to ruine, where it seem'd to raise.
These are, as som infamous Baud, or whore,
  Should praise a Matron. What could hurt her more?
But thou art proofe against them, and indeed
  Aboue th'ill fortune of them, or the need.
I, therefore will begin. Soule of the Age!
  The applause! delight! the wonder of our Stage!
My Shakespeare, rise; I will not lodge thee by
  Chaucer, or Spenser, or bid Beaumont lye
A little further, to make thee a roome:
  Thou art a Moniment, without a tombe,
And art aliue still, while thy Booke doth liue,
  And we haue wits to read, and praise to giue.
That I not mixe thee so, my braine excuses;
  I meane with great, but disproportion'd Muses:
For, if I thought my iudgement were of yeeres,
  I should commit thee surely with thy peeres.
And tell, how farre thou didstst our Lily out-shine,
  Or sporting Kid, or Marlowes mighty line.
And though thou hadst small Latine, and lesse Greeke,
  From thence to honour thee, I would not seeke
For names; but call forth thund'ring Æschilus,
  Euripides, and Sophocles to vs,
Paccuuius, Accius, him of Cordoua dead,
  To life againe, to heare thy Buskin tread,
And shake a Stage: Or, when thy Sockes were on,
  Leaue thee alone, for the comparison

Of all, that infolent Greece, *or haughtie* Rome
   fent forth, or fince did from their afhes come.
Triumph, my Britaine, *thou haft one to fhowe,*
   To whom all Scenes of Europe *homage owe.*
He was not of an age, but for all time !
   And all the Mufes ftill were in their prime,
when like Apollo *he came forth to warme*
   Our eares, or like a Mercury *to charme !*
Nature her felfe was proud of his defignes,
   And ioy'd to weare the drefsing of his lines !
which were fo richly fpun, and wouen fo fit,
   As, fince, fhe will vouchfafe no other Wit.
The merry Greeke, *'tart* Ariftophanes,
   Neat Terence, *witty* Plautus, *now not pleafe ;*
But antiquated, and deferted lye
   As they were not of Natures family.
Yet muft I not giue Nature all : Thy Art,
   My gentle Shakefpeare, *muft enioy a part.*
For though the Poets matter, Nature be,
   His Art doth giue the fafhion. And, that he,
Who cafts to write a liuing line, muft fweat,
   (fuch as thine are) and ftrike the fecond heat
Vpon the Mufes anuile : turne the fame,
   (And himfelfe with it) that he thinkes to frame ;
Or for the lawrell, he may gaine a fcorne,
   For a good Poet's made, as well as borne.
And fuch wert thou. Looke how the fathers face
   Liues in his ifsue, euen fo, the race
Of Shakefpeares *minde, and manners brightly fhines*
   In his well torned, and true-filed lines :
In each of which, he feemes to fhake a Lance,
   As brandifh't at the eyes of Ignorance.
Sweet Swan of Auon! *what a fight it were*
   To fee thee in our waters yet appeare,
And make thofe flights vpon the bankes of Thames,
   That fo did take Eliza, *and our* Iames !
But ftay, I fee thee in the Hemifphere
   Aduanc'd, and made a Conftellation there !
Shine forth, thou Starre of Poets, and with rage,
   Or influence, chide, or cheere the drooping Stage ;
Which, fince thy flight frõ hence, hath mourn'd like night,
   And defpaires day, but for thy Volumes light.

BEN: IONSON.

Signature 115.

This irregular acrostic is found in the poem signed by one L. Digges; and addressed *To The Memorie of the deceased Authour Maister W. Shakespeare.* (See p. 329.)

It is remarkable only in that if you begin to spell from the initial B of either ' Be ' or ' But,' which begin the last two lines; to the *right* or to the *left;* on the initials of the words; upwards and continuously until you have spelled BACON, you will arrive at the initial N of the word ' name ' each time you complete the spelling of the name itself.

The acrostic figure here in each of the four spellings is: —

```
                    O
              C        Name.
       A   C
          A
Be
But
```

Signature 116.

It is worth recording that if you begin to read on the first letter N in the first line of this poem by Digges ; to the right ; downwards; on all letters of all words ; spelling NOCAB SICNUARF, you will arrive at the initial F of the word ' fraught ': and that if you then begin to read from the last letter N of the last line; to the left; upwards; spelling NOCAB SICNUARF, you will again arrive at the initial F of the word ' fraught,' thus meeting on the common letter F, having spelled the name from the last letter N at either end of the string of letters.

The acrostic figure here is:—

Shake-speare, at leN
O
C
A
B
S
I
C
N
U
A
R
wit=Fraught
R
A
U
N
C
I
S
B
A
C
O
liue eterNally.

Compare this acrostic with those in the poems by Holland and I. M.

Signature 117.

It is worth recording that if you begin to read from the last letter N on the first line of the poem signed I. M. to the left; downwards; on all the letters of all the words; spelling NOCAB, you will arrive at the letter B of the word 'but'; and that if you begin to read from the last letter N of the last line; to the left; upwards; spelling NOCAB, you will again arrive at the same initial B of the same word 'but,' thus keying the name from the last letter N at either end of the string of letters to the common letter B of the same word 'but.'

The acrostic figure here is: —

<pre>
               sooNe
                 O
                 C
                 A
               But forth
                 A
                 C
                 O
        Re-entraNce to a Plaudite.
</pre>

Compare this acrostic with the previous one. It is the same device.

TO THE MEMORIE

of the deceafed Authour Maifter
W. SHAKESPEARE.

SHake-fpeare, *at length thy pious fellowes giue*
The world thy Workes: thy Workes,by which,out-liue
Thy Tombe, thy name muft · when that ftone is rent,
And Time diffolues thy Stratford Moniment,
Here we aliue fhall view thee ftill. This Booke,
When Braffe and Marble fade,fhall make thee looke
Fresh to all Ages: when Pofteritie
Shall loath what's new,thinke all is prodegie
That is not Shake-fpeares; eu'ry Line,each Verfe
Here fhall reuiue,redeeme thee from thy Herfe.
Nor Fire,nor cankring Age,as Nafo faid,
Of his,thy wit-fraught Booke fhall once inuade.
Nor fhall I e're beleeue, or thinke thee dead
(Though mift),vntill our bankrout Stage be fped
(Jmpofsible) with fome new ftraine t'out-do
Pafsions of Iuliet,and her Romeo;
Or till J heare a Scene more nobly take,
Then when thy half-Sword parlying Romans fpake.
Till thefe,till any of thy Volumes reft
Shall with more fire,more feeling be expreft,
Be fure,our Shake-fpeare, thou canft neuer dye,
But crown'd with Lawrell,liue eternally.

L. Digges.

To the memorie of M.W.Shake-fpeare.

VVEE wondred (Shake-fpeare)that thou went'ft fo foone
From the Worlds-Stage,to the Graues-Tyring-roome.
Wee thought thee dead, but this thy printed worth,
Tels thy Spectators,that thou went'ft but forth
To enter with applaufe. An Actors Art,
Can dye,and liue,to acte a fecond part.
That's but an Exit of Mortalitie;
This, a Re-entrance to a Plaudite.

I. M.

Signature 118.

It is worth recording that if you begin to read from the first letter N in the first line of the poem by Hugh Holland, to the right; downwards; on all the letters of all the words; spelling NOCAB NARF (=Fran Bacon), you will arrive at the letter F of the word 'of' ('Globe of heau'n'): and that if you begin to read from the first letter N of the last line of the poem; to the right; upwards; on all the letters of all the words; spelling NOCAB NARF (=Fran Bacon), you will again arrive at the same letter F of the same word 'of' ('Globe of heau'n'), thus keying the signature from the last letter N at either end of the string of letters to a common centre F of the word 'of.'

The acrostic figure here is:—

<pre>
            Those haN
                    O
                    C
                    A
                    B
                    N
                    A
                    R
        Globe oF heau'n
                    R
                    A
                    N
                    B
                    A
                    C
                    O
       The life yet of his liNes
</pre>

Compare this acrostic with those in the poems by Digges and I. M.

Vpon the Lines and Life of the Famous
Scenicke Poet, Maſter WILLIAM
SHAKESPEARE.

THose hands, which you ſo clapt, go now, and wring
You *Britaines* braue; for done are *Shakeſpeares* dayes :
His dayes are done, that made the dainty Playes,
Which made the Globe of heau'n and earth to ring.
Dry'de is that veine, dry'd is the *Theſpian* Spring,
Turn'd all to teares, and *Phœbus* clouds his rayes :
That corp's, that coffin now beſticke thoſe bayes,
Which crown'd him *Poet* firſt, then *Poets* King.
If *Tragedies* might any *Prologue* haue,
All thoſe he made, would ſcarſe make one to this :
Where *Fame*, now that he gone is to the graue
(Deaths publique tyring-houſe) the *Nuncius* is.
    For though his line of life went ſoone about,
    The life yet of his lines ſhall neuer out.

HVGH HOLLAND.

Signature 119.

This is perhaps the proper place to show the acrostics which are to be seen in the lines on the Monument at Stratford-on-Avon.

Begin to read from the initial S of the first word of the first line; to the right; downwards; on all the letters of all the words; spelling St Alban, you will arrive at the initial N of the word 'name.' Then continue to read from the initial N of the word 'name'; to the right or to the left; downwards throughout the rest of the lines and back again; spelling Nocab Sicnuarff, you will arrive by either route at the initial F of the word 'fast,' which is the last word of the first line.

The acrostic figure here is: —

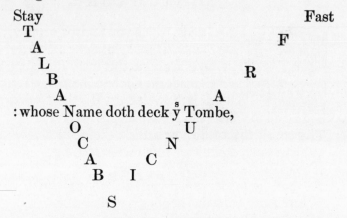

I was led to the discovery of this acrostic by the hypothesis that there might be a *double entente* in the words —

    Stay
    Read
    With in.

Ivdicio Pylivm, genio Socratem, arte Maronem
Terra tegit, popvlvs mæret, Olympvs habet

Stay Passenger why goest thov by so fast?
Read if thov canst, whom envious Death hath plast,
With in this monvment Shakspeare: with whome,
Qvick natvre dide: whose name, doth deck ẙ Tombe,
Far more, then cost: Sieh all, ẙ He hath writt,
Leaves living art, bvt page, to serve his witt.

OBIIT ANO DO 1616
ÆTATIS 53 DIE 23AP.

Signature 120.

This acrostic is found on the first page of *The Tempest.* It was shown to me by my friend Mr. W. L. Stoddard.

Note the large B^O with which the first line of the play opens.

Begin to read from the large initial B downwards and all the way around the first column; on the outside letters of the text; spelling BACONO, you will arrive at the capital O, or cipher, which is next to the large initial B.

It is easier to show this by a diagram than by an acrostic figure.

```
BOTESWAIN.........................E
T                                 E
B                                 L
H                                 D
Y                                 E
W                                 S
N                                 S
G                                 E
S                                 H
I                                 A
W                                 N
D                                 W
K                                 N
N                                 R
W                                 E
R                                 T
V                                 A
G                                 E
N                                 T
A                                 D
L                                 E
H                                 I
G                                 T
S                                 T
H                                 R
W                                 E
I                                 R
H                                 Y
I                                 S
G                                 N
O                                 N
H                                 R
D                                 E
                                  E
                                  R
BRINGHERTOTRYWITHMAINECOURSEAPLAGUE
```

THE TEMPEST.

Actus primus, Scena prima.

A tempestuous noise of Thunder and Lightning heard: En-
ter a Ship-master, and a Botefwaine.

Mafter.
Ote-fwaine.
Botef. Heere Mafter: What cheere?
Maft. Good: Speake to th' Mariners: fall
too't, yarely, or we run our felues a ground,
beftirre, beftirre. *Exit.*

Enter Mariners.

Botef. Heigh my hearts, cheerely, cheerely my harts:
yare, yare: Take in the toppe-fale: Tend to th' Mafters
whiftle: Blow till thou burft thy winde, if roome e-
nough.

Enter Alonfo, Sebaftian, Anthonio, Ferdinando,
Gonzalo, and others.

Alon. Good Botefwaine haue care: where's the Ma-
fter? Play the men.
Botef. I pray now keepe below.
Anth. Where is the Mafter, Bofon?
Botef. Do you not heare him? you marre our labour,
Keepe your Cabines: you do affift the ftorme.
Gonz. Nay, good be patient.
Botef. When the Sea is: hence, what cares thefe roa-
rers for the name of King? to Cabine; filence: trouble
vs not.
Gon. Good, yet remember whom thou haft aboord.
Botef. None that I more loue then my felfe. You are
a Counfellor, if you can command thefe Elements to filence, and worke the peace of the prefent, wee will not
hand a rope more, vfe your authoritie: If you cannot,
giue thankes you haue liu'd fo long, and make your
felfe readie in your Cabine for the mifchance of the
houre, if it fo hap. Cheerely good hearts: out of our
way I fay. *Exit.*
Gon. I haue great comfort from this fellow: methinks
he hath no drowning marke vpon him, his complexion
is perfect Gallowes: ftand faft good Fate to his hanging, make the rope of his deftiny our cable, for our
owne doth little aduantage: If he be not borne to bee
hang'd, our cafe is miferable. *Exit.*

Enter Botefwaine.

Botef. Downe with the top-Maft: yare, lower, lower,
bring her to Try with Maine-courfe. A plague——
A cry within. Enter Sebaftian, Anthonio & Gonzalo.

vpon this howling: they are lowder then the weather,
or our office: yet againe? What do you heere? Shal we
giue ore and drowne, haue you a minde to finke?
Sebaf. A poxe o' your throat, you bawling, blafphe-
mous incharitable Dog.
Botef. Worke you then.
Anth. Hang cur, hang, you whorefon infolent Noyfe-
maker, we are leffe afraid to be drownde, then thou art.
Gonz. I'le warrant him for drowning, though the
Ship were no ftronger then a Nutt-fhell, and as leaky as
an vnftanched wench.
Botef. Lay her a hold, a hold, fet her two courfes off
to Sea againe, lay her off.

Enter Mariners wet.

Mari. All loft, to prayers, to prayers, all loft.
Botef. What muft our mouths be cold?
Gonz. The King, and Prince, at prayers, let's affift them,
for our cafe is as theirs.
Sebaf. I'am out of patience.
An. We are meerly cheated of our liues by drunkards,
This wide-chopt-rafcall, would thou mightft lye drow-
ning the wafhing of ten Tides.
Gonz. Hee'l be hang'd yet,
Though euery drop of water fweare againft it,
And gape at widft to glut him. *A confufed noyfe within.*
Mercy on vs.
We fplit, we fplit, Farewell my wife, and children,
Farewell brother: we fplit, we fplit, we fplit.
Anth. Let's all finke with' King
Seb. Let's take leaue of him. *Exit.*
Gonz. Now would I giue a thoufand furlongs of Sea,
for an Acre of barren ground: Long heath, Browne
firrs, any thing; the wills aboue be done, but I would
faine dye a dry death. *Exit.*

Scena Secunda.

Enter Profpero and Miranda.

Mira. If by your Art (my deereft father) you haue
Put the wild waters in this Rore, alay them:
The skye it feemes would powre down ftinking pitch,
But that the Sea, mounting to th' welkins cheeke,
Dafhes the fire out. Oh! I haue fuffered
With thofe that I faw fuffer: A braue veffell

A   (Who

Signature 121.

The last Act of *The Tempest* contains several acrostics.

The 'Epilogue' has already been shown as a specimen on page 61.

Now note that the initial of the first word of Act v, Scene i, is the initial N of the word 'Now.' (See p. 340.)

Note also that the initial of the first word of the last line of the column is the B of the word 'Brim.'

Begin to read on the initial of the word 'Now,' which begins the first line of the block of type composing the first column of Act v, Scene i ; downwards ; on the initial *capitals* of the lines of the *text* (excluding stage-names); spelling NOCAB, you will arrive at the initial capital B of the word 'Brim.'

Begin to read up, in the same way from the initial capital B of the word 'Brim'; spelling BACON, you will arrive again at the initial capital N of the word 'Now'; thus keying the cipher both backwards and forwards.

Begin to read on the initial N of the word 'Now'; to the right; downwards; on the *capitals* of the text; spelling NOCAB, you will arrive at the initial B of the word 'Brim.'

Begin to read on the initial B of the word 'Brim'; to the right; upwards; on the capitals of the text; spelling BACON, you will arrive at the initial N of the word 'Now.'

Thus we have the name keyed four ways, forward and backward, in this first block of the text of the last Act of *The Tempest*.

The acrostic figure here is: —

Now
O
C
A
Brim

Signature 122.

Having found a signature in the first block of type in the text of this last Act of *The Tempest*, let us look at the last block of type in the text of the same Act. (See p. 343.)

Note that the initial of the last word of the first line of the block is the N of the word 'nuptial.'

Note also that the initial of the first word of the last line of the same block is the B of the word 'Be.'

Note the initials of the words at the beginning of this last line of the play: they are B F of the words 'Be free.'

Begin to read from the initial B of the word 'Be'; to the right; upwards; on the initials of the words of the *text;* spelling BACON, you will arrive at the initial N of the word 'nuptial.'

Begin to read from the same initial B of the word 'Be'; to the left; upwards; on the initials of the words of the text; spelling BACON, you will arrive at the initial N of the word 'nuptial.'

Begin to read from the initial N of the word 'nuptial'; to the left; downwards; on the initials of the words of the text; spelling backwards NOCAB, you will arrive at the initial B of the word 'Be.'

Begin to read from the initial N of the word 'nuptial'; to the right; downwards; on the initials of the words of the text; spelling backwards NOCAB, you will again arrive at the initial B of the word 'Be.'

Thus we have this name keyed *four* ways, and *forwards* and *backwards*, in this last block of the text of *The Tempest*.

The acrostic figure here is: —

                    Nuptial
                 O
              C
           A
Be free, and fare thou well:

Signature 123.

Another acrostic is to be found in this last Act of *The Tempest.* (See pp. 340–343.)

Note that the initial of the first word of the text of the Act is the initial N of the word ' Now.'

Note that the initial of the last word of the author, at the end of the Act, is the initial F of the word ' Finis.'

Begin to read from the initial F of the word ' Finis '; on the initial capitals of the first words of the lines of the *text* (excluding abbreviated stage-names and directions, but including the ' Epilogue ' and ' *Names of the Actors* '); back towards the beginning of the Act; spelling Fravncis Bacon, you will arrive at the initial N of the word ' Now,' which is the first word of the text of the Act.

Begin to read from the initial N of the word ' Now,' which is the first word of the last Act; on the initial capitals of the first words of the lines of the text; through the entire Act; spelling Nocab Sicnvarf, you will arrive at the initial F of the word ' Finis.'

The same result is given if the reader read from the same initial F to the same initial N; *up* one column and *down* another.

Thus we have found this carefully planned acrostic written forwards and backwards as to spelling, and in alternate as well as continuous direction; from the initial N of the first word of the text of the last Act, to the initial F of the word ' Finis,' which is presumably the author's last word.

The acrostic figures here are all alike, in a graphic: —
Now do's my Proiect gather to a head:

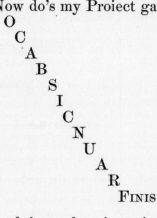

If the author of these plays is, as is generally supposed, speaking in the person of Prospero, his words have a new meaning for us when he says : —

'I will discase me and myself present.'

Pallas, the Spear-shaker, was born out of the head of Jove, fully cased in armour. There is no direct evidence that the poet was referring to Pallas here.

Ste. Put off that gowne (*Trinculo*) by this hand Ile
haue that gowne.

Tri. Thy grace shall haue it. (meane

Cal. The dropsie drowne this foole, what doe you
To doate thus on such luggage? let's alone
And doe the murther first: if he awake,
From toe to crowne hee'l fill our skins with pinches,
Make vs strange stuffe.

Ste. Be you quiet (*Monster*) Mistris line, is not this
my Ierkin? now is the Ierkin vnder the line: now Ierkin you are like to lose your haire, & proue a bald Ierkin.

Trin. Doe, doe; we steale by lyne and leuell, and't
like your grace.

Ste. I thank thee for that iest; heer's a garment for't:
Wit shall not goe vn-rewarded while I am King of this
Country: Steale by line and leuell, is an excellent passe
of pate: there's another garment for't.

Tri. Monster, come put some Lime vpon your fingers, and away with the rest.

Cal. I will haue none on't: we shall loose our time,
And all be turn'd to Barnacles, or to Apes
With foreheads villanous low.

Ste. Monster, lay to your fingers: helpe to beare this
away, where my hogshead of wine is, or Ile turne you
out of my kingdome: goe to, carry this.

Tri. And this.

Ste. I, and this.

*A noyse of Hunters heard. Enter diuers Spirits in shape
of Dogs and Hounds, hunting them about: Prospero
and Ariel setting them on.*

Pro. Hey *Mountaine*, hey.

Ari. Siluer: there it goes, *Siluer*.

Pro. Fury, Fury: there Tyrant, there: harke, harke.
Goe, charge my Goblins that they grinde their ioynts
With dry Convultions, shorten vp their sinewes
With aged Cramps, & more pinch-spotted make them,
Then Pard, or Cat o'Mountaine.

Ari. Harke, they rore.

Pro. Let them be hunted soundly: At this houre
Lies at my mercy all mine enemies:
Shortly shall all my labours end, and thou
Shalt haue the ayre at freedome: for a little
Follow, and doe me seruice. *Exeunt.*

Actus quintus: Scœna Prima.

Enter Prospero (in his Magicke robes) and Ariel.

Pro. Now do's my Proiect gather to a head:
My charmes cracke not: my Spirits obey, and Time
Goes vpright with his carriage: how's the day?

Ar. On the sixt hower at which time, my Lord
You said our worke should cease.

Pro. I did say so,
When first I rais'd the Tempest: say my Spirit,
How fares the King, and's followers?

Ar. Confin'd together
In the same fashion, as you gaue in charge,
Iust as you left them; all prisoners Sir
In the Line-groue which weather-fends your Cell,
They cannot boudge till your release: The King,
His Brother and yours, abide all three distracted,
And the remainder mourning ouer them,
Brim full of sorrow, and dismay: but chiefly

Him that you term'd Sir, the good old Lord *Gonzallo*,
His teares runs downe his beard like winters drops
From eaues of reeds: your charm so strongly works 'em
That if you now beheld them, your affections
Would become tender.

Pro. Dost thou thinke so, Spirit?

Ar. Mine would, Sir, were I humane.

Pro. And mine shall.
Hast thou (which art but aire) a touch, a feeling
Of their afflictions, and shall not my selfe,
One of their kinde, that rellish all as sharpely,
Passion as they, be kindlier mou'd then thou art?
Thogh with their high wrongs I am strook to th'quick,
Yet, with my nobler reason, gainst my furie
Doe I take part: the rarer Action is
In vertue, then in vengeance: they, being penitent,
The sole drift of my purpose doth extend
Not a frowne further: Goe, release them *Ariell*,
My Charmes Ile breake, their sences Ile restore,
And they shall be themselues.

Ar. Ile fetch them, Sir. *Exit.*

Pro. Ye Elues of hils, brooks, standing lakes & groues,
And ye, that on the sands with printlesse foote
Doe chase the ebbing-*Neptune*, and doe flie him
When he comes backe: you demy-Puppets, that
By Moone-shine doe the greene sowre Ringlets make,
Whereof the Ewe not bites: and you, whose pastime
Is to make midnight-Mushrumps, that reioyce
To heare the solemne Curfewe, by whose ayde
(Weake Masters though ye be) I haue bedymn'd
The Noone-tide Sun, call'd forth the mutenous windes,
And twixt the greene Sea, and the azur'd vault
Set roaring warre: To the dread ratling Thunder
Haue I giuen fire, and rifted *Ioues* stowt Oke
With his owne Bolt: The strong bass'd promontorie
Haue I made shake, and by the spurs pluckt vp
The Pyne, and Cedar. Graues at my command
Haue wak'd their sleepers, op'd, and let 'em forth
By my so potent Art. But this rough Magicke
I heere abiure: and when I haue requir'd
Some heauenly Musicke (which euen now I do)
To worke mine end vpon their Sences, that
This Ayrie-charme is for, I le breake my staffe,
Bury it certaine fadomes in the earth,
And deeper then did euer Plummet sound
Ile drowne my booke. *Solemne musicke.*

*Heere enters Ariel before: Then Alonso with a franticke ge-
sture, attended by Gonzalo. Sebastian and Anthonio in
like manner attended by Adrian and Francisco: They all
enter the circle which Prospero had made, and there stand
charm'd: which Prospero obseruing, speakes.*

A solemne Ayre, and the best comforter,
To an vnsetled fancie, Cure thy braines
(Now vselesse) boile within thy skull: there stand
For you are Spell-stopt.
Holy *Gonzallo*, Honourable man,
Mine eyes ev'n sociable to the shew of thine
Fall fellowly drops: The charme dissolues apace,
And as the morning steales vpon the night
(Melting the darkenesse) so their rising sences
Begin to chace the ignorant fumes that mantle
Their cleerer reason. O good *Gonzallo*
My true preseruer, and a loyall Sir,
To him thou follow'st; I will pay thy graces
Home both in word, and deede: Most cruelly

Didst

Did thou *Alonso*, vse me, and my daughter:
Thy brother was a furtherer in the Act,
Thou art pinch'd for't now *Sebastian*. Flesh, and bloud,
You, brother mine, that entertaine ambition,
Expelld remorse, and nature, whom, with *Sebastian*
(Whose inward pinches therefore are most strong)
Would heere haue kill'd your King: I do forgiue thee,
Vnnaturall though thou art: Their vnderstanding
Begins to swell, and the approching tide
Will shortly fill the reasonable shore
That now ly foule, and muddy: not one of them
That yet lookes on me, or would know me: *Ariell*,
Fetch me the Hat, and Rapier in my Cell,
I will discaserne, and my selfe present
As I was sometime *Millaine*: quickly Spirit,
Thou shalt ere long be free.

Ariell sings, and helps to attire him.
Where the Bee sucks, there suck I;
In a Cowslips bell, I lie,
There I cowch when Owles doe crie,
On the Batts backe I doe flie
after Sommer merrily.
Merrily, merrily, shall I liue now,
Vnder the blossom that hangs on the Bow.

Pro. Why that's my dainty *Ariell*: I shall misse
Thee, but yet thou shalt haue freedome: so, so, so.
To the Kings ship, inuisible as thou art,
There shalt thou finde the Marriners asleepe
Vnder the Hatches: the Master and the Boat-swaine
Being awake, enforce them to this place;
And presently, I pre'thee.

Ar. I drinke the aire before me, and returne
Or ere your pulse twice beate.   *Exit.*

Gon. All torment, trouble, wonder, and amazement
Inhabits heere: some heauenly power guide vs
Out of this fearefull Country.

Pro. Behold Sir King
The wronged Duke of *Millaine*, *Prospero*:
For more assurance that a liuing Prince
Do's now speake to thee, I embrace thy body,
And to thee, and thy Company, I bid
A hearty welcome.

Alo. Where thou bee'st he or no,
Or some inchanted trifle to abuse me,
(As late I haue beene) I not know: thy Pulse
Beats as of flesh, and blood: and since I saw thee,
Th'affliction of my minde amends, with which
I feare a madnesse held me: this must craue
(And if this be at all) a most strange story.
Thy Dukedome I resigne, and doe entreat
Thou pardon me my wrongs: But how shold *Prospero*
Be liuing, and be heere?

Pro. First, noble Frend,
Let me embrace thine age, whose honor cannot
Be measur'd, or confin'd.

Gonz. Whether this be,
Or be not, I'le not sweare.

Pro. You doe yet taste
Some subtleties o'th'Isle, that will not let you
Beleeue things certaine: Wellcome, my friends all,
But you, my brace of Lords; were I so minded
I heere could plucke his Highnesse frowne vpon you
And iustifie you Traitors: at this time
I will tell no tales.

Seb. The Diuell speakes in him.
Pro. No:

For you (most wicked Sir) whom to call brother
Would euen infect my mouth, I do forgiue
Thy rankest fault; all of them: and require
My Dukedome of thee, which, perforce I know
Thou must restore.

Alo. If thou beest *Prospero*
Giue vs particulars of thy preseruation,
How thou hast met vs heere, whom three howres since
Were wrackt vpon this shore? where I haue lost
(How sharp the point of this remembrance is)
My deere sonne *Ferdinand*.

Pro. I am woe for't, Sir.
Alo. Irreparable is the losse, and patience
Saies, it is past her cure.

Pro. I rather thinke
You haue not sought her helpe, of whose soft grace
For the like losse, I haue her soueraigne aid,
And rest my selfe content.

Alo. You the like losse?
Pro. As great to me, as late; and supportable
To make the deere losse, haue I meanes much weaker
Then you may call to comfort you; for I
Haue lost my daughter.

Alo. A daughter?
Oh heauens, that they were liuing both in *Naples*
The King and Queene there, that they were, I wish
My selfe were mudded in that oo-zie bed
Where my sonne lies: when did you lose your daughter?

Pro. In this last Tempest. I perceiue these Lords
At this encounter doe so much admire,
That they deuoure their reason, and scarce thinke
Their eies doe offices of Truth: Their words
Are naturall breath: but howsoeu'r you haue
Beene iustled from your sences, know for certain
That I am *Prospero*, and that very Duke
Which was thrust forth of *Millaine*, who most strangely
Vpon this shore (where you were wrackt) was landed
To be the Lord on't: No more yet of this,
For 'tis a Chronicle of day by day,
Not a relation for a break-fast, nor
Befitting this first meeting: Welcome, Sir;
This Cell's my Court: heere haue I few attendants,
And Subiects none abroad: pray you looke in:
My Dukedome since you haue giuen me againe,
I will requite you with as good a thing,
At least bring forth a wonder, to content ye
As much, as me my Dukedome.

Here Prospero discouers Ferdinand and Miranda, play-
ing at Chesse.

Mir. Sweet Lord, you play me false.
Fer. No my dearest loue,
I would not for the world.   (wrangle,
Mir. Yes, for a score of Kingdomes, you should
And I would call it faire play.

Alo. If this proue
A vision of the Island, one deere Sonne
Shall I twice loose.

Seb. A most high miracle.
Fer. Though the Seas threaten they are mercifull,
I haue curs'd them without cause.

Alo. Now all the blessings
Of a glad father, compasse thee about:
Arise, and say how thou cam'st heere.

Mir. O wonder!
How many goodly creatures are there heere
How beauteous mankinde is? O braue new world

R 3   That

That has ſuch people in't.

Pro. Tis new to thee.   (play?

Alo. What is this Maid, with whom thou was't at
Your eld'ſt aequaintance cannot be three houres :
Is ſhe the goddeſſe that hath ſeuer'd vs,
And brought vs thus together?

Fer. Sir, ſhe is mortall ;
But by immortall prouidence, ſhe's mine ;
I choſe her when I could not aske my Father
For his aduiſe : nor thought I had one : She
Is daughter to this famous Duke of *Millaine*,
Of whom, ſo often I haue heard renowne,
But neuer ſaw before : of whom I haue
Receiu'd a ſecond life ; and ſecond Father
This Lady makes him to me.

Alo. I am hers.
But O, how odly will it ſound, that I
Muſt aske my childe forgiueneſſe ?

Pro. There Sir ſtop,
Let vs not burthen our remembrances, with
A heauineſſe that's gon.

Gon. I haue inly wept,
Or ſhould haue ſpoke ere this : looke downe you gods
And on this couple drop a bleſſed crowne ;
For it is you, that haue chalk'd forth the way
Which brought vs hither.

Alo. I ſay Amen, *Gonzallo.*

Gon. Was *Millaine* thruſt from *Millaine*, that his Iſſue
Should become Kings of *Naples* ? O reioyce
Beyond a common ioy, and ſet it downe
With gold on laſting Pillers :In one voyage
Did *Claribell* her husband finde at *Tunis*,
And *Ferdinand* her brother, found a wife,
Where he himſelfe was loſt : *Proſpero,* his Dukedome
In a poore Iſle : and all of vs, our ſelues,
When no man was his owne.

Alo. Giue me your hands :
Let griefe and ſorrow ſtill embrace his heart,
That doth not wiſh you ioy.

Gon. Be it ſo, Amen.

*Enter Ariell, with the Maſter and Boatſwaine
amazedly following.*

O looke Sir, looke Sir, here is more of vs :
I propheſi'd, if a Gallowes were on Land
This fellow could not drowne : Now blasphemy,
That ſwear'ſt Grace ore-boord, not an oath on ſhore,
Haſt thou no mouth by land ?
What is the newes ?

Bot. The beſt newes is, that we haue ſafely found
Our King, and company : The next : our Ship,
Which but three glaſſes ſince, we gaue out ſplit,
Is tyte, and yare, and brauely rig'd, as when
We firſt put out to Sea.

Ar. Sir, all this ſeruice
Haue I done ſince I went.

Pro. My trickſey Spirit.

Alo. Theſe are not naturall euents, they ſtrengthen
From ſtrange, to ſtranger : ſay, how came you hither ?

Bot. If I did thinke, Sir, I were well awake,
I'ld ſtriue to tell you : we were dead of ſleepe,
And (how we know not) all clapt vnder hatches,
Where, but euen now, with ſtrange, and ſeuerall noyſes
Of roring, ſhrecking, howling, gingling chaines,
And mo diuerſitie of ſounds, all horrible.
We were awak'd : ſtraight way, at liberty ;
Where we, in all our trim, freſhly beheld

Our royall, good, and gallant Ship : our Maſter
Capring to eye her : on a trice, ſo pleaſe you,
Euen in a dreame, were we diuided from them,
And were brought moaping hither.

Ar. Was't well done ?

Pro. Brauely (my diligence) thou ſhalt be free.

Alo. This is as ſtrange a Maze, as ere men trod,
And there is in this buſineſſe, more then nature
Was euer conduct of : ſome Oracle
Muſt rectifie our knowledge.

Pro. Sir, my Leige,
Doe not infeſt your minde, with beating on
The ſtrangeneſſe of this buſineſſe, at pickt leiſure
(Which ſhall be ſhortly ſingle) I'le reſolue you,
(Which to you ſhall ſeeme probable) of euery
Theſe happend accidents : till when, be cheerefull
And thinke of each thing well : Come hither Spirit,
Set *Caliban*, and his companions free :
Vntye the Spell : How fares my gracious Sir ?
There are yet miſſing of your Companie
Some few odde Lads, that you remember not.

*Enter Ariell, driuing in Caliban, Stephano, and
Trinculo in their ſtolne Apparell.*

Ste. Euery man ſhift for all the reſt, and let
No man take care for himſelfe ; for all is
But fortune : *Coragio* Bully-Monſter *Coraſio.*

Tri. If theſe be true ſpies which I weare in my head,
here's a goodly ſight.

Cal. O *Setebos*, theſe be braue Spirits indeede :
How fine my Maſter is ? I am afraid
He will chaſtiſe me.

Seb. Ha, ha :
What things are theſe, my Lord *Anthonio* ?
Will money buy em ?

Ant. Very like : one of them
Is a plaine Fiſh, and no doubt marketable.

Pro. Marke but the badges of theſe men, my Lords,
Then ſay if they be true : This miſhapen knaue ;
His Mother was a Witch, and one ſo ſtrong
That could controle the Moone ; make flowes, and ebs,
And deale in her command, without her power :
Theſe three haue robd me, and this demy-diuell ;
(For he's a baſtard one) had plotted with them
To take my life : two of theſe Fellowes, you
Muſt know, and owne, this Thing of darkeneſſe, I
Acknowledge mine.

Cal. I ſhall be pincht to death.

Alo. Is not this *Stephano*, my drunken Butler ?

Seb. He is drunke now ;
Where had he wine ?

Alo. And *Trinculo* is reeling ripe : where ſhould they
Finde this grand Liquor that hath gilded 'em ?
How cam'ſt thou in this pickle ?

Tri. I haue bin in ſuch a pickle ſince I ſaw you laſt,
That I feare me will neuer out of my bones :
I ſhall not feare fly-blowing.

Seb. Why how now *Stephano* ?

Ste. O touch me not, I am not *Stephano*, but a Cramp.

Pro. You'ld be King o'the Iſle, Sirha ?

Ste. I ſhould haue bin a ſore one then.

Alo. This is a ſtrange thing as ere I look'd on.

Pro. He is as diſproportion'd in his Manners
As in his ſhape : Goe Sirha, to my Cell,
Take with you your Companions : as you looke
To haue my pardon, trim it handſomely.

Cal. I that I will : and Ile be wiſe hereafter,

And

And ſeeke for grace : what a thrice double Aſſe
Was I to take this drunkard for a god ?
And worſhip this dull foole ?
  Pro. Goe to, away.   (found it.
  Alo. Hence, and beſtow your luggage where you
Seb. Or ſtole it rather.
  Pro. Sir, I inuite your Highneſſe, and your traine
To my poore Cell : where you ſhall take your reſt
For this one night, which part of it, Ile waſte
With ſuch diſcourſe, as I not doubt, ſhall make it
Goe quicke away : The ſtory of my life,
And the particular accidents, gon by
Since I came to this Iſle : And in the morne
I'le bring you to your ſhip, and ſo to *Naples*,

Where I haue hope to ſee the nuptiall
Of theſe our deere-belou'd, ſolemnized,
And thence retire me to my *Millaine*, where
Euery third thought ſhall be my graue.
  Alo. I long
To heare the ſtory of your life ; which muſt
Take the eare ſtrangely.
  Pro. I'le deliuer all,
And promiſe you calme Seas, auſpicious gales,
And ſaile, ſo expeditious, that ſhall catch
Your Royall fleete farre off : My *Ariel* ; chicke
That is thy charge : Then to the Elements
Be free, and fare thou well : pleaſe you draw neere.
                    Exeunt omnes.

EPILOGVE,
ſpoken by *Proſpero.*

Now my Charmes are all ore-throwne,
  And what ſtrength I haue's mine owne.
Which is moſt faint : now 'tis true
I muſt be heere confinde by you,
Or ſent to *Naples*, Let me not
Since I haue my Dukedome got,
And pardon'd the deceiuer, dwell
In this bare Iſland, by your Spell,
But releaſe me from my bands
with the helpe of your good hands :
Gentle breath of yours, my Sailes
Muſt fill, or elſe my proiect failes,
which was to pleaſe : Now I want
Spirits to enforce : Art to inchant,
And my ending is deſpaire,
Vnleſſe I be relieu'd by praier
Which pierces ſo, that it aſſaults
Mercy it ſelfe, and frees all faults.
  As you from crimes would pardon'd be,
  Let your Indulgence ſet me free.   Exit.

The Scene, an vn-inhabited Iſland

Names of the Actors.

Alonſo, K. of Naples:
Sebaſtian his Brother.
Proſpero, the right Duke of Millaine.
Anthonio his brother, the vſurping Duke of Millaine.
Ferdinand, Son to the King of Naples.
Gonzalo, an honeſt old Counceller.
Adrian, & *Franciſco*, Lords.
Caliban, a ſaluage and deformed ſlaue.
Trinculo, a Ieſter.
Stephano, a drunken Butler.
Maſter of a Ship.
Boate-Swaine.
Marriners.
Miranda, daughter to Proſpero.
Ariell, an ayrie ſpirit.
Iris
Ceres
Iuno   } Spirits.
Nymphes
Reapers

FINIS.

THE

Signature 124.

This acrostic is found on the last page of the *Two Gentlemen of Verona.* The page is wrongly headed " The Merry Wiues of Windsor." (See p. 346.)

Begin to read from the initial B of the word ' Be,' which is the first word on the page; to the right; downwards; on the initials of the words of the text; spelling Bacono, you will arrive at the initial O of the word ' once ' (25th line from top).

Begin to read from the initial O of this word ' once'; to the right; downwards; on the initials of the words; spelling backwards Ocsicnarf, you will arrive at the initial F of the word 'Finis.'

The acrostic figure here is: —

Be thou ashamed, etc.
A
C
O
N
: if Once again, etc.
C
S
I
C
N
A
R
Finis.

The cipherer has also doubled this signature by treating both the columns as if they were one column: that is to say, he has read across both columns, and has adjusted the initials to the same figure, but has made it tie at another point.

Begin to read on the initial B of the word ' Be,' which is the first word on the page; to the right; downwards; on the initials of the words of the text; across both columns as one line; spelling BACONO, you will arrive at the initial O of the word 'of' (12th line from top: second column).

Begin to read from the initial O of this word 'of'; to the left; downwards; on the initials of the words of the text; still across both columns as one line; spelling backwards OCSICNARF, you will again arrive at the initial F of the word 'FINIS.'

The acrostic figure here is: —

Be thou ashamed, etc.

A

C

O

N

that I shall aske Of you

C

S

I

C

N

A

R

FINIS.

Be thou asham'd that I haue tooke vpon me,
Such an immodest rayment; if shame liue
In a disguise of loue?
It is the lesser blot modesty findes,
Women to change their shapes, then men their minds.

  Pro. Then men their minds? tis true: oh heuen, were man
But Constant, he were perfect; that one error.
Fils him with faults: makes him run through all th'sins;
Inconstancy falls-off, ere it begins:
What is in *Siluia's* face, but I may spie
More fresh in *Iulia's*, with a constant eye?

  Val. Come, come: a hand from either:
Let me be blest to make this happy close:
'Twere pitty two such friends should be long foes.

  Pro. Beare witnes (heauen) I haue my wish for euer.
  Iul. And I mine.
  Out-l. A prize: a prize: a prize.
  Val. Forbeare, forbeare I say: It is my Lord the *Duke*.
Your Grace is welcome to a man disgrac'd,
Banished *Valentine.*

  Duke. Sir *Valentine?*
  Thu. Yonder is *Siluia*: and *Siluia's* mine.
  Val. *Thurio* giue backe: or else embrace thy death:
Come not within the measure of my wrath:
Doe not name *Siluia* thine: if once againe,
Verona shall not hold thee: heere she stands,
Take but possession of her, with a Touch;
I dare thee, but to breath vpon my Loue.

  Thur. Sir *Valentine*, I care not for her, I:
I hold him but a foole that will endanger
His Body, for a Girle that loues him not:
I claime her not, and therefore she is thine.

  Duke. The more degenerate and base art thou
To make such meanes for her, as thou hast done,
And leaue her on such slight conditions.

Now, by the honor of my Ancestry,
I doe applaud thy spirit, *Valentine,*
And thinke thee worthy of an Empresse loue:
Know then, I heere forget all former greefes,
Cancell all grudge, repeale thee home againe,
Plead a new state in thy vn-riual'd merit,
To which I thus subscribe: Sir *Valentine,*
Thou art a Gentleman, and well deriu'd,
Take thou thy *Siluia*, for thou hast deseru'd her.

  Val. I thank your Grace, ẏ gift hath made me happy:
I now beseech you (for your daughters sake)
To grant one Boone that I shall aske of you.

  Duke. I grant it (for thine owne) what ere it be.
  Val. These banish'd men, that I haue kept withall,
Are men endu'd with worthy qualities,
Forgiue them what they haue committed here,
And let them be recall'd from their Exile:
They are reformed, ciuill, full of good,
And fit for great employment (worthy Lord.)

  Duke. Thou hast preuaild, I pardon them and thee:
Dispose of them, as thou knowst their deserts.
Come, let vs goe, we will include all iarres,
With Triumphes, Mirth, and rare solemnity.

  Val. And as we walke along, I dare be bold
With our discourse, to make your Grace to smile.
What thinke you of this Page (my Lord?)

  Duke. I think the Boy hath grace in him, he blushes.
  Val. I warrant you (my Lord) more grace, then Boy.
  Duke. What meane you by that saying?
  Val. Please you, Ile tell you, as we passe along,
That you will wonder what hath fortuned:
Come *Protheus*, 'tis your pennance, but to heare
The story of your Loues discouered.
That done, our day of marriage shall be yours,
One Feast, one house, one mutuall happinesse.   *Exeunt.*

The names of all the Actors.

Duke: Father to *Siluia.*
Valentine. }
Protheus. } the two Gentlemen.
Anthonio: father to *Protheus.*
Thurio: a foolish riuall to *Valentine.*

Eglamoure: Agent for *Siluia* in her escape.
Host: where *Iulia* lodges.
Out-lawes with *Valentine.*
Speed: a clownish seruant to *Valentine.*
Launce: the like to *Protheus.*
Panthion: seruant to *Antonio.*
Iulia: beloued of *Protheus.*
Siluia: beloued of *Valentine.*
Lucetta: waighting woman to *Iulia.*

FINIS.

THE

Signature 125.

This acrostic is found on page 50 of *The Merry Wiues of Windsor*, which is wrongly numbered 58. (See p. 349.)

Note that the initial of the first word in the first column is the initial B of the word 'Be'; and that the initial of the last word of the same column is the initial N of the word 'now.' Here we have B N to guide us at opposite corners.

Begin to read from the initial B of the word 'Be'; downwards; on the left-hand outside *letters* of the column; spelling Bacon, you will arrive at the initial N of the word 'now.'

Begin to read from the initial of the word 'now'; to the right and up the outside *letters* of the column; spelling Nocab, you will arrive at the initial B of the word 'Be' again; thus keying the cipher from corner to corner of the column.

The acrostic figure here is seen in a diagram.

BEGONE AND COMEWHENYOUARE CALLD MISTPAGEOMISTRISFORDWHATHAUEYOUDONE

M	U	R
M	S	E
R	E	N
M	Y	N
M	S	N
R	R	U
B	A	U
S	E	R
M	Y	N
M	E	E
S	U	R
B	E	E
M	I	E
S	U	E
M	E	H
M	E	M
H	M	H
T	S	E
F	Y	E
N	E	R
P	E	O
M	N	R
F	T	Y
F	D	H
W	D	E
M	Y	E
M	A	D
P	Y	E
F	R	E
I	U	A
H	S	E
T	N	E
A	E	Y
M	N	E
M	R	O
F	E	T
A	E	N
W	I	T
C	Y	T
F	T	N
H	T	R
M	E	L
F	E	T
T	I	E
C	E	K
O	N	T
I	M	E
P	D	E
T	T	T
M	E	S
F	E	H
C	F	Y
A	L	G
M	U	(?kt) K
A	T	E
F	T	E
M	E	Y
O	E	Y
R	T	E
T	Y	W
A	Y	E
F	E	D
T	S	H
M	N	N

WHATSTHEMATTER . . . . . . HOW NOW YOUSHALLSEESPORT . . . . ANON
Follow

Now note that if you treat both columns as one the same cipher will still key from and to the same points.

Note also that the cipherer seems to have been attracted by the *double entente* of the first line of the page.

Note also that the initial of the first word on the page is the initial B of the word 'Be': and that the initial of the last word of the page is the initial F of the word 'Follow.' If read upwards from lower to upper corner, they give us F B and point to the initial B from which this cipher proceeds.

Be gone, and come when you are call'd.

M.Page. Here comes little *Robin.*   (with you?

Mist.Ford. How now my Eyas-Musket, what newes

Rob. My M. Sir *Iohn* is come in at your backe doore (Mist.*Ford*,and requests your company.

M.Page. You litle Iack-a-lent,haue you bin true to vs

Rob. I, Ile be sworne: my Master knowes not of your being heere: and hath threatned to put me into euerlasting liberty, if I tell you of it: for he sweares he'll turne me away.

Mist.Pag. Thou'rt a good boy: this secrecy of thine shall be a Tailor to thee,and shal make thee a new doublet and hose. Ile go hide me.

Mi.Ford. Do so: go tell thy Master, I am alone: Mistris *Page,* remember you your *Qu.*

Mist.Pag. I warrant thee,if I do not act it, hisse me.

Mist.Ford. Go-too then: we'l vse this vnwholsome humidity,this grosse-watry Pumpion; we'll teach him to know Turtles from Iayes.

Fal. Haue I caught thee. my heauenly Iewell? Why now let me die,for I haue liu'd long enough: This is the period of my ambition: O this blessed houre.

Mist.Ford. O sweet Sir *Iohn.*

Fal. Mistris *Ford,* I cannot cog, I cannot prate (Mist. *Ford)* now shall I sin in my wish; I would thy Husband were dead, Ile speake it before the best Lord, I would make thee my Lady.

Mist.Ford. I your Lady Sir *Iohn?* Alas, I should bee a pittifull Lady.

Fal. Let the Court of France shew me such another: I see how thine eye would emulate the Diamond: Thou hast the right arched-beauty of the brow, that becomes the Ship-tyre,the Tyre-valiant, or any Tire of Venetian admittance.

Mist.Ford. A plaine Kerchiefe, Sir *Iohn?* My browes become nothing else,nor that well neither.

Fal. Thou art a tyrant to say so: thou wouldst make an absolute Courtier, and the firme fixture of thy foote, would giue an excellent motion to thy gate, in a semicircled Farthingale. I see what thou wert if Fortune thy foe, were not Nature thy friend: Come, thou canst not hide it.

Mist.Ford. Beleeue me, ther's no such thing in me.

Fal. What made me loue thee? Let that perswade thee. Ther's something extraordinary in thee: Come, I cannot cog, and say thou art this and that, like a-manie of these lisping-hauthorne buds, that come like women in mens apparrell, and smell like, Bucklers-berry in simple time: I cannot, but I loue thee, none but thee; and thou deseru'st it.

M.Ford. Do not betray me sir,I fear you loue M.*Page.*

Fal. Thou mightst as well say, I loue to walke by the Counter-gate, which is as hatefull to me, as the recke of a Lime-kill.

Mis Ford. Well, heauen knowes how I loue you, And you shall one day finde it.

Fal. Keepe in that minde, Ile deserue it.

Mist.Ford. Nay, I must tell you, so you doe; Or else I could not be in that minde.

Rob. Mistris *Ford,* Mistris *Ford:* heere's Mistris *Page* at the doore, sweating, and blowing, and looking wildely, and would needs speake with you presently.

Fal. She shall not see me, I will ensconce mee behinde the Arras.

M.Ford. Pray you do so, she's a very tatling woman. Whats the matter? How now?

Mist.Page. O mistris *Ford* what haue you done? You'r sham'd, y'are ouerthrowne, y'are vndone for euer.

M.Ford. What's the matter,good mistris *Page?*

M.Page. O weladay,mist.*Ford,* hauing an honest man to your husband,to giue him such cause of suspition.

M.Ford. What cause of suspition?

M.Page. What cause of suspition? Out vpon you: How am I mistooke in you?

M.Ford. Why (alas) what's the matter?

M.Page. Your husband's comming hether (Woman) with all the Officers in Windsor, to search for a Gentleman, that he sayes is heere now in the house; by your consent to take an ill aduantage of his absence: you are vndone.

M.Ford. 'Tis not so, I hope.

M.Page. Pray heauen it be not so, that you haue such a man heere: but 'tis most certaine your husband's comming, with halfe Windsor at his heeles, to serch for such a one, I come before to tell you: If you know your selfe cleere, why I am glad of it: but if you haue a friend here, conuey, conuey him out. Be not amaz'd, call all your senses to you, defend your reputation, or bid farwell to your good life for euer.

M.Ford. What shall I do? There is a Gentleman my deere friend: and I feare not mine owne shame so much, as his perill. I had rather then a thousand pound he were out of the house.

M.Page. For shame, neuer stand (you had rather,and you had rather:) your husband's heere at hand,bethinke you of some conueyance: in the house you cannot hide him. Oh, how haue you deceiu'd me? Looke, heere is a basket, if he be of any reasonable stature, he may creepe in heere, and throw fowle linnen vpon him, as if it were going to bucking: Or it is whiting time, send him by your two men to *Datchet*-Meade.

M.Ford. He's too big to go in there: what shall I do?

Fal. Let me see't, let me see't, O let me see't: Ile in, Ile in: Follow your friends counsell, Ile in.

M.Page. What Sir *Iohn Falstaffe?* Are these your Letters, Knight?

Fal. I loue thee, helpe mee away: let me creepe in heere: ile neuer——

M.Page. Helpe to couer your master (Boy:) Call your men (Mist.*Ford.*) You dissembling Knight.

M.Ford. What *Iohn,Robert,Iohn*; Go,take vp these cloathes heere,quickly: Wher's the Cowle-staffe? Look how you drumble? Carry them to the Landresse in Datchet mead: quickly, come.

Ford. 'Pray you come nere:if I suspect without cause, Why then make sport at me, then let me be your iest, I deserue it: How now? Whether beare you this?

Ser. To the Landresse forsooth?

M.Ford. Why, what haue you to doe whether they beare it? You were best meddle with buck-washing.

Ford. Bucke? I would I could wash my selfe of ý Bucke? Bucke, bucke, bucke, I bucke: I warrant you Bucke, And of the season too; it shall appeare.

Gentlemen, I haue dream'd to night, Ile tell you my dreame: heere, heere, heere bee my keyes, ascend my Chambers, search, seeke, finde out: Ile warrant wee'le vnkennell the Fox. Let me stop this way first: so,now vncape.

Page. Good master *Ford,* be contented: You wrong your selfe too much.

Ford. True (master *Page*) vp Gentlemen, You shall see sport anon:

Follow

Signature 126.

This acrostic is found on page 59 of *The Merry Wiues of Windsor*, which is wrongly numbered 51. (See p. 352.)

Note that the initial of the first word of the right-hand column is the B of the word 'Buckled': and that the initial of the last word in the column is the F of the word 'Ford.' Here we have B F, or F B, to guide us.

Begin to read from the initial B of the word 'Buckled'; to the right; downwards; on the initials of the words; spelling BACON, you will arrive at the initial N of the word 'not' (fifth line).

Begin to read from the initial F of the word 'Ford' (last word in the column); upwards; to the right; on the initials of the words; spelling FRAVNCIS BACON, you will arrive at the initial N of the word 'not'; thus keying the cipher from both the initials of the first and the last words on the column.

The acrostic figure here is: —

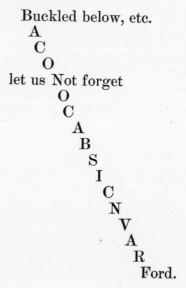

Signature 127.

While we are working on this page 51 of *The Merry Wiues of Windsor*, it may be observed that 'The Song' contains an independent signature. This acrostic was pointed out to me by my friend Mr. W. L. Stoddard. (See p. 352.)

Begin to read from the initial F of the word 'Fie,' which is the first word of the first line of the song; to the right; on all the letters of all the words; downwards; spelling Francisco Bacono, you will arrive at the initial O of the word ' out,' which is the last word of the song.

The acrostic figure here is: —

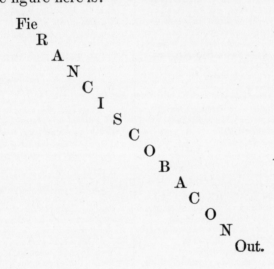

omnipotent Loue, how nere the God drew to the complexion of a Goose: a fault done first in the forme of a beast, (O Ioue, a beastly fault:) and then another fault, in the semblance of a Fowle, thinke on't (Ioue) a fowle-fault. When Gods haue hot backes, what shall poore men do? For me, I am heere a Windsor Stagge, and the fattest (I thinke) i'th Forrest. Send me a coole rut-time (Ioue) or who can blame me to pisse my Tallow? Who comes heere? my Doe?

M.Ford. Sir *Iohn?* Art thou there (my Deere?) My male-Deere?

Fal. My Doe, with the blacke Scut? Let the skie raine Potatoes: let it thunder, to the tune of Greenesleeues, haile-kissing Comfits, and snow Eringoes: Let there come a tempest of prouocation, I will shelter mee heere.

M. Ford. Mistris *Page* is come with me (sweet hart.)

Fal. Diuide me like a brib'd-Bucke, each a Haunch: I will keepe my sides to my selfe, my shoulders for the fellow of this walke; and my hornes I bequeath your husbands. Am I a Woodman, ha? Speake I like *Herne* the Hunter? Why, now is Cupid a child of conscience, he makes restitution. As I am a true spirit, welcome.

M.Page. Alas, what noise?

M.Ford. Heauen forgiue our sinnes.

Fal. What should this be?

M.Ford.M.Page. Away, away.

Fal. I thinke the diuell wil not haue me damn'd, Least the oyle that's in me should set hell on fire; He would neuer else crosse me thus.

Enter Fairies.

Qui. Fairies blacke, gray, greene, and white, You Moone-shine reuellers, and shades of night. You Orphan heires of fixed destiny, Attend your office, and your quality. Crier Hob-goblyn, make the Fairy Oyes.

Pist. Elues, list your names: Silence you aiery toyes. Cricket, to Windsor-chimnies shalt thou leape; Where fires thou find'st vnrak'd, and hearths vnswept, There pinch the Maids as blew as Bill-berry. Our radiant Queene, hates Sluts, and Sluttery.

Fal. They are Fairies, he that speaks to them shall die, Ile winke, and couch: No man their workes must eie.

Eu. Wher's *Bede?* Go you, and where you find a maid That ere she sleepe has thrice her prayers said, Raise vp the Organs of her fantasie, Sleepe she as sound as carelesse infancie, But those as sleepe, and thinke not on their sins, Pinch them armes, legs, backes, shoulders, sides, & shins.

Qu. About, about: Search Windsor Castle (Elues) within, and out. Strew good lucke (Ouphes) on euery sacred roome, That it may stand till the perpetuall doome, In state as wholsome, as in state 'tis fit, Worthy the Owner, and the Owner it. The seuerall Chaires of Order, looke you scowre With iuyce of Balme; and euery precious flowre, Each faire Instalment, Coate, and seu'rall Crest, With loyall Blazon, euermore be blest, And Nightly-meadow-Fairies, looke you sing Like to the *Garters*-Compasse, in a ring, Th'expressure that it beares: Greene let it be, Mote fertile-fresh then all the Field to see: And, *Hony Soit Qui Mal-y-Pence,* write In Emrold-tuffes, Flowres purple, blew, and white, Like Saphire-pearle, and rich embroiderie,

Buckled below faire Knight-hoods bending knee; Fairies vse Flowres for their characterie. Away, disperse: But till 'tis one a clocke, Our Dance of Custome, round about the Oke Of *Herne* the Hunter, let vs not forget. (set:

Euan. Pray you lock hand in hand: your selues in order And twenty glow-wormes shall our Lanthornes bee To guide our Measure round about the Tree. But stay, I smell a man of middle earth.

Fal. Heauens defend me from that Welsh Fairy, Least he transforme me to a peece of Cheese.

Pist. Vilde worme, thou wast ore-look'd euen in thy birth.

Qu. With Triall-fire touch me his finger end: If he be chaste, the flame will backe descend And turne him to no paine: but if he start, It is the flesh of a corrupted hart.

Pist. A triall, come.

Eua. Come: will this wood take fire?

Fal. Oh, oh, oh.

Qui. Corrupt, corrupt, and tainted in desire. About him (Fairies) sing a scornfull rime, And as you trip, still pinch him to your time.

The Song.

Fie on sinnefull phantasie: Fie on Lust, and Luxurie:
Lust is but a bloudy fire, kindled with vnchaste desire,
Fed in heart whose flames aspire,
As thoughts do blow them higher and higher.
Pinch him (Fairies) mutually: Pinch him for his villanie.
Pinch him, and burne him, and turne him about,
Till Candles, & Star-light, & Moone-shine be out.

Page. Nay do not flye, I thinke we haue watcht you now: Will none but *Herne* the Hunter serue your turne?

M. Page. I pray you come, hold vp the iest no higher. Now (good Sir *Iohn*) how like you *Windsor* wiues? See you these husband? Do not these faire yoakes Become the Forrest better then the Towne?

Ford. Now Sir, whose a Cuckold now? Mr *Broome, Falstaffes* a Knaue, a Cuckoldly knaue, Heere are his hornes Master *Broome:* And Master *Broome,* he hath enioyed nothing of *Fords,* but his Buck-basket, his cudgell, and twenty pounds of money, which must be paid to Mr *Broome,* his horses are arrested for it, Mr *Broome.*

M.Ford. Sir *Iohn,* we haue had ill lucke: wee could neuer meete: I will neuer take you for my Loue againe, but I will alwayes count you my Deere.

Fal. I do begin to perceiue that I am made an Asse.

Ford. I, and an Oxe too: both the proofes are extant.

Fal. And these are not Fairies: I was three or foure times in the thought they were not Fairies, and yet the guiltinesse of my minde, the sodaine surprize of my powers, droue the grossenesse of the foppery into a receiu'd beleefe, in despight of the teeth of all rime and reason, that they were Fairies. See now how wit may be made a Iacke-a-Lent, when 'tis vpon ill imployment.

Euant. Sir *Iohn Falstaffe,* serue Got, and leaue your desires, and Fairies will not pinse you.

Ford. Well said Fairy *Hugh.*

Euans. And leaue you your iealouzies too, I pray you.

Ford.

Signature 128.

These acrostics are found in the first column of *Measure for Measure*, in the Duke's first speech. (See p. 355.)

Begin to read from the initial O of the first word of the speech; to the right; on the terminals; downwards; spelling ONOCAB, you will arrive at the initial B of the word 'But' (sixth line of the speech).

Begin to read from the initial O of the first word of the last line of the speech; to the right; on terminals; upwards; spelling ONOCAB, you will arrive again at the initial B of the word 'But' (sixth line of the speech).

Begin to read from the terminal F of the first word of the speech; to the right; on the terminals; downwards; spelling FRANCISCO, you will arrive at the initial O of the word 'Our' (eighth line of the speech).

Begin to read from the terminal F of the first word of the last line of the speech; to the right; upwards; on the terminals; spelling FRANCISCO, you will again arrive at the initial O of the word 'Our' (eighth line of the speech).

The acrostic figures here are respectively: —

Of Gouernment, etc.

N
O
C
A

But that, etc.

A
C
O
N

Of our owne powre:

OF Gouernment, etc.

R
A
N
C
I
S
C

Our *Cities*, etc.

C
S
I
C
N
A
R

OF our owne powre:

Signature 129.

These acrostics are found on the first column of *Measure for Measure*, in the Duke's second speech. (See p. 355.)

Begin to read from the terminal O of the word *Angelo* (first word of the speech); to the left; on the terminals; downwards; spelling ONOCAB, you will arrive at the initial B of the word 'Both' (the first word of the last line in the column).

Begin to read from the initial A of the word *Angelo* (first word of the speech); to the right; on the terminals; downwards; spelling ANTONIO, you will arrive at the initial O of the word 'of' (ninth line of the speech).

Begin to read from the initial B of the word 'Both' (first word of the last line of the column); to the right; upwards; on the terminals; spelling BACONO, you will again arrive at the initial O of the word 'of' (ninth line of the speech).

The acrostic figures here are respectively:—

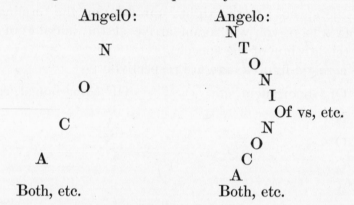

NOTE.—There are two acrostics, VERULAM, and F BACON, on the last page of this play. I hope to show these in another book.

MEASVRE,
For Meafure.

Actus primus, Scena prima.

Enter Duke, Efcalus, Lords.

Duke.
Scalus.

Efc. My Lord. (fold,

Duk. Of Gouernment,the properties to vn-
Would feeme in me t'affect fpeech & difcourfe,
Since I am put to know,that your owne Science
Excedes (in that) the lifts of all aduice
My ftrength can giue you : Then no more remaines
But that, to your fufficiency,as your worth is able,
And let them wotke : The nature of our People,
Our *Cities Inftitutions*, and the Termes
For Common Iuftice,y'are as pregnant in
As Art,and practife,hath inriched any
That we remember : There is our Commiffion,
From which,we would not haue you warpe ; call hither,
I fay, bid come before vs *Angelo* :
What figure of vs thinke you,he will beare.
For you muft know, we haue with fpeciall foule
Elected him our abfence to fupply ;
Lent him our terror,dreft him with our loue,
And giuen his Deputation all the Organs
Of our owne powre : What thinke you of it ?

Efc. If any in *Vienna* be of worth
To vndergoe fuch ample grace,and honour,
It is Lord *Angelo*.

Enter Angelo.

Duk. Looke where he comes.

Ang. Alwayes obedient to your Graces will,
I come to know your pleafure.

Duke. *Angelo* :
There is a kinde of Character in thy life,
That to th'obferuer, doth thy hiftory
Fully vnfold : Thy felfe,and thy belongings
Are not thine owne fo proper,as to wafte
Thy felfe vpon thy vertues ; they on thee :
Heauen doth with vs, as we,with Torches doe,
Not light them for themfelues : For if our vertues
Did not goe forth of vs, 'twere all alike
As if we had them not : Spirits are not finely tonch'd,
But to fine iffues : nor nature neuer lends
The fmalleft fcruple of her excellence,
But like a thrifty goddeffe,fhe determines
Her felfe the glory of a creditour,
Both thanks,and vfe ; but I do bend my fpeech

To one that can my part in him aduertife ;
Hold therefore *Angelo* :
In our remoue,be thou at full,our felfe :
Mortallitie and Mercie in *Vienna*
Liue in thy tongue,and heart : Old *Efcalus*
Though firft in queftion, is thy fecondary.
Take thy Commiffion.

Ang. Now good my Lord
Let there be fome more teft,made of my mettle,
Before fo noble, and fo great a figure
Be ftamp't vpon it.

Duk. No more euafion :
We haue with a leauen'd,and prepared choice.
Proceeded to you ; therefore take your honors :
Our hafte from hence is of fo quicke condition,
That it prefers it felfe, and leaues vnqueftion'd,
Matters of needfull value : We fhall write to you,
As time,and our concernings fhall importune,
How it goes with vs, and doe looke to know
What doth befall you here. So fare you well :
To th' hopefull execution doe I leaue you,
Of your Commiffions.

Ang. Yet giue leaue (my Lord,)
That we may bring you fomething on the way.

Duk. My hafte may not admit it,
Nor neede you (on mine honor) haue to doe
With any fcruple : your fcope is as mine owne,
So to inforce,or qualifie the Lawes
As to your foule feemes good : Giue me your hand,
Ile priuily away : I loue the people,
But doe not like to ftage me to their eyes :
Though it doe well, I doe not rellifh well
Their lowd applaufe,and Aues vehement ;
Nor doe I thinke the man of fafe difcretion
That do's affect it. Once more fare you well.

Ang. The heauens giue fafety to your purpofes.

Efc. Lead forth , and bring you backe in happineffe. *Exit.*

Duk. I thanke you, fare you well.

Efc. I fhall defire you, Sir,to giue me leaue
To haue free fpeech with you ; and it concernes me
To looke into the bottome of my place :
A powre I haue, but of what ftrength and nature,
I am not yet inftructed.

Ang. 'Tis fo with me : Let vs with-draw together,
And we may foone our fatisfaction haue
Touching that point.

Efc. Ile wait vpon your honor. *Exeunt.*

F *Scæna*

Signature 130.

This acrostic is found on the first page of *The Comedie of Errors*.

Begin to read from the initial F of the word ' fall,' which is the last word of the first line; to the left; downwards; on the initials of the words; spelling Francisco Bacono, you will arrive at the initial O of the word ' of ' in the line (see p. 358) : —

'My wife, not meanely prowd of two such boyes'

(thirteenth line from the top of the second column).

Now begin to read from the initial F of the word 'For,' which is the last word on the page; to the right; upwards; on the initials of the words; spelling Francisco Bacono, you will again arrive at the initial O of the same word ' of ' in the line

'My wife, not meanely prowd of two such boyes.'

The acrostic figure here is : —

```
    Fall
      R
       A
        N
         C
          I
           S
            C
             O
              B
               A
                C
                 O
                  N
                   Of two such boyes,
                  N
                 O
                C
               A
              B
             O
            C
           S
          I
         C
        N
       A
        R
         For
```

Signature 131.

This acrostic is found on the second page of *The Comedie of Errors*, which is wrongly numbered 88. (See p. 359.)

Begin to read from the initial F of the word 'For,' which is the first word of the first line in the first column; to the right; on initials; downwards; spelling Francisco Bacono, you will arrive at the initial O of the word 'oath' (nineteenth line from the bottom).

Now begin to read from the initial B of the word 'But,' which is the first word of the last line of the block of type (preceding the word *Exeunt*); to the right; upwards; or to the left; upwards; on the initials of the words of the text; spelling Bacono, you will arrive again at the initial O of the word 'oath.'

The acrostic figure here is: —

For we may pitty, etc.

R

A

N

C

I

S

C

O

B

A

C

O

N

my Oath, my dignity,

N

O

C

A

But to procrastinate, etc.

Exeunt.

The Comedie of Errors.

Actus primus, Scena prima.

Enter the Duke of Ephesus, with the Merchant of Siracusa, Iaylor, and other attendants.

Marchant.

Roceed *Solinus* to procure my fall,
And by the doome of death end woes and all.
  Duke. Merchant of *Siracusa* plead no more.
I am not partiall to infringe our Lawes;
The enmity and discord which of late
Sprung from the rancorous outrage of your Duke,
To Merchants our well-dealing Countrimen,
Who wanting gilders to redeeme their liues,
Haue seal'd his rigorous statutes with their bloyds,
Excludes all pitty from our threatning lookes:
For since the mortall and intestine iarres
Twixt thy seditious Countrimen and vs,
It hath in solemne Synodes beene decreed,
Both by the *Siracusians* and our selues,
To admit no traffike to our aduerse townes:
Nay more, if any borne at *Ephesus*
Be seene at any *Siracusian* Marts and Fayres:
Againe, if any *Siracusian* borne
Come to the Bay of *Ephesus*, he dies:
His goods confiscate to the Dukes dispose,
Vnlesse a thousand markes be leuied
To quit the penalty, and to ransome him:
Thy substance, valued at the highest rate,
Cannot amount vnto a hundred Markes,
Therefore by Law thou art condemn'd to die.
  Mer. Yet this my comfort, when your words are done,
My woes end likewise with the euening Sonne,
  Duk. Well *Siracusian*; say in briefe the cause
Why thou departedst from thy natiue home?
And for what cause thou cam'st to *Ephesus*.
  Mer. A heauier taske could not haue beene impos'd,
Then I to speake my griefes vnspeakeable:
Yet that the world may witnesse that my end
Was wrought by nature, not by vile offence,
Ile vtter what my sorrow giues me leaue.
In *Syracusa* was I borne, and wedde
Vnto a woman; happy but for me,
And by me; had not our hap beene bad:
With her I liu'd in ioy, our wealth increast
By prosperous voyages I often made
To *Epidamium*, till my factors death,
And he great care of goods at randone left,
Drew me from kinde embracements of my spouse;
From whom my absence was not sixe moneths olde,
Before her selfe (almost at fainting vnder

The pleasing punishment that women beare)
Had made prouision for her following me,
And soone, and safe, arriued where I was:
There had she not beene long, but she became
A ioyfull mother of two goodly sonnes:
And, which was strange, the one so like the other,
As could not be distinguish'd but by names.
That very howre, and in the selfe-same Inne,
A meane woman was deliuered
Of such a burthen Male, twins both, alike:
Those, for their parents were exceeding poore,
I bought, and brought vp to attend my sonnes.
My wife, not meanely prowd of two such boyes,
Made daily motions for our home returne:
Vnwilling I agreed, alas, too soone wee came aboord.
A league from *Epidamium* had we saild
Before the alwaies winde-obeying deepe
Gaue any Tragicke Instance of our harme:
But longer did we not retaine much hope;
For what obscured light the heauens did grant,
Did but conuay vnto our fearefull mindes
A doubtfull warrant of immediate death,
Which though my selfe would gladly haue imbrac'd,
Yet the incessant weepings of my wife,
Weeping before for what she saw must come,
And pitteous playnings of the prettie babes
That mourn'd for fashion, ignorant what to feare,
Forst me to seeke delayes for them and me,
And this it was: (for other meanes was none)
The Sailors sought for safety by our boate,
And left the ship then sinking ripe to vs.
My wife, more carefull for the latter borne,
Had fastned him vnto a small spare Mast,
Such as sea-faring men prouide for stormes:
To him one of the other twins was bound,
Whil'st I had beene like heedfull of the other.
The children thus dispos'd, my wife and I,
Fixing our eyes on whom our care was fixt,
Fastned our selues at eyther end the mast,
And floating straight, obedient to the streame,
Was carried towards *Corinth*, as we thought.
At length the sonne gazing vpon the earth,
Disperst those vapours that offended vs,
And by the benefit of his wished light
The seas waxt calme, and we discouered
Two shippes from farre, making amaine to vs:
Of *Corinth* that, of *Epidarus* this,
But ere they came, oh let me say no more,
Gather the sequell by that went before.
  Duk. Nay forward old man, doe not breake off so,

H   For

For we may pitty,though not pardon thee.

Merch. Oh had the gods done so,I had not now
Worthily tearm'd them mercilesse to vs:
For ere the ships could meet by twice fiue leagues,
We were encountred by a mighty rocke,
Which being violently borne vp,
Our helpefull ship was splitted in the midst;
So that in this vniust diuorce of vs,
Fortune had left to both of vs alike,
What to delight in,what to sorrow for,
Her part,poore soule,seeming as burdened
With lesser waight,but not with lesser woe,
Was carried with more speed before the winde,
And in our sight they three were taken vp
By Fishermen of *Corinth,*as we thought.
At length another ship had seiz'd on vs,
And knowing whom it was their hap to saue,
Gaue healthfull welcome to their ship-wrackt guests,
And would haue reft the Fishers of their prey,
Had not their backe beene very slow of saile;
And therefore homeward did they bend their course.
Thus haue you heard me seuer'd from my blisse,
That by misfortunes was my life prolong'd,
To tell sad stories of my owne mishaps.

Duke. And for the sake of them thou sorrowest for,
Doe me the fauour to dilate at full,
What haue befalne of them and they till now.

Merch. My yongest boy,and yet my eldest care,
At eighteene yeeres became inquisitiue
After his brother;and importun'd me
That his attendant,so his case was like,
Reft of his brother,but retain'd his name,
Might beare him company in the quest of him:
Whom whil'st I laboured of a loue to see,
I hazarded the losse of whom I lou'd.
Fiue Sommers haue I spent in farthest *Greece,*
Roming cleane through the bounds of *Asia,*
And coasting homeward,came to *Ephesus :*
Hopelesse to finde,yet loth to leaue vnsought
Or that,or any place that harbours men :
But heere must end the story of my life,
And happy were I in my timelie death,
Could all my trauells warrant me they liue.

Duke. Haplesse *Egeon* whom the fates haue markt
To beare the extremitie of dire mishap :
Now trust me,were it not against our Lawes,
Against my Crowne,my oath,my dignity,
Which Princes would they may not disanull,
My soule should sue as aduocate for thee :
But though thou art adiudged to the death,
And passed sentence may not be recal'd
But to our honours great disparagement :
Yet will I fauour thee in what I can;
Therefore Marchant,Ile limit thee this day
To seeke thy helpe by beneficiall helpe,
Try all the friends thou hast in *Ephesus,*
Beg thou,or borrow,to make vp the summe,
And liue: if no,then thou art doom'd to die:
Iaylor,take him to thy custodie.

Iaylor. I will my Lord.

Merch. Hopelesse and helpelesse doth *Egean* wend,
But to procrastinate his liuelesse end.   *Exeunt.*

Enter Antipholis Erotes, a Marchant, and Dromio.

Mer. Therefore giue out you are of *Epidamnum,*
Lest that your goods too soone be confiscate:

This very day a *Syracusian* Marchant
Is apprehended for a riuall here,
And not being able to buy out his life,
According to the statute of the towne,
Dies ere the wearie sunne set in the West :
There is your monie that I had to keepe.

Ant. Goe beare it to the Centaure,where we host,
And stay there *Dromio,*till I come to thee;
Within this houre it will be dinner time,
Till that Ile view the manners of the towne,
Peruse the traders,gaze vpon the buildings,
And then returne and sleepe within mine Inne,
For with long trauaile I am stiffe and wearie.
Get thee away.

Dro. Many a man would take you at your word,
And goe indeede,hauing so good a meane.   *Exit Dromio.*

Ant. A trustie villaine sir,that very oft,
When I am dull with care and melancholly,
Lightens my humour with his merry iests :
What will you walke with me about the towne,
And then goe to my Inne and dine with me?

E.Mar. I am inuited sir to certaine Marchants,
Of whom I hope to make much benefit :
I craue your pardon,soone at fiue a clocke,
Please you,Ile meete with you vpon the Mart,
And afterward consort you till bed time :
My present businesse cals me from you now.

Ant. Farewell till then : I will goe loose my selfe,
And wander vp and downe to view the Citie.

E.Mar. Sir, I commend you to your owne content.   *Exeunt.*

Ant. He that commends me to mine owne content,
Commends me to the thing I cannot get :
I to the world am like a drop of water,
That in the Ocean seekes another drop,
Who falling there to finde his fellow forth,
(Vnseene,inquisitiue) confounds himselfe.
So I,to finde a Mother and a Brother,
In quest of them (vnhappie a) loose my selfe.

Enter Dromio of Ephesus.

Here comes the almanacke of my true date :
What now? How chance thou art return'd so soone.

E.Dro. Return'd so soone, rather approacht too late:
The Capon burnes, the Pig fals from the spit;
The clocke hath strucken twelue vpon the bell :
My Mistris made it one vpon my cheeke :
She is so hot because the meate is colde :
The meate is colde, because you come not home:
You come not home,because you haue no stomacke :
You haue no stomacke,hauing broke your fast :
But we that know what 'tis to fast and pray,
Are penitent for your default to day.

Ant. Stop in your winde sir,tell me this I pray?
Where haue you left the mony that I gaue you.

E.Dro. Oh sixe pence that I had a wensday last,
To pay the Sadler for my Mistris crupper :
The Sadler had it Sir,I kept it not.

Ant. I am not in a sportiue humor now :
Tell me,and dally not,where is the monie?
We being strangers here,how dar'st thou trust
So great a charge from thine owne custodie.

E.Dro. I pray you iest sir as you sit at dinner :
I from my Mistris come to you in post:
If I returne I shall be post indeede.

For

Signature 132.

These acrostics are found on the last page of *The Comedie of Errors.* (See p. 362.)

Note that the initials of the last four words of the play are N. O. B. A. of the words 'not one before another.'

Frame the last Scene, which is headed: —

Exeunt omnes. Manet the two Dromio's and
two Brothers.

Begin to read from the initial A of the word 'another,' which is the last word of the text; to the left; upwards; on the initials of the text; throughout the text of the last Scene, and back again continuously; spelling ANTONIO, you will arrive at the initial O of the word 'one.'

Begin to read from the initial B of the word 'before,' which is the last word but one of the play; to the left; upwards; throughout the text of the last Scene, and back again continuously; spelling BACONO, you will again arrive at the initial O of the word 'one'; thus keying both words from the last two initials of the play to the same letter, which is the third initial from the end.

The acrostic figure here is: —

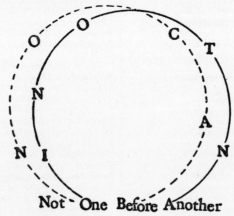

Not One Before Another

In the beginning of this play we have already found the signature of Francis Bacon, and here we have that of his brother Anthony.

Note the courteous dispute as to precedence in the last Scene.

Remember also that in William Rawley's biography of his master he tells us that Anthony was equal to him (Francis) in height of wit, though inferior to him in the endowments of learning and knowledge. (Spedding, vol. i, p. 5.)

Signature 133.

There is still another acrostic signature at this end of the play.

Begin to read from the initial F of the word 'FINIS'; to the right; upwards; on the *terminals* of *all* words on the last column; spelling FRANCIS BACON, you will arrive at the terminal N of the word ' anon.' (See p. 362.)

The acrostic figure here is: —

Come go with vs, wee'l looke to that anoN,

Key this signature by beginning to read from the terminal N of the word ' anoN '; to the left; downwards; on the terminals of all the words in the column; spelling NOCAB SICNARF, you will arrive at the initial F of the word ' FINIS.'

The acrostic figure here is the same as the last.

Note in these two acrostics what use seems to have been made of the *double entente* of the words, in the selection of a place in which to throw a signature.

Signature 135.

There is another acrostic in this column, 'weak,' because it depends upon the reader's quickness in being aware of a *double entente*.

Note the words 'strike vp Pipers' with which the play ends. I took the *double entente* of these words as a working hypothesis, and struck up the column until I came to the line (thirtieth from top; see p. 365) : —

'And heeres another.'

The next line above it is : —

'Fashioned to Beatrice.'

I therefore began to read from the F of the word 'Fashioned'; to the right; upwards; on the initials of the words; spelling FRANCIS BACON, I was not altogether surprised to arrive at the initial N of the word 'Nothing' again — the first word of the text of the column. I noted also that the signature is fashioned to Beatrice, for the word 'Bacon' begins upon the initial of the word 'Beatrice.'

Note also that the 'Bacon' part of this signature is not only to be read upwards, but can be read downwards either to the right or to the left. In other words, it can be read in three directions out of a possible four. If the reader has studied my chapter on *Method* he will realize that care is required to make any signature do this.

The acrostic figure here is : —

Nothing certainer.
O
  C
   A
    Beatrice
   S
   I
  C
  N
 A
 R
Fashioned to Beatrice.
And heeres another.

    .

     .

      .

       .

strike vp pipers.

Then this for whom we rendred vp this woe. *Exeunt.*

Enter Leonato, Bene. Marg. Vrsula, old man, Frier, Hero.

Frier. Did I not tell you she was innocent?

Leo. So are the *Prince* and *Claudio* who accus'd her,
Vpon the errour that you heard debated:
But *Margaret* was in some fault for this,
Although against her will as it appeares,
In the true course of all the question.

Old. Well, I am glad that all things sort so well.

Bene. And so am I, being else by faith enforc'd
To call young *Claudio* to a reckoning for it.

Leo. Well daughter, and you gentlewomen all,
Withdraw into a chamber by your selues,
And when I send for you, come hither mask'd:
The *Prince* and *Claudio* promis'd by this howre
To visit me, you know your office Brother,
You must be father to your brothers daughter,
And giue her to young *Claudio*. *Exeunt Ladies.*

Old. Which I will doe with confirm'd countenance.

Bene. Frier, I must intreat your paines, I thinke.

Frier. To doe what Signior?

Bene. To binde me, or vndoe me, one of them:
Signior *Leonato*, truth it is good Signior,
Your neece regards me with an eye of fauour.

Leo. That eye my daughter lent her, 'tis most true.

Bene. And I doe with an eye of loue requite her.

Leo. The sight whereof I thinke you had from me,
From *Claudio*, and the *Prince*, but what's your will?

Bened. Your answer sir is Enigmaticall,
But for my will, my will is, your good will
May stand with ours, this day to be conioyn'd,
In the state of honourable marriage,
In which (good Frier) I shall desire your helpe.

Leon. My heart is with your liking.

Frier. And my helpe.

Enter Prince and Claudio, with attendants.

Prin. Good morrow to this faire assembly.

Leo. Good morrow *Prince*, good morrow *Claudio*:
We heere attend you, are you yet determin'd,
To day to marry with my brothers daughter?

Claud. Ile hold my minde were she an Ethiope.

Leo. Call her forth brother, heres the Frier ready.

Prin. Good morrow *Benedicke*, why what's the matter?
That you haue such a Februarie face,
So full of frost, of storme, and clowdinesse.

Claud. I thinke he thinkes vpon the sauage bull:
Tush, feare not man, wee'll tip thy hornes with gold,
And all *Europa* shall reioyce at thee,
As once *Europa* did at lusty *Ioue*,
When he would play the noble beast in loue.

Ben. Bull *Ioue* sir, had an amiable low,
And some such strange bull leapt your fathers Cow,
A got a Calfe in that same noble feat,
Much like to you, for you haue iust his bleat.

Enter brother, Hero, Beatrice, Margaret, Vrsula.

Cla. For this I owe you: here comes other recknings.
Which is the Lady I must seize vpon?

Leo. This same is she, and I doe giue you her.

Cla. Why then she's mine, sweet let me see your face.

Leon. No that you shal not, till you take her hand,
Before this Frier, and sweare to marry her.

Clau. Giue me your hand before this holy Frier,
I am your husband if you like of me.

Hero. And when I liu'd I was your other wife,
And when you lou'd, you were my other husband.

Clau. Another *Hero*?

Hero. Nothing certainer.
One *Hero* died, but I doe liue,
And surely as I liue, I am a maid:

Prin. The former *Hero*, *Hero* that is dead.

Leon. Shee died my Lord, but whiles her slander liu'd.

Frier. All this amazement can I qualifie,
When after that the holy rites are ended,
Ile tell you largely of faire *Heroes* death:
Meane time let wonder seeme familiar,
And to the chappell let vs presently.

Ben. Soft and faire Frier, which is *Beatrice*?

Beat. I answer to that name, what is your will?

Bene. Doe not you loue me?

Beat. Why no, no more then reason.

Bene. Why then your Vncle, and the Prince, & *Claudio*,
haue beene deceiued, they swore you did.

Beat. Doe not you loue mee?

Bene. Troth no, no more then reason.

Beat. Why then my Cosin *Margaret* and *Vrsula*
Are much deceiu'd, for they did sweare you did.

Bene. They swore you were almost sicke for me.

Beat. They swore you were wel-nye dead for me.

Bene. 'Tis no matter, then you doe not loue me?

Beat. No truly, but in friendly recompence.

Leon. Come Cosin, I am sure you loue the gentlemā.

Clau. And Ile be sworne vpon't, that he loues her,
For heres a paper written in his hand,
A halting sonnet of his owne pure braine,
Fashioned to *Beatrice*.

Hero. And heeres another,
Writ in my cosins hand, stolne from her pocket,
Containing her affection vnto *Benedicke*.

Bene. A miracle, here's our owne hands against our
hearts: come I will haue thee, but by this light I take
thee for pittie.

Beat. I would not denie you, but by this good day, I
yeeld vpon great perswasion, & partly to saue your life,
for I was told, you were in a consumption.

Leon. Peace I will stop your mouth.

Prin. How dost thou *Benedicke* the married man?

Bene. Ile tell thee what Prince: a Colledge of witte-
crackers cannot flout mee out of my humour, dost thou
thinke I care for a Satyre or an Epigram? no, if a man will
be beaten with braines, a shall weare nothing handsome
about him: in briefe, since I do purpose to marry, I will
thinke nothing to any purpose that the world can say a-
gainst it, and therefore neuer flout at me, for I haue said
against it: for man is a giddy thing, and this is my conclusion: for thy part *Claudio*, I did thinke to haue beaten
thee, but in that thou art like to be my kinsman, liue vn-
bruis'd, and loue my cousin.

Cla. I had well hop'd ȳ wouldst haue denied *Beatrice*, ȳ
I might haue cudgel'd thee out of thy single life, to make
thee a double dealer, which out of questiō thou wilt be,
if my Cousin do not looke exceeding narrowly to thee.

Bene. Come, come, we are friends, let's haue a dance
ere we are married, that we may lighten our own hearts,
and our wiues heeles.

Leon. Wee'll haue dancing afterward.

Bene. First, of my vvord, therfore play musick. *Prince,*
thou art sad, get thee a vvife, get thee a vvife, there is no
staff more reuerend then one tipt with horn. *Enter Mes.*

Messen. My Lord, your brother *Iohn* is tane in flight,
And brought with armed men backe to *Messina*.

Bene. Thinke not on him till to morrow, ile deuise
thee braue punishments for him: strike vp Pipers. *Dance.*

L   *FINIS.*

Signature 136.

This acrostic is found on the last page of *Loues Labour's Lost*.

Note the two stanzas sung by *Winter*. They contain two capitals O. Each capital O is in the same relative position in the stanza.

Note the initials of the words above each O: they are $\begin{smallmatrix}\text{fowle}\\\text{Owle}\end{smallmatrix}$ in the upper stanza; and $\begin{smallmatrix}\text{bowle}\\\text{Owle}\end{smallmatrix}$ in the lower stanza. We thus have $\begin{smallmatrix}\text{F}\\\text{O}\end{smallmatrix}$ and $\begin{smallmatrix}\text{B}\\\text{O}\end{smallmatrix}$ to guide us in each stanza respectively.

Begin to read from the initial F of the word 'fowle'; to the right, *or to the left ;* downwards and back again; on the initials of the words; spelling FRANCISCO, you will arrive at the initial O of the word 'Owle' in the upper stanza.

Follow on continuously, without stopping on the O; still on the initials of the words; spelling BACONO, you will arrive at the initial O of the word 'Owle' in the lower stanza.

Note the simplicity of this cipher. It is keyed to the right or to the left by the easy expedient of excluding all ciphers or O's except the two which end the names of the signature.

Now begin to read from the initial B of the word 'bowle'; to the right or to the left; downwards and back throughout the whole of the two stanzas until you have spelled BACONO: you will again arrive at the initial O of the word 'Owle' in the upper stanza.

The complete acrostic figure of the combined signatures is: —

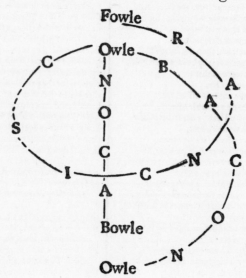

Ile marke no words that smoothfac'd wooers say.
Come when the King doth to my Ladie come:
Then if I haue much loue, Ile giue you some.

Dum. Ile serue thee true and faithfully till then.

Kath. Yet sweare not, least ye be forsworne agen.

Lon. What saies *Maria*?

Mari. At the tweluemonths end,
Ile change my blacke Gowne, for a faithfull friend.

Lon. Ile stay with patience: but the time is long.

Mari. The liker you, few taller are so yong.

Ber. Studies my Ladie? Mistresse, looke on me,
Behold the window of my heart, mine eie:
What humble suite attends thy answer there,
Impose some seruice on me for my loue.

Ros. Oft haue I heard of you my Lord *Berowne*,
Before I saw you: and the worlds large tongue
Proclaimes you for a man repleate with mockes,
Full of comparisons, and wounding floutes:
Which you on all estates will execute,
That lie within the mercie of your wit.
To weed this Wormewood from your fruitfull braine,
And therewithall to win me, if you please,
Without the which I am not to be won:
You shall this tweluemonth terme from day to day,
Visite the speechlesse sicke, and still conuerse.
With groaning wretches: and your taske shall be,
With all the fierce endeuour of your wit,
To enforce the pained impotent to smile.

Ber. To moue wilde laughter in the throate of death?
It cannot be, it is impossible.
Mirth cannot moue a soule in agonie.

Ros. Why that's the way to choke a gibing spirit,
Whose influence is begot of that loose grace,
Which shallow laughing hearers giue to fooles:
A iests prosperitie, lies in the eare
Of him that heares it, neuer in the tongue
Of him that makes it: then, if sickly eares,
Deaft with the clamors of their owne deare grones,
Will heare your idle scornes; continue then,
And I will haue you, and that fault withall.
But if they will not, throw away that spirit,
And I shal finde you emptie of that fault,
Right ioyfull of your reformation.

Ber. A tweluemonth? Well: befall what will befall,
Ile iest a tweluemonth in an Hospitall.

Qu. I sweet my Lord, and so I take my leaue.

King. No Madam, we will bring you on your way.

Ber. Our woing doth not end like an old Play:
Iacke hath not Gill: these Ladies courtesie
Might wel haue made our sport a Comedie.

Kin. Come sir, it wants a tweluemonth and a day,
And then 'twil end.

Ber. That's too long for a play.

Enter Braggart.

Brag. Sweet Maiesty vouchsafe me.

Qu. Was not that Hector?

Dum. The worthie Knight of Troy.

Brag. I wil kisse thy royal finger, and take leaue.
I am a Votarie, I haue vow'd to *Iaquenetta* to holde the
Plough for her sweet loue three yeares. But most esteemed greatnesse, wil you heare the Dialogue that the two
Learned men haue compiled, in praise of the Owle and
the Cuckow? It should haue followed in the end of our
shew.

Kin. Call them forth quickely, we will do so.

Brag. Holla, Approach.

Enter all.

This side is *Hiems*, Winter.
This *Ver*, the Spring: the one maintained by the Owle,
Th'other by the Cuckow.
Ver, begin.

The Song.

When Dasies pied, and Violets blew,
And Cuckow-buds of yellow hew:
And Ladie-smockes all siluer white,
Do paint the Medowes with delight.
The Cuckow then on euerie tree,
Mockes married men, for thus sings he,
Cuckow.
Cuckow, Cuckow: O word of feare,
Vnpleasing to a married eare.

When Shepheards pipe on Oaten strawes,
And merrie Larkes are Ploughmens clockes:
When Turtles tread, and Rookes and Dawes,
And Maidens bleach their summer smockes:
The Cuckow then on euerie tree
Mockes married men; for thus sings he,
Cuckow.
Cuckow, Cuckow: O word of feare,
Vnpleasing to a married eare.

Winter.

When Isicles hang by the wall,
And Dicke the Shepheard blowes his naile;
And Tom beares Logges into the hall,
And Milke comes frozen home in paile:
When blood is nipt, and waies be fowle,
Then nightly sings the staring Owle
Tu-whit to-who.
   A merrie note,
   While greasie Ione doth keele the pot.

When all aloud the winde doth blow,
And coffing drownes the Parsons saw:
And birds sit brooding in the snow,
And Marrians nose lookes red and raw:
When roasted Crabs hisse in the bowle,
Then nightly sings the staring Owle,
Tu-whit to who:
   A merrie note,
   While greasie Ione doth keele the pot.

Brag. The Words of Mercurie,
Are harsh after the songs of Apollo:
You that way; we this way.

Exeunt omnes.

FINIS.

Signature 137.

This acrostic is found on page 153, which is wrongly numbered 151, in *A Midsommer nights Dreame.*

Note that the first word of the *text* on the page is the word 'Be,' and that its initial is B.

Begin to read from this initial B of the first word on the page; to the right or to the left; downwards; on the initials of the words of the text; spelling BACON, you will arrive at the word 'name' in the twenty-first line —

'Your name honest Gentleman?'

This acrostic is 'weak,' as it ends nowhere in position. But I deem it of possible value in that it ends on the word 'name.'

The acrostic figure here is: —

Be kinde, etc.
A
C
O
Your Name honest Gentleman?

Tita. Be kinde and curteous to this Gentleman,
Hop in his walkes, and gambole in his eies,
Feede him with Apricocks, and Dewberries,
With purple Grapes, greene Figs, and Mulberries,
The honie-bags steale from the humble Bees,
And for night-tapers crop their waxen thighes,
And light them at the fierie-Glow-wormes eyes,
To haue my loue to bed, and to arise:
And plucke the wings from painted Butterflies,
To fan the Moone-beames from his sleeping eies.
Nod to him Elues, and doe him curtesies.

1. Fai. Haile mortall, haile.
2. Fai. Haile.
3. Fai. Haile.

Bot. I cry your worships mercy hartily; I beseech your worships name.

Cob. Cobweb.

Bot. I shall desire you of more acquaintance, good Master *Cobweb*: if I cut my finger, I shall make bold with you.
Your name honest Gentleman?

Peas. Pease blossome.

Bot. I pray you commend mee to mistresse *Squash*, your mother, and to master *Peascod* your father. Good master *Pease-blossome*, I shal desire of you more acquaintance to. Your name I beseech you sir?

Mus. Mustard-seede.

Peas. Pease-blossome.

Bot. Good master *Mustard seede*, I know your patience well: that same cowardly gyant-like Oxe-beefe hath deuoured many a gentleman of your house. I promise you, your kindred hath made my eyes water ere now. I desire you more acquaintance, good Master *Mustard-seede.*

Tita. Come waite vpon him, lead him to my bower.
The Moone me-thinks, lookes with a watrie eie,
And when she weepes, weepe euerie little flower,
Lamenting some enforced chastitie.
Tye vp my louers tongue, bring him silently. *Exit.*

Enter King of Pharies, solus.

Ob. I wonder if *Titania* be awak't?
Then what it was that next came in her eye,
Which she must dote on, in extremitie.

Enter Pucke.

Here comes my messenger: how now mad spirit,
What night-rule now about this haunted groue?

Puck. My Mistris with a monster is in loue,
Neere to her close and consecrated bower,
While she was in her dull and sleeping hower,
A crew of patches, rude Mechanicals,
That worke for bread vpon *Athenian* stals,
Were met together to rehearse a Play,
Intended for great *Theseus* nuptiall day:
The shallowest thick-skin of that barren sort,
Who *Piramus* presented, in their sport,
Forsooke his Scene, and entred in a brake,
When I did him at this aduantage take,
An Asses nole I fixed on his head.
Anon his *Thisbie* must be answered,
And forth my Mimmick comes: when they him spie;
As Wilde-geese, that the creeping Fowler eye,
Or russed-pated choughes, many in sort
(Rising and cawing at the guns report)
Seuer themselues, and madly sweepe the skye:

So at his sight, away his fellowes flye,
And at our stampe, here ore and ore one fals;
He murther cries, and helpe from *Athens* cals.
Their sense thus weake, lost with their fears thus strong,
Made senselesse things begin to do them wrong.
For briars and thornes at their apparell snatch,
Some sleeues, some hats, from yeelders all things catch,
I led them on in this distracted feare,
And left sweete *Piramus* translated there:
When in that moment (so it came to passe)
Tytania waked, and straightway lou'd an Asse.

Ob. This fals out better then I could deuise:
But hast thou yet lacht the *Athenians* eyes,
With the loue iuyce, as I did bid thee doe?

Rob. I tooke him sleeping (that is finisht to)
And the *Athenian* woman by his side,
That when he wak't, of force she must be eyde.

Enter Demetrius and Hermia.

Ob. Stand close, this is the same *Athenian.*
Rob. This is the woman, but not this the man.
Dem. O why rebuke you him that loues you so?
Lay breath so bitter on your bitter foe.

Her. Now I but chide, but I should vse thee worse.
For thou (I feare) hast giuen me cause to curse,
If thou hast slaine *Lysander* in his sleepe,
Being ore shooes in bloud, plunge in the deepe, and kill me too:
The Sunne was not so true vnto the day,
As he to me. Would he haue stollen away,
From sleeping *Hermia*? Ile beleeue as soone
This whole earth may be bord, and that the Moone
May through the Center creepe, and so displease
Her brothers noonetide, with th'*Antipodes.*
It cannot be but thou hast murdred him,
So should a mutrherer looke, so dead, so grim.

Dem. So should the murderer looke, and so should I,
Pierst through the heart with your sterne cruelty:
Yet you the murderer looks as bright as cleare,
As yonder *Venus* in her glimmering sphaere.

Her. What's this to my *Lysander*? where is he?
Ah good *Demetrius*, wilt thou giue him me?

Dem. I'de rather giue his carkasse to my hounds.

Her. Out dog, out cur, thou driu'st me past the bounds
Of maidens patience. Hast thou slaine him then?
Henceforth be neuer numbred among men:
Oh, once tell true, euen for my sake,
Durst thou a lookt vpon him, being awake?
And hast thou kill'd him sleeping? O braue tutch:
Could not a worme, an Adder do so much?
An Adder did it: for with doubler tongue
Then thine (thou serpent) neuer Adder stung.

Dem. You spend your passion on a mispri'sd mood,
I am not guiltie of *Lysanders* blood:
Nor is he dead for ought that I can tell.

Her. I pray thee tell me then that he is well.

Dem. And if I could, what should I get therefore?

Her. A priuiledge, neuer to see me more;
And from thy hated presence part I: see me no more
Whether he be dead or no. *Exit.*

Dem. There is no following her in this fierce vaine,
Here therefore for a while I will remaine.
So sorrowes heauinesse doth heauier grow:
For debt that bankrout slip doth sorrow owe,
Which now in some slight measure it will pay,

If

Signature 138.

This acrostic is found on the last page of *A Midsommer nights Dreame.* (See p. 375.)

(See p. 375.)

Note the initials
B
F
F
of the words
By
From
Following
which are the four-teenth, fifteenth, and sixteenth lines of Puck's speech.

Begin to read from the initial F of the word 'Following'; to the right; upwards; throughout the column and continuously down the next column; on the initials of the words; spelling FRANCISCO BACONO, you will arrive at the initial O of the word 'owner,' third line from bottom of 'The Song.'

Begin to read from the initial B of the word 'By'; to the right; downwards; on the initials of the words of the text; throughout the column and continuously up the next; spelling BACONO, you will arrive again at the initial O of the same word 'owner,' having keyed the cipher.

The acrostic figure here is: —

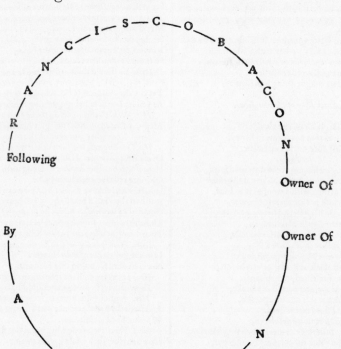

Signature 139.

Now note that the initials of the first and last words of the first line of the second column are the initials B and F of the words ' By ' and ' fier.' (See p. 375.)

Begin to read from the initial B of the word 'By'; to the right; downwards; on the initials of the words of all lines; spelling BACONO, you will again arrive at the initial O of the word 'owner.'

Begin to read from the initial F of the word ' fier'; to the left; downwards; on the initials of the words of all lines; spelling FRAN-CISCO, you will arrive at the initial O of the word ' of,' which comes next to the word ' owner.'

The acrostic figure here is:—

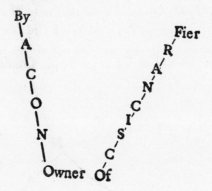

This acrostic is weak, as the two names do not meet upon the same initial O. But it is sufficiently remarkable as it is.

The complete acrostic on this page may be represented thus: —

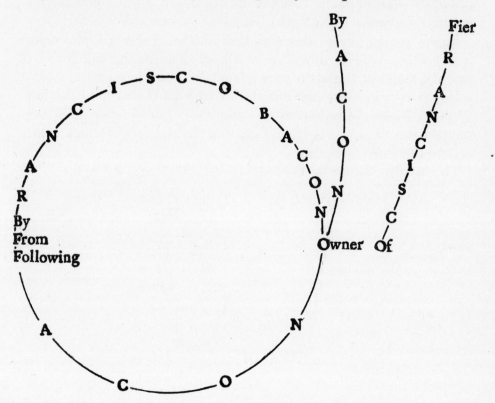

Signature 140.

There is still another acrostic in this last page of *A Midsommer nights Dreame.* (See p. 375.)

The fun begins when *Pucke* enters.

Begin to read from the initial N of the first word of Pucke's speech; to the right; downwards; throughout the remaining text of the play; on the initials of the words of the text; spelling Nocab Sicnuarff, you will arrive at the initial F of the word 'Finis.'

The acrostic figure here is:—

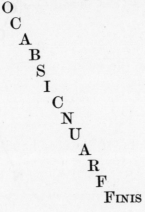

      Pucke. Now the hungry Lyons rores,

Signature 141.

As I am reading the proofs I see that I have missed another acrostic on the last page of *A Midsommer nights Dreame.* It follows here.

Begin to read from the initial B of the word 'By,' which begins the first line of the second column; to the right; downwards; on the terminals of the words; spelling BACONO, you will arrive at the initial O of the word 'of' (eighteenth line from top).

Begin now to read from the initial F of the word 'FINIS'; to the right; upwards; on the terminals of the words; spelling FRANCISCO, you will again arrive at the initial O of the word 'of' (eighteenth line from top).

The acrostic here is: —

<pre>
        By the dead and drowsie fier
        A
          C
            O
              N
And the blots Of Natures hand,   —
              C
            S
          I
        C
      N
    A
  R
  FINIS.
</pre>

And farwell friends, thus *Thisbie* ends ;
Adieu, adieu, adieu.

Duk. Moon-ſhine & Lion are left to burie the dead.

Deme. I, and Wall too.

Bot. No, I aſſure you, the wall is downe, that parted their Fathers. Will it pleaſe you to ſee the Epilogue, or to heare a Bergomask dance, betweene two of our company?

Duk. No Epilogue, I pray you; for your play needs no excuſe. Neuer excuſe ; for when the plaiers are all dead, there need none to be blamed. Marry, if hee that writ it had plaid *Piramus*, and hung himſelfe in *Thisbies* garter, it would haue beene a fine Tragedy : and ſo it is truely, and very notably diſcharg'd. But come, your Burgomaske ; let your Epilogue alone.
The iron tongue of midnight hath told twelue.
Louers to bed, 'tis almoſt Fairy time.
I ſeare we ſhall out-ſteepe the comming morne,
As much as we this night haue ouer-watcht.
This palpable groſſe play hath well beguil'd
The heauy gate of night. Sweet friends to bed.
A fortnight hold we this ſolemnity.
In nightly Reuels; and new iollitie.   *Exeunt.*

Enter Pucke.

Puck. Now the hungry Lyons rores,
And the Wolfe beholds the Moone :
Whileſt the heauy ploughman ſnores,
All with weary taske fore-done.
Now the waſted brands doe glow,
Whil'ſt the ſcritch-owle, ſcritching loud,
Puts the wretch that lies in woe,
In remembrance of a ſhrowd.
Now it is the time of night,
That the graues, all gaping wide,
Euery one lets forth his ſpright,
In the Church-way paths to glide.
And we Fairies, that do runne,
By the triple *Hecates* teame,
From the preſence of the Sunne,
Following darkeneſſe like a dreame,
Now are frollicke ; not a Mouſe
Shall diſturbe this hallowed houſe.
I am ſent with broome before,
To ſweep the duſt behinde the doore.

Enter King and Queene of Fairies, with their traine.

Ob. Through the houſe giue glimmering light,

By the dead and drowſie fier,
Euerie Elfe and Fairie ſpright,
Hop as light as bird from brier,
And this Ditty after me, ſing and dance it trippinglie.

Tita. Firſt rehearſe this ſong by roate,
To each word a warbling note,
Hand in hand, with Fairie grace,
Will we ſing and bleſſe this place.

The Song

Now vntill the breake of day,
Through this houſe each Fairy ſtray.
To the beſt Brids-bed will we,
Which by vs ſhall bleſſed be :
And the iſſue there create,
Euer ſhall be fortunate :
So ſhall all the couples three,
Euer true in louing be :
And the blots of Natures hand,
Shall not in their iſſue ſtand.
Neuer mole, harelip, nor ſcarre,
Nor marke prodigious, ſuch as are
Deſpiſed in Natiuitie,
Shall vpon their children be.
With this field dew conſecrate,
Euery Fairy take his gate,
And each ſeuerall chamber bleſſe,
Through this Pallace with ſweet peace,
Euer ſhall in ſafety reſt,
And the owner of it bleſt.
Trip away, make no ſtay ;
Meet me all by breake of day.

Robin. If we ſhadowes haue offended,
Thinke but this (and all is mended)
That you haue but ſlumbred heere,
While theſe viſions did appeare.
And this weake and idle theame,
No more yeelding but a dreame,
Gentles, doe not reprehend.
If you pardon, we will mend.
And as I am an honeſt *Pucke*,
If we haue vnearned lucke,
Now to ſcape the Serpents tongue,
We will make amends ere long :
Elſe the *Pucke* a lyar call.
So good night vnto you all.
Giue me your hands, if we be friends,
And *Robin* ſhall reſtore amends.

FINIS.

Signature 142.

This acrostic is found on the first page of *The Merchant of Venice.*
(See p. 378.)

Note the arrangement of the initials at the head of the text $\boxed{I}^{N}_{B.}$

Note also that the initials of the words at the bottom corners of
the page are N of the word 'Nor,' and the B of the word 'By.'

Here we have two N B's to attract our attention.

Begin to read from the capital B of the word 'By,' which is at the
extreme lower right-hand corner of the page; to the right *or* to the
left; upwards; on the *capitals* alone; spelling BACON, you will arrive

at the capital N in the monogram at the head of the page $\boxed{I}^{N}$;

thus keying the signature from corner to corner of the page.

The acrostic figure here is: —

$$\boxed{I}^{N}$$

O

C

A

By

Signature 143.

This acrostic is found upon the pages 164 and 165 of *The Merchant of Venice.* They are incorrectly numbered 162 and 163. (See pp. 379–380.)

Note that the initial of the first word of the first line of the first column of page 162 is B of the word ' By.'

Note also that the initial of the first word of the last line of page 163 is B of the word ' Be.'

Here again we shall deal solely with the *capitals* throughout the text.

Begin to read from the capital B of the word ' By,' at the top left-hand corner of page 162; to the right; downwards; on the capital letters of the *text;* spelling BACONO, you will arrive at the capital O of the line: —

'O my *Antonio*, had I but the meanes.'

Begin to read from the capital B of the word ' Be,' at the beginning of the last line of page 163; to the right; upwards throughout the text of all columns; spelling BACONO, you will again arrive at the capital O in the line: —

'O my *Antonio*, had I but the meanes,'

and keying the cipher.

The acrostic figure here is: —

By being peevish?
  A
    C
      O
       N
        O my Antonio, had I but the meanes
       N
        O
         C
          A
          Be assured you may.

chooses you, wil no doubt neuer be chosen by any rightly, but one who you shall rightly loue: but what warmth is there in your affection towards any of these Princely suters that are already come?.

Por. I pray thee ouer-name them, and as thou namest them, I will describe them, and according to my description leuell at my affection.

Ner. First there is the Neopolitane Prince.

Por. I that's a colt indeede, for he doth nothing but talke of his horse, and hee makes it a great appropriation to his owne good parts that he can shoo him himselfe: I am much afraid my Ladie his mother plaid false with a Smyth.

Ner. Than is there the Countie Palentine.

Por. He doth nothing but frowne (as who should say, and you will not haue me, choose: he heares merrie tales and smiles not, I feare hee will proue the weeping Phylosopher when he growes old, being so full of vnmannerly sadnesse in his youth.) I had rather to be married to a deaths head with a bone in his mouth, then to either of these: God defend me from these two.

Ner. How say you by the French Lord, Mounsier *Le Boune*?

Pro. God made him, and therefore let him passe for a man, in truth I know it is a sinne to be a mocker, but he, why he hath a horse better then the Neopolitans, a better bad habite of frowning then the Count Palentine, he is euery man in no man, if a Trassell sing, he fals straight a capring, he will fence with his own shadow. If I should marry him, I should marry twentie husbands: if hee would despise me, I would forgiue him, for if he loue me to madnesse, I should neuer requite him.

Ner. What say you then to *Fauconbridge*, the yong Baron of *England*?

Por. You know I say nothing to him, for hee vnderstands not me, nor I him: he hath neither *Latine*, *French*, nor *Italian*, and you will come into the Court & sweare that I haue a poore pennie-worth in the *English*: hee is a proper mans picture, but alas who can conuerse with a dumbe show? how odly be is suited, I thinke he bought his doublet in *Italie*, his round hose in *France*, his bonnet in *Germanie*, and his behauiour euery where.

Ner. What thinke you of the other Lord his neighbour?

Por. That he hath a neighbourly charitie in him, for he borrowed a boxe of the eare of the *Englishman*, and swore he would pay him againe when hee was able: I thinke the *Frenchman* became his suretie, and seald vnder for another.

Ner. How like you the yong *Germaine*, the Duke of *Saxonies* Nephew?

Por. Very vildely in the morning when hee is sober, and most vildely in the afternoone when hee is drunke: when he is best, he is a little worse then a man, and when he is worst he is little better then a beast: and the worst fall that euer fell, I hope I shall make shift to goe without him.

Ner. If he should offer to choose, and choose the right Casket, you should refuse to performe your Fathers will, if you should refuse to accept him.

Por. Therefore for feare of the worst, I pray thee set a deepe glasse of Reinish-wine on the contrary Casket, for if the diuell be within, and that temptation without, I know he will choose it. I will doe any thing *Nerrissa* ere I will be married to a spunge.

Ner. You neede not feare Lady the hauing any of these Lords, they haue acquainted me with their determinations, which is indeede to returne to their home, and to trouble you with no more suite, vnlesse you may be won by some other sort then your Fathers imposition, depending on the Caskets.

Por. If I liue to be as olde as *Sibilla*, I will dye as chaste as *Diana*: vnlesse I be obtained by the manner of my Fathers will: I am glad this parcell of wooers are so reasonable, for there is not one among them but I doate on his verie absence: and I wish them a faire departure.

Ner. Doe you not remember Ladie in your Fathers time, a *Venecian*, a Scholler and a Souldior that came hither in companie of the Marquesse of *Mountferrat*?

Por. Yes, yes, it was *Bassanio*, as I thinke, so was hee call'd.

Ner. True Madam, hee of all the men that euer my foolish eyes look'd vpon, was the best deseruing a faire Lady.

Por. I remember him well, and I remember him worthy of thy praise.

Enter a Seruingman.

Ser. The foure Strangers seeke you Madam to take their leaue: and there is a fore-runner come from a fift, the Prince of *Moroco*, who brings word the Prince his Maister will be here to night.

Por. If I could bid the fift welcome with so good heart as I can bid the other foure farewell, I should be glad of his approach: if he haue the condition of a Saint, and the complexion of a diuell, I had rather hee should shriue me then wiue me. Come *Nerrissa*, sirra go before; whiles wee shut the gate vpon one wooer, another knocks at the doore. *Exeunt.*

Enter Bassanio with Shylocke the Iew.

Shy. Three thousand ducates, well.

Bass. I sir, for three months.

Shy. For three months, well.

Bass. For the which, as I told you, Anthonio shall be bound.

Shy. Anthonio shall become bound, well.

Bass. May you sted me? Will you pleasure me? Shall I know your answere.

Shy. Three thousand ducats for three months, and Anthonio bound.

Bass. Your answere to that.

Shy. Anthonio is a good man.

Bass. Haue you heard any imputation to the contrary.

Shy. Ho no, no, no, no: my meaning in saying he is a good man, is to haue you vnderstand me that he is sufficient, yet his meanes are in supposition: he hath an Argosie bound to Tripolis, another to the Indies, I vnderstand moreouer vpon the Ryalta, he hath a third at Mexico, a fourth for England and other ventures hee hath squandred abroad, but ships are but boords, Saylers but men, there be land rats, and water rats, water theeues, and land theeues, I meane Pyrats, and then there is the perrill of waters, windes, and rocks; the man is notwithstanding sufficient, three thousand ducats, I thinke I may take his bond.

Bas. Be assured you may.

Iew. I

Signature 144.

This acrostic is found on the last page of *As you like it.* (See p. 383.)

Note that the last two lines of the play are: —

'beards, or good faces, or sweet breaths, will for my kind
　　offer, when I make curt'sie, bid me farewell.'

Treat these two lines as if they were a string of letters.

Begin to read from the initial B of the word 'beards'; to the right and downwards; throughout all letters of all words in the two lines in the usual way; spelling BACONO, you will arrive at the initial O of the word 'offer.'

The acrostic figure here is:—

Beards
A
C
O
N
Offer

Note that this acrostic may also be read from the initial O of the word 'offer'; to the right; upwards, and ending on the initial B of the word 'beards.' Seventy-eight letters are in this string.

Signature 146.

This acrostic is found on the first page of *The Taming of the Shrew.*

Note the last line on the page, and in it the words 'name: but' —

'I haue forgot your name: but sure that part.'

Begin to read on the initial B of the word 'but'; to the right; on the *initials* of the *outside words* of the two columns taken together; completely around the page; spelling Bacon, you will arrive at the initial N of the word 'name.'

The acrostic figure here is:—

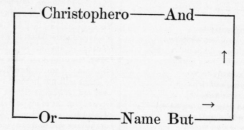

Note that the complete sentence is: —

'I haue forgot your name: but sure that part
Was aptly fitted, and naturally performed.'

THE
Taming of the Shrew.

Actus primus. Scœna Prima.

Enter Begger and Hostes, Christophero Sly.

Begger.

ILe pheeze you infaith.

Host. A paire of stockes you rogue.

Beg. Y'are a baggage, the *Slies* are no Rogues. Looke in the Chronicles, we came in with *Richard Conqueror* : therefore *Paucas pallabris*, let the world slide : Sessa.

Host. You will not pay for the glasses you haue burst?

Beg. No, not a deniere: go by S. *Ieronimie*, goe to thy cold bed, and warme thee.

Host. I know my remedie, I must go fetch the Headborough.

Beg. Third, or fourth, or fift Borough, Ile answere him by Law. Ile not budge an inch boy: Let him come, and kindly.   *Falles asleepe.*

Winde hornes. Enter a Lord from hunting with his traine.

Lo. Huntsman I charge thee, tender wel my hounds,
Brach *Meriman*, the poore Curre is imbost,
And couple *Clowder* with the deepe-mouth'd brach,
Saw'st thou not boy how *Siluer* made it good
At the hedge corner, in the couldest fault,
I would not loose the dogge for twentie pound.

Hunts. Why *Belman* is as good as he my Lord,
He cried vpon it at the meerest losse,
And twice to day pick'd out the dullest sent,
Trust me, I take him for the better dogge.

Lord. Thou art a Foole, if *Eccho* were as fleete,
I would esteeme him worth a dozen such:
But sup them well, and looke vnto them all,
To morrow I intend to hunt againe.

Hunts. I will my Lord.

Lord. What's heere? One dead, or drunke? See doth he breath?

2.Hun. He breath's my Lord. Were he not warm'd with Ale, this were a bed but cold to sleep so soundly.

Lord. Oh monstrous beast, how like a swine he lyes.
Grim death, how foule and loathsome is thine image :
Sirs, I will practise on this drunken man.
What thinke you, if he were conuey'd to bed,
Wrap'd in sweet cloathes: Rings put vpon his fingers :
A most delicious banquet by his bed,
And braue attendants neere him when he wakes,
Would not the begger then forget himselfe?

1.Hun. Beleeue me Lord, I thinke he cannot choose.

2.H. It would seem strange vnto him when he wak'd

Lord. Euen as a flatt'ring dreame, or worthles fancies.

Then take him vp, and manage well the iest :
Carrie him gently to my fairest Chamber,
And hang it round with all my wanton pictures:
Balme his foule head in warme distilled waters,
And burne sweet Wood to make the Lodging sweete:
Procure me Musicke readie when he wakes,
To make a dulcet and a heauenly sound :
And if he chance to speake, be readie straight
(And with a lowe submissiue reuerence)
Say, what is it your Honor wil command :
Let one attend him with a siluer Bason
Full of Rose-water, and bestrew'd with Flowers,
Another beare the Ewer: the third a Diaper,
And say wilt please your Lordship coole your hands.
Some one be readie with a costly suite,
And aske him what apparrel he will weare :
Another tell him of his Hounds and Horse,
And that his Ladie mournes at his disease,
Perswade him that he hath bin Lunaticke,
And when he sayes he is, say that he dreames,
For he is nothing but a mightie Lord :
This do, and do it kindly, gentle sirs,
It wil be pastime passing excellent,
If it be husbanded with modestie.

1.Hunts. My Lord I warrant you we wil play our part
As he shall thinke by our true diligence
He is no lesse then what we say he is.

Lord. Take him vp gently, and to bed with him,
And each one to his office when he wakes.
                                              Sound trumpets.
Sirrah, go see what Trumpet 'tis that sounds,
Belike some Noble Gentleman that meanes
(Trauelling some iourney) to repose him heere.

Enter Seruingman.

How now? who is it?

Ser. An't please your Honor, Players
That offer seruice to your Lordship.

Enter Players.

Lord. Bid them come neere:
Now fellowes, you are welcome.

Players. We thanke your Honor.

Lord. Do you intend to stay with me to night?

2.Player. So please your Lordshippe to accept our dutie.

Lord. With all my heart. This fellow I remember,
Since once he plaide a Farmers eldest sonne,
'Twas where you woo'd the Gentlewoman so well:
I haue forgot your name : but sure that part

Was

Signature 147.

This acrostic is found in *The Taming of the Shrew*, on page 214, which is wrongly numbered 212, in the facsimile edited by J. O. Halliwell-Phillipps.

Note that the initial of the first word of the last line in the first column is the B of the word 'Baptista.'

Begin to read from the initial B of the word 'Baptista'; to the right; upwards; on the initials of the words; spelling BACONO, you will arrive at the initial O of the word ' offence.'

Now begin at the diagonally opposite corner of the block of type which begins with the line: —

      ' Gentlemen, God saue you. If I may be bold.'

Begin to read from the initial B of the word 'bold '; to the right; downwards; on the initials of the words; spelling BACONO, you will arrive at the initial O of the word ' offence' again: and thus keying the cipher.

The acrostic figure here is : —

<pre>
                        If I may be Bold
                                    A
                                C
                              O
                            N
        is it any   Offence
                    N
                  O
                C
              A
        Baptista is a noble Gentleman.
</pre>

Vpon agreement from vs to his liking.
Will vndertake to woo curst *Katherine*,
Yea, and to marrie her, if her dowrie please.

  Gre. So said, so done, is well:
Hortensio, haue you told him all her faults?

  Petr. I know she is an irkesome brawling scold:
If that be all Masters, I heare no harme.

  Gre. No, sayst me so, friend? What Countreyman?

  Petr. Borne in *Verona*, old *Butonios* sonne:
My father dead, my fortune liues for me,
And I do hope, good dayes and long, to see.

  Gre. Oh sir, such a life with such a wife, were strange:
But if you haue a stomacke, too't a Gods name,
You shal haue me assisting you in all.
But will you woo this Wilde-cat?

  Petr. Will I liue?

  Gru. Wil he woo her? I: or Ile hang her.

  Petr. Why came I hither, but to that intent?
Thinke you, a little dinne can daunt mine eares?
Haue I not in my time heard Lions rore?
Haue I not heard the sea, puft vp with windes,
Rage like an angry Boare, chafed with sweat?
Haue I not heard great Ordnance in the field?
And heauens Artillerie thunder in the skies?
Haue I not in a pitched battell heard
Loud larums, neighing steeds, & trumpets clangue?
And do you tell me of a womans tongue?
That giues not halfe so great a blow to heare,
As wil a Chesse-nut in a Farmers fire.
Tush, tush, feare boyes with bugs.

  Gru. For he feares none.

  Grem. *Hortensio* hearke:
This Gentleman is happily attriu'd,
My minde presumes for his owne good, and yours.

  Hor. I promist we would be Contributors,
And beare his charge of wooing whatsoere.

  Gremio. And so we wil, prouided that he win her.

  Gru. I would I were as sure of a good dinner.

Enter Tranio braue, and Biondello.

  Tra. Gentlemen God saue you. If I may be bold
Tell me I beseech you, which is the readiest way
To the house of Signior *Baptista Minola*?

  Bion. He that ha's the two faire daughters: ist he you
meane?

  Tra. Euen he *Biondello*.

  Gre. Hearke you sir, you meane not her to——

  Tra. Perhaps him and her sir, what haue you to do?

  Petr. Not her that chides sir, at any hand I pray.

  Tranio. I loue no chiders sir: *Biondello*, let's away.

  Luc. Well begun *Tranio*.

  Hor. Sir, a word ere you go:
Are you a sutor to the Maid you talke of, yea or no?

  Tra. And if I be sir, is it any offence?

  Gremio. No: if without more words you will get you
hence.

  Tra. Why sir, I pray are not the streets as free
For me, as for you?

  Gre. But so is not she.

  Tra. For what reason I beseech you.

  Gre. For this reason if you'l kno,
That she's the choise loue of Signior *Gremio*.

  Hor. That she's the chosen of signior *Hortensio*.

  Tra. Softly my Masters: If you be Gentlemen
Do me this right: heare me with patience.
Baptista is a noble Gentleman,

To whom my Father is not all vnknowne,
And were his daughter fairer then she is,
She may more sutors haue, and me for one.
Faire *Ladaes* daughter had a thousand wooers,
Then well one more may faire *Bianca* haue;
And so she shall: *Lucentio* shal make one,
Though *Paris* came, in hope to speed alone.

  Gre. What, this Gentleman will out-talke vs all.

  Luc. Sir giue him head, I know hee'l proue a Iade.

  Petr. *Hortensio*, to what end are all these words?

  Hor. Sir, let me be so bold as aske you,
Did you yet euer see *Baptistas* daughter?

  Tra. No sir, but heare I do that he hath two:
The one, as famous for a scolding tongue,
As is the other, for beauteous modestie.

  Petr. Sir, sir, the first's for me, let her go by.

  Gre. Yea, leaue that labour to great *Hercules*,
And let it be more then *Alcides* twelue.

  Petr. Sir vnderstand you this of me (insooth)
The yongest daughter whom you hearken for,
Her father keepes from all accesse of sutors,
And will not promise her to any man,
Vntill the elder sister first be wed.
The yonger then is free, and not before.

  Tranio. If it be so sir, that you are the man
Must steed vs all, and me amongst the rest:
And if you breake the ice, and do this seeke,
Atchieue the elder: set the yonger free,
For our accesse, whose hap shall be to haue her,
Wil not so gracelesse be, to be ingrate.

  Hor. Sir you say wel, and wel you do conceiue,
And since you do professe to be a sutor,
You must as we do, gratifie this Gentleman,
To whom we all rest generally beholding.

  Tranio. Sir, I shal not be slacke, in signe whereof,
Please ye we may contriue this afternoone,
And quaffe carowses to our Mistresse health,
And do as aduersaries do in law,
Striue mightily, but eate and drinke as friends.

  Gru. Bion. Oh excellent motion: fellowes let's be gon.

  Hor. The motions good indeed, and be it so,
Petruchio, I shal be your *Been venuto*.   *Exeunt.*

Enter Katherina and Bianca.

  Bian. Good sister wrong me not, nor wrong your self,
To make a bondmaide and a slaue of mee,
That I disdaine: but for these other goods,
Vnbinde my hands, Ile pull them off my selfe,
Yea all my raiment, to my petticoate,
Or what you will command me, wil I do,
So well I know my dutie to my elders.

  Kate. Of all thy sutors heere I charge tel
Whom thou lou'st best: see thou dissemble not.

  Bianca. Beleeue me sister, of all the men aliue,
I neuer yet beheld that speciall face,
Which I could fancie, more then any other.

  Kate. Minion thou lyest: Is't not *Hortensio*?

  Bian. If you affect him sister, heere I sweare
Ile pleade for you my selfe, but you shal haue him.

  Kate. Oh then belike you fancie riches more,
You wil haue *Gremio* to keepe you faire.

  Bian. Is it for him you do enuie me so?
Nay then you iest, and now I wel perceiue
You haue but iested with me all this while.
I prethee sister Kate, vntie my hands.

  Ka. If that be iest, then all the rest was so. *Strikes her*
                                                        Enter

Signature 148.

This acrostic is found on the first two (facing) pages of *All's Well that Ends Well.* (See pp. 390–391.)

Note the capital N at the upper right-hand corner of the ornamental

initial at the head of the text on the first page of the play $\boxed{\text{I}}^{\text{N}}$

We shall use the *capitals* only.

Begin to spell from the capital N at the upper right-hand of the initial; to the right; downwards; throughout the whole of the text of the two pages; on the *capitals* alone; spelling backwards NOCAB SICNVARF, you will arrive at the capital F of the last word ('Friends') of the right-hand page; having keyed the signature clear across the two pages from opposite corners.

The acrostic figure here is: —

I N
O
C
A
B
S
I
C
N
V
A
R

remember thy   Friends.

ALL'S
Well, that Ends Well.

Actus primus. Scœna Prima.

Enter yong Bertram Count of Rossillion, his Mother, and
Helena, Lord Lafew, all in blacke.

Mother.

IN deliuering my sonne from me, I burie a second husband.

Ros. And I in going Madam, weep ore my
fathers death anew; but I must attend his maiesties command, to whom I am now in Ward, euermore
in subiection.

Laf. You shall find of the King a husband Madame,
you sir a father. He that so generally is at all times good,
must of necessitie hold his vertue to you, whose worthi-
nesse would stirre it vp where it wanted rather then lacke
it where there is such abundance.

Mo. What hope is there of his Maiesties amendment?

Laf. He hath abandon'd his Phisitions Madam, vnder whose practises he hath persecuted time with hope,
and finds no other aduantage in the processe, but onely
the loosing of hope by time.

Mo. This yong Gentlewoman had a father, O that
had; how sad a passage tis, whose skill was almost as
great as his honestie, had it stretch'd so far, would haue
made nature immortall, and death should haue play for
lacke of worke. Would for the Kings sake hee were liuing, I thinke it would be the death of the Kings disease.

Laf. How call'd you the man you speake of Madam?

Mo. He was famous sir in his profession, and it was
his great right to be so : *Gerard de Narbon.*

Laf. He was excellent indeed Madam, the King very
latelie spoke of him admiringly, and mourningly : hee
was skilfull enough to haue liu'd stil, if knowledge could
be set vp against mortallitie.

Ros. What is it (my good Lord)the King languishes
of?

Laf. A Fistula my Lord.

Ros I heard not of it before.

Laf. I would it were not notorious. Was this Gentlewoman the Daughter of *Gerard de Narbon* ?

Mo. His sole childe my Lord, and bequeathed to my
ouer looking. I haue those hopes of her good, that her
education promises her dispositions shee inherits, which
makes faire gifts fairer: for where an vncleane mind carries vertuous qualities, there commendations go with
pitty, they are vertues and traitors too : in her they are
the better for their simplenesse; she deriues her honestie,
and atcheeues her goodnesse.

Lafew. Your commendations Madam get from her
teares.

Mo. 'Tis the best brine a Maiden can season her praise
in. The remembrance of her father neuer approches her
heart, but the tirrany of her sorrowes takes all liuelihood
from her cheeke. No more of this *Helena*, go too, no
more least it be rather thought you affect a sorrow, then
to haue.

Hell. I doe affect a sorrow indeed, but I haue it too.

Laf. Moderate lamentation is the right of the dead,
excessiue greefe the enemie to the liuing.

Mo. If the liuing be enemie to the greefe, the excesse
makes it soone mortall.

Ros. Maddam I desire your holie wishes.

Laf. How vnderstand we that ?

Mo. Be thou blest *Bertrame*, and succeed thy father,
In manners as in shape : thy blood and vertue
Contend for Empire in thee, and thy goodnesse
Share with thy birth-right. Loue all, trust a few,
Doe wrong to none : be able for thine enemie
Rather in power then vse : and keepe thy friend
Vnder thy owne lifes key. Be checkt for silence,
But neuer tax'd for speech. What heauen more wil,
That thee may furnish, and my prayers plucke downe,
Fall on thy head. Farwell my Lord,
'Tis an vnseason'd Courtier, good my Lord
Aduise him.

Laf. He cannot want the best
That shall attend his loue.

Mo. Heauen blesse him : Farwell *Bertram.*

*Ro.*The best wishes that can be forg'd in your thoghts
be seruants to you : be comfortable to my mother, your
Mistris, and make much of her.

Laf. Farewell prettie Lady, you must hold the credit of your father.

Hell. O were that all, I thinke not on my father,
And these great teares grace his remembrance more
Then those I shed for him. What was he like?
I haue forgott him. My imagination
Carries no fauour in't but *Bertrams*.
I am vndone, there is no liuing, none,
If *Bertram* be away. 'Twere all one,
That I should loue a bright particuler starre,
And think to wed it, he is so aboue me
In his bright radience and colaterall light,

Must

Muſt I be comforted, not in his ſphere;
Th'ambition in my loue thus plagues it ſelfe:
The hind that would be mated by the Lion
Muſt die for loue. 'Twas prettie, though a plague
To ſee him euerie houre to ſit and draw
His arched browes, his hawking eie, his curles
In our hearts-table: heart too capeable
Of euerie line and tricke of his ſweet fauour.
But now he's gone, and my idolatrous fancie
Muſt ſanctifie his Reliques. Who comes heere?

Enter Parrolles.

One that goes with him: I loue him for his ſake,
And yet I know him a notorious Liar,
Thinke him a great way foole, ſolie a coward,
Yet theſe fixt euils ſit ſo fit in him,
That they take place, when Vertues ſteely bones
Lookes bleake i'th cold wind: withall, full ofte we ſee
Cold wiſedome waighting on ſuperfluous follie.

Par. Saue you faire Queene.
Hel. And you Monarch.
Par. No.
Hel. And no.
Par. Are you meditating on virginitie?
Hel. I, you haue ſome ſtaine of ſouldier in you: Let
mee aske you a queſtion. Man is enemie to virginitie,
how may we barracado it againſt him?
Par. Keepe him out.
Hel. But he aſſailes, and our virginitie though vali-
ant, in the defence yet is weak: vnfold to vs ſome war-
like reſiſtance.
Par. There is none: Man ſetting downe before you,
will vndermine you, and blow you vp.
Hel. Bleſſe our poore Virginity from vnderminers
and blowers vp. Is there no Military policy how Virgins might blow vp men?
Par. Virginity beeing blowne downe, Man will
quicklier be blowne vp: marry in blowing him downe
againe, with the breach your ſelues made, you loſe your
City. It is not politicke, in the Common-wealth of
Nature, to preſerue virginity. Loſſe of Virginitie, is
rationall encreaſe, and there was neuer Virgin goe, till
virginitie was firſt loſt. That you were made of, is mettall to make Virgins. Virginitie, by beeing once loſt,
may be ten times found: by being euer kept, it is euer
loſt: 'tis too cold a companion: Away with't.
Hel. I will ſtand for't a little, though therefore I die
a Virgin.
Par. There's little can bee ſaide in't, 'tis againſt the
rule of Nature. To ſpeake on the part of virginitie, is
to accuſe your Mothers; which is moſt infallible diſo-
bedience. He that hangs himſelfe is a Virgin: Virginitie murthers it ſelfe, and ſhould be buried in highwayes
out of all ſanctified limit, as a deſperate Offendreſſe a-
gainſt Nature. Virginitie breedes mites, much like a
Cheeſe, conſumes it ſelfe to the very payring, and ſo
dies with feeding his owne ſtomacke. Beſides, Virginitie is peeuiſh, proud, ydle, made of ſelfe-loue, which
is the moſt inhibited ſinne in the Cannon. Keepe it not,
you cannot chooſe but looſe by't. Out with't: within
ten yeare it will make it ſelfe two, which is a goodly increaſe, and the principall it ſelfe not much the worſe.
Away with't.
Hel. How might one do ſir, to looſe it to her owne
liking?

Par. Let mee ſee. Marry ill, to like him that ne're
it likes. 'Tis a commodity wil loſe the gloſſe with lying:
The longer kept, the leſſe worth: Off with't while 'tis
vendible. Anſwer the time of requeſt, Virginitie like
an olde Courtier, weares her cap out of faſhion, richly
ſuted, but vnſuteable, iuſt like the brooch & the tooth-
pick, which were not now: your Date is better in your
Pye and your Porredge, then in your cheeke: and your
virginity, your old virginity, is like one of our French
wither'd peares, it lookes ill, it eates drily, marry 'tis a
wither'd peare: it was formerly better, marry yet 'tis a
wither'd peare: Will you any thing with it?
Hel. Not my virginity yet:
There ſhall your Maſter haue a thouſand loues,
A Mother, and a Miſtreſſe, and a friend,
A Phenix, Captaine, and an enemy,
A guide, a Goddeſſe, and a Soueraigne,
A Counſellor, a Traitoreſſe, and a Deare:
His humble ambition, proud humility:
His iarring, concord: and his diſcord, dulcet:
His faith, his ſweet diſaſter: with a world
Of pretty fond adoptious chriſtendomes
That blinking Cupid goſſips. Now ſhall he:
I know not what he ſhall, God ſend him well,
The Courts a learning-place, and he is one.
Par. What one iſaith?
Hel. That I wiſh well, 'tis pitty.
Par. What's pitty?
Hel. That wiſhing well had not a body in't,
Which might be felt, that we the poorer borne,
Whoſe baſer ſtarres do ſhut vs vp in wiſhes,
Might with effects of them follow our friends,
And ſhew what vve alone muſt thinke, which neuer
Returnes vs thankes.

Enter Page.

Pag. Monſieur *Parrolles*,
My Lord cals for you.
Par. Little *Hellen* farewell, if I can remember thee, I
will thinke of thee at Court.
Hel. Monſieur *Parolles*, you were borne vnder a
charitable ſtarre.
Par. Vnder *Mars* I.
Hel. I eſpecially thinke, vnder *Mars*.
Par. Why vnder *Mars*?
Hel. The warres hath ſo kept you vnder, that you
muſt needes be borne vnder *Mars*.
Par. When he was predominant.
Hel. When he was retrograde I thinke rather.
Par. Why thinke you ſo?
Hel. You go ſo much backward when you fight.
Par. That's for aduantage.
Hel. So is running away,
When feare propoſes the ſaſetie:
But the compoſition that your valour and feare makes
in you, is a vertue of a good wing, and I like the
weare well.
Paroll. I am ſo full of buſineſſes, I cannot anſwere
thee acutely: I will returne perfect Courtier, in the
which my inſtruction ſhall ſerue to naturalize thee, ſo
thou wilt be capeable of a Courtiers councell, and vn-
derſtand what aduice ſhall thruſt vppon thee, elſe thou
dieſt in thine vnthankfulnes, and thine ignorance makes
thee away, farewell: When thou haſt leyſure, ſay thy
praiers: when thou haſt none, remember thy Friends:

V. 2   Get

Signature 149.

This acrostic is found in *All's Well that Ends Well*, on pages 249 and 250, which are wrongly numbered 251 and 252. (See pp. 394, 395.)

Note the initials B O of the words 'But O' in the line at the top of the right-hand column of page 251.

Treat both these wrongly numbered pages as one page.

Begin to read from the initial O of the line at the top of the right-hand column of page 251; to the right; on the *initials* of the *outside* words of the text of the two pages; spelling ONOCAB (i. e. BACONO), you will arrive at the initial B of the word 'But,' having keyed the cipher by completely circling the initials of the outside words of the whole of the two wrongly numbered pages.

The acrostic figure here is: —

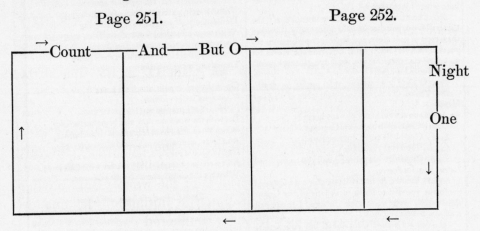

Page 251.   Page 252.

This figure shows the four columns and the words which are involved in the cipher.

Signature 150.

This acrostic is found on the last page of *Twelfe Night*.

Note the initials of the first words of the last three lines of the

F   For

text preceding the 'Clowne's Song.' They are B of the But

O   Orsino's.

Treat the last two lines as if they were a string of letters.

Begin to read from the letter B of the word 'But'; to the right; on all the letters of all words in the two lines; spelling BACONO, you will arrive at the initial letter O of the word 'Orsino': having keyed the name from end to end of the string of letters; thus:—

BUTWHENINOTHERHABITESYOUARESEENEENEEUQSEICNAFSIHDNASIRTSIMSONISRO

The acrostic figure here is:—

But
A
C
O
N
Orsino's Mistris and, etc.

Signature 151.

Now begin to read from the initial B of the same word 'But'; to the right, *or to the left;* downwards; on the *initials* of all words in all lines; to the end of the 'Clownes Song' and back again continuously; spelling BACONO, you will again arrive at the initial O of the word 'Orsino': having keyed the cipher, to the right or to the left, and from end to end of the string.

The acrostic figure here is:—

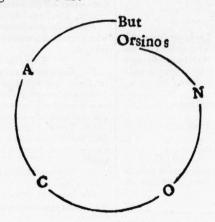

Or fay, tis not your feale, not your inuention :
You can fay none of this. Well, grant it then,
And tell me in the modeſtie of honor,
Why you haue giuen me ſuch cleare lights of fauour,
Bad me come ſmiling, and croſſe-garter'd to you,
To put on yellow ſtockings, and to frowne
Vpon ſir *Toby*, and the lighter people :
And acting this in an obedient hope,
Why haue you ſuffer'd me to be impriſon'd,
Kept in a darke houſe, viſited by the Prieſt,
And made the moſt notorious gecke and gull,
That ere inuention plaid on ? Tell me why ?

Ol. Alas *Maluolio*, this is not my writing,
Though I confeſſe much like the Charracter :
But out of queſtion, tis *Marias* hand.
And now I do bethinke me, it was ſhee
Firſt told me thou waſt mad ; then cam'ſt in ſmiling,
And in ſuch formes, which heere were preſuppos'd
Vpon thee in the Letter : prethee be content,
This practice hath moſt ſhrewdly paſt vpon thee :
But when we know the grounds, and authors of it,
Thou ſhalt be both the Plaintiffe and the Iudge
Of thine owne cauſe.

Fab. Good Madam heare me ſpeake,
And let no quarrell, nor no braule to come,
Taint the condition of this preſent houre,
Which I haue wondred at. In hope it ſhall not,
Moſt freely I confeſſe my ſelfe, and *Toby*
Set this deuice againſt *Maluolio* heere,
Vpon ſome ſtubborne and vncourteous parts
We had conceiu'd againſt him. *Maria* writ
The Letter, at ſir *Tobyes* great importance,
In recompence whereof, he hath married her :
How with a ſportfull malice it was follow'd,
May rather plucke on laughter then reuenge,
If that the iniuries be iuſtly weigh'd,
That haue on both ſides paſt

Ol. Alas poore Foole, how haue they baffel'd thee ?

Clo. Why ſome are borne great, ſome atchieue greatneſſe, and ſome haue greatneſſe throwne vpon them. I
was, one ſir, in this Enterlude, one ſir *Topas* ſir, but that's

all one : By the Lord Foole, I am not mad : but do you remember, Madam, why laugh you at ſuch a barren raſcall,
and you ſmile not he's gag'd : and thus the whirlegigge
of time, brings in his reuenges.

Mal. Ile be reueng'd on the whole packe of you ?

Ol. He hath bene moſt notoriouſly abus'd.

Du. Purſue him, and entreate him to a peace :
He hath not told vs of the Captaine yet,
When that is knowne, and golden time conuents
A ſolemne Combination ſhall be made
Of our deere ſoules. Meane time ſweet ſiſter,
We will not part from hence. *Cesario* come
(For ſo you ſhall be while you are a man :)
But when in other habites you are ſeene,
Orſino's Miſtris, and his fancies Queene.   *Exeunt*

Clowne ſings
When that I was and a little tine boy,
  with hey, ho, the winde and the raine :
A fooliſh thing was but a toy,
  for the raine it raineth euery day.

But when I came to mans eſtate,
  with hey ho, &c.
Gainſt Knaues and Theeues men ſhut their gate,
  for the raine, &c.

But when I came alas to wiue,
  with hey ho, &c.
By ſwaggering could I neuer thriue,
  for the raine, &c.

But when I came vnto my beds,
  with hey ho &c.
With toſſpottes ſtill had drunken heades,
  for the raine, &c.

A great while ago the world begon,
  hey ho, &c.
But that's all one, our Play is done,
  and wee'l ſtriue to pleaſe you euery day.

FINIS.

Signature 153.

These acrostics are found in *The life and death of King John*, on the first two pages of the play. (See pp. 402–403.)

Note that the ornamental monogram at the beginning of the play is **N**⁰· This looks as if it may be the tail end of an acrostic.

By turning the page we find what may be the fore end of the acrostic in the initials of the first words of the last two lines of the second page of the play. They are $\frac{F}{B}$ of the words $\frac{For}{But}$

Begin to read from the initial B of the word 'But'; upwards; on the initials of the first words of all lines of the text; spelling Bacon, you will arrive at the initial N of the word 'Nay,' which is the initial of the first word of the first line of the column.

Here we have the name keyed from the first initial of the last line in the column to the first initial of the first line of the same column.

The acrostic figure here is: —

Nay I would have you go, etc.
O
C
A
But who comes, etc.

Signature 154.

Now begin to read from the initial F of the word ' For'; to the left; downwards; up the next column and down the next, and so on; on the *capitals* as they fall throughout the text; spelling FRANCIS BACON, you will arrive at the large $\boxed{\text{N}}$ with which the play begins, and from which we began by assuming it to be the tail end of a signature.

The acrostic figure here is:—

NOCABSICNAR For it shall strew the footsteps of my rising:
But who comes, etc.

The life and death of King Iohn.

Actus Primus, Scæna Prima.

Enter King Iohn, Queene Elinor, Pembroke, Essex, and Sa-
lisbury, with the Chattylion of France.

King Iohn.

OW say *Chatillion*, what would *France* with vs ?
  Chat. Thus (after greeting) speakes the King
    of France,
In my behauiour to the Maiesty,
The borrowed Maiesty of *England* heere.
  Elea. A strange beginning : borrowed Maiesty ?
  K.Iohn. Silence (good mother) heare the Embassie.
  Chat. Philip of *France*, in right and true behalfe
Of thy deceased brother, *Geffreyes* sonne,
Arthur Plantaginet, laies most lawfull claime
To this faire Iland, and the Territories :
To *Ireland, Poyctiers, Aniowe, Torayne, Maine,*
Desiring thee to lay aside the sword
Which swaies vsurpingly these seuerall titles,
And put the same into yong *Arthurs* hand,
Thy Nephew, and right royall Soueraigne.
  K.Iohn. What followes if we disallow of this ?
  Chat. The proud controle of fierce and bloudy warre,
To inforce these rights, so forcibly with-held,
  K.Io. Heere haue we war for war, & bloud for bloud,
Controlement for controlement : so answer *France.*
  Chat. Then take my Kings defiance from my mouth,
The farthest limit of my Embassie.
  K.Iohn. Beare mine to him, and so depart in peace,
Be thou as lightning in the eies of *France* ;
For ere thou canst report, I will be there.
The thunder of my Cannon shall be heard.
So hence : be thou the trumpet of our wrath,
And sullen presage of your owne decay :
An honourable conduct let him haue,
Pembroke looke too't : farewell *Chattillion.*

Exit Chat. and Pem.

  Ele. What now my sonne, haue I not euer said
How that ambitious *Constance* would not cease
Till she had kindled *France* and all the world,
Vpon the right and party of her sonne.
This might haue beene preuented, and made whole
With very easie arguments of loue,
Which now the mannage of two kingdomes must
With fearefull bloudy issue arbitrate.
  K.Iohn. Our strong possession, and our right for vs.
  Eli. Your strong possessiō much more then your right,
Or else it must go wrong with you and me,
So much my conscience whispers in your eare,

Which none but heauen, and you, and I, shall heare.

Enter a Sheriffe.

  Essex. My Liege, here is the strangest controuersie
Come from the Country to be iudg'd by you
That ere I heard : shall I produce the men ?
  K.Iohn. Let them approach :
Our Abbies and our Priories shall pay
This expeditious charge : what men are you ?

Enter Robert Faulconbridge, and Philip.

  Philip. Your faithfull subiect, I a gentleman,
Borne in *Northamptonshire,* and eldest sonne
As I suppose, to *Robert Faulconbridge,*
A Souldier by the Honor-giuing-hand
Of *Cordelion,* Knighted in the field.
  K.Iohn. What art thou ?
  Robert. The son and heire to that same *Faulconbridge.*
  K.Iohn. Is that the elder, and art thou the heyre ?
You came not of one mother then it seemes.
  Philip. Most certain of one mother, mighty King,
That is well knowne, and as I thinke one father :
But for the cerraine knowledge of that truth,
I put you o're to heauen, and to my mother ;
Of that I doubt, as all mens children may.
  Eli. Out on thee rude man, ŷ dost shame thy mother,
And wound her honor with this diffidence.
  Phil. I Madame ? No, I haue no reason for it,
That is my brothers plea, and none of mine,
The which if he can proue, a pops me out,
At least from faire fiue hundred pound a yeere :
Heauen guard my mothers honor, and my Land.
  K.Iohn. A good blunt fellow : why being yonget born
Doth he lay claime to thine inheritance ?
  Phil. I know not why, except to get the land :
But once he slanderd me with bastardy :
But where I be as true begot or no,
That still I lay vpon my mothers head,
But that I am as well begot my Liege
(Faire fall the bones that tooke the paines for me)
Compare our faces, and be Iudge your selfe
If old Sir *Robert* did beget vs both,
And were our father, and this sonne like him :
O old sir *Robert* Father, on my knee
I giue heauen thankes I was not like to thee.
  K.Iohn. Why what a mad-cap hath heauen lent vs here?
  Elen. He hath a tricke of *Cordelions* face,
The accent of his tongue affecteth him :
Doe you not read some tokens of my sonne
In the large composition of this man ?

a   *K.Ioh.*

K. Iohn. Mine eye hath well examined his parts,
And findes them perfect *Richard* : firra speake,
What doth moue you to claime your brothers land.

Philip. Becaufe he hath a half-face like my father :
With halfe that face would he haue all my land,
A halfe-fac'd groat, fiue hundred pound a yeere?

Rob. My gracious Liege, when that my father liu'd,
Your brother did imploy my father much.

Phil. Well fir, by this you cannot get my land,
Your tale muft be how he employ'd my mother.

Rob And once difpatch'd him in an Embaffie
To *Germany*, there with the Emperor
To treat of high affaires touching that time :
Th'aduantage of his abfence tooke the King,
And in the meane time foiourn'd at my fathers ;
Where how he did preuaile, I fhame to fpeake:
But truth is truth, large lengths of feas and fhores
Betweene my father, and my mother lay,
As I haue heard my father fpeake himfelfe
When this fame lufty gentleman was got :
Vpon his death-bed he by will bequeath'd
His lands to me, and tooke it on his death
That this my mothers fonne was none of his;
And if he were, he came into the world
Full fourteene weekes before the courfe of time :
Then good my Liedge let me haue what is mine,
My fathers land, as was my fathers will.

K. Iohn. Sirra, your brother is Legittimate,
Your fathers wife did after wedlocke beare him :
And if fhe did play falfe, the fault was hers,
Which fault lyes on the hazards of all husbands
That marry wiues : tell me, how if my brother
Who as you fay, tooke paines, to get this fonne,
Had of your father claim'd this fonne for his,
Infooth, good friend, your father might haue kept.
This Calfe, bred from his Cow from all the world :
Infooth he might : then if he were my brothers,
My brother might not claime him, nor your father,
Being none of his, refufe him : this concludes,
My mothers fonne did get your fathers heyre,
Your fathers heyre muft haue your fathers land.

Rob. Shal then my fathers Will be of no force,
To difpoffeffe that childe which is not his.

Phil. Of no more force to difpoffeffe me fir,
Then was his will to get me, as I thinke.

Eli. Whether hadft thou rather be a *Faulconbridge*,
And like thy brother to enioy thy land :
Or the reputed fonne of *Cordelion*,
Lord of thy prefence, and no land befide.

Baft. Madam, and if my brother had my fhape
And I had his, fir *Roberts* his like him,
And if my legs were two fuch riding rods,
My armes, fuch eele-skins ftuft, my face fo thin,
That in mine eare I durft not fticke a rofe,
Left men fhould fay, looke where three farthings goes,
And to his fhape were heyre to all this land,
Would I might neuer ftirre from off this place,
I would giue it euery foot to haue this face :
It would not be fir nobbe in any cafe.

Elinor. I like thee well: wilt thou forfake thy fortune,
Bequeath thy land to him, and follow me?
I am a Souldier, and now bound to *France.*

Baft. Brother, take you my laud, Ile take my chances
Your face hath got fiue hundred pound a yeere,
Yet fell your face for fiue pence and 'tis deere:
Madam, Ile follow you vnto the death.

Elinor. Nay, I would haue you go before me thither.

Baft. Our Country manners giue our betters way.

K. Iohn. What is thy name?

Baft. Philip my Liege, fo is my name begun,
Philip, good old Sir *Roberts* wiues eldeft fonne.

K. Iohn. From henceforth beare his name
Whofe forme thou beareft :
Kneele thou downe *Philip*, but rife more great,
Arife Sir *Richard*, and *Plantagenet.*

Baft. Brother by th'mothers fide, giue me your hand,
My father gaue me honor, yours gaue land :
Now bleffed be the houre by night or day
When I was got, Sir *Robert* was away.

Ele. The very fpirit of *Plantaginet* :
I am thy grandame *Richard*, call me fo.

Baft. Madam by chance, but not by truth, what tho;
Something about a little from the right,
In at the window, or elfe ore the hatch :
Who dares not ftirre by day, muft walke by night,
And haue is haue, how euer men doe catch:
Neere or farre off, well wonne is ftill well fhot,
And I am I, how ere I was begot.

K. Iohn. Goe, *Faulconbridge*, now haft thou thy defire,
A landleffe Knight, makes thee a landed Squire :
Come Madam, and come *Richard*, we muft fpeed
For *France*, for *France*, for it is more then need.

Baft. Brother adieu, good fortune come to thee,
For thou waft got i'th way of honefty.

Exeunt all but baftard.

Baft. A foot of Honor better then I was,
But many a many foot of Land the worfe.
Well, now can I make any *Ioane* a Lady,
Good den Sir *Richard*, Godamercy fellow,
And if his name be *George*, Ile call him *Peter*;
For new made honor doth forget mens names :
'Tis two refpectiue, and too fociable
For your conuerfion, now your traueller,
Hee and his tooth-picke at my worfhips meffe,
And when my knightly ftomacke is fuffis'd,
Why then I fucke my teeth, and catechize
My picked man of Countries : my deare fir,
Thus leaning on mine elbow I begin,
I fhall befeech you ; that is queftion now,
And then comes anfwer like an Abfey booke :
O fir, fayes anfwer, at your beft command,
At your employment, at your feruice fir
No fir, faies queftion, I fweet fir at yours,
And fo ere anfwer knowes what queftion would,
Sauing in Dialogue of Complement,
And talking of the Alpes and Appenines,
The Perennean and the riuer *Poe*,
It drawes toward fupper in conclufion fo.
But this is worfhipfull fociety,
And fits the mounting fpirit like my felfe ;
For he is but a baftard to the time
That doth not fmoake of obferuation,
And fo am I whether I fmacke or no :
And not alone in habit and deuice,
Exterior forme, outward accoutrement ;
But from the inward motion to deliuer
Sweet, fweet, fweet poyfon for the ages tooth,
Which though I will not practice to deceiue,
Yet to auoid deceit I meane to learne;
For it fhall ftrew the footfteps of my rifing :
But who comes in fuch hafte in riding robes?

What

Signature 155.

This acrostic is found in the first page of *The life and death of King Richard the Second.*

Begin to read from the large initial 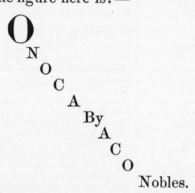 which begins the play; to the right; on the *capitals* of the *text;* spelling backwards ONOCAB, you will arrive at the initial capital B of the word 'By' (twenty-seventh line, second column).

Now begin to read from the initial N of the word 'Nobles,' which is the last word in the text on the page; to the left; upwards; on the capitals of the words of the text; spelling backwards NOCAB, you will arrive at the same initial B of the same word 'By' (twenty-seventh line, second column).

This last name is keyed by reading it downwards from the initial of the word 'By'; to the right; downwards; on the capitals; spelling BACON, you will arrive at the capital N of the word 'Nobles.'

The acrostic figure here is:—

O
  N
    O
      C
        A
         By
        A
         C
          O
           Nobles.

It is to be noted here that the word 'Nobles' is not capitalised in the Quarto of 1597.

The life and death of King Richard the Second.

Actus Primus, Scæna Prima.

Enter King Richard, Iohn of Gaunt, with other Nobles and Attendants.

King Richard.
OLd *Iohn of Gaunt*, time-honoured Lancaster,
Haſt thou according to thy oath and band
Brought hither *Henry* Herford thy bold ſon:
Heere to make good ÿ boiſtrous late appeale,
Which then our leyſure would not let vs heare,
Againſt the Duke of Norfolke, *Thomas Mowbray?*

Gaunt. I haue my Liege.

King. Tell me moreouer, haſt thou ſounded him,
If he appeale the Duke on ancient malice,
Or worthily as a good ſubiect ſhould
On ſome knowne ground of treacherie in him.

Gaunt As neere as I could ſift him on that argument,
On ſome apparant danger ſeene in him,
Aym'd at your Highneſſe, no inueterate malice.

Kin. Then call them to our preſence face to face,
And frowning brow to brow, our ſelues will heare
Th'accuſer, and the accuſed, freely ſpeake;
High ſtomack d are they both, and full of ire,
In rage, deafe as the ſea; haſtie as fire.

Enter Bullingbrooke and Mowbray.

Bul. Many yeares of happy dayes befall
My gracious Soueraigne, my moſt louing Liege.

Mow. Each day ſtill better others happineſſe,
Vntill the heauens enuying earths good hap,
Adde an immortall title to your Crowne.

King. We thanke you both, yet one but flatters vs,
As well appeareth by the cauſe you come,
Namely, to appeale each other of high treaſon.
Cooſin of Hereford, what doſt thou obiect
Againſt the Duke of Norfolke, *Thomas Mowbray?*

Bul. Firſt, heauen be the record to my ſpeech,
In the deuotion of a ſubiects loue,
Tendering the precious ſafetie of my Prince,
And free from other misbegotten hate,
Come I appealant to this Princely preſence.
Now *Thomas Mowbray* do I turne to thee,
And marke my greeting well : for what I ſpeake,
My body ſhall make good vpon this earth,
Or my diuine ſoule anſwer it in heauen.
Thou art a Traitor, and a Miſcreant;
Too good to be ſo, and too bad to liue,
Since the more faire and chriſtall is the skie,

The vglier ſeeme the cloudes that in it flye :
Once more, the more to aggrauate the note,
With a foule Traitors name ſtuffe I thy throte,
And wiſh (ſo pleaſe my Soueraigne) ere I moue,
What my tong ſpeaks, my right drawn ſword may proue

Mow. Let not my cold words heere accuſe my zeale:
'Tis not the triall of a Womans warre,
The bitter clamour of two eager tongues,
Can arbitrate this cauſe betwixt vs twaine :
The blood is hot that muſt be cool'd for this.
Yet can I not of ſuch tame patience boaſt,
As to be huſht, and nought at all to ſay.
Firſt the faire reuerence of your Highneſſe curbes mee,
From giuing reines and ſpurres to my free ſpeech,
Which elſe would poſt, vntill it had return'd
Theſe tearmes of treaſon, doubly downe his throat.
Setting aſide his high bloods royalty,
And let him be no Kinſman to my Liege,
I do defie him, and I ſpit at him,
Call him a ſlanderous Coward, and a Villaine :
Which to maintaine, I would allow him oddes,
And meete him, were I tide to runne a foote,
Euen to the frozen ridges of the Alpes,
Or any other ground inhabitable,
Where euer Engliſhman durſt ſet his foote.
Meane time, let this defend my loyaltie,
By all my hopes moſt falſely doth he lie.

Bul. Pale trembling Coward, there I throw my gage,
Diſclaiming heere the kindred of a King,
And lay aſide my high bloods Royalty,
Which feare, not reuerence makes thee to except.
If guilty dread hath left thee ſo much ſtrength,
As to take vp mine Honors pawne, then ſtoope.
By that, and all the rites of Knight-hood elſe,
Will I make good againſt thee arme to arme,
What I haue ſpoken, or thou canſt deuiſe.

Mow. I take it vp, and by that ſword I ſweare,
Which gently laid my Knight-hood on my ſhoulder,
Ile anſwer thee in any faire degree,
Or Chiualrous deſigne of knightly triall :
And when I mount, aliue may I not light,
If I be Traitor, or vniuſtly fight.

King. What doth our Coſin lay to *Mowbraies* charge?
It muſt be great that can inherite vs,
So much as of a thought ot ill in him.

Bul. Looke what I ſaid, my life ſhall proue it true,
That *Mowbray* hath receiu'd eight thouſand Nobles,

In

Signature 156.

This acrostic is found in the first two pages of *The First Part of Henry the Fourth,* in which the paging jumps from 46 to 49.   (See pp. 408–409.)

This is a weak acrostic, but it is remarkable, as it is the only instance in which I have found an *open,* barefaced acrostic of Bacon's name.

Bacon's name was sometimes latinised into Baco, sometimes into Baconus. In this case the former is used. We shall find it by reading from the capital O at the upper right-hand of the big initial

downwards; on the capital of the first word in each line in the first column, up on the capitals of the next column, and down on the capitals of the third column (treating the front initials of the columns as if they were on a string); spelling backwards ONOCAB, you will arrive at the initial B of the word 'But,' beginning the fourth line from the end of the Scene:—

'But come your selfe with speed to vs againe.'

Now note the initials of the first words of the five lines at which we have arrived by spelling ONOCAB from the first O. They are:—

Our
Cosin
At
But come
For

Read these initials upwards, they give us F BACO; the latinised form sometimes used for Bacon's name.

The acrostic figure here is: —

S	O	N			Our holy purpose, etc.
	F		O		Cosin
	A			C	A	At
	T					But come
						For

Note that the Latin name forms the end or 'butt' of the acrostic, whereas if it were a strong instead of a weak acrostic the butt would be the initial of the first word of the last line of the Scene.

The First Part of Henry the Fourth,
with the Life and Death of HENRY
Sirnamed HOT-SPVRRE.

Aᶜtus Primus. Scœna Prima.

Enter the King, Lord Iohn of Lancaſter, Earle of Weſtmerland, with others.

King.

SO ſhaken as we are, ſo wan with care,
Finde we a time for frighted Peace to pant,
And breath ſhortwinded accents of new broils
To be commenc'd in Stronds a-farre remote :
No more the thirſty entrance of this Soile,
Shall daube her lippes with her owne childrens blood :
No more ſhall trenching Warre channell her fields,
Nor bruiſe her Flowrets with the Armed hooſes
Of hoſtile paces. Thoſe oppoſed eyes,
Which like the Meteors of a troubled Heauen,
All of one Nature, of one Subſtance bred,
Did lately meete in the inteſtine ſhocke,
And furious cloze of ciuill Butchery,
Shall now in mutuall well-beſeeming rankes
March all one way, and be no more oppos'd
Againſt Acquaintance, Kindred, and Allies.
The edge of Warre, like an ill-ſheathed knife,
No more ſhall cut his Maſter. Therefore Friends,
As farre as to the Sepulcher of Chriſt,
Whoſe Souldier now vnder whoſe bleſſed Croſſe,
We are impreſſed and ingag'd to fight,
Forthwith a power of Engliſh ſhall we leuie,
Whoſe armes were moulded in their Mothers wombe,
To chace theſe Pagans in thoſe holy Fields,
Ouer whoſe Acres walk'd thoſe bleſſed feete
Which fourteene hundred yeares ago were nail'd
For our aduantage on the bitter Croſſe.
But this our purpoſe is a tweluemonth old,
And bootleſſe 'tis to tell you we will go :
Therefore we meete not now. Then let me heare
Of you my gentle Couſin Weſtmerland,
What yeſternight our Councell did decree,
In forwarding this deere expedience.

Weſt. My Liege : This haſte was hot in queſtiō,
And many limits of the Charge ſet downe
But yeſternight : when all athwart there came
A Poſt from Wales, loaden with heauy Newes ;
Whoſe worſt was, That the Noble *Mortimer*,
Leading the men of Hereford ſhire to fight
Againſt the irregular and wilde *Glendower*,
Was by the rude hands of that Welſhman taken,
And a thouſand of his people butchered :

Vpon whoſe dead corpes there was ſuch miſuſe,
Such beaſtly, ſhameleſſe transformation,
By thoſe Welſhwomen done, as may not be
(Without much ſhame) re-told or ſpoken of.

King It ſeemes then, that the tidings of this broile,
Brake off our buſineſſe for the Holy land.

Weſt. This matcht with other like, my gracious Lord.
Farre more vneuen and vnwelcome Newes
Came from the North, and thus it did report :
On Holy-roode day, the gallant *Hotſpurre* there,
Young *Harry Percy*, and braue *Archibald*,
That euer-valiant and approoued Scot,
At *Holmeden* met, where they did ſpend
A ſad and bloody houre :
As by diſcharge of their Artillerie,
And ſhape of likely-hood the newes was told :
For he that brought them, in the very heate
And pride of their contention, did take horſe,
Vncertaine of the iſſue any way.

King. Heere is a deere and true induſtrious friend,
Sir *Walter Blunt*, new lighted from his Horſe,
Strain'd with the variation of each ſoyle,
Betwixt that *Holmedon*, and this Seat of ours :
And he hath brought vs ſmooth and welcome newes.
The Earle of *Dowglas* is diſcomfited,
Ten thouſand bold Scots, two and twenty Knights
Balk'd in their owne blood did Sir *Walter* ſee
On *Holmedons* Plaines. Of Priſoners, *Hotſpurre* tooke
Mordake Earle of Fife, and eldeſt ſonne
To beaten *Dowglas*, and the Earle of *Atholl*,
Of *Murry*, *Angus*, and *Menteith*.
And is not this an honourable ſpoyle ?
A gallant prize ? Ha Coſin, is it not ? Infaith it is.

Weſt. A Conqueſt for a Prince to boaſt of.

King. Yea, there thou mak'ſt me ſad, & mak'ſt me ſin,
In enuy, that my Lord Northumberland
Should be the Father of ſo bleſt a Sonne :
A Sonne, who is the Theame of Honors tongue ;
Among'ſt a Groue, the very ſtraighteſt Plant,
Who is ſweet Fortunes Minion, and her Pride :
Whil'ſt I by looking on the praiſe of him,
See Ryot and Diſhonor ſtaine the brow
Of my yong *Harry* O that it could be prou'd,
That ſome Night-tripping-Faiery, had exchang'd
In Cradle-clothes, our Children where they lay,
And call'd mine *Percy*, his *Plantagenet* :

The

Then would I haue his *Harry*, and he mine :
But let him from my thoughts. What thinke you Coze
Of this young *Percies* pride ? The Priſoners
Which he in this aduenture hath ſurpriz'd,
To his owne vſe he keepes, and ſends me word
I ſhall haue none but *Mordake* Earle of *Fife*.

Weſt. This is his Vnckles teaching. This is Worceſter
Maleuolent to you in all Aſpects :
Which makes him prune himſelfe, and briſtle vp
The creſt of Youth againſt your Dignity.

King. But I haue ſent for him to anſwer this:
And for this cauſe a-while we muſt neglect
Our holy purpoſe to Ieruſalem.
Coſin, on Wedneſday next, our Councell we will hold
At Windſor, and ſo informe the Lords :
But come your ſelfe with ſpeed to vs againe,
For more is to be ſaid, and to be done,
Then out of anger can be vttered.

Weſt. I will my Liege. *Exeunt*

Scæna Secunda.

Enter Henry Prince of Wales, Sir Iohn Falſtaffe, and Pointz.

Fal. Now *Hal*, what time of day is it Lad ?

Prince. Thou art ſo fat-witted with drinking of olde Sacke, and vnbuttoning thee after Supper, and ſleeping vpon Benches in the afternoone, that thou haſt forgotten to demand that truely, which thou wouldeſt truly know. What a diuell haſt thou to do with the time of the day ? vnleſſe houres were cups of Sacke, and minutes Capons, and clockes the tongues of Bawdes, and dialls the ſignes of Leaping-houſes, and the bleſſed Sunne himſelfe a faire hot Wench in Flame-coloured Taffata ; I ſee no reaſon, why thou ſhouldeſt bee ſo ſuperfluous, to demaund the time of the day.

Fal. Indeed you come neere me now *Hal*, for we that take Purſes, go by the Moone and ſeuen Starres, and not by Phœbus hee, that wand'ring Knight ſo faire. And I prythee ſweet Wagge, when thou art King, as God ſaue thy Grace, Maieſty I ſhould ſay, for Grace thou wilte haue none.

Prin. What, none ?

Fal. No, not ſo much as will ſerue to be Prologue to an Egge and Butter.

Prin. Well, how then ? Come roundly, roundly.

Fal. Marry then, ſweet Wagge, when thou art King, let not vs that are Squires of the Nights bodie, bee call'd Theeues of the Dayes beautie. Let vs be *Dianaes* Forreſters, Gentlemen of the Shade, Minions of the Moone ; and let men ſay, we be men of good Gouernment, being gouerned as the Sea is, by our noble and chaſt miſtris the Moone, vnder whoſe countenance we ſteale.

Prin. Thou ſay'ſt well, and it holds well too : for the fortune of vs that are the Moones men, doeth ebbe and flow like the Sea, beeing gouerned as the Sea is, by the Moone : as for proofe. Now a Purſe of Gold moſt reſolutely ſnatch'd on Monday night, and moſt diſſolutely ſpent on Tueſday Morning ; got with ſwearing, Lay by : and ſpent with crying, Bring in : now, in as low an ebbe as the foot of the Ladder, and by and by in as high a flow as the ridge of the Gallowes.

Fal. Thou ſay'ſt true Lad : and is not my Hoſteſſe of the Tauerne a moſt ſweet Wench ?

Prin. As is the hony, my old Lad of the Caſtle : and is not a Buffe Ierkin a moſt ſweet robe of durance ?

Fal. How now ? how now mad Wagge ? What in thy quips and thy quiddities ? What a plague haue I to doe with a Buffe-Ierkin ?

Prin. Why, what a poxe haue I to doe with my Hoſteſſe of the Tauerne?

Fal. Well, thou haſt call'd her to a reck'ning many a time and oft.

Prin. Did I euer call for thee to pay thy part ?

Fal. No, Ile giue thee thy due, thou haſt paid al there.

Prin. Yea and elſewhere, ſo farre as my Coine would ſtretch, and where it would not, I haue vs'd my credit.

Fal. Yea, and ſo vs'd it, that were it heere apparant, that thou art Heire apparant. But I prythee ſweet Wag, ſhall there be Gallowes ſtanding in England when thou art King ? and reſolution thus fobb'd as it is, with the ruſtie curbe of old Father Anticke the Law? Doe not thou when thou art a King, hang a Theefe.

Prin. No, thou ſhalt.

Fal. Shall I? O rare! Ile be a braue Iudge.

Prin. Thou iudgeſt falſe already. I meane, thou ſhalt haue the hanging of the Theeues, and ſo become a rare Hangman.

Fal. Well *Hal*, well : and in ſome ſort it iumpes with my humour, as well as waiting in the Court, I can tell you.

Prin. For obtaining of ſuites ?

Fal. Yea, for obtaining of ſuites, whereof the Hangman hath no leane Wardrobe. I am as Melancholly as a Gyb-Cat, or a lugg'd Beare.

Prin. Or an old Lyon, or a Louers Lute.

Fal. Yea, or the Drone of a Lincolnſhire Bagpipe.

Prin. What ſay'ſt thou to a Hare, or the Melancholly of Moore Ditch ?

Fal. Thou haſt the moſt vnſauoury ſmiles, and art indeed the moſt comparatiue raſcallieſt, ſweet yong Prince. But *Hal*, I prythee trouble me no more with vanity, I wold thou and I knew, where a Commodity of good names were to be bought : an olde Lord of the Councell rated me the other day in the ſtreet about you ſir ; but I mark'd him not, and yet hee talk'd very wiſely, but I regarded him not, and yet he talkt wiſely, and in the ſtreet too.

Prin. Thou didſt well: for no man regards it.

Fal. O, thou haſt damnable iteration, and art indeede able to corrupt a Saint. Thou haſt done much harme vnto me *Hall*, God forgiue thee for it. Before I knew thee *Hal*, I knew nothing: and now I am (if a man ſhold ſpeake truly) little better then one of the wicked. I muſt giue ouer this life, and I will giue it ouer : and I do not, I am a Villaine. Ile be damn'd for neuer a Kings ſonne in Chriſtendome.

Prin. Where ſhall we take a purſe to morrow, Iacke?

Fal. Where thou wilt Lad, Ile make one : and I doe not, call me Villaine, and baffle me.

Prin. I ſee a good amendment of life in thee : From Praying, to Purſe-taking.

Fal. Why, *Hal*, 'tis my Vocation *Hal* : 'Tis no ſin for a man to labour in his Vocation.

Pointz. Now ſhall wee know if Gads hill haue ſet a Watch. O, if men were to be ſaued by merit, what hole in Hell were hot enough for him ? This is the moſt omnipotent Villaine, that euer cryed, Stand, to a true man.

Prin. Good morrow *Ned*.

Pointz.

Signature 159.

Pages 89 and 90 of *The Second Part of King Henry the Fourth* are wrongly numbered 91 and 92.

On page 89 (91), if you read across both columns on the last line of the page, beginning on the initial N of the word 'Nor'; on all letters of the words; spelling NOCAB, you will arrive at the initial B of the name *Bullingbrooke*. The signature thus runs from the first letter of the first word to the first letter of the last word.

If you care to capitalize the letters, the figure may be shown thus: —

'NOr do i as an enemie to peaCe hAue since mis-carryed vnder Bullingbrooke'
NO············ ····· ····C· ·A·· ····· ·· ······ ···· B···········

Compare this signature with that on the first page of *Pericles*.

Haſt. Wee haue ſent forth alreadie.

Biſh. 'Tis well done.
My Friends, and Brethren (in theſe great Affaires)
I muſt acquaint you, that I haue receiu'd
New-dated Letters from *Northumberland*:
Their cold intent, tenure, and ſubſtance thus.
Here doth hee wiſh his Perſon, with ſuch Powers
As might hold ſortance with his Qualitie,
The which hee could not leuie: whereupon
Hee is retyr'd, to ripe his growing Fortunes,
To Scotland; and concludes in heartie prayers,
That your Attempts may ouer-liue the hazard,
And feareſull meeting of their Oppoſite.

Mow. Thus do the hopes we haue in him, touch ground,
And daſh themſelues to pieces.

Enter a Meſſenger.

Haſt. Now? what newes?

Meſſ. Weſt of this Forreſt, ſcarcely off a mile,
In goodly forme, comes on the Enemie:
And by the ground they hide, I iudge their number
Vpon, or neere, the rate of thirtie thouſand.

Mow. The iuſt proportion that we gaue them out,
Let vs ſway-on, and face them in the field.

Enter Weſtmerland.

Biſh. What well-appointed Leader fronts vs here?

Mow. I thinke it is my Lord of Weſtmerland.

Weſt. Health, and faire greeting from our Generall,
The Prince, Lord *Iohn*, and Duke of Lancaſter.

Biſh. Say on (my Lord of Weſtmerland) in peace:
What doth concerne your comming?

Weſt. Then (my Lord)
Vnto your Grace doe I in chiefe addreſſe
The ſubſtance of my Speech. If that Rebellion
Came like it ſelfe, in baſe and abiect Routs,
Led on by bloodie Youth, guarded with Rage,
And countenanc'd by Boyes, and Beggerie:
I ſay, if damn'd Commotion ſo appeare,
In his true, natiue, and moſt proper ſhape,
You (Reuerend Father, and theſe Noble Lords)
Had not beene here, to dreſſe the ougly forme
Of baſe, and bloodie Inſurrection,
With your faire Honors. You, Lord Arch-biſhop,
Whoſe Sea is by a Ciuill Peace maintain'd,
Whoſe Beard, the Siluer Hand of Peace hath touch'd,
Whoſe Learning, and good Letters, Peace hath tutor'd,
Whoſe white Inueſtments figure Innocence,
The Doue, and very bleſſed Spirit of Peace.
Wherefore doe you ſo ill tranſlate your ſelfe,
Out of the Speech of Peace, that beares ſuch grace,
Into the harſh and boyſtrous Tongue of Warre?
Turning your Bookes to Graues, your Inke to Blood,
Your Pennes to Launces, and your Tongue diuine
To a lowd Trumpet, and a Point of Warre.

Biſh. Wherefore doe I this? ſo the Queſtion ſtands.
Brieſely to this end: Wee are all diſeas'd,
And with our ſurfetting, and wanton howres,
Haue brought our ſelues into a burning Feuer,
And wee muſt bleede for it: of which Diſeaſe,
Our late King *Richard* (being infected) dy'd.
But (my moſt Noble Lord of Weſtmerland)
I take not on me here as a Phyſician,
Nor doe I, as an Enemie to Peace,

Troope in the Throngs of Militarie men:
But rather ſhew a while like feareſull Warre,
To dyet ranke Mindes, ſicke of happineſſe,
And purge th'obſtructions, which begin to ſtop
Our very Veines of Life: heare me more plainely.
I haue in equall ballance iuſtly weigh'd,
What wrongs our Arms may do, what wrongs we ſuffer,
And finde our Griefes heauier then our Offences.
Wee ſee which way the ſtreame of Time doth runne,
And are enforc'd from our moſt quiet there,
By the rough Torrent of Occaſion,
And haue the ſummarie of all our Griefes
(When time ſhall ſerue) to ſhew in Articles;
Which long ere this, wee offer'd to the King,
And might, by no Suit, gayne our Audience:
When wee are wrong'd, and would vnfold our Griefes,
Wee are deny'd acceſſe vnto his Perſon,
Euen by thoſe men, that moſt haue done vs wrong.
The dangers of the dayes but newly gone,
Whoſe memorie is written on the Earth
With yet appearing blood; and the examples
Of euery Minutes inſtance (preſent now)
Hath put vs in theſe ill-beſeeming Armes:
Not to breake Peace, or any Branch of it,
But to eſtabliſh here a Peace indeede,
Concurring both in Name and Qualitie.

Weſt. When euer yet was your Appeale deny'd?
Wherein haue you beene galled by the King?
What Peere hath beene ſuborn'd, to grate on you,
That you ſhould ſeale this lawleſſe bloody Booke
Of forg'd Rebellion, with a Seale diuine?

Biſh. My Brother generall, the Common-wealth,
I make my Quarrell, in particular.

Weſt. There is no neede of any ſuch redreſſe:
Or if there were, it not belongs to you.

Mow. Why not to him in part, and to vs all,
That feele the bruizes of the dayes before,
And ſuffer the Condition of theſe Times
To lay a heauie and vnequall Hand vpon our Honors?

Weſt. O my good Lord *Mowbray*,
Conſtrue the Times to their Neceſſities,
And you ſhall ſay (indeede) it is the Time,
And not the King, that doth you iniuries.
Yet for your part, it not appeares to me,
Either from the King, or in the preſent Time,
That you ſhould haue an ynch of any ground
To build a Griefe on: were you not reſtor'd
To all the Duke of Norfolkes Seignories,
Your Noble, and right well-remembred Fathers?

Mow. What thing, in Honor, had my Father loſt,
That need to be reuiu'd, and breath'd in me?
The King that lou'd him, as the State ſtood then,
Was forc'd, perforce compell'd to baniſh him:
And then, that *Henry Bullingbrooke* and hee
Being mounted, and both rowſed in their Seates,
Their neighing Courſers daring of the Spurre,
Their armed Staues in charge, their Beauers downe,
Their eyes of fire, ſparkling through ſights of Steele,
And the lowd Trumpet blowing them together:
Then, then, when there was nothing could haue ſtay'd
My Father from the Breaſt of *Bullingbrooke*;
O, when the King did throw his Warder downe,
(His owne Life hung vpon the Staffe hee threw)
Then threw hee downe himſelfe, and all their Liues,
That by Indictment, and by dint of Sword,
Haue ſince miſ-carryed vnder *Bullingbrooke*.

gg 3   *Weſt.* You

Signature 161.

These acrostics are found in the 'Epilogue' to the first and second parts of *Henry the Fourth*. The page bears no page-number. (See p. 419.)

Note that the *capital* initials down the *outside* left-hand side of the 'Epilogue' are

F
F
B

Note also the capitals clustered against the large ornamental F.

F IRST
   M
   A

The capital R in this cluster is of interest because there is not one initial R in the whole page.

Note that the M falls under the I R, and that the A falls under the M. Here we have the suggestion of the word 'FIRMA.'

Begin to read from the big F of the word 'FIRST'; to the right; downwards; treating the capitals FIRST as if they were initials; on the initials of the words of the text; spelling FIRMA, you will arrive at the capital A in the cluster. Go on continuously on the initials of the words; downwards and throughout the 'Epilogue' and back, until you have spelled MEDIOCRIA: you will again arrive at the capital A in the cluster. The same result will happen if you begin to read from the capital M in the cluster to the left; downwards; throughout the 'Epilogue'; on the initials (but treating F I R S T as initials); spelling MEDIOCRIA FIRMA; at the end of the spelling of each word you will arrive at the same capital A in the cluster; having spelled Bacon's posy or motto.

Note that 'Firma' is the Latin word for 'Signature.' Here, perhaps, is a *double entente*, a hint to some fellow cipherer.

Signature 162.

F I R S T MYFEARETHENMYCURTSIELASTMYSPEECH
M Y FEAREISYOURDISPLEASUREMYCURTSIEMYDUTIE
A N D MYSPEECHTOBEGGEYOURPARDONSIFYOULOOKEFORA

These are the first three lines, begun by the word 'F I R S T,' and
the front capitals of which contain the word F I R M A

Begin to read on the large initial F; to the right; downwards; on
all the letters of all the words; spelling Firma Mediocria, you
will arrive at the last letter (A) of the third line.

The acrostic figure here is: —

F I R M A M E D I O C R I A

If you looke for   A

Signature 163.

Now begin to read from the capital B of the word 'But' at the beginning of the last line of the 'Epilogue'; to the right; upwards; on the initials of the words (until you come to F I R S T, which we still count as initials); spelling BACONOCSICNARF, you will arrive at the big initial F of the word 'F I R S T.'

The acrostic figure here is:—

F^R
   A
    N
     C
      I
       S
        C

Dance out Of your debt

       N

      O

     C

   A

But

Signature 164.

Begin to read from the capital B of the word 'But' again; to the left; upwards; on the initials of the words; spelling BACONO, you will arrive at the initial O of the word 'One,' which begins 'One word more.'

The acrostic figure here is:—

One word more,
N
O
C
A
But (indeed) to pray for the Queene.

EPILOGVE.

FIRST, *my Feare: then, my Curtsie: last, my Speech.*
My Feare, is your Displeasure: My Curtsie, my Dutie:
And my Speech, to Begge your Pardons. If you looke for a
good Speech now, you vndoe me: For what I haue to say, is
of mine owne making: and what (indeed) I should say, will
(I doubt) prooue mine owne marring. But to the Purpose,
and so to the Venture. Be it knowne to you (as it is very
well) I was lately heere in the end of a displeasing Play, to pray your Patience
for it, and to promise you a Better: I did meane (indeede) to pay you with this,
which if (like an ill Venture) it come vnluckily home, I breake: and you, my gentle Creditors lose. Heere I promist you I would be, and heere I commit my Bodie
to your Mercies: Bate me some, and I will pay you some, and (as most Debtors do)
promise you infinitely.

If my Tongue cannot entreate you to acquit me: will you command me to vse
my Legges? And yet that were but light payment, to Dance out of your debt: But
a good Conscience, will make any possible satisfaction, and so will I. All the Gentlewomen heere, haue forgiuen me, if the Gentlemen will not, then the Gentlemen
do not agree with the Gentlewowen, which was neuer seene before, in such an Assembly.

One word more, I beseech you: if you be not too much cloid with Fat Meate,
our humble Author will continue the Story (with Sir Iohn in it) and make you
merry, with faire Katherine of France: where (for any thing I know) Falstaffe shall dye of a sweat, vnlesse already he be kill'd with your hard Opinions:
For Old-Castle dyed a Martyr, and this is not the man. My Tongue is wearie,
when my Legs are too, I will bid you good night; and so kneele downe before.you:
But (indeed) to pray for the Queene.

Signature 165.

This acrostic is found in 'The Actors Names' of *The Life of Henry the Fift*.

I was attracted by the devotion of a whole page in the front of the play to 'The Actors Names'; and by the curious arrangement of the list. It is worth recording that if you begin to read from the capital initial B of the name 'Bullcalfe'; upwards; to the right or to the left; on the capitals alone; spelling BACON, you will arrive at the capital initial N of the word 'NAMES.'

Also, if you begin again to read from the capital initial B of the word 'Bullcalfe'; upwards; to the right or to the left; on the capitals alone; spelling BEN IONSON, you will again arrive at the initial N of the word 'NAMES.'

The acrostic figure here is:—

NAMES	NAMES
RVMOVR	RVMOVR
Clarence	Sonnes
Arch	Northumberland
Bullcalfe	Of
	Iustices
	Northumberlands
	Epilogue
	Bullcalfe

Note the initials $\frac{F}{B}$ of the words $\frac{\text{Feeble}}{\text{Bullcalfe}}$; and the initials $\frac{B}{I}$ of the words $\frac{\text{Both}}{\text{Iustices}}$; and that the name BACON begins from the word 'Bullcalfe' and the name IONSON from the word 'Iustices.'

THE
ACTORS
NAMES.

RVMOVR the Presentor.
King *Henry* the Fourth.
Prince *Henry*, afterwards Crowned King *Henrie* the Fift.
Prince *Iohn* of Lancaster.
Humphrey of Gloucester. } Sonnes to *Henry* the Fourth, & brethren to *Henry* 5.
Thomas of Clarence.

Northumberland.
The Arch Byshop of Yorke.
Mowbray.
Hastings.   } Opposites against King *Henrie* the
Lord Bardolfe.   Fourth.
Trauers.
Morton.
Coleuile.

Warwicke.   Pointz.
Westmerland.   Falstaffe.
Surrey.   } Of the Kings   Bardolphe. } Irregular
Gowre.   Partie.   Pistoll.   Humorists.
Harecourt.   Peto.
Lord Chiefe Iustice.   Page.

Shallow.   } Both Country
Silence.   Iustices.
Dauie, Seruant to Shallow.   Drawers   Northumberlands Wife.
Phang, and Snare, 2. Serieants   Beadles.   Percies Widdow.
Mouldie.   Groomes   Hostesse Quickly.
Shadow,   Doll Teare-sheete.
Wart.   } Country Soldiers   Epilogue.
Feeble.
Bullcalfe.

Signature 166.

This acrostic is found on the last page (95) of *The Life of Henry the Fift.*

Begin to read on the letter F of the word 'FINIS'; to the right; upwards; on the terminals of the words of the 'Chorus'; spelling FFRANCIS BACON, you will arrive at the terminal N of the word 'Pen,' which is the last word of the first line of the 'Chorus.'

The acrostic figure here is :—

Exet. Onely he hath not yet subscribed this :
Where your Maiestie demands, That the King of France
hauing any occasion to write for matter of Graunt, shall
name your Highnesse in this forme, and with this addition, in French : *Nostre trescher filæ Henry Roy d'Angleterre
Heretere de Fraunce :* and thus in Latine ; *Præclarissimus
Filius noster Henricus Rex Angliæ & Heres Franciæ.*

France. Nor this I haue not Brother so deny'd,
But your request shall make me let it passe.

England. I pray you then, in loue and deare allyance,
Let that one Article ranke with the rest,
And thereupon giue me your Daughter.

France. Take her faire Sonne, and from her blood rayse vp
Issue to me, that the contending Kingdomes
Of France and England, whose very shoares looke pale,
With enuy of each others happinesse,
May cease their hatred, and this deare Coniunction
Plant Neighbour-hood and Christian-like accord
In their sweet Bosomes that neuer Warre aduance
His bleeding Sword twixt England and faire France.

Lords Amen.

King Now welcome *Kate*, and beare me witnesse all,
That here I kisse her as my Soueraigne Queene.
Flourish

Quee God, the best maker of all Marriages,
Combine your hearts in one, your Realmes in one :
As Man and Wife being two, are one in loue,
So be there twixt your Kingdomes such a Spousall,
That neuer may ill Office, or fell Iealousie,
Which troubles oft the Bed of blessed Marriage,
Thrust in betweene the Pation of these Kingdomes,
To make diuorce of their incorporate League :
That English may as French, French Englishmen,
Receiue each other God speake this Amen.

All. Amen.

King. Prepare we for our Marriage : on which day,
My Lord of Burgundy wee'le take your Oath
And all the Peeres, for suretie of our Leagues.
Then shall I sweare to *Kate*, and you to me,
And may our Oathes well kept and prosp'rous be.
Senet   *Exeunt.*

Enter Chorus.

Thus farre with rough, and all-vnable Pen,
Our bending Author hath pursu'd the Story,
In little roome confining mightie men,
Mangling by starts the full course of their glory.
Small time : but in that small, most greatly liued
This Starre of England. Fortune made his Sword;
By which, the Worlds best Garden he atchieued :
And of it left his Sonne Imperiall Lord.
Henry the Sixt, in Infant Bands crown'd King
Of France and England, did this King succeed :
Whose State so many had the managing,
That they lost France, and made his England bleed :
Which oft our Stage hath showne ; and for their sake,
In your faire minds let this acceptance take.

FINIS.

Signature 167.

This acrostic is found on the first page of *The First Part of Henry the Sixt*. (See p. 428.)

Note the block of type at the top of the second column, which begins with the word 'Name' and which is broken off with the word 'bright—'.

Begin to read from the initial N of the word 'Name'; to the right; on the initials of the words of the text; downwards; spelling NOCAB, you will arrive at the initial B of the word 'bright—

The acrostic figure here is:—

Name
O
C
A
Bright—

Begin to read from the initial N of the word 'Name'; to the *left;* on the initials of the words of the text; downwards; spelling NOCAB, you will arrive at the initial B of the word 'bright—'; thus keying the cipher by reading either to the right or to the left.

The acrostic figure here is:—

Name
O
C
A
Bright —

Signature 168.

Now note on the second page of the play that the initials of the first two words of the first two lines of the second column are $\frac{F}{B}$ of the words $\frac{Farwell}{Bonfires.}$ (See p. 429.)

Treat the initials of the first words of all the lines of the text as if they were on a string, and begin to read from the initial F of the word 'Farwell'; down the column; up the next; down the next, etc.; spelling F BACON, you will again arrive at the initial N of the word 'Name,' which began the cipher on the first page. Thus we have this cipher doubly keyed from well-defined points in the typography.

The acrostic figure here is: —

Farwell
Bonfires
A
C
O
Name

Signature 169.

Begin again to read from the initial F of the word 'Farwell'; to the right (first word, second column, second page); downward; on all the capitals in the *text;* up the next column; down the next, etc.; spelling FRAVNCIS BACON, you will still arrive at the initial N of the word 'Name,' with which we began the cipher on the first page.

The acrostic figure here is: —

Farwell
R
A
V
N
C
I
S
B
A
C
O
Name

Signature 170.

Begin to read from the initial N of the word 'night,' which is the last word of the first line of the play; downwards; on the initials of the last words of the lines; and up the initials of the last words of the lines on the next column; spelling backwards NOCAB, you will arrive at the initial B of the word 'bright,' with which we ended the first signature in the play. (See p. 428.)

The acrostic figure here is: —

Night
O
C
A
Bright

We thus have the words 'night' and 'bright,' the initials of which are the end letters of the name BACON, keyed from opposite ends of four facing columns.

Signature 171.

This acrostic is found in the last block of type of the second column of the first page of *The First Part of Henry the Sixt;* that is to say, in the block of type which follows the words '*Enter a Messenger.*'

We have already found the acrostic name BACON in the upper block of type in this column.

Begin to read from the initial M of the word 'Miseries,' which is the last word in the column; to the left; upwards; on the terminals; spelling MALUREV (= Verulam), you will arrive at the initial terminal V of the word 'vs'd,' in the line:—

'*Exe.* How were they lost? what trecherie was vs'd?'

Begin again to read from this initial terminal 'v' of the word 'vs'd'; to the left; upwards; on the terminals; spelling VERULAM, you will arrive at the initial M of the word 'My,' thus keying the title from the initial of the last word to the initial of the first word. This is a 'weak' acrostic.

The acrostic figure here is: —

My honourable Lords, health to you all:

A
  L
    U
     R
      E
       Vs'd [21st line from bottom.]
       E
       R
      U
     L
      A
       Miseries.

Enter

Note that in reading this acrostic the title must be spelled with the letters Verulam, and not with the letters Uerulam, i. e., 'MalureV' and not 'MalureU.' Though the V and U are often used for one another in the lower case, they were not so used in the initial capitals. A capital V was often used for a capital U, but a capital U was not used for a capital V.

The first Part of Henry the Sixt.

Actus Primus. Scœna Prima.

Dead March.

Enter the Funerall of King Henry the Fift, attended on by the Duke of Bedford, Regent of France ; the Duke of Gloster, Protector; the Duke of Exeter War-wicke, the Bishop of Winchester, and the Duke of Somerset.

Bedford.

HVng be y heauens with black, yield day to night;
Comets importing change of Times and States,
Brandish your crystall Tresses in the Skie,
And with them scourge the bad reuolting Stars,
That haue consented vnto Henries death :
King Henry the Fift, too famous to liue long,
England ne're lost a King of so much worth.

Glost. England ne re had a King vntill his time:
Vertue he had, deseruing to command,
His brandisht Sword did blinde men with his beames,
His Armes spred wider then a Dragons Wings :
His sparkling Eyes, replcat with wrathfull fire,
More dazled and droue back his Enemies,
Then mid-day Sunne, fierce bent against their faces.
What should I say? his Deeds exceed all speech :
He ne're lift vp his Hand, but conquered.

Exe. We mourne in black, why mourn we not in blood?
Henry is dead, and neuer shall reuiue:
Vpon a Woodden Coffin we attend;
And Deaths dishonourable Victorie,
We with our stately presence glorifie,
Like Captiues bound to a Triumphant Carre.
What? shall we curse the Planets of Mishap,
That plotted thus our Glories ouerthrow?
Or shall we thinke the subtile-witted French,
Coniurers and Sorcerers, that afraid of him,
By Magick Verses haue contriu'd his end.

Winch. He was a King, blest of the King of Kings.
Vnto the French, the dreadfull Iudgement-Day
So dreadfull will not be, as was his sight.
The Battailes of the Lord of Hosts he fought :
The Churches Prayers made him so prosperous,

Glost. The Church? where is it?
Had not Church-men pray'd,
His thred of Life had not so soone decay'd.
None doe you like, but an effeminate Prince,
Whom like a Schoole-boy you may ouer-awe.

Winch. Gloster, what ere we like, thou art Protector,
And lookest to command the Prince and Realme.
Thy Wife is prowd, she holdeth thee in awe,
More then God or Religious Church-men may.

Glost. Name not Religion, for thou lou'st the Flesh,
And ne're throughout the yeere to Church thou go'st,
Except it be to pray against thy foes.

Bed. Cease, cease these Iarres, & rest your minds in peace:
Let's to the Altar: Heralds wayt on vs;
In stead of Gold, wee'le offer vp our Armes,
Since Armes auayle not, now that Henry's dead,
Posteritie await for wretched yeeres,
When at their Mothers moistned eyes, Babes shall suck,
Our Ile be made a Nourish of salt Teares,
And none but Women left to wayle the dead.
Henry the Fift, thy Ghost I inuocate:
Prosper this Realme, keepe it from Ciuill Broyles,
Combat with aduerse Planets in the Heauens;
A farre more glorious Starre thy Soule will make,
Then Iulius Cæsar, or bright----

Enter a Messenger.

Mess. My honourable Lords, health to you all :
Sad tidings bring I to you out of France,
Of losse of slaughter, and discomfiture:
Guyen, Champaigne, Rheimes, Orleance,
Paris, Guysors, Poictiers, are all quite lost.

Bedf. What say'st thou man, before dead Henry's Coarse?
Speake softly, or the losse of those great Townes
Will make him burst his Lead, and rise from death.

Glost. Is Paris lost? is Roan yeelded vp?
If Henry were recall'd to life againe,
These news would cause him once more yeeld the Ghost.

Exe. How were they lost? what trecherie was vs'd?

Mess. No trecherie, but want of Men and Money.
Amongst the Souldiers this is muttered,
That here you maintaine seuerall Factions :
And whil'st a Field should be dispatcht and fought,
You are disputing of your Generals.
One would haue lingring Warres, with little cost;
Another would flye swift, but wanteth Wings :
A third thinkes, without expence at all,
By guilefull faire words, Peace may be obtayn'd.
Awake, awake, English Nobilitie,
Let not slouth dimme your Honors, new begot;
Cropt are the Flower-de-Luces in your Armes
Of Englands Coat, one halfe is cut away.

Exe. Were our Teares wanting to this Funerall,
These Tidings would call forth her flowing Tides.

Bedf. Me they concerne, Regent I am of France :
Giue me my steeled Coat, Ile fight for France.
Away with these disgracefull wayling Robes;
Wounds will I lend the French in stead of Eyes,
To weepe their intermissiue Miseries.

Enter

Enter to them another Messenger.

Mess. Lords view these Letters, full of bad mischance.
France is reuolted from the English quite,
Except some petty Townes, of no import.
The Dolphin *Charles* is crowned King in Rheimes:
The Bastard of Orleance with him is ioyn'd:
Reynold, Duke of Aniou, doth take his part,
The Duke of Alanson flyeth to his side.   *Exit.*

Exe. The Dolphin crown d King? all flye to him?
O whither shall we flye from this reproach?
Glost. We will not flye, but to our enemies throats.
Bedford, if thou be slacke, Ile fight it out.
Bed. *Gloster,* why doubtst thou of my forwardnesse?
An Army haue I muster'd in my thoughts,
Wherewith already France is ouer-run.

Enter another Messenger.

Mess. My gracious Lords, to adde to your laments,
Wherewith you now bedew King *Henries* hearse,
I must informe you of a dismall fight,
Betwixt the stout Lord *Talbot,* and the French.
Win. What? wherein *Talbot* ouercame, is't so?
3.Mess. O no: wherein Lord *Talbot* was o'rethrown!
The circumstance Ile tell you more at large.
The tenth of August last, this dreadfull Lord,
Retyring from the Siege of Orleance,
Hauing full scarce six thousand in his troupe,
By three and twentie thousand of the French
Was round incompassed, and set vpon:
No leysure had he to enranke his men.
He wanted Pikes to set before his Archers:
In stead whereof, sharpe Stakes pluckt out of Hedges
They pitched in the ground confusedly,
To keepe the Horsemen off, from breaking in.
More then three houres the fight continued:
Where valiant *Talbot,* aboue humane thought,
Enacted wonders with his Sword and Lance.
Hundreds he sent to Hell, and none durst stand him:
Here, there, and euery where enrag'd, he slew.
The French exclaym'd, the Deuill was in Armes,
All the whole Army stood agaz'd on him.
His Souldiers spying his vndaunted Spirit,
A *Talbot,* a *Talbot,* cry'd out amaine,
And rusht into the Bowels of the Battaile.
Here had the Conquest fully beene seal'd vp,
If Sir *Iohn Falstaffe* had not play'd the Coward.
He being in the Vauward, plac't behinde,
With purpose to relieue and follow them,
Cowardly fled, not hauing struck one stroake.
Hence grew the generall wrack and massacre:
Enclosed were they with their Enemies.
A base Wallon, to win the Dolphins grace,
Thrust *Talbot* with a Speare into the Back,
Whom all France, with their chiefe assembled strength,
Durst not presume to looke once in the face.
Bedf. Is *Talbot* slaine then? I will slay my selfe,
For liuing idly here, in pompe and ease,
Whil'st such a worthy Leader, wanting ayd,
Vnto his dastard foe-men is betray'd.
3.Mess. O no, he liues, but is tooke Prisoner,
And Lord *Scales* with him, and Lord *Hungerford:*
Most of the rest slaughter'd, or tooke likewise.
Bedf. His Ransome there is none but I shall pay.
Ile hale the Dolphin headlong from his Throne,
His Crowne shall be the Ransome of my friend:
Foure of their Lords Ile change for one of ours.

Farwell my Masters, to my Taske will I,
Bonfires in France forthwith I am to make,
To keepe our great Saint *Georges* Feast withall.
Ten thousand Souldiers with me I will take,
Whose bloody deeds shall make all Europe quake.
3.Mess. So you had need, for Orleance is besieg'd,
The English Army is growne weake and faint:
The Earle of Salisbury craueth supply,
And hardly keepes his men from mutinie,
Since they so few, watch such a multitude.
Exe. Remember Lords your Oathes to *Henry* sworne:
Eyther to quell the Dolphin vtterly,
Or bring him in obedience to your yoake.
Bedf. I doe remember it, and here take my leaue,
To goe about my preparation.   *Exit Bedford.*
Glost. Ile to the Tower with all the hast I can,
To view th'Artillerie and Munition,
And then I will proclayme young *Henry* King.
    Exit Gloster.
Exe. To Eltam will I, where the young King is,
Being ordayn'd his speciall Gouernor,
And for his safetie there Ile best deuise.   *Exit.*
Winch. Each hath his Place and Function to attend:
I am left out; for me nothing remaines:
But long I will not be Iack out of Office.
The King from Eltam I intend to send,
And sit at chiefest Sterne of publique Weale.
    Exit.

Sound a Flourish.

*Enter Charles, Alanson, and Reignier, marching
with Drum and Souldiers.*

Charles. Mars his true mouing, euen as in the Heauens,
So in the Earth, to this day is not knowne.
Late did he shine vpon the English side:
Now we are Victors, vpon vs he smiles.
What Townes of any moment, but we haue?
At pleasure here we lye, neere Orleance:
Otherwhiles, the famisht English, like pale Ghosts,
Faintly besiege vs one houre in a moneth.
Alan. They want their Porredge, & their fat Bul Beeues:
Eyther they must be dyeted like Mules,
And haue their Prouender ty'd to their mouthes,
Or pitteous they will looke, like drowned Mice.
Reignier. Let's rayse the Siege: why liue we idly here?
Talbot is taken, whom we wont to feare:
Remayneth none but mad-brayn'd *Salisbury,*
And he may well in fretting spend his gall,
Nor men nor Money hath he to make Warre.
Charles. Sound, sound Alarum, we will rush on them.
Now for the honour of the forlorne French:
Him I forgiue my death, that killeth me,
When he sees me goe back one foot, or flye.   *Exeunt.*

*Here Alarum, they are beaten back by the
English, with great losse.*

Enter Charles, Alanson, and Reignier.

Charles. Who euer saw the like? what men haue I?
Dogges, Cowards, Dastards: I would ne're haue fled,
But that they left me 'midst my Enemies.
Reignier. *Salisbury* is a desperate Homicide,
He fighteth as one weary of his life:
The other Lords, like Lyons wanting foode,
Doe rush vpon vs as their hungry prey.

    k 3   *Alans. Froy-*

Signature 173.

This acrostic is found on the last two pages, 145 and 146, of *The Second Part of Henry the Sixt.* (See pp. 434, 435.)

Begin to read from the initial F of the word 'FINIS'; upwards; on the initials of the first words of the lines of the *text;* down the same on the next column; up the next, as on a string; spelling FRAN BACON, you will arrive at the initial N of the word 'Now,' which begins the first line of the second column of the preceding page of the play (p. 145).

Now note that the initial of the first word of the bottom line of that column is the B of the word 'But.'

Begin to read from the initial B of this word 'But'; up the initials of the first words of the lines of the text; spelling BACON, you will arrive at the initial N again of the same word 'Now' on which we ended the previous cipher.

The acrostic figure here is: —

      Now

  O   O

  C   C

  A   A

  But then,   B

               N

                  A

                    R

                      FINIS

If you oppose your selues to match Lord Warwicke.

Clif. Hence heape of wrath, foule indigested lumpe,
As crooked in thy manners, as thy shape.

Yor. Nay we shall heate you thorowly anon.

Clif. Take heede least by your heate you burne your selues:

King. Why Warwicke, hath thy knee forgot to bow?
Old Salsbury, shame to thy siluer haire,
Thou mad misleader of thy brain-sicke sonne,
What wilt thou on thy death-bed play the Ruffian?
And seeke for sorrow with thy Spectacles?
Oh where is Faith? Oh, where is Loyalty?
If it be banisht from the frostie head,
Where shall it finde a harbour in the earth?
Wilt thou go digge a graue to finde out Warre,
And shame thine honourable Age with blood?
Why art thou old, and want'st experience?
Or wherefore doest abuse it, if thou hast it?
For shame in dutie bend thy knee to me,
That bowes vnto the graue with mickle age.

Sal. My Lord, I haue considered with my selfe
The Title of this most renowned Duke,
And in my conscience, do'repute his grace
The rightfull heyre to Englands Royall seate.

King. Hast thou not sworne Allegeance vnto me?

Sal. I haue.

Ki. Canst thou dispense with heauen for such an oath?

Sal. It is great sinne, to sweare vnto a sinne;
But greater sinne to keepe a sinfull oath:
Who can be bound by any solemne Vow
To do a murd'rous deede, to rob a man,
To force a spotlesse Virgins Chastitie,
To reaue the Orphan of his Patrimonie,
To wring the Widdow from her custom'd right,
And haue no other reason for this wrong,
But that he was bound by a solemne Oath?

Qu. A subtle Traitor needs no Sophister.

King. Call Buckingham, and bid him arme himselfe.

Yorke. Call Buckingham, and all the friends thou hast,
I am resolu'd for death and dignitie.

Old Clif. The first I warrant thee, if dreames proue true

War. You were best to go to bed, and dreame againe,
To keepe thee from the Tempest of the field.

Old Clif. I am resolu'd to beare a greater storme,
Then any thou canst coniure vp to day:
And that Ile write vpon thy Burgonet,
Might I but know thee by thy housed Badge.

War. Now by my Fathers badge, old *Newils* Crest,
The rampant Beare chain'd to the ragged staffe,
This day Ile weare aloft my Burgonet,
As on a Mountaine top, the Cedar shewes,
That keepes his leaues inspight of any storme,
Euen to affright thee with the view thereof.

Old Clif. And from thy Burgonet Ile rend thy Beare,
And tread it vnder foot with all contempt,
Despight the Bearard, that protects the Beare.

Yo. Clif. And so to Armes victorious Father,
To quell the Rebels, and their Complices.

Rich. Fie, Charitie for shame, speake not in spight,
For you shall sup with Iesu Christ to night.

Yo Clif. Foule stygmaticke that's more then thou canst tell.

Ric. If not in heauen, you'l surely sup in hell. *Exeunt*

Enter Warwicke.

War. Clifford of Cumberland, 'tis Warwicke calles:
And if thou dost not hide thee from the Beare,

Now when the angrie Trumpet sounds alarum,
And dead mens cries do fill the emptie ayre,
Clifford I say, come forth and fight with me,
Proud Northerne Lord, Clifford of Cumberland,
Warwicke is hoarse with calling thee to armes.

Enter Yorke.

War. How now my Noble Lord? What all a-foot.

Yor. The deadly handed Clifford slew my Steed:
But match to match I haue encountred him,
And made a prey for Carrion Kytes and Crowes
Euen of the bonnie beast he loued so well.

Enter Clifford.

War. Of one or both of vs the time is come.

Yor. Hold Warwick: seek thee out some other chace
For I my selfe must hunt this Deere to death.

War. Then nobly Yorke, 'tis for a Crown thou fightst:
As I intend Clifford to thriue to day,
It greeues my soule to leaue theee vnassail'd. *Exit War.*

Clif. What seest thou in me Yorke?
Why dost thou pause?

Yorke. With thy braue bearing should I be in loue,
But that thou art so fast mine enemie.

Clif. Nor should thy prowesse want praise & esteeme,
But that 'tis shewne ignobly, and in Treason.

Yorke. So let it helpe me now against thy sword,
As I in iustice, and true right expresse it.

Clif. My soule and bodie on the action both.

Yor. A dreadfull lay, addresse thee instantly.

Clif. La fin Corrone les enmenes.

Yor. Thus Warre hath giuen thee peace, for y art still,
Peace with his soule, heauen if it be thy will.

Enter yong Clifford.

Clif. Shame and Confusion all is on the rout,
Feare frames disorder, and disorder wounds
Where it should guard. O Warre, thou sonne of hell,
Whom angry heauens do make their minister,
Throw in the frozen bosomes of our part,
Hot Coales of Vengeance. Let no Souldier flye.
He that is truly dedicate to Warre,
Hath no selfe-loue: nor he that loues himselfe,
Hath not essentially, but by circumstance
The name of Valour. O let the vile world end,
And the premised Flames of the Last day,
Knit earth and heauen together.
Now let the generall Trumpet blow his blast,
Particularities, and pettie sounds
To cease. Was't thou ordain'd (deere Father)
To loose thy youth in peace, and to atchieeue
The Siluer Liuery of aduised Age,
And in thy Reuerence, and thy Chaire-dayes, thus
To die in Ruffian battell? Euen at this sight,
My heart is turn'd to stone: and while 'tis mine,
It shall be stony. Yorke, not our old men spares:
No more will I their Babes, Teares Virginall,
Shall be to me, euen as the Dew to Fire,
And Beautie, that the Tyrant oft reclaimes,
Shall to my flaming wrath, be Oyle and Flax:
Henceforth, I will not haue to do with pitty.
Meet I an infant of the house of Yorke,
Into as many gobbits will I cut it
As wilde *Medea* yong *Absirtis* did.
In cruelty, will I seeke out my Fame.
Come thou new ruine of olde Cliffords house:
As did *Æneas* old *Anchyses* beare,
So beare I thee vpon my manly shoulders:
But then, *Æneas* bare a liuing loade;

o 3   Nothing

Nothing so heauy as these woes of mine.

Enter Richard, and Somerset to fight.

Rich. So lye thou there:
For vnderneath an Ale-house paltry signe,
The Castle in S. *Albons*, Somerset
Hath made the Wizard famous in his death:
Sword, hold thy temper; Heart, be wrathfull still:)
Priests pray for enemies, but Princes kill.
       Fight.   *Excursions.*

Enter King, Queene, and others.

Qu. Away my Lord, you are slow, for shame away.
King. Can we outrun the Heauens? Good *Margaret*
stay.
  Qu. What are you made of? You'l nor fight nor fly:
Now is it manhood, wisedome, and defence,
To giue the enemy way, and to secure vs
By what we can, which can no more but flye.
           Alarum a farre off.
If you be tane, we then should see the bottome
Of all our Fortunes: but if we haply scape,
(As well we may, if not through your neglect)
We shall to London get, where you are lou'd,
And where this breach now in our Fortunes made
May readily be stopt.

Enter Clifford.

Clif. But that my hearts on future mischeefe set,
I would speake blasphemy ere bid you flye:
But flye you must: Vncureable discomfite
Reignes in the hearts of all our present parts.
Away for your releefe, and we will liue
To see their day, and them our Fortune giue.
Away my Lord, away.   *Exeunt*

Alarum. Retreat. Enter Yorke, Richard, Warwicke,
and Soldiers, with Drum & Colours.

Yorke. Of Salsbury, who can report of him,
That Winter Lyon, who in rage forgets
Aged contusions, and all brush of Time:
And like a Gallant, in the brow of youth,
Repaires him with Occasion. This happy day
Is not it selfe, nor haue we wonne one foot,
If Salsbury be lost.
  Rich. My Noble Father:
Three times to day I holpe him to his horse,
Three times bestrid him: Thrice I led him off,
Perswaded him from any further act:
But still where danger was, still there I met him,
And like rich hangings in a homely house,
So was his Will, in his old feeble body,
But Noble as he is, looke where he comes.
Enter Salisbury.

Sal. Now by my Sword, well hast thou fought to day:
By'th'Masse so did we all. I thanke you *Richard.*
God knowes how long it is I haue to liue:
And it hath pleas'd him that three times to day
You haue defended me from imminent death.
Well Lords, we haue not got that which we haue,
'Tis not enough our foes are this time fled,
Being opposites of such repayring Nature.
  Yorke. I know our safety is to follow them,
For (as I heare) the King is fled to London,
To call a present Court of Parliament:
Let vs pursue him ere the Writs go forth.
What sayes Lord Warwicke, shall we after them?
  War. After them: nay before them if we can:
Now by my hand (Lords) 'twas a glorious day.
Saint Albons battell wonne by famous *Yorke*,
Shall be eterniz'd in all Age to come.
Sound Drumme and Trumpets, and to London all,
And more such dayes as these, to vs befall.   *Exeunt.*

FINIS.

Signature 174.

These acrostics are found in *The third Part of King Henry the Sixt.*

I find no acrostic in the front of the play.

Pages 165 and 166 are wrongly numbered 167 and 168. (See pp. 438, 439.)

Note on the wrongly numbered page 167 the passage which follows the direction, '*Takes off his Crowne,*' in the left-hand column; and ends before the direction, '*They leade him out forcibly.*'

We shall treat the block of type between these two directions, which is devoted to the uncrowning of King Edward.

Begin to read from the initial B of the word 'But'; to the right; downwards; on the initials of the words of the text; spelling BACON, you will arrive at the initial N of the word 'Now,' which is the initial of the first word of the last line of the passage with which we are dealing.

This name may be keyed by reading it from the same point to the same point, but downwards to the left instead of to the right.

The acrostic figure here is: —

      But Henry now shall, etc.
      A
      C
      O
      Now for a-while farewell, etc.

Signature 175.

We now turn to the next page, 168, which is also wrongly numbered. (See p. 439.)

Note that the initial of the last word of the first line of the first column of the page is the F of the word 'free.'

Note also that the last two words of the last line of the same column are 'by mee.'

Begin to read from the initial F of the word 'free'; to the right; on the initials of the words of the text; downwards; spelling FRAUNCIS BACON, you will arrive at the initial N of the word 'no' in the bracketed phrase '(for I command no more).'

Now begin to read from the initial B of the word 'by,' in the phrase 'by mee' at the bottom of the column; to the left; upwards; on the initials of the words of the text; spelling BACON, you will arrive at the initial N of the same word 'no' in the bracketed phrase '(for I command no more)'; thus keying the cipher.

The acrostic figure here is:—

But Warwicke, after God, thou set'st me Free
<pre>
                              R
                              A
                              V
                              N
                              C
                              I
                              S
                              B
                              A
                              C
                              O
        (for I command No more)
                              O
                              C
                              A
                           By mee.
</pre>

I regard this as a 'weak' acrostic, but print it, as it is sufficiently remarkable as it stands.

K. Edw. Yea, Brother of Clarence,
Art thou here too?
Nay then I see, that *Edward* needs must downe.
Yet *Warwicke*, in despight of all mischance,
Of thee thy selfe, and all thy Complices,
Edward will alwayes beare himselfe as King:
Though Fortunes mallice ouerthrow my State,
My minde exceedes the compasse of her Wheele.

Warw. Then for his minde, be *Edward* Englands King,

Takes off his Crowne.

But *Henry* now shall weare the English Crowne,
And be true King indeede: thou but the shadow.
My Lord of Somerset, at my request,
See that forthwith Duke *Edward* be conuey'd
Vnto my Brother Arch-Bishop of Yorke:
When I haue fought with *Pembrooke*, and his fellowes,
Ile follow you, and tell what answer
Lewis and the Lady *Bona* send to him.
Now for a-while farewell good Duke of Yorke.

They leade him out forcibly.

K. Ed. What Fates impose, that men must needs abide;
It boots not to resist both winde and tide. *Exeunt.*
Oxf. What now remaines my Lords for vs to do,
But march to London with our Soldiers?
War. I, that's the first thing that we haue to do,
To free King *Henry* from imprisonment,
And see him seated in the Regall Throne. *exit.*

Enter Riuers, and Lady Gray.

Riu. Madam, what makes you in this sodain change?
Gray. Why Brother *Riuers*, are you yet to learne
What late misfortune is befalne King *Edward*?
Riu. What losse of some pitcht battell
Against *Warwicke*?
Gray. No, but the losse of his owne Royall person.
Riu. Then is my Soueraigne slaine?
Gray. I almost slaine, for he is taken prisoner,
Either betrayd by falshood of his Guard,
Or by his Foe surpriz'd at vnawares:
And as I further haue to vnderstand,
Is new committed to the Bishop of Yorke,
Fell Warwickes Brother, and by that our Foe.
Riu. These Newes I must confesse are full of greefe,
Yet gracious Madam, beare it as you may,
Warwicke may loose, that now hath wonne the day.
Gray. Till then, faire hope must hinder liues decay:
And I the rather waine me from dispaire
For loue of *Edwards* Off-spring in my wombe:
This is it that makes me bridle passion,
And beare with Mildnesse my misfortunes crosse:
I, I, for this I draw in many a teare,
And stop the rising of blood-sucking sighes,
Least with my sighes or teares, I blast or drowne
King *Edwards* Fruite, true heyre to th'English Crowne.
Riu. But Madam,
Where is Warwicke then become?
Gray. I am inform'd that he comes towards London,
To set the Crowne once more on *Henries* head,
Guesse thou the rest, King *Edwards* Friends must downe.
But to preuent the Tyrants violence,
(For trust not him that hath once broken Faith)
Ile hence forthwith vnto the Sanctuary,

To saue (at least) the heire of *Edwards* right:
There shall I rest secure from force and fraud:
Come therefore let vs flye, while we may flye,
If *Warwicke* take vs, we are sure to dye. *exeunt.*

Enter Richard, Lord Hastings, and Sir William Stanley.

Rich. Now my Lord *Hastings*, and Sir *William Stanley*
Leaue off to wonder why I drew you hither,
Into this theefest Thicket of the Parke.
Thus stand the case: you know our King, my Brother,
Is prisoner to the Bishop here, at whose hands
He hath good vsage, and great liberty,
And often but attended with weake guard,
Come hunting this way to disport himselfe.
I haue aduertis'd him by secret meanes,
That if about this houre he make this way,
Vnder the colour of his vsuall game,
He shall heere finde his Friends with Horse and Men,
To set him free from his Captiuitie.

Enter King Edward, and a Huntsman with him.

Huntsman. This way my Lord,
For this way lies the Game.
King Edw. Nay this way man,
See where the Huntsmen stand.
Now Brother of Gloster, Lord Hastings, and the rest,
Stand you thus close to steale the Bishops Deere?
Rich. Brother, the time and case, requireth hast,
Your horse stands ready at the Parke-corner.
King Ed. But whether shall we then?
Hast. To Lyn my Lord,
And shipt from thence to Flanders.
Rich. Wel guest beleeue me, for that was my meaning
K. Ed. *Stanley*, I will requite thy forwardnesse.
Rich. But wherefore stay we? 'tis no time to talke.
K. Ed. Huntsman, what say'st thou?
Wilt thou go along?
Hunts. Better do so, then tarry and be hang'd.
Rich. Come then away, lets ha no more adoo.
K. Ed. Bishop farwell,
Sheeld thee from *Warwickes* frowne,
And pray that I may re-possesse the Crowne. *exeunt*

Flourish. Enter King Henry the sixt, Clarence, Warwicke, Somerset, young Henry, Oxford, Mountague, and Lieutenant.

K. Hen. M. Lieutenant, now that God and Friends
Haue shaken *Edward* from the Regall seate,
And turn'd my captiue state to libertie,
My feare to hope, my sorrowes vnto ioyes,
At our enlargement what are thy due Fees?
Lieu. Subiects may challenge nothing of their Sou'rains
But, if an humble prayer may preuaile,
I then craue pardon of your Maiestie.
K. Hen. For what, Lieutenant? For well vsing me?
Nay, be thou sure, Ile well requite thy kindnesse.
For that it made my imprisonment, a pleasure:
I, such a pleasure, as incaged Birds
Conceiue; when after many moody Thoughts,
At last, by Notes of Houshold harmonie,
They quite forget their losse of Libertie.

q   But

But *Warwicke*, after God, thou set'st me free,
And chiefely therefore, I thanke God, and thee,
He was the Author, thou the Inftrument.
Therefore that I may conquer Fortunes fpight,
By liuing low, where Fortune cannot hurt me,
And that the people of this bleffed Land
May not be punifht with my thwarting ftarres,
Warwicke, although my Head ftill weare the Crowne,
I here refigne my Gouernment to thee,
For thou art fortunate in all thy deed.
Warw. Your Grace hath ftill beene fam'd for vertuous,
And now may feeme as wife as vertuous,
By fpying and auoiding Fortunes malice,
For few men rightly temper with the Starres:
Yet in this one thing let me blame your Grace,
For chufing me, when *Clarence* is in place.
Clar. No *Warwicke*, thou art worthy of the fway,
To whom the Heau'ns in thy Natiuitie,
Adiudg'd an Oliue Branch, and Lawrell Crowne,
As likely to be bleft in Peace and Warre:
And therefore I yeeld thee my free confent.
Warw. And I chufe *Clarence* onely for Protector.
King. *Warwick* and *Clarence*, giue me both your Hands:
Now ioyne your Hands, & with your Hands your Hearts,
That no diffention hinder Gouernment:
I make you both Protectors of this Land,
While I my felfe will lead a priuate Life,
And in deuotion fpend my latter dayes,
To finnes rebuke, and my Creators prayfe.
Warw. What anfweres *Clarence* to his Soueraignes
will?
Clar. That he confents, if *Warwicke* yeeld confent,
For on thy fortune I repofe my felfe.
Warw. Why then, though loth, yet muft I be content:
Wee'le yoake together, like a double fhadow
To *Henries* Body, and fupply his place;
I meane, in bearing weight of Gouernment,
While he enioyes the Honor, and his eafe.
And *Clarence*, now then it is more then needfull,
Forthwith that *Edward* be pronounc'd a Traytor,
And all his Lands and Goods confifcate.
Clar. What elfe? and that Succeffion be determined.
Warw. I, therein *Clarence* fhall not want his part.
King. But with the firft, of all your chiefe affaires,
Let me entreat (for I command no more)
That *Margaret* your Queene, and my Sonne *Edward*,
Be fent for, to returne from France with fpeed:
For till I fee them here, by doubtfull feare,
My ioy of libertie is halfe eclips'd.
Clar. It fhall bee done, my Soueraigne, with all
fpeede.
King. My Lord of Somerfet, what Youth is that,
Of whom you feeme to haue fo tender care?
Somerf. My Liege, it is young *Henry*, Earle of Rich-
mond.
King. Come hither, Englands Hope:
Layes his Hand on his Head.
If fecret Powers fuggeft but truth
To my diuining thoughts,
This prettie Lad will proue our Countries bliffe.
His Lookes are full of peacefull Maieftie,
His Head by nature fram'd to weare a Crowne,
His Hand to wield a Scepter, and himfelfe
Likely in time to bleffe a Regall Throne:
Make much of him, my Lords; for this is hee
Muft helpe you more, then you are hurt by mee.

Enter a Pofte.

Warw. What newes, my friend?
Pofte. That *Edward* is efcaped from your Brother,
And fled (as hee heares fince) to Burgundie.
Warw. Vnfauorie newes: but how made he efcape?
Pofte. He was conuey'd by *Richard*, Duke of Glofter,
And the Lord *Haftings*, who attended him
In fecret ambufh, on the Forreft fide,
And from the Bifhops Huntfmen refcu'd him:
For Hunting was his dayly Exercife.
Warw. My Brother was too careleffe of his charge.
But let vs hence, my Soueraigne, to prouide
A falue for any fore, that may betide.   *Exeunt.*

Manet Somerfet, Richmond, and Oxford.

Som. My Lord, I like not of this flight of *Edwards*:
For doubtleffe, *Burgundie* will yeeld him helpe,
And we fhall haue more Warres befor't be long.
As *Henries* late prefaging Prophecie
Did glad my heart, with hope of this young *Richmond*:
So doth my heart mif-giue me, in thefe Conflicts,
What may befall him, to his harme and ours.
Therefore, Lord *Oxford*, to preuent the worft,
Forthwith wee'le fend him hence to Brittanie,
Till ftormes be paft of Ciuill Enmitie.
Oxf. I: for if *Edward* re-poffeffe the Crowne,
'Tis like that *Richmond*, with the reft, fhall downe.
Som. It fhall be fo: he fhall to Brittanie.
Come therefore, let's about it fpeedily.   *Exeunt.*

Flourifh. Enter Edward, Richard, Haftings,
and Souldiers.

Edw. Now Brother *Richard*, Lord *Haftings*, and the reft,
Yet thus farre Fortune maketh vs amends,
And fayes, that once more I fhall enterchange
My wained ftate, for *Henries* Regall Crowne.
Well haue we pafs'd, and now re-pafs'd the Seas,
And brought defired helpe from Burgundie,
What then remaines, we being thus arriu'd
From Rauenfpurre Hauen, before the Gates of Yorke,
But that we enter, as into our Dukedome?
Rich. The Gates made faft?
Brother, I like not this.
For many men that ftumble at the Threfhold,
Are well fore-told, that danger lurkes within.
Edw. Tufh man, aboadments muft not now affright vs:
By faire or foule meanes we muft enter in,
For hither will our friends repaire to vs.
Haft. My Liege, Ile knocke once more, to fummon
them.

Enter on the Walls, the Maior of Yorke,
and his Brethren.

Maior. My Lords,
We were fore-warned of your comming,
And fhut the Gates, for fafetie of our felues;
For now we owe allegeance vnto *Henry*.
Edw. But, Mafter Maior, if *Henry* be your King,
Yet *Edward*, at the leaft, is Duke of Yorke.
Maior. True, my good Lord, I know you for no
leffe.
Edw. Why, and I challenge nothing but my Dukedome,
As being well content with that alone.
                                        Rich. But

Signature 176.

This acrostic is found on the last page of *The Third Part of King Henry the Sixt.* (See p. 443.)

We shall deal solely with the text after the word '*Flourish*' and the entry of the King, down to the word 'Finis.'

Begin to read from the initial F of the word '*Flourish*'; to the right; on all initials; downward; throughout the column and over into the next column; spelling Frauncis Bacon, you will arrive at the initial N of the word ' not ' in the line (tenth from the top): —

'For yet I am not look'd on in the world.'

Now begin to read from the initial F of the word 'Finis'; to the right; upwards; on the initials of the words of the text; spelling Francis Bacon, you will arrive at the initial N of the same word ' not ' in the line quoted above.

I regard this as a weak acrostic, inasmuch as the word Frauncis is spelled Francis in the second acrostic half of the figure. But this is not a serious objection. The name was spelled with and without the U or V; and it was often spelled by Bacon with two small F's, thus, ' ffrauncis,' or ' ffrancis.' It is possible that the cipherer counted one V of a VV, in which case the two sides of the figure would be precisely similar.

The acrostic figure here is: —
Flourish

    R
      A
        U
          N
            C
              I
                S
                  B
                    A
                      C
                        O
For yet I am   O   Not look'd on, etc.
                    C
                  A
                B
              S
            I
          C
        N
      A
    R
FINIS

Signature 177.

The text of this passage seems to have been played with also.

Begin to read from the initial O of the word 'Once' at the beginning of the passage after the word '*Flourish*'; to the right; downwards; on the initials of the words, and over on the next column; spelling ONOCAB, you will arrive at the initial B of the word 'Boy,' in the line: —

'Come hither Besse, and let me kisse my Boy.'

Now begin to read from the initial F of the word 'For,' which begins the last line of the text; upwards; to the right; on the initials of the words of the *text;* spelling FRANCISCONOCAB, you will again arrive at the initial B of the same word 'Boy'; thus keying the cipher.

The figure seems to show how the sense of the text suggested the *double entente* which is apparent in the mechanism of the figure.

The acrostic figure here is: —

Once more we sit in Englands Royall Throne,
        N
                O
                        C
                                A
Come hither Besse, and let me kisse my   Boy.
                                A
                        C
                O
                N
I Seale vpon the lips Of this sweet Babe
                C
                S
        I
        C
    N
  A
R
For heere I hope begins our lasting ioy.

Note that the verb 'Seale' is spelled with a capital initial.

And so I was, which plainly signified,
That I should snarle, and bite, and play the dogge:
Then since the Heauens haue shap'd my Body so,
Let Hell make crook'd my Minde to answer it.
I haue no Brother, I am like no Brother:
And this word [Loue] which Gray-beards call Diuine,
Be resident in men like one another,.
And not in me: I am my selfe alone.
Clarence beware, thou keep'st me from the Light,
But I will sort a pitchy day for thee:
For I will buzze abroad such Prophesies,
That *Edward* shall be fearefull of his life,
And then to purge his feare, Ile be thy death.
King *Henry*, and the Prince his Son are gone,
Clarence thy turne is next, and then the rest,
Counting my selfe but bad, till I be best.
Ile throw thy body in another roome,
And Triumph *Henry*, in thy day of Doome.   *Exit.*

*Flourish. Enter King, Queene, Clarence, Richard, Hastings,
Nurse, and Attendants.*

    King. Once more we sit in Englands Royall Throne.
Re-purchac'd with the Blood of Enemies:
What valiant Foe-men, like to Autumnes Corne,
Haue we mow'd downe in tops of all their pride?
Three Dukes of Somerset, threefold Renowne,
For hardy and vndoubted Champions:
Two *Cliffords*, as the Father and the Sonne,
And two Northumberlands: two brauer men,
Ne're spurr'd their Coursers at the Trumpets sound.
With them, the two braue Beares, *Warwick* & *Montague*,
That in their Chaines fetter'd the Kingly Lyon,
And made the Forrest tremble when they roar'd.

Thus haue we swept Suspition from our Seate,
And made our Footstoole of Security.
Come hither *Besse*, and let me kisse my Boy:
Yong *Ned*, for thee, thine Vnckles, and my selfe,
Haue in our Armors watcht the Winters night,
Went all asoote in Summers scalding heate,
That thou might'st repossesse the Crowne in peace,
And of our Labours thou shalt reape the gaine.
    Rich. Ile blast his Haruest, if your head were laid,
For yet I am not look'd on in the world.
This shoulder was ordain'd so thicke, to heaue,
And heaue it shall some waight, or breake my backe,
Worke thou the way, and that shalt execute.
    King. Clarence and Gloster, loue my louely Queene,
And kis your Princely Nephew Brothers both.
    Cla. The duty that I owe vnto your Maiesty,
I Seale vpon the lips of this sweet Babe.
    Cla. Thanke Noble *Clarence*, worthy brother thanks.
    Rich. And that I loue the tree fró whence ÿ sprang'st:
Witnesse the louing kisse I giue the Fruite,
To say the truth, so *Iudas* kist his master,
And cried all haile, when as he meant all harme.
    King. Now am I seated as my soule delights,
Hauing my Countries peace, and Brothers loues.
    Cla. What will your Grace haue done with *Margaret*,
Reynard her Father, to the King of France
Hath pawn'd the Sicils and Ierusalem,
And hither haue they sent it for her ransome.
    King. Away with her, and waft her hence to France:
And now what rests, but that we spend the time
With stately Triumphes, mirthfull Comicke shewes,
Such as befits the pleasure of the Court.
Sound Drums and Trumpets, farwell sowre annoy,
For heere I hope begins our lasting ioy.   *Exeunt omnes*

FINIS.

Signature 178.

This acrostic is found on the first page of *The Tragedy of Richard the Third*.

Begin to read from the initial B of the word ' Brother,' which is the first word of the last line of the first column; upwards; on the capital initials of the first words of each line; spelling BACONO, you will arrive at the capital O at the upper right hand of the large N^O; thus keying the acrostic from bottom to top of the first column of the same sized capitals.

The acrostic figure here is: —

N Ow is the Winter, etc.
N
O
C
A
Brother, good day: etc.

It is also worth observing that if you begin to read from the initial B of the word ' Brother,' which is the last word of the text of the second column; to the right; on the outside letters of the text of the page; upwards; spelling BACONO, you will again arrive at the capital O, next to the large capital N.

Again, begin to read from the initial B of the word ' Brother,' which is the last word of the text of the second column; to the left; on the outside letters of the page; upwards; spelling BACONO, you will again arrive at the capital O, next to the large capital N.

The name is thus keyed to the same point in three routes, from the capital B of the word ' Brother,' at the left-hand bottom corner of the first column, in the one case; and at the right-hand bottom corner of the second column, in the second place; and in each case, on the outside letters of the text of the page.

The Tragedy of Richard the Third:
with the Landing of Earle Richmond, and the
Battell at Bosworth Field.

Actus Primus, Scœna Prima.

Enter Richard Duke of Gloster, solus.

Ow is the Winter of our Discontent,
Made glorious Summer by this Son of Yorke:
And all the clouds that lowr'd vpon our house
In the deepe bosome of the Ocean buried.
Now are our browes bound with Victorious Wreathes,
Our bruised armes hung vp for Monuments;
Our sterne Alarums chang'd to merry Meetings;
Our dreadfull Marches, to delightfull Measures.
Grim-visag'd Warre, hath smooth'd his wrinkled Front:
And now, in stead of mounting Barbed Steeds,
To fright the Soules of fearfull Aduersaries,
He capers nimbly in a Ladies Chamber,
To the lasciuious pleasing of a Lute.
But I, that am not shap'd for sportiue trickes,
Nor made to court an amorous Looking-glasse:
I, that am Rudely stampt, and want loues Maiesty,
To strut before a wonton ambling Nymph:
I, that am curtail'd of this faire Proportion,
Cheated of Feature by dissembling Nature,
Deform'd, vn-finish'd, sent before my time
Into this breathing World, scarse halfe made vp,
And that so lamely and vnfashionable,
That dogges barke at me, as I halt by them.
Why I (in this weake piping time of Peace)
Haue no delight to passe away the time,
Vnlesse to see my Shadow in the Sunne,
And descant on mine owne Deformity.
And therefore, since I cannot proue a Louer,
To entertaine these faire well spoken dayes,
I am determined to proue a Villaine,
And hate the idle pleasures of these dayes.
Plots haue I laide, Inductions dangerous,
By drunken Prophesies, Libels, and Dreames,
To set my Brother *Clarence* and the King
In deadly hate, the one against the other:
And if King *Edward* be as true and iust,
As I am Subtle, False, and Treacherous,
This day should *Clarence* closely be mew'd vp:
About a Prophesie, which sayes that G,
Of *Edwards* heyres the murtherer shall be.
Diue thoughts downe to my soule, here *Clarence* comes.

Enter Clarence, and Brakenbury, guarded.
Brother, good day: What meanes this armed guard

That waites vpon your Grace?
  Cla. His Maiesty tendring my persons safety,
Hath appointed this Conduct, to conuey me to th'Tower
  Rich. Vpon what cause?
  Cla. Because my name is *George*.
  Rich. Alacke my Lord, that fault is none of yours:
He should for that commit your Godfathers.
O belike, his Maiesty hath some intent,
That you should be new Christned in the Tower,
But what's the matter *Clarence*, may I know?
  Cla. Yea *Richard*, when I know: but I protest
As yet I do not: But as I can learne,
He hearkens after Prophesies and Dreames,
And from the Crosse-row pluckes the letter G:
And sayes, a Wizard told him, that by G,
His issue disinherited should be.
And for my name of *George* begins with G,
It followes in his thought, that I am he.
These (as I learne) and such like toyes as these,
Hath moou'd his Highnesse to commit me now.
  Rich. Why this it is, when men are rul'd by Women:
'Tis not the King that sends you to the Tower,
My Lady *Grey* his Wife, *Clarence* 'tis shee,
That tempts him to this harsh Extremity.
Was it not shee, and that good man of Worship,
Anthony Woodeuile her Brother there,
That made him send Lord *Hastings* to the Tower?
From whence this present day he is deliuered?
We are not safe *Clarence*, we are not safe.
  Cla. By heauen, I thinke there is no man secure
But the Queenes Kindred, and night-walking Heralds,
That trudge betwixt the King, and Mistris *Shore*.
Heard you not what an humble Suppliant
Lord *Hastings* was, for her deliuery?
  Rich. Humbly complaining to her Deitie,
Got my Lord Chamberlaine his libertie.
Ile tell you what, I thinke it is our way,
If we will keepe in fauour with the King,
To be her men, and weare her Liuery.
The iealous ore-worne Widdow, and her selfe,
Since that our Brother dub'd them Gentlewomen,
Are mighty Gossips in our Monarchy.
  Bra. I beseech your Graces both to pardon me,
His Maiesty hath straightly giuen in charge,
That no man shall haue priuate Conference
(Of what degree soeuer) with your Brother.
                                        Rich.

Signature 180.

Begin to read from the initial capital B of the word 'Beyond,' at the lower right-hand corner of the page; to the right; up through the two columns of the *Actus Primus;* on *all* the capitals of *all* the words; spelling Bacono, you will arrive at the capital O in the word **G**Ood.

The acrostic figure here is: —

> **G**Ood morrow, and well met.
>   N
>   O
>   C
>   A
>   Beyond.

The Famous History of the Life of
King HENRY the Eight.

THE PROLOGVE.

I Come no more to make you laugh, Things now,
That beare a Weighty, and a Serious Brow,
Sad, high, and working, full of State and woe:
Such Noble Scænes, as draw the Eye to flow
We now present. Those that can Pitty, heere
May (if they thinke it well) let fall a Teare,
The Subiect will deserue it. Such as giue
Their Money out of hope they may beleeue,
May heere finde Truth too. Those that come to see
Onely a show or two, and so agree,
The Play may passe: If they be still, and willing,
Ile vndertake may see away their shilling
R chly in two short houres. Onely they
That come to heare a Merry, Bawdy Play,
A noyse of Targets: Or to see a Fellow
In a long Motley Coate, garded with Yellow,
Will be deceyu'd. For gentle Hearers, know
To ranke our chosen Truth with such a show
As Foole, and Fight is, beside forfeyting
Our owne Braines, and the Opinion that we bring
To make that onely true, we now intend,
Will leaue vs neuer an vnderstanding Friend.
Therefore, for Goodnesse sake, and as you are knowne
The First and Happiest Hearers of the Towne,
Be sad, as we would make ye. Thinke ye see
The very Persons of our Noble Story,
As they were Liuing: Thinke you see them Great,
And follow'd with the generall throng, and sweat
Of thousand Friends: Then, in a moment, see
How soone this Mightinesse, meets Misery:
And if you can be merry then, Ile say,
A Man may weepe vpon his Wedding day.

Actus Primus. Scœna Prima.

*Enter the Duke of Norfolke at one doore. At the other,
the Duke of Buckingham, and the Lord
Aburgauenny.*

Buckingham.

Good morrow, and well met. How haue ye done
Since last we saw in France?

Norf. I thanke your Grace:
Healthfull, and euer since a fresh Admirer
Of what I saw there.

Buck. An vntimely Ague
Staid me a Prisoner in my Chamber, when
Those Sunnes of Glory, those two Lights of Men
Met in the vale of Andren.

Nor. 'Twixt Guynes and Arde,
I was then present, saw them salute on Horsebacke,
Beheld them when they lighted, how they clung
In their Embracement, as they grew together,
Which had they,
What foure Thron'd ones could haue weigh'd
Such a compounded one?

Buck. All the whole time
I was my Chambers Prisoner.

Nor. Then you lost
The view of earthly glory · Men might say
Till this time Pompe was single, but now married
To one aboue it selfe. Each following day
Became the next dayes master, till the last
Made former Wonders, it's. To day the French,
All Clinquant all in Gold, like Heathen Gods
Shone downe the English; and to morrow, they
Made Britaine, India: Euery man that stood,
Shew'd like a Mine. Their Dwarfish Pages were
As Cherubins, all gilt: the Madams too,
Not vs'd to toyle, did almost sweat to beare
The Pride vpon them, that their very labour
Was to them, as a Painting. Now this Maske
Was cry'de incompareable; and th'ensuing night,
Made it a Foole, and Begger. The two Kings
Equall in lustre, were now best, now worst
As presence did present them: Him in eye,
Still him in praise, and being present both,
'Twas said they saw but one, and no Discerner
Durst wagge his Tongue in censure, when these Sunnes
(For so they phrase 'em) by their Heralds challeng'd
The Noble Spirits to Armes, they did performe

E 3   Beyond

Signature 181.

This acrostic is found in the last page of *The Life of King Henry the Eight*. (See p. 453.)

Note that the initials of the last two words of the last two lines of the first column are $\frac{N}{F}$ of the words $\frac{\text{Name}}{\text{flourish}}$

Begin to read from the initial F of the word 'flourish'; to the left; upwards; throughout the column and back; on the initials of the words; spelling FRAUNCIS BACON, you will arrive at the initial N of the word 'Name.'

Begin to read from the same initial F of the same word 'flourish'; to the right; upwards; throughout the column and back; on the initials of the words; spelling FRAUNCIS BACON, you will arrive again at the same initial N of the word 'Name'; thus we key the cipher by reading it in two directions.

The acrostic figure here is:—

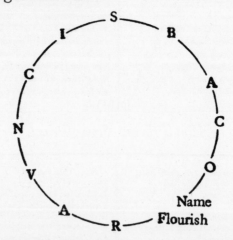

Note that in this play page 216 is wrongly numbered 218. I can see no acrostic in it.

Signature 182.

This acrostic is found in 'The Epilogue' on the last page of *The Life of King Henry the Eight*. (See p. 453.)

Begin to read from the initial T of the word 'THE' ('THE EPILOGUE'); to the right; downwards; through the whole 'Epilogue'; on all the letters of the words; spelling TINEVNI NOCAB ARF (Fra Bacon invenit), you will arrive at the initial F of the word 'FINIS.'

The acrostic figure here is:—

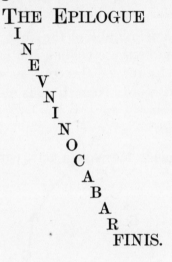

THE EPILOGUE
  I
   N
    E
     V
      N
       I
        N
         O
          C
           A
            B
             A
              R
               FINIS.

Signature 183.

This acrostic is found on the last column of the last page of *The Life of King Henry the Eight.*

Begin to read from the terminal S of the word ' branches,' which is the last word of the first line; to the left; downwards; on the terminals; spelling SAINT ALBANOCABSICNARFF, you will arrive at the initial F of the word ' FINIS.'

The acrostic figure here is: —

And like a Mountaine Cedar, reach his brancheS

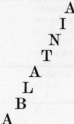

```
                          A
                         I
                        N
                       T
                      A
                     L
                    B
                   A
Thou hast made me Now a man, neuer before
                 O
                C
               A
              B
             S
            I
           C
          N
         A
        R
       F
      FINIS
```

Observe that in reading this acrostic, the words ' The Epilogue ' are common to both columns, and are therefore counted as a line here.

Holy and Heauenly thoughts still Counsell her:
She shall be lou'd and fear'd. Her owne shall blesse her;
Her Foes shake like a Field of beaten Corne,
And hang their heads with sorrow:
Good growes with her.
In her dayes, Euery Man shall eate in safety,
Vnder his owne Vine what he plants; and sing
The merry Songs of Peace to all his Neighbours.
God shall be truely knowne, and those about her,
From her shall read the perfect way of Honour,
And by those claime their greatnesse; not by Blood.
Nor shall this peace sleepe with her: But as when
The Bird of Wonder dyes, the Mayden Phoenix,
Her Ashes new create another Heyre,
As great in admiration as her selfe.
So shall she leaue her Blessednesse to One,
(When Heauen shal call her from this clowd of darknes)
Who, from the sacred Ashes of her Honour
Shall Star-like rise, as great in fame as she was,
And so stand fix'd. Peace, Plenty, Loue, Truth, Terror,
That were the Seruants to this chosen Infant,
Shall then be his, and like a Vine grow to him;
Where euer the bright Sunne of Heauen shall shine,
His Honour, and the greatnesse of his Name,
Shall be, and make new Nations. He shall flourish,

And like a Mountaine Cedar, reach his branches,
To all the Plaines about him: Our Childrens Children
Shall see this, and blesse Heauen.
  Kin. Thou speakest wonders.
  Cran. She shall be to the happinesse of England,
An aged Princesse; many dayes shall see her,
And yet no day without a deed to Crowne it.
Would I had knowne no more: But she must dye,
She must, the Saints must haue her; yet a Virgin,
A most vnspotted Lilly shall she passe
To th' ground, and all the World shall mourne her.
  Kin. O Lord Archbishop
Thou hast made me now a man, neuer before
This happy Child, did I get any thing.
This Oracle of comfort, ha's so pleas'd me,
That when I am in Heauen, I shall desire
To see what this Child does, and praise my Maker.
I thanke ye all. To you my good Lord Maior,
And you good Brethren, I am much beholding:
I haue receiu'd much Honour by your presence,
And ye shall find me thankfull. Lead the way Lords,
Ye must all see the Queene, and she must thanke ye,
She will be sicke els. This day, no man thinke
'Has businesse at his house; for all shall stay:
This Little-One shall make it Holy-day.   *Exeunt.*

THE EPILOGVE.

'Tis ten to one, this Play can neuer please
  All that are heere: Some come to take their ease,
And sleepe an Act or two; but those we feare
W'haue frighted with our Trumpets: so 'tis cleare,
They'l say tis naught. Others to heare the City
Abus'd extreamly, and to cry that's witty,
Which wee haue not done neither; that I feare
All the expected good w'are like to heare.
For this Play at this time, is onely in
The mercifull construction of good women,
For such a one we shew'd'em: If they smile,
And say twill doe; I know within a while,
  All the best men are ours; for 'tis ill hap,
  If they hold, when their Ladies bid'em clap.

FINIS.

Signature 184.

While we are dealing with *Henry the Eight*, we may as well notice a very pretty example of a cipher, thrown into a song. It occurs on page 218, in the 'Song' which stands in the left-hand column.

Note the plan of the initials: —

O^{Rpheus}

O Rpheus
And
Bow

.
.
.
.
.

Fall asleep, etc.

Begin to read from the initial F of the word 'Fall,' which is the first word of the last line; to the right; on all the letters of all the words; upwards; spelling FRANCISCO, you will arrive at the letter O in the word 'Billowes.' Continue to spell from the O of the word 'Billowes'; still going upwards; spelling ONOCAB, you will arrive at the B of the word 'Bow,' which is immediately under the large O.

The acrostic figure here is: —

      O R
        A
    Bow themselves, etc.
       A
        C
         O
          N
        BILLOWES
          C
         S
        I
        C
       N
       A
      R
     F

Ora Francisco Bacono.

Latinists may possibly object to this reading; in which case they may amuse themselves by discovering the word 'pro,' which is in the first three lines of the poem.

As we shall have other specimens planned like this, we may as well give the song in its detail: —

ORPHEUSWITHHISLUTEMADETREES
OANDTHEMOUNTAINETOPSTHATFREEZE
BOWTHEMSELUESWHENHEDIDSING
TOHISMUSICKEPLANTSANDFLOWERS
EUERSPRUNGASSUNNEANDSHOWERS
THEREHADMADEALASTINGSPRING
EUERYTHINGTHATHEARDHIMPLAY
EUENTHEBILLOWESOFTHESEA
HUNGTHEIRHEADS&THENLAYBY
INSWEETMUSICKEISSUCHART
KILLINGCARE&GRIEFEOFHEART
FALLASLEEPEORHEARINGDYE

The letters under which I have placed a mark are those of the cipher.

Actus Tertius. Scena Prima.

Enter Queene and her Women as at worke.

Queen. Take thy Lute wench,
My Soule growes sad with troubles,
Sing, and disperse 'em if thou canst: leaue working:

SONG.

Orpheus with his Lute made Trees,
    And the Mountaine tops that freeze,
Bow themselues when he did sing
To his Musicke, Plants and Flowers
Euer sprung; as Sunne and Showers,
    There had made a lasting Spring.
Euery thing that heard him play,
Euen the Billowes of the Sea,
Hung their heads, & then lay by.
In sweet Musicke is such Art,
Killing care, & griefe of heart,
Fall asleepe, or hearing dye.

Enter a Gentleman.

Queen. How now?

Gent. And't please your Grace, the two great Cardinals
Wait in the presence.

Queen. Would they speake with me?

Gent. They wil'd me say so Madam.

Queen. Pray their Graces
To come neere: what can be their busines
With me, a poore weake woman, falne from fauour?
I doe not like their comming; now I thinke on't,
They should bee good men, their affaires as righteous:
But all Hoods, make not Monkes.

Enter the two Cardinalls, Wolsey & Campian.

Wolf. Peace to your Highnesse.

Queen. Your Graces find me heere part of a Houswife,
(I would be all) against the worst may happen:
What are your pleasures with me, reuerent Lords?

Wol. May it please you Noble Madam, to withdraw
Into your priuate Chamber; we shall giue you
The full cause of our comming.

Queen. Speake it heere.
There's nothing I haue done yet o' my Conscience
Deserues a Corner: would all other Women
Could speake this with as free a Soule as I doe.
My Lords, I care not (so much I am happy
Aboue a number) if my actions
Were tri'de by eu'ry tongue, eu'ry eye saw 'em,
Enuy and base opinion set against 'em,
I know my life so euen. If your busines
Seeke me out, and that way I am Wife in;
Out with it boldly. Truth loues open dealing.

Card. *Tanta est erga te mentis integritas Regina serenissima.*

Queen. O good my Lord, no Latin;
I am not such a Truant since my comming,
As not to know the Language I haue liu'd in: (ous:
A strange Tongue makes my cause more strange, suspiti-
Pray speake in English; heere are some will thanke you,
If you speake truth, for their poore Mistris sake;
Beleeue me she ha's had much wrong. Lord Cardinall,
The willing'st sinne I euer yet committed,
May be absolu'd in English.

Card. Noble Lady,

I am sorry my integrity shoul breed,
(And seruice to his Maiesty and you)
So deepe suspition, where all faith was meant;
We come not by the way of Accusation,
To taint that honour euery good Tongue blesses;
Nor to betray you any way to sorrow;
You haue too much good Lady: But to know
How you stand minded in the waighty difference
Betweene the King and you, and to deliuer
(Like free and honest men) our iust opinions,
And comforts to our cause.

Camp. Most honour d Madam,
My Lord of Yorke, out of his Noble nature,
Zeale and obedience he still bore your Grace,
Forgetting (like a good man) your late Censure
Both of his truth and him (which was too farre)
Offers, as I doe, in a signe of peace,
His Seruice, and his Counsell.

Queen. To betray me.
My Lords, I thanke you both for your good wills,
Ye speake like honest men, (pray God ye proue so)
But how to make ye sodainly an Answere
In such a poynt of weight, so neere mine Honour,
(More neere my Life I feare) with my weake wit;
And to such men of grauity and learning;
In truth I know not. I was set at worke,
Among my Maids, full little (God knowes) looking
Either for such men, or such businesse;
For her sake that I haue beene, for I feele
The last fit of my Greatnesse; good your Graces
Let me haue time and Councell for my Cause:
Alas, I am a Woman frendlesse, hopelesse.

Wol. Madam,
You wrong the Kings loue with these feares,
Your hopes and friends are infinite.

Queen. In England,
But little for my profit can you thinke Lords,
That any English man dare giue me Councell?
Or be a knowne friend 'gainst his Highnes pleasure,
(Though he be growne so desperate to be honest)
And liue a Subiect? Nay forsooth, my Friends,
They that must weigh out my afflictions,
They that my trust must grow to, liue not heere,
They are (as all my other comforts) far hence
In mine owne Countrey Lords.

Camp. I would your Grace
Would leaue your greefes, and take my Counsell.

Queen. How Sir?

Camp. Put your maine cause into the Kings protection,
Hee's louing and most gracious. 'Twill be much,
Both for your Honour better, and your Cause:
For if the tryall of the Law o'retake ye,
You'l part away disgrac'd.

Wol. He tels you rightly.

Queen. Ye tell me what ye wish for both, my ruine:
Is this your Christian Councell? Out vpon ye.
Heauen is aboue all yet; there sits a Iudge,
That no King can corrupt.

Camp. Your rage mistakes vs.

Queen. The more shame for ye; holy men I thought ye,
Vpon my Soule two reuerend Cardinall Vertues;
But Cardinall Sins, and hollow hearts I feare ye:
Mend 'em for shame my Lords: Is this your comfort?
The Cordiall that ye bring a wretched Lady?
A woman lost among ye, laugh't at, scornd?
I will not wish ye halfe my miseries,

Signature 186.

Begin to read from the large initial I at the head of the text; to the left; downwards (note that the I brackets the two top lines); on the initials of the words; spelling INVENIT F BACON, you will arrive at the initial N of the first word 'Now' of the last line.

Note that the initials of F BACON fall on the initials of the words ('faire Beholders') which are in brackets, sixth line from the bottom.

Here the acrostic figure is: —

I NT
t T
  H
N
V
E
N
I
T
Faire
Beholders
A
C
O
Now good, etc.

Signature 188.

This acrostic is found in *The Tragedy of Coriolanus*, page 1.
Note the first line of the play:—

B Efore we proceed any further, heare me speake.

Note now the eleventh and twelfth lines: —

'No more talking on't; Let it be done, away, away
One word, good Citizens.'

Begin to read from the initial O of the word 'One'; to the right;
upwards; on the initials of the words of the text; spelling ONOCAB,

you will arrive at the initial **B** of the first line of the play.

Begin to read from the same big B; to the left; downwards; on
the initials of the words of the text; spelling BACONO, you will arrive
at the initial O of the word 'One'; thus keying the cipher.

In a correct sense this is not an acrostic because there is no visible
point for the base or butt. We rely here entirely on the amusing
double entente of the text itself.

B Efore we proceed any further, heare me speake.
A
C
O
N
One word, good Citizens.

Before the belching Whale; then is he yonder,
And there the straying Greekes, ripe for his edge,
Fall downe before him, like the mowers fwath;
Here, there, and euery where, he leaues and takes;
Dexteritie fo obaying appetite,
That what he will, he does, and does fo much,
That proofe is call'd impoffibility.

Enter Vliffes.

Vlif. Oh, courage, courage Princes: great *Achilles*
Is arming, weeping, curfing, vowing vengeance;
Patroclus wounds haue rouz'd his drowzie bloud,
Together with his mangled *Myrmidons,*
That nofeleffe, handleffe, hackt and chipt, come to him;
Crying on *Hector. Aiax* hath loft a friend,
And foames at mouth, and he is arm'd, and at it:
Roaring for *Troylus*; who hath done to day,
Mad and fantafticke execution;
Engaging and redeeming of himfelfe.
With fuch a careleffe force, and forceleffe care,
As if that luck in very fpight of cunning, bad him win all.

Enter Aiax.

Aia. Troylus thou coward Troylus.   *Exit.*
Dio. I, there, there.
Neft. So, fo, we draw together.   *Exit.*

Enter Achilles.

Achil. Where is this *Hector?*
Come, come, thou boy-queller, fhew thy face:
Know what it is to meete *Achilles* angry.
Hector, wher's *Hector?* I will none but *Hector.*   *Exit.*

Enter Aiax.

Aia. Troylus, thou coward Troylus, fhew thy head.

Enter Diomed.

Diom. Troylus, I fay, wher's *Troylus?*
Aia. What would'ft thou?
Diom. I would correct him.
Aia. Were I the Generall,
Thou fhould'ft haue my office.
Ere that correction: *Troylus* I fay, what *Troylus?*

Enter Troylus.

Troy. Oh traitour *Diomed!*
Turne thy falfe face thou traytor,
And pay thy life thou oweft me for my horfe.
Dio. Ha, art thou there?
Aia. Ile fight with him alone, ftand *Diomed.*
Dio. He is my prize, I will not looke vpon.
Troy. Come both you coging Greekes, haue at you
both.   *Exit Troylus.*

Enter Hector.

Hect. Yea *Troylus?* O well fought my yongeft Brother.

Enter Achilles.

Achil. Now doe I fee thee; haue at thee *Hector.*
Hect. Paufe if thou wilt.
Achil. I doe difdaine thy curtefie, proud Troian;
Be happy that my armes are out of vfe:
My reft and negligence befriends thee now,
But thou anon fhalt heare of me againe:
Till when, goe feeke thy fortune.   *Exit.*
Hect. Fare thee well:
I would haue beene much more a frefher man,
Had I expected thee: how now my Brother?

Enter Troylus.

Troy. Aiax hath tane *Æneas*; fhall it be?
No, by the flame of yonder glorious heauen,
He fhall not carry him: Ile be tane too,
Or bring him off: Fate heare me what I fay;

I wreake not, though thou end my life to day.   *Exit.*

Enter one in Armour.

Hect. Stand, ftand, thou Greeke,
Thou art a goodly marke:
No? wilt thou not? I like thy armour well,
Ile frufh it, and vnlocke the riuets all,
But Ile be maifter of it: wilt thou not beaft abide?
Why then flye on, Ile hunt thee for thy hide.   *Exit.*

Enter Achilles with Myrmidons.

Achil. Come here about me you my *Myrmidons:*
Marke what I fay; attend me where I wheele:
Strike not a ftroake, but keepe your felues in breath;
And when I haue the bloudy *Hector* found,
Empale him with your weapons round about:
In felleft manner execute your arme.
Follow me firs, and my proceedings eye;
It is decreed, *Hector* the great muft dye.   *Exit.*

Enter Therfites, Menelaus, and Paris.

Ther. The Cuckold and the Cuckold maker are at it:
now bull, now dogge, lowe; *Paris* lowe; now my double hen'd fparrow; lowe *Paris,* lowe; the bull has the
game: ware hornes ho?

Exit Paris and Menelaus.

Enter Baftard.

Baft. Turne flaue and fight.
Ther. What art thou?
Baft. A Baftard Sonne of Priams.
Ther. I am a Baftard too, I loue Baftards, I am a Baftard begot, Baftard inftructed, Baftard in minde, Baftard
in valour, in euery thing illegitimate: one Beare will not
bite another, and wherefore fhould one Baftard? take
heede, the quarrel's moft ominous to vs: if the Sonne of a
whore fight for a whore, he tempts iudgement: farewell
Baftard.
Baft. The diuell take thee coward.   *Exeunt.*

Enter Hector.

Hect. Moft putrified core fo faire without?
Thy goodly armour thus hath coft thy life:
Now is my daies worke done; Ile take good breath:
Reft Sword, thou haft thy fill of bloud and death.

Enter Achilles and his Myrmidons.

Achil. Looke *Hector* how the Sunne begins to fet;
How vgly night comes breathing at his heeles,
Euen with the vaile and darking of the Sunne.
To clofe the day vp, *Hectors* life is done.
Hect. I am vnarm'd, forgoe this vantage Greeke.
Achil. Strike fellowes, ftrike, this is the man I feeke.
So Illion fall thou: now Troy finke downe;
Here lyes thy heart, thy finewes, and thy bone.
On *Myrmidons,* cry you all a maine,
Achilles hath the mighty *Hector* flaine.   *Retreat.*
Harke, a retreat vpon our Grecian part.
Gree. The Troian Trumpets founds the like my Lord.
Achi. The dragon wing of night ore-fpreds the earth
And ftickler-like the Armies feperates
My halfe fupt Sword, that frankly would haue fed,
Pleas'd with this dainty bed; thus goes to bed.
Come, tye his body to my horfes tayle;
Along the field, I will the Troian traile.   *Exeunt.*

Sound Retreat. *Shout.*

Enter Agamemnon, Aiax, Menelaus, Neftor,
Diomed, and the reft marching.

Aga. Harke, harke, what fhout is that?
Neft. Peace Drums.

Sol Achille

Signature 187.

This acrostic is found in the left-hand column of the last page but one in *Troylus and Cressida*. This page *faces* the last page of the play.

Begin to read from the initial B of the first word of the first line of the column; down the column on the initial capitals of the first words of the lines; spelling BACONO, you will arrive at the initial O of the first word of the last line.

The acrostic figure here is : —

>   Before the, etc.
>   A
>   C
>   O
>   N
>   Or bring, etc.

Observe that if you begin to read from the initial B of the first word of the first line in the column; to the right; downwards; on the capitals of all the words (text and stage-directions); spelling BACONO, you will arrive at the initial O of the first word of the last line.

Observe again, that if you begin to read from the initial O of the first word of the last line in the column; to the right; upwards; on the capitals of all words (text and stage-directions); spelling ONOCAB, you will arrive at the initial B of the first word of the first line in the column.

We have here the name BACONO keyed to and from the same points by three routes in the same column.

The acrostic figure will be the same in each case.

The Prologue.

IN Troy there lyes the Scene : From Iles of Greece
The Princes Orgillous, their high blood chaf'd
Haue to the Port of Athens sent their shippes
Fraught with the ministers and instruments
Of cruell Warre : Sixty and nine that wore
Their Crownets Regall, from th' Athenian bay
Put forth toward Phrygia, and their vow is made
To ransacke Troy, within whose strong emures
The rauish'd Helen, Menelaus Queene,
With wanton Paris sleepes, and that's the Quarrell.
To Tenedos they come,
And the deepe-drawing Barke do there disgorge
Their warlike frautage : now on Dardan Plaines
The fresh and yet vnbruised Greekes do pitch
Their braue Pauillions.Priams six-gated City,
Dardan and Timbria, Helias, Chetas, Troien,
And Antenonidus with massie Staples
And corresponsiue and fulfilling Bolts
Stirre vp the Sonnes of Troy.
Now Expectation tickling skittish spirits,
On one and other side, Troian and Greeke,
Sets all on hazard. And hither am J come,
A Prologue arm'd, but not in confidence
Of Authors pen, or Actors voyce ; but suited
Jn like conditions, as our Argament ;
To tell you (faire Beholders) that our Play
Leapes ore the vaunt and firstlings of those broyles,
Beginning in the middle : starting thence away,
To what may be digested in a Play :
Like, or finde fault, do as your pleasures are,
Now good, or bad, 'tis but the chance of Warre.

The Tragedy of Coriolanus:

Actus Primus. Scœna Prima.

Enter a Company of Mutinous Citizens, with Staues,
Clubs, and other weapons.

1. Citizen.

BEfore we proceed any further, heare me speake.

All. Speake, speake.

1. Cit. You are all resolu'd rather to dy then to famish?

All. Resolu'd, resolu'd.

1. Cit. First you know, *Caius Martius* is chiefe enemy to the people.

All. We know't, we know't.

1. Cit. Let vs kill him, and wee'l haue Corne at our own price. Is't a Verdict?

All. No more talking on't; Let it be done, away, away

2. Cit. One word, good Citizens.

1. Cit. We are accounted poore Citizens, the Patricians good: what Authority surfets one, would releeue vs. If they would yeelde vs but the superfluitie while it were wholsome, wee might guesse they releeued vs humanely: But they thinke we are too deere, the leannesse that afflicts vs, the obiect of our misery, is as an inuentory to particularize their abundance, our sufferance is a gaine to them. Let vs reuenge this with our Pikes, ere we become Rakes. For the Gods know, I speake this in hunger for Bread, not in thirst for Reuenge.

2. Cit. Would you proceede especially against *Caius Martius.*

All. Against him first: He's a very dog to the Commonalty.

2. Cit. Consider you what Seruices he ha's done for his Country?

1. Cit. Very well, and could bee content to giue him good report for't, but that hee payes himselfe with beeing proud.

All. Nay, but speak not maliciously.

1. Cit. I say vnto you, what he hath done Famouslie, he did it to that end: though soft conscienc'd men can be content to say it was for his Countrey, he did it to please his Mother, and to be partly proud, which he is, euen to the altitude of his vertue.

2. Cit. What he cannot helpe in his Nature, you account a Vice in him; You must in no way say he is couetous.

1. Cit. If I must not, I neede not be barren of Accusations he hath faults (with surplus) to tyre in repetition.

Showts within.

What showts are these? The other side a'th City is risen: why stay we prating heere? To th'Capitoll.

All. Come, come.

1. Cit. Soft, who comes heere?

Enter Menenius Agrippa.

2. Cit. Worthy *Menenius Agrippa*, one that hath alwayes lou'd the people.

1. Cit. He's one honest enough, wold al the rest wer so.

Men. What work's my Countrimen in hand? Where go you with Bats and Clubs? The matter Speake I pray you.

2. Cit. Our busines is not vnknowne to th'Senat; they haue had inkling this fortnight what we intend to do, w now wee'l shew em in deeds: they say poore Suters haue strong breaths, they shal know we haue strong arms too.

Menen. Why Masters, my good Friends, mine honest Neighbours, will you vndo your selues?

2. Cit. We cannot Sir, we are vndone already.

Men. I tell you Friends, most charitable care Haue the Patricians of you for your wants. Your suffering in this dearth, you may as well Strike at the Heauen with your staues, as lift them Against the Roman State, whose course will on The way it takes: cracking ten thousand Curbes Of more strong linke assunder, then can euer Appeare in your impediment. For the Dearth, The Gods, not the Patricians make it, and Your knees to them (not armes) must helpe. Alacke, You are transported by Calamity Therher, where more attends you, and you slander The Helmes o'th State; who care for you like Fathers, When you curse them, as Enemies.

2. Cit. Care for vs? True indeed, they nere car'd for vs yet. Suffer vs to famish, and their Store-houses cramm'd with Graine: Make Edicts for Vsurie, to support Vsurers; repeale daily any wholsome Act established against the rich, and prouide more piercing Statutes daily, to chaine vp and restraine the poore. If the Warres eate vs not vppe, they will; and there's all the loue they beare vs.

Menen. Either you must Confesse your selues wondrous Malicious, Or be accus'd of Folly. I shall tell you A pretty Tale, it may be you haue heard it, But since it serues my purpose, I will venture To scale't a little more.

2. Citizen. Well, Ile heare it Sir: yet you must not thinke To fobbe off our disgrace with a tale: . But and't please you deliuer.

Men. There was a time, when all the bodies members Rebell'd against the Belly; thus accus'd it: That onely like a Gulfe it did remaine

a 2

I'th

Signature 189.

This acrostic is found on the last column of *The Tragedie of Coriolanus*.

Begin to read from the initial F of the word 'Flattered'; to the right; downwards; on the initials of the words of the *text;* spelling Francis Bacon, you will arrive at the initial N of the word 'Noble' in the last line. The acrostic figure here is:—

Flattered your Volcians, etc.
R
A
N
C
I
S
B
A
C
O
Noble
Memory
Assist.

In a spirit of amusement let me point out that if I had been the cipherer I should have made this a strong instead of a weak acrostic[1] by using the initials of the last two words of the text. The acrostic would then run from the initial F of the first word of the column to the initial A of the last, and the acrostic figure would then read:—

FRANCIS. BACON. M.A.

So far as I can see there is no reason to suppose that this latter complete figure is not intentional.

Note that there is no V or U in Francis; and note also that the name could be spelled Ffrancis, if the reader prefers it that way.

Note that the eighth line from the bottom reads:—
'Helpe three a'th'cheefest Souldiers, Ile be one,'
and not as most modern reprints have it:—
'Helpe three o' th',' etc.
As this letter 'a' is essential to the signature, the misprint is curiously fortunate if it was a typographical accident.

[1] Spedding (vol. viii, p. 305) says, 'and being so near Cambridge he made use of the opportunity to take his degree of Master of Arts; which was conferred upon him in a special congregation, the usual exercises and ceremonies being dispensed with, on the 27th of July [1594]. Spedding refers to Blackbourne, vol. i, p. 217.

Auf. He approaches, you shall heare him.

Enter Coriolanus marching with Drumme, and Colours. The Commoners being with him.

Corio. Haile Lords, I am return'd your Souldier
No more infected with my Countries loue
Then when I parted hence : but still subsisting
Vnder your great Command You are to know,
That prosperously I haue attempted, and
With bloody passage led your Warres, euen to
The gates of Rome : Our spoiles we haue brought home
Doth more then counterpoize a full third part
The charges of the Action. We haue made peace
With no lesse Honor to the *Antiates*
Then shame to th'Romaines. And we heere deliuer
Subscrib'd by th'Consuls, and Patricians,
Together with the Seale a'th Senat, what
We haue compounded on.

Auf. Read it not Noble Lords,
But tell the Traitor in the highest degree
He hath abus'd your Powers.

Corio. Traitor? How now?

Auf. I Traitor, *Martius.*

Corio. *Martius?*

Auf. I *Martius, Caius Martius* · Do'st thou thinke
Ile grace thee with that Robbery, thy stolne name
Coriolanus in Corioles?
You Lords and Heads a'th'State, perfidiously
He ha's betray'd your businesse, and giuen vp
For certaine drops of Salt, your City *Rome* ·
I say your City to his Wife and Mother,
Breaking his Oath and Resolution, like
A twist of rotten Silke, neuer admitting
Counsaile a'th'warre : But at his Nurses teares
He whin'd and roar'd away your Victory,
That Pages blush'd at him, and men of heart
Look'd wond'ring each at others.

Corio. Hear'st thou Mars?

Auf. Name not the God, thou boy of Teares.

Corio. Ha?

Aufid. No more

Corio. Measurelesse Lyar, thou hast made my heart
Too great for what containes it. Boy? Oh Slaue.
Pardon me Lords, 'tis the first time that euer
I was forc'd to scoul'd. Your iudgments my graue Lords
Must giue this Curre the Lye : and his owne Notion,
Who weares my stripes imprest vpon him, that
Must beare my beating to his Graue, shall ioyne
To thrust the Lye vnto him.

1 Lord. Peace both, and heare me speake.

Corio. Cut me to peeces Volces men and Lads,
Staine all your edges on me. Boy, false Hound ·
If you haue writ your Annales true, 'tis there,
That like an Eagle in a Doue-coat, I

Flatter'd your Volcians in *Corioles*
Alone I did it, Boy

Auf. Why Noble Lords,
Will you be put in minde of his blinde Fortune,
Which was your shame, by this vnholy Braggart?
'Fore your owne eyes, and eares?

All Consp. Let him dye for't

All People. Teare him to peeces, do it presently:
He kill'd my Sonne, my daughter, he kill'd my Cosine
Marcus, he kill'd my Father.

2 Lord. Peace hoe : no outrage, peace :
The man is Noble, and his Fame folds in
This Orbe o'th'earth : His last offences to vs
Shall haue Iudicious hearing. Stand *Auffidius,*
And trouble not the peace.

Corio. O that I had him, with six *Auffidiusses,* or more :
His Tribe, to vse my lawfull Sword.

Auf. Insolent Villaine.

All Consp. Kill, kill, kill, kill, kill him.

Draw both the Conspirators, and kils Martius, who falles, Auffidius stands on him.

Lords Hold, hold, hold, hold.

Auf My Noble Masters, heare me speake.

1. Lord. O *Tullus*

2. Lord. Thou hast done a deed, whereat
Valour will weepe.

3 Lord. Tread not vpon him Masters, all be quiet,
Put vp your Swords.

Auf My Lords,
When you shall know (as in this Rage
Prouok'd by him, you cannot) the great danger
Which this mans life did owe you, you'l reioyce
That he is thus cut off. Please it your Honours
To call me to your Senate, Ile deliuer
My selfe your loyall Seruant, or endure
Your heauiest Censure

1 Lord. Beare from hence his body,
And mourne you for him. Let him be regarded
As the most Noble Coarse, that euer Herald
Did follow to his Vrne.

2. Lord His owne impatience,
Takes from *Auffidius* a great part of blame.
Let's make the Best of it.

Auf My Rage is gone,
And I am strucke with sorrow. Take him vp:
Helpe three a'th'cheefest Souldiers, Ile be one.
Beate thou the Drumme that it speake mournfully
Traile your steele Pikes. Though in this City hee
Hath widdowed and vnchilded many a one,
Which to this houre bewaile the Iniury,
Yet he shall haue a Noble Memory. Assist.

Exeunt bearing the Body of Martius. A dead March Sounded.

FINIS.

Signature 190.

This acrostic is found in the first and second pages of *The Lamentable Tragedy of Titus Andronicus* (see pp. 470 and 471).

Note that the two capitals of the first word of the play are N^O

I can see no other indication of an acrostic in this play, but let us suppose that these first two letters N^O indicate the tail letters of an acrostic; that is to say, the last two letters in the name of Francis Bacon. In order to find the head of the cipher we scan the page, find nothing, turn the page and 'Loe!' or 'Lo!' stares us in the face. The word is remarkable, and halts us also, because it is deliberately printed on two lines (as any printer can see); thus, L_{oe}.

Now note the capitals of the next two lines; they are $\frac{R}{F}$ and $\frac{B}{A}$ of the words $\frac{Returnes}{From}$ and $\frac{Bay}{Anchorage}$

Here we have Bacon's initials F R A B, or Fra B, 'Anchorage,' and a place 'From which to Return.' Let us return from the word 'From.'

Begin to read from the initial F of the word 'From'; to the right; upwards; on the capitals of the *text;* down the next column (p. 31); and up the next; spelling FRAVNCIS BACON, you will arrive at the large initial N with which the play opens.

The acrostic figure here is: —

N
  O
   C
    A
    B
     S
      I
       C
        N
         V
          A
           R

From whence at first she
weighed her anchorage:

The Lamentable Tragedy of
Titus Andronicus.

Actus Primus   Scœna Prima.

*Flourish. Enter the Tribunes and Senators aloft And then
enter Saturninus and his Followers at one doore,
and Bassianus and his Followers at the
other, with Drum & Colours.*

Saturninus.

Oble Patricians, Patrons of my right,
Defend the iustice of my Cause with Armes.
And Countrey-men, my louing Followers,
Pleade my Successiue Title with your Swords.
I was the first borne Sonne, that was the last
That wore the Imperiall Diadem of Rome :
Then let my Fathers Honours liue in me,
Nor wrong mine Age with this indignitie.

Bassianus. Romaines, Friends, Followers,
Fauourers of my Right :
If euer *Bassianus*, *Cæsars* Sonne,
Were gracious in the eyes of Royall Rome,
Keepe then this passage to the Capitoll ·
And suffer not Dishonour to approach
Th'Imperiall Seate to Vertue : consecrate
To Iustice, Continence, and Nobility :
But let Desert in pure Election shine ;
And Romanes, fight for Freedome in your Choice.

Enter Marcus Andronicus aloft with the Crowne.

Princes, that striue by Factions, and by Friends
Ambitiously for Rule and Empery :
Know, that the people of Rome for whom we stand
A speciall Party, haue by Common voyce
In Election for the Romane Emperie,
Chosen *Andronicus*, Sur-named *Pious*,
For many good and great deserts to Rome.
A Nobler man, a brauer Warriour,
Lives not this day within the City Walles.
He by the Senate is accited home
From weary Warres against the barbarous *Cothes*,
That with his Sonnes (a terror to our Foes)
Hath yoak'd a Nation strong, train'd vp in Armes
Ten yeares are spent, since first he vndertooke
This Cause of Rome, and chasticed with Armes
Our Enemies pride. Fiue times he hath return'd
Bleeding to Rome, bearing his Valiant Sonnes
In Coffins from the Field.
And now at last, laden with Honours Spoyles,
Returnes the good *Andronicus* to Rome,
Renowned *Titus*, flourishing in Armes.

Let vs intreat, by Honour of his Name,
Whom (worthily) you would haue now succeede,
And in the Capitoll and Senates right,
Whom you pretend to Honour and Adore,
That you withdraw you, and abate your Strength,
Dismisse your Followers, and as Suters should,
Pleade your Deserts in Peace and Humblenesse

Saturnine. How fayre the Tribune speakes,
To calme my thoughts
Bassia. Marcus Andronicus, so I do affie
In thy vprightnesse and Integrity
And so I Loue and Honor thee, and thine,
Thy Noble Brother *Titus*, and his Sonnes,
And Her (to whom my thoughts are humbled all)
Gracious *Lauinia*, Romes rich Ornament,
That I will heere dismisse my louing Friends :
And to my Fortunes, and the Peoples Fauour,
Commit my Cause in ballance to be weigh'd.
Exit Souldiours
Saturnine Friends, that haue beene
Thus forward in my Right,
I thanke you all, and heere Dismisse you all,
And to the Loue and Fauour of my Countrey,
Commit my Selfe, my Person, and the Cause ·
Rome, be as iust and gracious vnto me,
As I am confident and kinde to thee.
Open the Gates, and let me in.
Bassia. Tribunes, and me, a poore Competitor.
Flourish.   *They go vp into the Senat house.*

Enter a Captaine.
Cap Romanes make way : the good *Andronicus*,
Patron of Vertue, Romes best Champion,
Successefull in the Battailes that he fights,
With Honour and with Fortune is return'd,
From whence he circumscribed with his Sword,
And brought to yoke the Enemies of Rome

*Sound Drummes and Trumpets. And then enter two of Titus
Sonnes ; After them, two men bearing a Coffin couered
with blacke, then two other Sonnes   After them, Titus
Andronicus, and then Tamora the Queene of Gothes, &
her two Sonnes Chiron and Demetrius, with Aaron the
Moore, and others as many as can bee · They set downe the
Coffin, and Titus speakes.*

Andronicus. Haile Rome
Victorious in thy Mourning Weedes :

Loe,

Loe as the Barke that hath discharg'd his fraught,
Returnes with precious lading to the Bay,
From whence at first she wegth'd her Anchorage :
Commeth *Andronicus* bound with Lawrell bowes,
To resalute his Country with his teares,
Teares of true ioy for his returne to Rome,
Thou great defender of this Capitoll,
Stand gracious to the Rites that we intend,
Romaines, of fiue and twenty Valiant Sonnes,
Halfe of the number that King *Priam* had,
Behold the poore remaines aliue and dead!
These that Suruiue, let Rome reward with Loue?
These that I bring vnto their latest home,
With buriall amongst their Aunceltors.
Heere Gothes haue giuen me leaue to sheath my Sword:
Titus vnkinde, and carelesse of thine owne,
Why suffer'st thou thy Sonnes vnburied yet,
To houer on the dreadfull shore of Stix ?
Make way to lay them by their Bretheren.

They open the Tombe.

There greete in silence as the dead are wont,
And sleepe in peace, slaine in your Countries warres :
O sacred receptacle of my ioyes,
Sweet Cell of vertue and Noblitie,
How many Sonnes of mine hast thou in store,
That thou wilt neuer render to me more ?
Luc. Giue vs the proudest prisoner of the Gothes,
That we may hew his limbes, and on a pile
Ad manus fratrum, sacrifice his flesh :
Before this earthly prison of their bones,
That so the shadowes be not vnappeas'd,
Nor we disturb'd with prodigies on earth.
Tit. I giue him you, the Noblest that Suruiues,
The eldest Son of this distressed Queene.
Tam. Stay Romaine Bretheren gracious Conqueror,
Victorious *Titus*, rue the teares I shed,
A Mothers teares in passion for her sonne :
And if thy Sonnes were euer deere to thee,
Oh thinke my sonnes to be as deere to mee.
Sufficeth not, that we are brought to Rome
To beautifie thy Triumphs, and returne
Captiue to thee, and to thy Romaine yoake,
But must my Sonnes be slaughtred in the streetes,
For Valiant doings in their Countries cause ?
O ! If to fight for King and Common-weale,
Were piety in thine, it is in these.
Andronicus, staine not thy Tombe with blood.
Wilt thou draw neere the nature of the Gods ?
Draw neere them then in being mercifull.
Sweet mercy is Nobilities true badge,
Thrice Noble *Titus*, spare my first borne sonne.
Tit. Patient your selfe Madam, and pardon me.
These are the Brethren, whom you Gothes beheld
Aliue and dead, and for their Bretheren slaine,
Religiously they aske a sacrifice :
To this your sonne is markt, and die he must,
T'appease their groaning shadowes that are gone.
Luc. Away with him, and make a fire straight,
And with our Swords vpon a pile of wood,
Let's hew his limbes till they be cleane consum'd.

Exit Sonnes with Alarbus.

Tamo. O cruell irreligious piety.
Chi. Was euer Scythia halfe so barbarous?
Dem. Oppose me Scythia to ambitious Rome,

Alarbus goes to rest, and we suruiue,
To tremble vnder *Titus* threatning lookes,
Then Madam stand resolu'd, but hope withall,
The selfe same Gods that arm'd the Queene of Troy
With opportunitie of sharpe reuenge
Vpon the Thracian Tyrant in his Tent,
May fauour *Tamora* the Queene of Gothes,
(When Gothes were Gothes, and *Tamora* was Queene)
To quit the bloody wrongs vpon her foes.

Enter the Sonnes of Andronicus againe.

Luci. See Lord and Father, how we haue perform'd
Our Romaine rightes, *Alarbus* limbs are lopt,
And intrals feede the sacrifising fire,
Whose smoke like incense doth perfume the skie.
Remaineth nought but to interre our Brethren,
And with low'd Larums welcome them to Rome.
Tit. Let it be so, and let *Andronicus*
Make this his latest farewell to their soules.

Flourish.

Then Sound Trumpets, and lay the Coffins in the Tombe.

In peace and Honour rest you heere my Sonnes,
Romes readiest Champions, repose you heere in rest,
Secure from worldly chaunces and mishaps :
Heere lurks no Treason, heere no enuie swels,
Heere grow no damned grudges, heere are no stormes,
No noyse, but silence and Eternall sleepe,
In peace and Honour rest you heere my Sonnes.

Enter Lauinia.

Laui. In peace and Honour, liue Lord *Titus* long,
My Noble Lord and Father, liue in Fame :
Loe at this Tombe my tributarie teares,
I render for my Bretherens Obsequies.
And at thy feete I kneele, with teares of ioy
Shed on the earth for thy returne to Rome.
O blesse me heere with thy victorious hand,
Whose Fortune Romes best Citizens applau'd.
Ti. Kind Rome,
That hast thus louingly reseru'd
The Cordiall of mine age to glad my hart,
Lauinia liue, out-liue thy Fathers dayes :
And Fames eternall date for vertues praise.
Marc. Long liue Lord *Titus*, my beloued brother,
Gracious Triumpher in the eyes of Rome.
Tit. Thankes Gentle Tribune,
Noble brother *Marcus*.
Mar. And welcome, Nephews from successfull wars,
You that suruiue and you that sleepe in Fame :
Faire Lords your Fortunes are all alike in all,
That in your Countries seruice drew your Swords.
But safer Triumph is this Funerall Pompe,
That hath aspir'd to *Solons* Happines,
And Triumphs ouer chaunce in honours bed.
Titus Andronicus, the people of Rome,
Whose friend in iustice thou hast er er bene,
Send thee by me their Tribune and their trust,
This Palliament of white and spotlesse Hue,
And name thee in Election for the Empire,
With these our late deceased Emperours Sonnes :
Be *Candidatus* then and put it on,
And helpe to set a head on headlesse Rome.
Tit. A better head her Glorious body fits,
Then his that shakes for age and feeblenesse:

                                                    What

Signature 191.

This acrostic is found on the first page of *The Tragedie of Romeo and Juliet.*

Begin to read from the terminal O of the word ' No,' which is the last word in the first column; to the left; upwards; on the terminals of *all words and part words in the column and the heading of the play ;* spelling ONOCAB OCSICNARF (Francisco Bacono), you will arrive at the terminal F of the word ' OF ' in the heading 'THE TRAGEDIE OF.'

The acrostic figure here is: —

THE TRAGEDIE OF

Gre. NO

This acrostic was found for me by Mr. W. L. Stoddard.

An acrostic is found on the last page of *The Tragedie of Romeo and Juliet.*

As the text and the figure of the acrostic are the same as the corresponding text and figure found in the so-called second Quarto, it has been found convenient to print the facsimile from the Folio alongside that taken from the second Quarto, in chapter XIII. The reader is therefore referred to that chapter for this signature; it will be found on page 530.

THE TRAGEDIE OF
ROMEO and IVLIET.

Actus Primus. Scœna Prima.

Enter Sampson and Gregory with Swords and Bucklers,
of the House of Capulet.

Sampson.

Gregory: A my word wee'l not carry coales.
Greg. No, for then we should be Colliars.
Samp. I meane, if we be in choller, wee'l draw.
Greg. I, While you liue, draw your necke out
o'th Collar.
Samp. I strike quickly, being mou'd.
Greg. But thou art not quickly mou'd to strike.
Samp. A dog of the house of *Mountague*, moues me.
Greg. To moue, is to stir: and to be valiant, is to stand:
Therefore, if thou art mou'd, thou runst away.
Samp. A dogge of that house shall moue me to stand.
I will take the wall of any Man or Maid of *Mountagues*.
Greg. That shewes thee a weake slaue, for the weakest goes to the wall.
Samp. True, and therefore women being the weaker
Vessels, are euer thrust to the wall: therefore I will push
Mountagues men from the wall, and thrust his Maides to
the wall. (their men.
Greg. The Quarrell is betweene our Masters, and vs
Samp. 'Tis all one, I will shew my selfe a tyrant: when
I haue fought with the men, I will bee ciuill with the
Maids, and cut off their heads.
Greg. The heads of the Maids?
Sam. I, the heads of the Maids, or their Maiden-heads,
Take it in what sence thou wilt.
Greg. They must take it sence, that feele it.
Samp. Me they shall feele while I am able to stand:
And 'tis knowne I am a pretty peece of flesh.
Greg. 'Tis well thou art not Fish: If thou had'st, thou
had'st beene poore Iohn. Draw thy Toole, here comes of
the House of the *Mountagues*.

Enter two other Seruingmen.

Sam. My naked weapon is out: quarrel, I wil back thee
Gre. How? Turne thy backe, and run.
Sam. Feare me not.
Gre. No marry: I feare thee.
Sam. Let vs take the Law of our sides: let them begin.
Gr. I wil frown as I passe by, & let thē take it as they list.
Sam. Nay, as they dare. I wil bite my Thumb at them,
which is a disgrace to them, if they beare it.
Abra. Do you bite your Thumbe at vs sir?
Samp. I do bite my Thumbe, sir.
Abra. Do you bite your Thumb at vs, sir?
Sam. Is the Law of our side, if I say I? *Gre.* No.

Sam. No sir, I do not bite my Thumbe at you sir: but
I bite my Thumbe sir.
Greg. Do you quarrell sir?
Abra. Quarrell sir? no sir. (as you
Sam. If you do sir, I am for you, I serue as good a man
Abra. No better? *Samp.* Well sir.

Enter Benuolio.

Gr. Say better: here comes one of my masters kinsmen.
Samp. Yes, better.
Abra. You Lye.
Samp. Draw if you be men. *Gregory*, remember thy
washing blow. *They Fight.*
Ben. Part Fooles, put vp your Swords, you know not
what you do.

Enter Tibalt.

Tyb. What art thou drawne, among these heartlesse
Hindes? Turne thee *Benuolio*, looke vpon thy death.
Ben. I do but keepe the peace, put vp thy Sword,
Or manage it to part these men with me.
Tyb. What draw, and talke of peace? I hate the word
As I hate hell, all *Mountagues*, and thee:
Haue at thee Coward. *Fight.*

Enter three or foure Citizens with Clubs.

Offi. Clubs, Bils, and Partisons, strike, beat them down
Downe with the *Capulets*, downe with the *Mountagues*.

Enter old Capulet in his Gowne, and his wife.

Cap. What noise is this? Giue me my long Sword ho.
Wife. A crutch, a crutch: why call you for a Sword?
Cap. My Sword I say: Old *Mountague* is come,
And flourishes his Blade in spight of me.

Enter old Mountague, & his wife.

Moun. Thou villaine *Capulet*. Hold me not, let me go
2.Wife. Thou shalt not stir a foote to seeke a Foe.

Enter Prince Eskales, with his Traine.

Prince Rebellious Subiects, Enemies to peace,
Prophaners of this Neighbor-stained Steele,
Will they not heare? What hoe, you Men, you Beasts,
That quench the fire of your pernitious Rage,
With purple Fountaines issuing from your Veines:
On paine of Torture, from those bloody hands
Throw your mistemper'd Weapons to the ground,
And heare the Sentence of your mooued Prince.
Three ciuill Broyles, bred of an Ayery word,
By thee old *Capulet* and *Mountague*,
Haue thrice disturb'd the quiet of our streets,
And made *Verona's* ancient Citizens
Cast by their Graue beseeming Ornaments,
To wield old Partizans, in hands as old,

Cankred

Signature 192.

This acrostic is found on the last page of *Timon of Athens*. (See p. 477.)

Begin to read from the initial F of the word 'Finis'; to the right ; upwards ; on the initials of the words of the text of the first column; spelling Francisco Bacono, you will arrive at the initial O of the word 'out,' which is the last word of the first line of the first column, and the end of the string of letters on that column.

The acrostic figure here is :—

Out
N
O
C
A
B
O
C
S
I
C
N
A
R
FINIS.

Signature 193.

While we are dealing with the last page of *Timon of Athens*, we may as well observe the amusing way in which the 'Epitaph' seems to have been used. (See p. 477.)

Begin to read from the initial S of the word 'strike,' which is the last word of the text of the play; to the left; upwards; on the initials of the words; spelling Saint Alban, you will arrive at the initial N of the word 'name.' The acrostic figure here is: —

Seek not my Name
A
B
L
A
T
N
I
A
Strike.

Signature 194.

Here is still another acrostic in the 'Epitaph' at the end of *Timon of Athens*. (See p. 477.)

Begin to read from the initial N of the word 'name,' on which we ended the last signature (193); to the left; downwards; on the terminals; spelling Nocab Sicnvarf, you will arrive at the initial F of the word 'Finis.' The acrostic figure here is: —

Seek not my Name:
O
C
A
B
S
I
C
N
V
A
R
FINIS.

I hope to have a later opportunity to show the acrostics which I have found on the pages of this play which bear irregular numbers.

Signature 195.

This acrostic is also found in the last page of *Timon of Athens.*

Begin to read from the terminal F of the word ' of,' in the page-heading; to the right; downwards; on the terminals; spelling FFRANCIS BACON, you will arrive at the initial terminal N of the word ' name ' in the ' Epitaph.'

The complete figure of this and the two foregoing acrostics is:—

```
Timon oF
        F
        R
        A
        N
        C
        I
         S
          B
          A
          C
          O
Seek not my Name
          O A
          C   B
          A     L
          B       A
          S         T
          I           N
          C             I
          N               A
          V                   Strike
          A
          R
        FINIS
```

Who were the motiues that you firft went out,
(Shame that they wanted, cunning in exceffe)
Hath broke their hearts. March, Noble Lord,
Into our City with thy Banners fpred,
By decimation and a tythed death ;
If thy Reuenges hunger for that Food
Which Nature loathes, take thou the deftin'd tenth,
And by the hazard of the fpotted dye,
Let dye the fpotted.

   1 All haue not offended :
For thofe that were, it is not fquare to take
On thofe that are, Reuenge : Crimes, like Lands
Are not inherited, then deere Countryman,
Bring in thy rankes, but leaue without thy rage,
Spare thy Athenian Cradle, and thofe Kin
Which in the blufter of thy wrath muft fall
With thofe that haue offended, like a Shepheard,
Approach the Fold, and cull th'infected forth,
But kill not altogether.

   2 What thou wilt,
Thou rather fhalt inforce it with thy fmile,
Then hew too't, with thy Sword.

   1 Set but thy foot
Againft our rampyr'd gates, and they fhall ope :
So thou wilt fend thy gentle heart before,
To fay thou't enter Friendly.

   2 Throw thy Gloue,
Or any Token of thine Honour elfe,
That thou wilt vfe the warres as thy redreffe,
And not as our Confufion : All thy Powers
Shall make their harbour in our Towne, till wee
Haue feal'd thy full defire.

   Alc Then there's my Gloue,
Defend and open your vncharged Ports,
Thofe Enemies of *Timons.* and mine owne,
Whom you your felues fhall fet out for reproofe,
Fall and no more ; and to attone your feares
With my more Noble meaning, not a man
Shall paffe his quarter, or offend the ftreame
Of Regular Iuftice in your Cities bounds,
But fhall be remedied to your publique Lawes
At heauieft anfwer.

   Both. 'Tis moft Nobly fpoken.
   Alc. Defcend, and keepe your words.
          Enter a Meffenger.
   Mef. My Noble Generall, *Timon* is dead,
Entomb'd vpon the very hemme o'th'Sea,
And on his Grauestone, this Infculpture which
With wax I brought away : whofe foft Impreffion
Interprets for my poore ignorance.

    Alcibiades reades the Epitaph.
Heere lies a wretched Coarfe, of wretched Soule bereft,
Seek not my name: A Plague confume you, wicked Caitifs left:
Heere lye I Timon, who aliue, all liuing men did hate,
Paffe by, and curfe thy fill, but paffe and ftay not here thy gate.
Thefe well expreffe in thee thy latter fpirits:
Though thou abhorrd'ft in vs our humane griefes,
Scornd'ft our Braines flow, and thofe our droplets, which
From niggard Nature fall ; yet Rich Conceit
Taught thee to make vaft Neptune weepe for aye
On thy low Graue, on faults forgiuen. Dead
Is Noble *Timon*, of whofe Memorie
Heereafter more. Bring me into your Citie,
And I will vfe the Oliue, with my Sword :
Make war breed peace ; make peace ftint war, make each
Prefcribe to other, as each others Leach.
Let our Drummes ftrike.   *Exeunt.*

FINIS.

Signature 196.

This acrostic is found on the last page of *The Tragedie of Julius Cæsar*. (See p. 481.) *The Alarum* sounds and Clitus cries to Brutus: —

Fly my Lord, flye.

Begin to read from the initial F of the word 'Fly'; to the right; downwards; on the initials of the words; throughout the whole of the remaining text of the play and back again continuously; spelling FRAVNCIS (or FFRAVNCIS) BACON BARON VERVLAM, you will arrive at the initial M of the word 'my.'

Begin again to read from the same initial F, and read in precisely the same way but in the reverse direction, to the left instead of to the right at the start; you will again arrive at the initial M of the word 'my,' having spelled FRAVNCIS BACON BARON VERVLAM.

Here we have this extraordinary signature keyed from and to the same points and in opposite directions.

The acrostic figure here is shown in conjunction with the next figure, on page 480.

Signature 197.

Now note in reading either way we ended the spelling of FF or FRAVNCIS BACON on the initial N of the word 'Nature' (second column, twenty-second line), whether reading to the left or to the right. In other words, the initial N was a keyed point.

Begin therefore to read from the initial N of the word 'Nature'; to the right; downwards; on all the letters, this time, of all the words of the text; spelling backwards NOCAB SICNVARFF, you will arrive at the initial F of the word 'FINIS.'

The acrostic figure here is: —

Nature might stand up,

                    O
                   C
                  A
                 B
                S
               I
              C
             N
            V
           A
          R
         F
        FINIS

Now note that I can see no signature on the first page of the play, but observe that the opening word of the play is H Ence

It was the possible *double entente* of this opening word which drove me at once to the end of the play for the cipher.

The combined acrostic figures for signatures 196 and 197 are:—

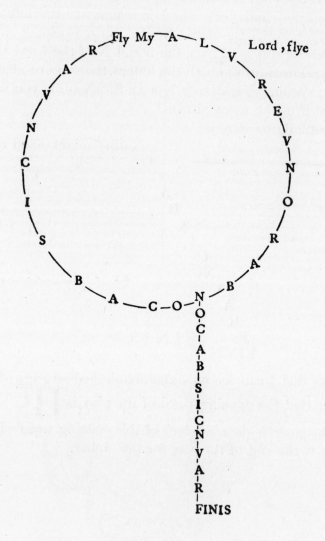

Cly. Fly, flye my Lord, there is no tarrying heere.
Bru. Farewell to you, and you, and you *Volumnius.*
Strato, thou haſt bin all this while aſleepe:
Farewell to thee, to *Strato,* Countrymen:
My heart doth ioy, that yet in all my life,
I found no man, but he was true to me.
I ſhall haue glory by this looſing day
More then *Octauius,* and *Marke Antony,*
By this vile Conqueſt ſhall attaine vnto.
So fare you well at once, for *Brutus* tongue
Hath almoſt ended his liues Hiſtory:
Night hangs vpon mine eyes, my Bones would reſt,
That haue but labour'd, to attaine this houre.

        Alarum.   Cry within, Flye, flye, flye.
Cly. Fly my Lord, flye.
Bru. Hence: I will follow:
I prythee *Strato,* ſtay thou by thy Lord,
Thou art a Fellow of a good reſpect:
Thy life hath had ſome ſmatch of Honor in it,
Hold then my Sword, and turne away thy face, ⎫
While I do run vpon it. Wilt thou *Strato?*
Stra. Giue me your hand firſt. Fare you wel my Lord.
Bru. Farewell good *Strato.* ——*Cæsar,* now be ſtill,
I kill'd not thee with halfe ſo good a will.   *Dyes.*

    Alarum. Retreat. Enter Antony, Octauius, Meſſala,
                Lucillius, and the Army.
Octa. What man is that?

Meſſa. My Maſters man. *Strato,* where is thy Maſter?
Stra. Free from the Bondage you are in *Meſſala,*
The Conquerors can but make a fire of him:
For *Brutus* onely ouercame himſelfe,
And no man elſe hath Honor by his death.
Lucil. So *Brutus* ſhould be found. I thank thee *Brutus*
That thou haſt prou'd *Lucillius* ſaying true.
Octa. All that ſeru'd *Brutus,* I will entertaine them.
Fellow, wilt thou beſtow thy time with me?
Stra. I, if *Meſſala* will preferre me to you.
Octa. Do ſo, good *Meſſala.*
Meſſa. How dyed my Maſter *Strato?*
Stra. I held the Sword, and he did run on it.
Meſſa. Octauius, then take him to follow thee,
That did the lateſt ſeruice to my Maſter.
Ant. This was the Nobleſt Roman of them all:
All the Conſpirators ſaue onely hee,
Did that they did, in enuy of great *Cæsar:*
He, onely in a generall honeſt thought,
And common good to all, made one of them.
His life was gentle, and the Elements
So mixt in him, that Nature might ſtand vp,
And ſay to all the world; This was a man.
Octa. According to his Vertue, let vs vſe him
Withall Reſpect, and Rites of Buriall:
Within my Tent his bones to night ſhall ly,
Moſt like a Souldier ordered Honourably:
So call the Field to reſt, and let's away,
To part the glories of this happy day.   *Exeunt omnes.*

FINIS.

Signature 198.

This signature is found in Act 1; Scene 1; of *The Tragedie of Macbeth*. (See p. 485.) Begin to read from the large W which is the initial of the first word of the text of the Scene; to the right; downwards; on all the letters of all the words; spelling WILL SHAKESPEARE, you will arrive at the terminal E of the word 'ayre,' which is the last word in the Scene.

The acrostic figure here is: —

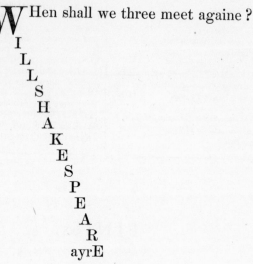

WHen shall we three meet againe?
I
L
L
S
H
A
K
E
S
P
E
A
R
ayrE

Signature 199.

This acrostic is found on the second column of the first page of *The Tragedie of Macbeth*. (See p. 485.)

Begin to read from the initial O, which is the first word of the first line; to the right; downwards; on the terminals; spelling ONOCAB OCSICNARF, you will arrive at the initial F of the word 'faint' (twentieth line from top).

Begin to read from the terminal N of 'Gentleman,' which is the last word of the first line; to the left; downwards; on terminals; spelling NOCAB SICNVARF, you will again arrive at the initial F of the word 'faint' (twentieth line from top).

Begin to read from the initial F of the word 'faint'; to the right; downwards; on the terminals; spelling FRANCISCO BACONO, you will arrive at the terminal O of the word 'No,' which is the last word on the page.

The complete acrostic figure here is: —

O   valiant Cousin, worthy GentlemaN.

```
N                                   O
 O                                 C
  C                               A
   A                             B
    B                           S
     O                         I
      C                       N
       S                     C
        I                   N
         C                 V
          N               A
         A   A           R
        R   R           
         Faint
              R
               A
                N
                 C
                  I
                   S
                    C
                     O
                      B
                       A
                        C
                         O
                          N
              King.      NO
```

Signature 200.

This acrostic is found on the first page of *The Tragedie of Macbeth.*

Begin to read from the initial B of 'Battlements,' the last word of the last line of the first column; to the left; upwards; on the initials of the words of the text; spelling Bacon, you will arrive at the initial N of the word 'Name' (eighth line up).

Begin to read from the initial N of this word 'Name'; to the left; downwards; on the initials of the text; spelling Nocab, you will arrive at the initial B of the word 'Battlements'; thus keying the name from two points in two directions.

The acrostic figure here is: —

Name

O

C

A

Battlements

THE TRAGEDIE OF
MACBETH.

Actus Primus. Scœna Prima.

Thunder and Lightning. Enter three Witches.

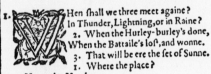

1. Hen shall we three meet againe?
In Thunder, Lightning, or in Raine?
2. When the Hurley-burley's done,
When the Battaile's lost, and wonne.
3. That will be ere the set of Sunne.
1. Where the place?
2. Vpon the Heath.
3. There to meet with *Macbeth*.
1. I come, *Gray-Malkin*.
All. *Padock* calls anon: faire is foule, and foule is faire,
Houer through the fogge and filthie ayre.   *Exeunt.*

Scena Secunda.

Alarum within. Enter King Malcome, Donal-
baine, Lenox, with attendants, meeting
a bleeding Captaine.

King. What bloody man is that? he can report,
As seemeth by his plight, of the Reuolt
The newest state.
Mal. This is the Serieant,
Who like a good and hardie Souldier fought
'Gainst my Captiuitie: Haile braue friend;
Say to the King, the knowledge of the Broyle,
As thou didst leaue it.
Cap. Doubtfull it stood,
As two spent Swimmers, that doe cling together,
And choake their Art: The mercilesse *Macdonwald*
(Worthie to be a Rebell, for to that
The multiplying Villanies of Nature
Doe swarme vpon him) from the Westerne Isles
Of Kernes and Gallowgrosses is supply'd,
And Fortune on his damned Quarry smiling,
Shew'd like a Rebells Whore: but all's too weake:
For braue *Macbeth* (well hee deserues that Name)
Disdayning Fortune, with his brandisht Steele,
Which smoak'd with bloody execution
(Like Valours Minion) caru'd out his passage,
Till hee fac'd the Slaue:
Which neu'r shooke hands, nor bad farwell to him,
Till he vnseam'd him from the Naue toth' Chops,
And fix'd his Head vpon our Battlements.

King. 'O valiant Cousin, worthy Gentleman.
Cap. As whence the Sunne 'gins his reflection,
Shipwracking Stormes, and direfull Thunders:
So from that Spring, whence comfort seem'd'to come,
Discomfort swells: Marke King of Scotland, marke,
No sooner Iustice had, with Valour arm'd,
Compell'd these skipping Kernes to trust their heeles,
But the Norweyan Lord, surueying vantage,
With surbusht Armes, and new supplyes of men,
Began a fresh assault.
King. Dismay'd not this our Captaines, *Macbeth* and
Banquoh?
Cap. Yes, as Sparrowes, Eagles;
Or the Hare, the Lyon:
If I say sooth, I must report they were
As Cannons ouer-charg'd with double Cracks,
So they doubly redoubled stroakes vpon the Foe:
Except they meant to bathe in reeking Wounds,
Or memorize another *Golgotha*,
I cannot tell: but I am faint,
My Gashes cry for helpe.
King. So well thy words become thee, as thy wounds,
They smack of Honor both: Goe get him Surgeons.

Enter Rosse and Angus.

Who comes here?
Mal. The worthy *Thane* of Rosse.
Lenox. What a haste lookes through his eyes?
So should he looke, that seemes to speake things strange.
Rosse. God saue the King.
King. Whence cam'st thou, worthy *Thane*?
Rosse. From Fiffe, great King,
Where the Norweyan Banners flowt the Skie,
And fanne our people cold.
Norway himselfe, with terrible numbers,
Assisted by that most disloyall Traytor,
The *Thane* of Cawdor, began a dismall Conflict,
Till that *Bellona's* Bridegroome, lapt in proofe,
Confronted him with selfe-comparisons,
Point against Point, rebellious Arme 'gainst Arme,
Curbing his lauish spirit: and to conclude,
The Victorie fell on vs.
King. Great happinesse.
Rosse. That now *Sweno*, the Norwayes King,
Craues composition:
Nor would we deigne him buriall of his men,
Till he disbursed, at Saint *Colmes* ynch,
Ten thousand Dollars, to our generall vse.

King. No

Signature 201.

This acrostic is found on the last page of *The Tragedie of Macbeth*. Note the *Flourish* before and after Malcolm's last speech.

Begin to read from the initial F of the upper 'Flourish'; to the right; downwards; on all letters of all words; spelling FRAUNCIS BACON, you will arrive at the letter N in the word 'TyraNny' (enlarged for your convenience). Now continue down; to the right; from the N of the word 'TyraNny'; spelling NOCAB SICNVARFF, you will arrive at the initial F of the lower word 'Flourish.'

The acrostic figure here is:—

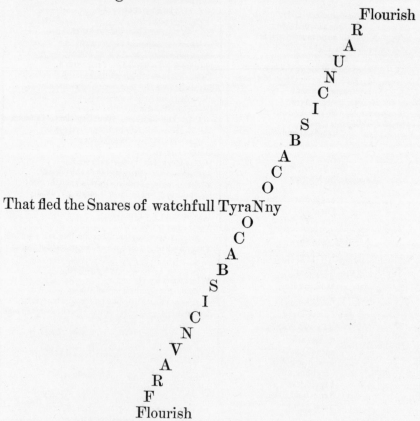

Note that the upper name is spelled with one F, while the lower has FF; an immaterial difference, but it puts the figure in the class of 'weak' acrostics.

Seemes bruited. Let me finde him Fortune,
And more I begge not.   *Exit.*   *Alarums.*

Enter Malcolme and Seyward.

Sey. This way my Lord, the Castles gently rendred :
The Tyrants people, on both sides do fight,
The Noble Thanes do brauely in the Warre,
The day almost it selfe professes yours,
And little is to do.

Malc. We haue met with Foes
That strike beside vs.

Sey. Enter Sir, the Castle.   *Exeunt.*   *Alarum*

Enter Macbeth.

Macb. Why should I play the Roman Foole, and dye
On mine owne sword? whiles I see liues, the gashes
Do better vpon them.

Enter Macduffe.

Macd. Turne Hell-hound, turne.

Macb. Of all men else I haue auoyded thee :
But get thee backe, my soule is too much charg'd
With blood of thine already.

Macd. I haue no words,
My voice is in my Sword, thou bloodier Villaine
Then tearmes can giue thee out.   *Fight: Alarum*

Macb. Thou loosest labour,
As easie may'st thou the intrenchant Ayre
With thy keene Sword impresse, as make me bleed :
Let fall thy blade on vulnerable Crests,
I beare a charmed Life, which must not yeeld
To one of woman borne.

Macd. Dispaire thy Charme,
And let the Angell whom thou still hast seru'd
Tell thee, *Macduffe* was from his Mothers womb
Vntimely ript.

Macb. Accursed be that tongue that tels mee so ;
For it hath Cow'd my better part of man :
And be these Iugling Fiends no more beleeu'd,
That palter with vs in a double sence,
That keepe the word of promise to our eare,
And breake it to our hope. Ile not fight with thee.

Macd. Then yeeld thee Coward,
And liue to be the shew, and gaze o'th'time.
Wee'l haue thee, as our rarer Monsters are
Painted vpon a pole, and vnder-writ,
Heere may you see the Tyrant.

Macb. I will not yeeld
To kisse the ground before young *Malcolmes* feet,
And to be baited with the Rabbles curse.
Though Byrnane wood be come to Dunsinane,
And thou oppos'd, being of no woman borne,
Yet I will try the last. Before my body,
I throw my warlike Shield : Lay on *Macduffe*,
And damn'd be him, that first cries hold, enough.
        Exeunt fighting.   *Alarums.*

Enter Fighting, and Macbeth slaine.

Retreat, and Flourish. Enter with Drumme and Colours,
Malcolm, Seyward, Rosse, Thanes, & Soldiers.

Mal. I would the Friends we misse, were safe arriu'd.

Sey. Some must go off : and yet by these I see,
So great a day as this is cheapely bought.

Mal. Macduffe is missing, and your Noble Sonne.

Rosse Your son my Lord, ha's paid a souldiers debt,
He onely liu'd but till he was a man,
The which no sooner had his Prowesse confirm'd
In the vnshrinking station where he fought,
But like a man he dy'de.

Sey. Then he is dead?

Rosse. I, and brought off the field : your cause of sorrow
Must not be measur'd by his worth, for then
It hath no end.

Sey. Had he his hurts before?

Rosse. I, on the Front.

Sey. Why then, Gods Soldier be he :
Had I as many Sonnes, as I haue haires,
I would not wish them to a fairer death:
And so his Knell is knoll'd.

Mal. Hee's worth more sorrow,
And that Ile spend for him.

Sey. He's worth no more,
They say he parted well, and paid his score,
And so God be with him. Here comes newer comfort.

Enter Macduffe; with Macbeths head.

Macd. Haile King, for so thou art.
Behold where stands
Th'Vsurpers cursed head : the time is free :
I see thee compast with thy Kingdomes Pearle,
That speake my salutation in their minds :
Whose voyces I desire alowd with mine.
Haile King of Scotland.

All. Haile King of Scotland.   *Flourish.*

Mal. We shall not spend a large expence of time,
Before we reckon with your seuerall loues,
And make vs euen with you. My Thanes and Kinsmen
Henceforth be Earles, the first that euer Scotland
In such an Honor nam'd : What's more to do,
Which would be planted newly with the time,
As calling home our exil'd Friends abroad,
That fled the Snares of watchfull Tyranny,
Producing forth the cruell Ministers
Of this dead Butcher, and his Fiend-like Queene ;
Who (as 'tis thought) by selfe and violent hands,
Tooke off her life. This, and what needfull else
That call's vpon vs, by the Grace of Grace,
We will performe in measure, time, and place :
So thankes to all at once, and to each one,
Whom we inuite, to see vs Crown'd at Scone.
        Flourish.   *Exeunt Omnes.*

FINIS.

Signature 202.

This acrostic is found on the first column of the first page of *The Tragedie of Hamlet, Prince of Denmarke* (see page 491), in the first Folio.

Begin to read on the large ornamental letter W, with which the first line of the text begins; to the right; on all letters of *all* words (including stage-directions); downwards; spelling WILLIAM SHAKE-SPEARE,[1] you will arrive at the initial E of the word ' *Exit.*'

Begin to read from the initial F of the name ' *Fran,*' which stands under the words ' Who's there ? '; to the right; downwards; on all the letters of *all* the words; spelling FRANCIS BACON, you will arrive at the letter N in the word ' thaNkes' (ninth line).

Begin to read from the initial F of the word '*Fran,*' which follows the word ' *Exit*'; to the right; upwards; on all the letters of all the words; spelling FRANCIS BACON, you will again arrive at the same letter N of the word ' thaNkes.'

[1] N. B.—The name William Shakespeare may be spelled with or without the hyphen.

The complete acrostic figure here is : —

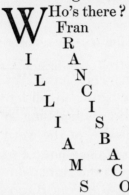

```
W Ho's there?
    Fran
    R
I      A
  L    N
   L   C
    I   I s
     A   B
      A   a c
       M  . o
       M    o
        S
For this releefe much thaNkes
          H    o
          A    C
          K    a
          E    b s
           S    i
            P    c n
             E    a
              A    r
              R    r
                Exit  Fran
```

Note the line which immediately precedes the words ' *Exit Fran.*' It is:—

Fra. Barnardo ha's my place: giue you goodnight.

Now note the name that runs from the first F to the last N in this line: —

FRA. BArnardo ha's my plaCe: giue yOu goodNight.
FRA. BA..................C..........O........N......

Compare this signature with that found in the Quarto of 1604. (See p. 547.)

Note the position of the line: —

Fr a n. Barnardo hath my place, giue you good night.
FRAN BA........................C........O..........N......

THE TRAGEDIE OF

HAMLET, Prince of Denmarke.

Actus Primus. Scœna Prima.

Enter Barnardo and Francisco two Centinels.

Barnardo.

Ho's there?

Fran. Nay answer me. Stand & vnfold your selfe.

Bar. Long liue the King.

Fran. Barnardo?

Bar. He.

Fran. You come most carefully vpon your houre.

Bar. 'Tis now strook twelue, get thee to bed *Francisco.*

Fran. For this releefe much thankes: 'Tis bitter cold, And I am sicke at heart.

Barn. Haue you had quiet Guard?

Fran. Not a Mouse stirring.

Barn. Well, goodnight. If you do meet *Horatio* and *Marcellus,* the Riuals of my Watch, bid them make hast.

Enter Horatio and Marcellus.

Fran. I thinke I heare them. Stand: who's there?

Hor. Friends to this ground.

Mar. And Leige-men to the Dane.

Fran. Giue you good night.

Mar. O farwel honest Soldier, who hath relieu'd you?

Fra. Barnardo ha's my place: giue you goodnight.

Exit Fran.

Mar. Holla *Barnardo.*

Bar. Say, what is *Horatio* there?

Hor. A peece of him.

Bar. Welcome *Horatio,* welcome good *Marcellus.*

Mar. What, ha's this thing appear'd againe to night.

Bar. I haue seene nothing.

Mar. Horatio saies, 'tis but our Fantasie, And will not let beleefe take hold of him Touching this dreaded sight, twice seene of vs, Therefore I haue intreated him along With vs, to watch the minutes of this Night, That if againe this Apparition come, He may approue our eyes, and speake to it.

Hor. Tush, tush, 'twill not appeare.

Bar. Sit downe a-while, And let vs once againe assaile your eares, That are so fortified against our Story, What we two Nights haue seene.

Hor. Well, sit we downe, And let vs heare *Barnardo* speake of this.

Barn. Last night of all, When yond same Starre that's Westward from the Pole Had made his course t'illume that part of Heauen

Where now it burnes, *Marcellus* and my selfe, The Bell then beating one.

Mar. Peace, breake thee of: *Enter the Ghost.* Looke where it comes againe.

Barn. In the same figure, like the King that's dead.

Mar. Thou art a Scholler; speake to it *Horatio.*

Barn. Lookes it not like the King? Marke it *Horatio.*

Hora. Most like: It harrowes me with fear & wonder

Barn. It would be spoke too.

Mar. Question it *Horatio.*

Hor. What art thou that vsurp'st this time of night, Together with that Faire and Warlike forme In which the Maiesty of buried Denmarke Did sometimes march: By Heauen I charge thee speake.

Mar. It is offended.

Barn. See, it stalkes away.

Hor. Stay: speake; speake: I Charge thee, speake.

Exit the Ghost.

Mar. 'Tis gone, and will not answer.

Barn. How now *Horatio?* You tremble & look pale: Is not this something more then Fantasie? What thinke you on't?

Hor. Before my God, I might not this beleeue Without the sensible and true auouch Of mine owne eyes.

Mar. Is it not like the King?

Hor. As thou art to thy selfe, Such was the very Armour he had on, When th'Ambitious Norwey combatted: So frown'd he once, when in an angry parle He smot the sledded Pollax on the Ice. 'Tis strange.

Mar. Thus twice before, and iust at this dead houre, With Martiall stalke, hath he gone by our Watch.

Hor. In what particular thought to work, I know not: But in the grosse and scope of my Opinion, This boades some strange erruption to our State.

Mar. Good now sit downe, & tell me he that knowes Why this same strict and most obseruant Watch, So nightly toyles the subiect of the Land, And why such dayly Cast of Brazon Cannon And Forraigne Mart for Implements of warre: Why such impresse of Ship-wrights, whose sore Taske Do's not diuide the Sunday from the weeke, What might be toward, that this sweaty hast Doth make the Night ioynt-Labourer with the day: Who is't that can informe me?

Hor. That can I,

At

Signature 203.

These acrostics are found in the last page of *The Tragedie of Hamlet,* p. 282, but wrongly numbered 280.

Note that the initials of the first words of the first and last lines of Horatio's last speech are O and O of the words 'Of' and 'On.' In other words they are two ciphers.

Begin to read from the initial O of the word 'Of'; to the right; on all the letters of all the words; downwards; spelling ONOCAB, you will arrive at the letter B of the word ' be.'

Begin to read from the initial O of the word 'On'; to the right; on all the letters of all the words; upwards; spelling ONOCAB, you will arrive again at the letter B of the word ' be.'

Here we have a cipher keyed from two ends of a paragraph to a central point.

The acrostic figure here is: —

<pre>
                Of that I shall haue, etc.
                N
                 O
                  C
                   A
But let this same Be presently performed
                   A
                  C
                 O
                N
                On plots, etc.
                Beare, etc.
                For, etc.
</pre>

That *Rosincrance* and *Guildensterne* are dead :
Where should we haue our thankes ?
   Hor. Not from his mouth,
Had it th'abilitie of life to thanke you :
He neuer gaue command'ment for their death.
But since so iumpe vpon this bloodie question,
You from the Polake warres, and you from England
Are heere arriued. Giue order that these bodies
High on a stage be placed to the view,
And let me speake to th'yet vnknowing world,
How these things came about. So shall you heare)
Of carnall, bloudie, and vnnaturall acts,
Of accidentall iudgements, casuall slaughters
Of death's put on by cunning, and forc'd cause,
And in this vpshot, purposes mistooke,
Falne on the Inuentors heads. All this can I
Truly deliuer.
      For. Let vs hast to heare it,
And call the Noblest to the Audience.
For me, with sorrow, I embrace my Fortune,
I haue some Rites of memory in this Kingdome,

Which are ro claime, my vantage doth
Inuite me,
   Hor. Of that I shall haue alwayes cause to speake,
And from his mouth
Whose voyce will draw on more :
But let this same be presently perform'd,
Euen whiles mens mindes are wilde,
Lest more mischance
On plots, and errors happen.
   For. Let foure Captaines
Beare *Hamlet* like a Soldier to the Stage,
For he was likely, had he beene put on
To haue prou'd most royally :
And for his passage,
The Souldiours Musicke,and the rites of Warre
Speake lowdly for him.
Take vp the body ; Such a sight as this
Becomes the Field, but heere shewes much amis.
Go, bid the Souldiers shoote.
    Exeunt Marching : after the which, a Peale of
        Ordenance are shot off.

FINIS.

Signature 204.

This acrostic is found in the speech by Hamlet which is headed in the Folio *Manet Hamlet*. It is the speech made by Hamlet to himself when he is alone for the first time. It is found on the third page of the play. (See p. 495.)

Note that the initials of the first words of the first and last lines respectively are O and B of the words 'Oh' and 'But.'

Begin to read from the initial B of the word 'But'; to the right; upwards; on the initials of the words of the text; spelling Bacono, you will arrive at the initial O of the word 'Oh.'

The acrostic figure is:—

Oh that this too too solid Flesh, would melt,

N

O

C

A

But breake my heart, for I must hold my tongue.

It is worth recording that I was directed to this acrostic by noticing that the numbering of the page 156 jumps to 257 on the next page. As I could find nothing on either of these pages I amused myself by adding their page-numbers together. This yields 413. I then counted 413 lines from the top line on the right-hand column on page 257 back towards the beginning of the play. The 414th line from my starting-point is: '*Manet Hamlet.*'

This statement may be verified by any one who has access to a facsimile of the first Folio. It should be in any well-equipped library.

You told vs of some suite. What is't *Laertes* ?
You cannot speake of Reason to the Dane,
And loose your voyce. What would'st thou beg *Laertes*,
That shall not be my Offer, not thy Asking ?
The Head is not more Natiue to the Heart,
The Hand more Instrumentall to the Mouth,
Then is the Throne of Denmarke to thy Father.
What would'st thou haue *Laertes* ?

Laer. Dread my Lord,
Your leaue and fauour to returne to France,
From whence, though willingly I came to Denmarke
To shew my duty in your Coronation,
Yet now I must confesse, that duty done,
My thoughts and wishes bend againe towards France,
And bow them to your gracious leaue and pardon.

King. Haue you your Fathers leaue ?
What sayes *Pollonius* ?

Pol. He hath my Lord:
I do beseech you giue him leaue to go.

King. Take thy faire houre *Laertes*, time be thine,
And thy best graces spend it at thy will :
But now my Cosin *Hamlet*, and my Sonne ?

Ham. A little more then kin, and lesse then kinde.

King. How is it that the Clouds still hang on you ?

Ham. Not so my Lord, I am too much i'th'Sun.

Queen. Good *Hamlet* cast thy nightly colour off,
And let thine eye looke like a Friend on Denmarke.
Do not for euer with thy veyled lids
Seeke for thy Noble Father in the dust ;
Thou know'st 'tis common, all that liues must dye,
Passing through Nature, to Eternity.

Ham. I Madam, it is common.

Queen. If it be ;
Why seemes it so particular with thee.

Ham. Seemes Madam ? Nay, it is : I know not Seemes:
'Tis not alone my Inky Cloake (good Mother)
Nor Customary suites of solemne Blacke,
Nor windy suspiration of forc'd breath,
No, nor the fruitfull Riuer in the Eye,
Nor the deiected hauiour of the Visage,
Together with all Formes, Moods, shewes of Griefe,
That can denote me truly. These indeed Seeme,
For they are actions that a man might play :
But I haue that Within, which passeth show ;
These, but the Trappings, and the Suites of woe.

King. 'Tis sweet and commendable
In your Nature *Hamlet*,
To giue these mourning duties to your Father :
But you must know, your Father lost a Father,
That Father lost, lost his, and the Suruiuer bound
In filiall Obligation, for some terme
To do obsequious Sorrow. But to perseuer
In obstinate Condolement, is a course
Of impious stubbornnesse. 'Tis vnmanly greefe,
It shewes a will most incorrect to Heauen,
A Heart vnfortified, a Minde impatient,
An Vnderstanding simple, and vnschool'd :
For, what we know must be, and is as common
As any the most vulgar thing to sence,
Why should we in our peeuish Opposition
Take it to heart ? Fye, 'tis a fault to Heauen,
A fault against the Dead, a fault to Nature,
To Reason most absurd, whose common Theame
Is death of Fathers, and who still hath cried,
From the first Coarse, till he that dyed to day,
This must be so. We pray you throw to earth

This vnpreuayling woe, and thinke of vs
As of a Father ; For let the world take note,
You are the most immediate to our Throne,
And with no lesse Nobility of Loue,
Then that which deerest Father beares his Sonne,
Do I impart towards you. For your intent
In going backe to Schoole in Wittenberg,
It is most retrograde to our desire :
And we beseech you, bend you to remaine
Heere in the cheere and comfort of our eye,
Our cheefest Courtier Cosin, and our Sonne

Qu. Let not thy Mother lose her Prayers *Hamlet* :
I prythee stay with vs, go not to Wittenberg.

Ham. I shall in all my best
Obey you Madam.

King. Why 'tis a louing, and a faire Reply,
Be as our selfe in Denmarke. Madam come,
This gentle and vnforc'd accord of *Hamlet*
Sits smiling to my heart ; in grace whereof,
No iocond health that Denmarke drinkes to day,
But the great Cannon to the Clowds shall tell,
And the Kings Rouce, the Heauens shall bruite againe,
Respeaking earthly Thunder. Come away. *Exeunt*

Manet Hamlet.

Ham. Oh that this too too solid Flesh, would melt,
Thaw, and resolue it selfe into a Dew :
Or that the Euerlasting had not fixt
His Cannon 'gainst Selfe-slaughter. O God, O God !
How weary, stale, flat, and vnprofitable
Seemes to me all the vses of this world ?
Fie on't ? Oh fie, fie, 'tis an vnweeded Garden
That growes to Seed : Things rank, and grosse in Nature
Posse sse it meerely. That it should come to this :
But two months dead : Nay, not so much ; not two,
So excellent a King, that was to this
Hiperion to a Satyre : so louing to my Mother,
That he might not beteene the windes of heauen
Visit her face too roughly. Heauen and Earth
Must I remember : why she would hang on him,
As if encrease of Appetite had growne
By what it fed on ; and yet within a month ?
Let me not thinke on't : Frailty, thy name is woman.
A little Month, or ere those shooes were old,
With which she followed my poore Fathers body
Like *Niobe*, all teares. Why she, euen she.
(O Heauen ! A beast that wants discourse of Reason
Would haue mourn'd longer) married with mine Vnkle,
My Fathers Brother : but no more like my Father,
Then I to *Hercules*. Within a Moneth ?
Ere yet the salt of most vnrighteous Teares
Had left the flushing of her gauled eyes,
She married. O most wicked speed, to post
With such dexterity to Incestuous sheets :
It is not, nor it cannot come to good.
But breake my heart, for I must hold my tongue.

Enter Horatio, Barnard, and Marcellus.

Hor. Haile to your Lordship.

Ham. I am glad to see you well :
Horatio, or I do forget my selfe.

Hor. The same my Lord,
And your poore Seruant euer.

Ham. Sir my good friend,
Ile change that name with you :
And what make you from Wittenberg *Horatio* ?

Mar-

Signature 205.

This acrostic is found on page 258 of *The Tragedie of Hamlet.*

I noticed that the paging of this play skips from page 156 to 257, and that 259 is repeated where 279 should be. This led me to scan all these pages. I noticed that the last two lines of the first column of page 258 are: —

> *Hor.* Good my Lord tell it.
> *Ham.* No you'l reveale it.

I also noticed that the initial of the first word of the first line is the B of 'But.'

Begin to read from this initial B of the word 'But'; downwards; on the initials of the first word of the lines of the text; spelling BACON, you will arrive at the initial N of the word 'No,' which is the first word of the last line.

The acrostic figure here is: —

> But soft, methinkes I sent the, etc.
> A
> C
> O
> No you'l reveale it.

If the wrong paging of this play is intended, or if advantage has been taken of it, to attract the reader, I cannot see any method by which it does so; except in the instances to which I have already called attention.

But foft, me thinkes I fent the Mornings Ayre;
Briefe let me be : Sleeping within mine Orchard,
My cuftome alwayes in the afternoone;
Vpon my fecure hower thy Vncle ftole
With iuyce of curfed Hebenon in a Violl,
And in the Porches of mine eares did poure
The leaperous Diftilment; whofe effect
Holds fuch an enmity with bloud of Man,
That fwift as Quick-filuer, it courfes through
The naturall Gates and Allies of the Body;
And with a fodaine vigour it doth poffet
And curd, like Aygre droppings into Milke,
The thin and wholfome blood : fo did it mine;
And a moft inftant Tetter bak'd about,
Moft Lazar-like, with vile and loathfome cruft,
All my fmooth Body.
Thus was I, fleeping, by a Brothers hand,
Of Life, of Crowne, and Queene at once difpatcht;
Cut off euen in the Bloffomes of my Sinne,
Vnhouzzled, difappointed, vnnaneld,
No reckoning made, but fent to my account
With all my imperfections on my head;
Oh horrible Oh horrible, moft horrible:
If thou haft nature in thee beare it not;
Let not the Royall Bed of Denmarke be
A Couch for Luxury and damned Inceft.
But howfoeuer thou purfueft this Act,
Taint not thy mind; nor let thy Soule contriue
Againft thy Mother ought; leaue her to heauen,
And to thofe Thornes that in her bofome lodge,
To pricke and fting her. Fare thee well at once;
The Glow-worme fhowes the Matine to be neere,
And gins to pale his vneffectuall Fire:
Adue, adue, *Hamlet* : remember me.   *Exit.*
    Ham Oh all you hoft of Heauen! Oh Earth; what els?
And fhall I couple Hell? Oh fie: hold my heart;
And you my finnewes, grow not inftant Old;
But beare me ftiffely vp: Remember thee?
I, thou poore Ghoft, while memory holds a feate
In this diftracted Globe: Remember thee?
Yes, from the Table of my Memory,
Ile wipe away all triuiall fond Records,
All fawes of Bookes, all formes, all prefures paft,
That youth and obferuation coppied there;
And thy Commandment all alone fhall liue
Within the Booke and Volume of my Braine,
Vnmixt with bafer matter; yes, yes, by Heauen:
Oh moft pernicious woman!
Oh Villaine, Villaine, fmiling damned Villaine!
My Tables, my Tables; meet it is I fet it downe,
That one may fmile, and fmile and be a Villaine;
At leaft I'm fure it may be fo in Denmarke;
So Vnckle there you are: now to my word;
It is; Adue, Adue, Remember me: I haue fworn't.
    Hor & Mar.within. My Lord, my Lord.
        Enter Horatio and Marcellus.
Mar. Lord *Hamlet.*
Hor. Heauen fecure him.
Mar. So be it.
Hor. Illo, ho, ho, my Lord.
Ham. Hillo, ho, ho, boy; come bird, come.
Mar. How ift my Noble Lord?
Hor. What newes, my Lord?
Ham. Oh wonderfull!
Hor. Good my Lord tell it.
Ham. No you'l reueale it.

Hor. Not I, my Lord, by Heauen.
Mar. Nor I, my Lord.   (think it?
Ham. How fay you then, would heart of man once
But you'l be fecret?
    Both. I, by Heau'n, my Lord.
Ham. There's nere a villaine dwelling in all Denmarke
But hee's an arrant knaue.
Hor. There needs no Ghoft my Lord, come from the
Graue, to tell vs this.
Ham. Why right, you are i'th' right;
And fo, without more circumftance at all,
I hold it fit that we fhake hands, and part:
You, as your bufines and defires fhall point you:
For euery man ha's bufineffe and defire,
Such as it is : and for mine owne poore part,
Looke you, Ile goe pray.
Hor. Thefe are but wild and hurling words, my Lord.
Ham. I'm forry they offend you heartily:
Yes faith heartily.
Hor. There's no offence my Lord.
Ham. Yes, by Saint *Patricke,* but there is my Lord,
And much offence too, touching this Vifion heere :
It is an honeft Ghoft, that let me tell you:
For your defire to know what is betweene vs,
O'remafter't as you may. And now good friends,
As you are Friends, Schollers and Soldiers,
Giue me one poore requeft.
Hor. What is't my Lord? we will.
Ham Neuer make known what you haue feen to night.
    Both. My Lord we will not.
Ham Nay, but fwear't.
Hor. Infaith my Lord, not I.
Mar. Nor I my Lord : in faith.
Ham. Vpon my fword.
Marcell. We haue fworne my Lord already.
Ham Indeed, vpon my fword Indeed
Gho. Sweare.   *Ghoft cries vnder the Stage.*
Ham. Ah ha boy, fayeft thou fo. Art thou there true-
penny? Come one you here this fellow in the felleredge
Confent to fweare.
Hor. Propofe the Oath my Lord.
Ham Neuer to fpeake of this that you haue feene.
Sweare by my fword.
Gho. Sweare.
Ham. Hic & vbique? Then wee'l fhift for grownd,
Come hither Gentlemen,
And lay your hands againe vpon my fword,
Neuer to fpeake of this that you haue heard:
Sweare by my Sword.
Gho. Sweare.   (faft?
Ham. Well faid old Mole, can'ft worke i'th' ground fo
A worthy Pioner, once more remoue good friends.
Hor. Oh day and night: but this is wondrous ftrange
Ham. And therefore as a ftranger giue it welcome.
There are more things in Heauen and Earth, *Horatio,*
Then are dream't of in our Philofophy. But come,
Here as before, neuer fo helpe you mercy,
How ftrange or odde fo ere I beare my felfe;
(As I perchance heereafter fhall thinke meet
To put an Anticke difpofition on:)
That you at fuch time feeing me, neuer fhall
With Armes encombred thus, or thus, head fhake;
Or by pronouncing of fome doubtfull Phrafe;
As well, we know, or we could and if we would,
Or if we lift to fpeake; or there be and if there might,
Or fuch ambiguous giuing out to note,

                                                    That

Signature 206.

This acrostic is found on the first page of *The Tragedie of King Lear.*

Begin to read on the initial (capital) N of the word 'Nothing,' which is the last word of the text of the second column; to the right, or to the left; on all the roman capital letters; upwards; through one column after another; spelling NOCAB SICNARF, you will arrive at the capital letter F of the word 'OF,' which is the last word of the first line of the title ('THE TRAGEDIE OF').

The reading may be made with the same results if all capitals, of every kind, are used.

The acrostic figure here is: —

THE TRAGEDIE OF
R
A
N
C
I
S
B
A
C
O
Nothing?

THE TRAGEDIE OF
KING LEAR.

Actus Primus. Scœna Prima.

Enter Kent, Glouuefter, and Edmond.

Kent.

Thought the King had more affected the Duke of *Albany*, then *Cornwall*.

Glou. It did alwayes feeme fo to vs : But now in the diuifion of the Kingdome, it ap-peares not which of the Dukes hee valewes moft, for qualities are fo weigh'd, that curiofity in nei-ther, can make choife of eithers moity.

Kent. Is not this your Son, my Lord?

Glou. His breeding Sir, hath bin at my charge. I haue fo often blufh'd to acknowledge him, that now I am braz'd too't.

Kent. I cannot conceiue you.

Glou. Sir, this yong Fellowes mother could ; where-vpon fhe grew round womb'd, and had indeede (Sir) a Sonne for her Cradle, ere fhe had a husband for her bed. Do you fmell a fault ?

Kent. I cannot wifh the fault vndone, the iffue of it, being fo proper.

Glou. But I haue a Sonne, Sir, by order of Law, fome yeere elder then this ; . who, yet is no deerer in my ac-count, though this Knaue came fomthing fawcily to the world before he was fent for : yet was his Mother fayre, there was good fport at his making, and the horfon muft be acknowledged. Doe you know this Noble Gentle-man, *Edmond*?

Edm. No, my Lord.

Glou. My Lord of Kent :
Remember him heereafter, as my Honourable Friend.

Edm. My feruices to your Lordfhip.

Kent. I muft loue you, and fue to know you better.

Edm. Sir, I fhall ftudy deferuing.

Glou. He hath bin out nine yeares, and away he fhall againe. The King is comming.

Sennet. Enter King Lear, Cornwall, Albany, Gonerill, Re-gan, Cordelia, and attendants.

Lear. Attend the Lords of France & Burgundy, Glofter.

Glou. I fhall, my Lord.   *Exit.*

Lear. Meane time we fhal expreffe our darker purpofe.
Giue me the Map there. Know, that we haue diuided
In three our Kingdome : and 'tis our faft intent,
To fhake all Cares and Bufineffe from our Age,
Conferring them on yonger ftrengths, while we
Vnburthen'd crawle toward death. Our fon of *Cornwal*,
And you our no leffe louing Sonne of *Albany*,

We haue this houre a conftant will to publifh
Our daughters feuerall Dowers, that future ftrife
May be preuented now. The Princes, *France* & *Burgundy*,
Great Riuals in our yongeft daughters loue,
Long in our Court, haue made their amorous foiourne,
And heere are to be anfwer'd. Tell me my daughters
(Since now we will diueft vs both of Rule,
Intereft of Territory, Cares of State)
Which of you fhall we fay doth loue vs moft,
That we, our largeft bountie may extend
Where Nature doth with merit challenge. *Gonerill*,
Our eldeft borne, fpeake firft.

Gon. Sir, I loue you more then word can weild ∮ matter,
Deerer then eye-fight, fpace, and libertie,
Beyond what can be valewed, rich or rare,
No leffe then life, with grace, health, beauty, honor;
As much as Childe ere lou'd, or, Father found.
A loue that makes breath poore, and fpeech vnable,
Beyond all manner of fo much I loue you.

Cor. What fhall *Cordelia* fpeake ? Loue, and be filent.

Lear. Of all thefe bounds euen from this Line, to this,
With fhadowie Forrefts, and with Champains rich'd
With plenteous Riuers, and wide-skirted Meades
We make thee Lady. To thine and *Albanies* iffues
Be this perpetuall. What fayes our fecond Daughter?
Our deereft *Regan*, wife of *Cornwall*?

Reg. I am made of that felfe-mettle as my Sifter,
And prize me at her worth. In my true heart,
I finde fhe names my very deede of loue :
Onely fhe comes too fhort, that I profeffe
My felfe an enemy to all other ioyes,
Which the moft precious fquare of fenfe profeffes,
And finde I am alone felicitate
In your deere Highneffe loue.

Cor. Then poore *Cordelia*,
And yet not fo, fince I am fure my loue's
More ponderous then my tongue.

Lear. To thee, and thine hereditarie euer,
Remaine this ample third of our faire Kingdome,
No leffe in fpace, validitie, and pleafure
Then that conferr'd on *Gonerill*. Now our Ioy,
Although our laft and leaft : to whofe yong loue,
The Vines of France, and Milke of Burgundie,
Striue to be intereft. What can you fay, to draw
A third, more opilent then your Sifters? fpeake.

Cor. Nothing my Lord.

Lear. Nothing ?

qq 3   *Cor.*

Signature 207.

This acrostic is found on the page facing the last page of *The Tragedie of King Lear*. It is wrongly numbered 38 instead of 308. (See p. 503.)

Observe the phrase '(O fault)' in brackets, four lines from the foot of the left-hand column. In the Quarto of 1608 this phrase is '(O Father).'

Observe also the initial of the first word in Edgar's speech is the letter B of the word 'By,' and the initial of the first word of the last line in the same speech is the B of the word 'Burst.'

Begin to read from the initial B of the word 'By'; to the right; downwards; on the initials of the words of the text; throughout the speech and back continuously until you have spelled BACONO: you will arrive at the letter O in the bracketed phrase '(O fault).'

Begin to read from the initial B of the word 'Burst'; to the right; upwards; on the initials of the words; spelling BACONO, you will arrive again at the letter O in the phrase '(O fault).'

The acrostic thus reads to a common point from the initial of the first word of the first line of Edgar's speech, and from the initial of the first word of the last line of the same speech.

The acrostic figure here is: —

By nursing them my Lord.
A
  C
    O
     N
      (O fault)
     N
    O
  C
A
Burst smilingly.

Now begin to read from the initial F of the word 'fault,' to the right; upwards; on the initials of the words of the text; spelling FRAVNCIS BACON, you will arrive at the initial N of the word 'name.'

Now begin to read from the initial A, the first word of the first line, on the column; to the right; downwards; on the initials of the words of the text; spelling ANTHONIE BACON, you will arrive again at the initial N of the word 'name.'

The acrostic figure here is:—

```
                A most Toad-spotted Traitor.
                  N
                   T
                    H
                     O
                      N
                       I
                        E
                         B
                          A
                           C
                            O                    : hold Sir,
        Thou worse then any Name, reade thine owne euill:
                            O
                           C
                          A
                         B
                        S
                       I
                      C
                     N
                    V
                   A
                    R
                (O Fault)
```

A moſt Toad-ſpotted Traitor. Say thou no,
This Sword,this arme,and my beſt ſpirits are bent
To proue vpon thy heart,whereto I ſpeake,
Thou lyeſt.

   Baſt. In wiſedome I ſhould aske thy name,
But ſince thy out-ſide lookes ſo faire and Warlike,
And that thy tongue(ſome ſay) of breeding breathes,
What ſafe,and nicely I might well delay,
By rule of Knight-hood,I diſdaine and ſpurne:
Backe do I toſſe theſe Treaſons to thy head,
With the hell-hated Lye,ore-whelme thy heart,
Which for they yet glance by,and ſcarely bruiſe,
This Sword of mine ſhall giue them inſtant way,
Where they ſhall reſt for euer. *Trumpets ſpeake.*

   Alb. Saue him,ſaue him.   *Alarums. Fights.*

   Gon. This is practiſe *Gloſter*,
By th'law of Warre,thou waſt not bound to anſwer,
An vnknowne oppoſite:thou art not vanquiſh'd,
But cozend,and beguild.

   Alb. Shut your mouth Dame,
Or with this paper ſhall I ſtop it : hold Sir,
Thou worſe then any name,reade thine owne euill :
No tearing Lady,I perceiue you know it.

   Gon. Say if I do,the Lawes are mine not thine,
Who can arraigne me for't ?   *Exit.*

   Alb. Moſt monſtrous ! O,know'ſt thou this paper?

   Baſt. Aske me not what I know.

   Alb. Go after her,ſhe's deſperate,gouerne her.

   Baſt. What you haue charg'd me with,
That haue I done,
And more,much more,the time will bring it out.
'Tis paſt,and ſo am I : But what art thou
That haſt this Fortune on me ? If thou'rt Noble,
I do forgiue thee.

   Edg. Let's exchange charity:
I am no leſſe in blood then thou art *Edmond*,
If more,the more th'haſt wrong'd me.
My name is *Edgar* and thy Fathers Sonne,
The Gods are iuſt,and of our pleaſant vices
Make inſtruments to plague vs :
The darke and vitious place where thee he got,
Coſt him his eyes.

   Baſt. Th'haſt ſpoken right,'tis true,
The Wheele is come full circle,I am heere.

   Alb. Me thought thy very gate did propheſie
A Royall Nobleneſſe : I muſt embrace thee,
Let ſorrow ſplit my heart,if euer I
Did hate thee,or thy Father.

   Edg. Worthy Prince I know't.

   Alb. Where haue you hid your ſelfe ?
How haue you knowne the miſeries of your Father?

   Edg. By nurſing them my Lord. Liſt a breefe tale,
And when 'tis told,O that my heart would burſt.
The bloody proclamation to eſcape
That follow'd me ſo neere,(O our liues ſweetneſſe,
That we the paine of death would hourely dye,
Rather then die at once)taught me to ſhift
Into a mad-mans rags,t'aſſume a ſemblance
That very Dogges diſdain'd : and in this habit
Met I my Father with his bleeding Rings ,
Their precious Stones new loſt:became his guide,
Led him,begg'd for him,ſau'd him from diſpaire.
Neuer(O fault)reueal'd my ſelfe vnto him,
Vntill ſome halfe houre paſt when I was arm'd,
Not ſure,though hoping of this good ſucceſſe,
I ask'd his bleſſing,and from firſt to laſt

Told him our pilgrimage. But his flaw'd heart
(Alacke too weake the conflict to ſupport)
Twixt two extremes of paſſion,ioy and greefe,
Burſt ſmilingly.

   Baſt. This ſpeech of yours hath mou'd me,
And ſhall perchance do good,but ſpeake you on,
You looke as you had ſomething more to ſay.

   Alb. If there be more,more woſull,hold it in,
For I am almoſt ready to diſſolue,
Hearing of this.

Enter a Gentleman.

   Gen. Helpe,helpe : O helpe.

   Edg. What kinde of helpe ?

   Alb. Speake man.

   Edg. What meanes this bloody Knife ?

   Gen. 'Tis hot,it ſmoakes, it came euen from the heart
of——O ſhe's dead.

   Alb. Who dead? Speake man.

   Gen. Your Lady Sir,your Lady; and her Siſter
By her is poyſon'd : ſhe confeſſes it.

   Baſt. I was contracted to them both,all three
Now marry in an inſtant.

   Edg. Here comes *Kent*.

Enter Kent.

   Alb. Produce the bodies,be they aliue or dead ;
      Gonerill and Regans bodies brought out.
This iudgement of the Heauens that makes vs tremble.
Touches vs not with pitty O,is this he ?
The time will not allow the complement
Which very manners vrges.

   Kent. I am come
To bid my King and Maſter aye good night.
Is he not here ?

   Alb. Great thing of vs forgot,
Speake *Edmund*,where's the King ?and where's *Cordelia*?
Seeſt thou this obiect *Kent*?

   Kent. Alacke,why thus ?

   Baſt. Yet *Edmund* was belou'd:
The one the other poiſon'd for my ſake,
And after ſlew herſelfe.

   Alb. Euen ſo. couer their faces.

   Baſt. I pant for life : ſome good I meane to do
Deſpight of mine owne Nature. Quickly ſend,
(Be briefe in it) to th'Caſtle for my Writ
Is on the life of *Lear*,and on *Cordelia* :
Nay,ſend in time.

   Alb. Run,run,O run.

   Edg. To who my Lord? Who ha's the Office?
Send thy token of repreeue.

   Baſt. Well thought on,take my Sword,
Giue it the Captaine.

   Edg. Haſt thee for thy life.

   Baſt. He hath Commiſſion from thy Wife and me,
To hang *Cordelia* in the priſon,and
To lay the blame vpon her owne diſpaire,
That ſhe for-did her ſelfe.

   Alb. The Gods defend her,beare him hence awhile.

Enter Lear with Cordelia in his armes.

   Lear. Howle,howle,howle: O your are men of ſtones,
Had I your tongues and eyes,Il'd vſe them ſo,
That Heauens vault ſhould crack : ſhe's gone for euer.
I know when one is dead,and when one liues,
She's dead as earth :Lend me a Looking-glaſſe,

            If

Signature 208.

This acrostic is found on the last page of *The Tragedie of King Lear.*

I noticed that the Quarto of 1608 did not contain the words '*Exeunt with a dead March.*' So I began to read from the initial M of the word 'March'; to the left; on the initials of the words; excluding abbreviated stage-names; spelling backwards MALVREV, i. e. Verulam, I arrived at the initial V of the word ' Very,' which follows the ' *Enter a messenger.*'

The acrostic figure here is : —

Very bootlesse
E
R
V
L
A
Exeunt with a dead March

If that her breath will mist or staine the stone,
Why then she liues.
  Kent. Is this the promis'd end?
  Edg. Or image of that horror.
  All. Fall and cease.
  Lear. This feather stirs, she liues: if it be so,
It is a chance which do's redeeme all sorrowes
That euer I haue felt.
  Kent. O my good Master.
  Lear. Prythee away.
  Edg. 'Tis Noble *Kent* your Friend.
  Lear. A plague vpon you Murderors, Traitors all,
I might haue sau'd her, now she's gone for euer:
Cordelia, Cordelia, stay a little. Ha:
What is't thou saist? Her voice was euer soft,
Gentle, and low, an excellent thing in woman.
I kill'd the Slaue that was a hanging thee.
  Gent. 'Tis true (my Lords) he did
  Lear. Did I not fellow?
I haue seene the day, with my good biting Faulchion
I would haue made him skip: I am old now,
And these same crosses spoile me. Who are you?
Mine eyes are not o'th' best, Ile tell you straight.
  Kent. If Fortune brag of two, she lou'd and hated,
One of them we behold.
  Lear. This is a dull sight, are you not *Kent*?
  Kent. The same: your Seruant *Kent*,
Where is your Seruant *Caius*?
  Lear. He's a good fellow, I can tell you that,
He'le strike and quickly too, he's dead and rotten.
  Kent. No my good Lord, I am the very man.
  Lear. Ile see that straight.
  Kent. That from your first of difference and decay,
Haue follow'd your sad steps.
  Lear. Your are welcome hither.
  Kent. Nor no man else:
All's cheerlesse, darke, and deadly,
Your eldest Daughters haue fore-done themselues,
And desperately are dead
  Lear. I so I thinke.
  Alb. He knowes not what he saies, and vaine is it

That we present vs to him.

     Enter a Messenger.
  Edg. Very bootlesse.
  Mess. Edmund is dead my Lord.
  Alb. That's but a trifle heere:
You Lords and Noble Friends, know our intent,
What comfort to this great decay may come,
Shall be appli'd. For vs we will resigne,
During the life of this old Maiesty
To him our absolute power, you to your rights,
With boote, and such addition as your Honours
Haue more then merited. All Friends shall
Taste the wages of their vertue, and all Foes
The cup of their deseruings: O see, see.
  Lear. And my poore Foole is hang'd: no, no, no life?
Why should a Dog, a Horse, a Rat haue life,
And thou no breath at all? Thou'lt come no more,
Neuer, neuer, neuer, neuer, neuer.
Pray you vndo this Button. Thanke you Sir,
Do you see this? Looke on her? Looke her lips,
Looke there, looke there.   *He dies.*
  Edg. He faints, my Lord, my Lord.
  Kent. Breake heart, I prythee breake.
  Edg. Looke vp my Lord.
  Kent. Vex not his ghost, O let him passe, he hates him,
That would vpon the wracke of this tough world
Stretch him out longer.
  Edg. He is gon indeed.
  Kent. The wonder is, he hath endur'd so long,
He but vsurpt his life.
  Alb. Beare them from hence, our present businesse
Is generall woe: Friends of my soule, you twaine,
Rule in this Realme, and the gor'd state sustaine.
  Kent. I haue a iourney Sir, shortly to go,
My Master calls me, I must not say no.
  Edg. The waight of this sad time we must obey,
Speake what we feele, not what we ought to say:
The oldest hath borne most, we that are yong,
Shall neuer see so much, nor liue so long.

     Exeunt with a dead March.
        ss3

FINIS.

Signature 209.

This acrostic is found on the first page of *The Tragedie of Othello.* (See p. 509.)

Begin to read from the large initial **N** to the right; downwards; on the capitals of the words of the text; spelling NOCAB SICNARF, you will arrive at the initial F of the word 'For' (twentieth line, second column). [Fig. 1.]

Begin again to read from the large initial **N** down the first letter of every line until you have spelled NOCAB: you will arrive at the initial B of the word 'But' (nineteenth line, second column). [Fig. 2.]

Now read these last six lines of Iago's speech (the letters of the cipher are printed in capitals). They are: —

> But seeming so, for my peculiAr end:
> fOr wheN my Outward aCtion doth demonstrate
> the natiue aCt, and figure of my heart
> in Complement externe, 'tIS not long after
> but I will weare my heart vpon my sleeue
> FoR dAwes to pecke at; i am Not what i am.

Observe that the initials of the first words of the first two lines of the passage are $\frac{B}{F}$, and also that the initials of the first words of the last two lines are also $\frac{B}{F}$.

Observe also that if you begin to read from the initial B of the word 'But,' which is the first word of the first line; to the right; on all the letters of all words; downwards; spelling Bacono, you will arrive at the letter O of the word 'For' on the second line of the passage. [Fig. 3.]

Begin to read from the initial F of the word 'For,' which is the first word of the last line of the passage; to the right; upwards; on all the letters of all the words; spelling Francisco, you will again arrive at the letter O of the word 'For.' [Fig. 3.]

The acrostic figures here are:—

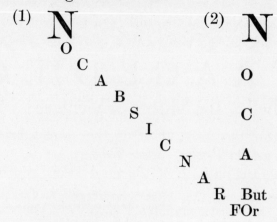

(3) But seeming so, for my peculiar end:

  A
  C
  O
  N
 FOr
  C
  S
  I
  C
  N
  A
  R

For Dawes to pecke at; I am not what I am.

THE TRAGEDIE OF
Othello, the Moore of Venice.

Actus Primus. Scœna Prima.

Enter Rodorigo, and Iago.

Rodorigo.

Euer tell me, I take it much vnkindly
That thou (*Iago*) who haft had my purse,
As if ÿ strings were thine, should'st know of this.
Ia. But you'l not heareme. If euer I did dream
Of such a matter, abhorre me.
Rodo. Thou told'st me,
Thou did'st hold him in thy hate.
Iago. Despise me
If I do not. Three Great-ones of the Cittie,
(In personall suite to make me his Lieutenant)
Off-capt to him: and by the faith of man
I know my price, I am worth no worsse a place.
But he (as louing his owne pride, and purposes)
Euades them, with a bumbast Circumstance,
Horribly stufft with Epithites of warre,
Non-suites my Mediators. For certes, saies he,
I haue already chose my Officer. And what was he?
For-footh, a great Arithmatician,
One *Michaell Cassio*, a *Florentine*,
(A Fellow almost damn'd in a faire Wife)
That neuer set a Squadron in the Field,
Nor the deuision of a Battaile knowes
More then a Spinster. Vnlesse the Bookish Theoricke:
Wherein the Tongued Consuls can propose
As Masterly as he. Meere pratle (without practise)
Is all his Souldiership. But he (Sir) had th'election;
And I (of whom his eies had seene the proofe
At Rhodes, at Ciprus, and on others grounds
Christen'd, and Heathen) must be be-leed, and calm'd
By Debitor, and Creditor. This Counter-caster,
He (in good time) must his Lieutenant be,
And I (blesse the marke) his Mooreships Auntient.
　Rod. By heauen, I rather would haue bin his hangman.
　Iago. Why, there's no remedie.
'Tis the cursse of Seruice;
Preferment goes by Letter, and affection;
And not by old gradation, where each second
Stood Heire to th'first. Now Sir, be iudge your selfe,
Whether I in any iust terme am Affin'd
To loue the *Moore*?
　Rod. I would not follow him then.
　Iago. O Sir content you.
I follow him, to serue my turne vpon him.
We cannot all be Masters, nor all Masters

Cannot be truely follow'd. You shall marke
Many a dutious and knee-crooking knaue;
That (doting on his owne obsequious bondage)
Weares out his time, much like his Mast ers Asse,
For naught but Prouender, & when he's old Casheer'd.
Whip me such honest knaues. Others there are
Who trym'd in Formes, and visages of Dutie,
Keepe yet their hearts attending on themselues,
And throwing but showes of Seruice on their Lords
Doe well thriue by them.
And when they haue lin'd their Coates
Doe themselues Homage.
These Fellowes haue some soule,
And such a one do I professe my selfe. For (Sir)
It is as sure as you are *Rodorigo*,
Were I the Moore, I would not be *Iago* :
In following him, I follow but my selfe.
Heauen is my Iudge, not I for loue and dutie,
But seeming so, for my peculiar end :
For when my outward Action doth demonstrate
The natiue act, and figure of my heart
In Complement extrerne, 'tis not long after
But I will weare my heart vpon my sleeue
For Dawes to pecke at ; I am not what I am.
　Rod. What a fall Fortune do's the Thicks-lips owe
If he can carry't thus?
　Iago. Call vp her Father :
Rowse him, make after him, poyson his delight,
Proclaime him in the Streets, Incense her kinsmen,
And though he in a fertile Clymate dwell,
Plague him with Flies: though that his Ioy be Ioy,
Yet throw such chances of vexation on't,
As it may loose some colour.
　Rodo. Heere is her Fathers house, Ile call aloud.
　Iago. Doe, with like timerous accent, and dire yell,
As when (by Night and Negligence) the Fire
Is spied in populus Citties.
　Rodo. What hoa : *Brabantio*, Siginor *Brabantio*, hoa.
　Iago. Awake: what hoa, *Brabantio* : Theeues, Theeues.
Looke to your house, your daughter, and your Bags,
Theeues, Theeues.
　Bra. About. What is the reason of this terrible
Summons? What is the matter there?
　Rodo. Signior is all your Familie within?
　Iago. Are your Doores lock'd?
　Bra. Why? Wherefore ask you this?
　Iago. Sir, y'are rob'd, for shame put on your Gowne,
Your

Signature 210.

This signature is found on the last page of *The Tragedie of Othello.*

Begin to read on the terminal N of the word 'weapon,' which is at the end of the first line; to the left; downwards; through the text, the word 'FINIS,' and the list of names of the actors, and over on to the next column; on the terminals; spelling NOCAB, you will arrive at the initial terminal B of the word 'be' in the first line of the second column.

Begin to read from the terminal N of the word 'Curtezan,' which is the last word in the second column; to the left; upwards; on the terminals; through the names of the actors, the word 'FINIS,' and the words of the text; spelling NOCAB, you will arrive again at the initial terminal B of the word 'be' in the first line of the second column; thus keying the cipher from opposite ends of the string of letters to a common centre.

The acrostic figure here is: —

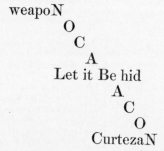

```
        weapoN
             O
              C
               A
        Let it Be hid
               A
              C
             O
        CurtezaN
```

The reader will observe that the word 'FINIS' is common to both columns.

Caſ This did I feare, but thought he had no weapon;
For he was great of heart.
    Lod Oh Sparton Dogge:
More fell then Anguiſh, Hunger, or the Sea:
Looke on the Tragicke Loading of this bed:
This is thy worke:
The Obiect poyſons Sight,

Let it be hid. *Cratiano*, keepe the houſe,
And ſeize vpon the Fortunes of the Moore,
For they ſucceede on , ɔu. To you, Lord Gouernor,
Remainer th eCenſure of this helliſh villaine:
The Time, the Place, the Torture, oh inforce it ⁏
My ſelfe will ſtraight aboord, and to the State,
This heauie Act, with heauie heart relate.   *Exeunt.*

FINIS.

The Names of the Actors.
(:*⁎*:)

 Thello, *the Moore.*
Brabantio, *Father to Deſdemona.*
Caſſio, *an Honourable Lieutenant.*
Iago, *a Villaine.*
Rodorigo, *a gull'd Gentleman.*
Duke *of Venice*

Senators.
Montano, *Gouernour of Cyprus.*
Gentlemen of Cyprus.
Lodouico, *and* Gratiano, *two Noble Venetians.*
Saylors.
Clowne.

Deſdemona, *wife to Othello.*
Æmilia, *wife to Iago.*
Bianca, *a Curtezan.*

Signature 211.

This acrostic is found on the last page of *The Tragedie of Anthony and Cleopatra.*

Begin to read from the initial O of the word ' Oh,' which is the first word of the text on the page; to the right; downwards; on initials; through the text to the end of the play; spelling ONOCAB OCSICNARF, you will arrive at the initial F of the word ' FINIS.'

On turning back to the last lines of the previous page it is amusing to find that they are:—

> *Enter Cæsar and all his Traine, marching.*
> *All.* A way there, a way for Cæsar.

The signature begins on the next word over the page.

Oh sir, you are too sure an Augurer:

N
  O
    C
     A
       B
        O
         C
          S
           I
            C
             N
              A
               R
                 FINIS

Dol. Oh sir, you are too sure an Augurer:
That you did feare, is done.

Cæsar. Brauest at the last,
She leuell'd at our purposes, and being Royall
Tooke her owne way : the manner of their deaths,
I do not see them bleede.

Dol. Who was last with them?

1 Guard. A simple Countryman, that broght hir Figs:
This was his Basket.

Cæsar. Poyson'd then.

1.Guard. Oh *Cæsar.:*
This *Charmian* liu'd but now, she stood and spake :
I found her trimming vp the Diadem;
On her dead Mistris tremblingly she stood,
And on the sodaine dropt.

Cæsar. Oh Noble weakenesse :
If they had swallow'd poyson, 'twould appeare
By externall swelling : but she lookes like sleepe,
As she would catch another *Anthony*
In her strong toyle of Grace.

Dol. Heere on her brest,
There is a vent of Bloud, and something blowne,
The like is on her Arme.

1.Guard. This is an Aspickes traile,
And these Figge-leaues haue slime vpon them, such
As th'Aspicke leaues vpon the Caues of Nyle.

Cæsar. Most probable
That so she dyed : for her Physitian tels mee
She hath pursu'de Conclusions infinite
Of easie wayes to dye. Take vp her bed,
And beare her Women from the Monument,
She shall be buried by her *Anthony*.
No Graue vpon the earth shall clip in it
A payre so famous : high euents as these
Strike those that make them : and their Story is
No lesse in pitty, then his Glory which
Brought them to be lamented. Our Army shall
In solemne shew, attend this Funerall,
And then to Rome. Come *Dolabella,* see
High Order, in this great Solmemnity. *Exeunt omnes*

FINIS.

Signature 212.

This signature is found in *The Tragedie of Cymbeline*, on page 379, wrongly numbered 389. (See p. 517.)

Note the lines with which the page opens. They run:—

> You'l giue me leaue to spare, when you shall finde
> You neede it not.

Post. Proceed.

Iach. First, etc.

The possible *double entente* of this opening on a wrongly numbered page gave me a lead.

Begin to read from the initial F of the word ' finde,' which is the last word of the first line on the column; downwards; on the initials of the last words of the lines; spelling F BACONO, you will arrive at the initial O of the last word of the last line in the column, ' or.'

The acrostic figure here is:—

> You'l giue me leaue to spare, when you shall Finde
> B
> A
> C
> O
> N
> Or

Signature 213.

This acrostic is also found in *The Tragedie of Cymbeline*, on page 379, which is wrongly numbered 389. (See p. 517.)

Note the first two lines of the first column. They are:—

> You'l giue me leaue to spare, when you shall finde
> You neede it not.

The possible *double entente* of these lines is, ' You 'll excuse my liberality when you find that you have enough without it.'

Begin to read on the initial F of the word ' finde ' (at the end of the first line); down the first and then the second column; on the initial of each end word of each line; spelling FRANCIS BACON, you will arrive at the initial N of the word ' not,' which is the last word of the text of the second column.

Begin again to read from the initial F of the word ' finde ' (at the end of the first line of the first column); down the first and then the second column; on the initial of each end word of each line; spelling FRANCISCO BACONO, you will arrive at the initial O of the word ' Or,' which is the last word on the page (i. e. the last word on the last typographical line).

The two acrostic figures here are: —

You shall Finde

R
A
N
C
I
S
B
A
C
O
Not

Finde

R
A
N
C
I
S
C
O
B
A
C
O
N
Or

You'l giue me leaue to spare, when you shall finde
You neede it not.

Post. Proceed.

Iach. First, her Bed-chamber
(Where I confesse I slept not, but professe
Had that was well worth watching) it was hang'd
With Tapistry of Silke and Siluer, the Story
Proud *Cleopatra*, when she met her Roman,
And *Sidnus* swell'd aboue the Bankes, or for
The presse of Boates, or Price. A peece of Worke
So brauely doue, so rich, that it did striue
In Workemanship, and Value, which I wonder'd
Could be so rarely, and exactly wrought.
Since the true life on't was ————

Post. This is true:
And this you might haue heard of heere, by me,
Or by some other.

Iach. More particulars
Must iustifie my knowledge.

Post. So they must,
Or doe your Honour iniury.

Iach. The Chimney
Is South the Chamber, and the Chimney-peece
Chaste *Dian*, bathing : neuer saw I figures
So likely to report themselues ; the Cutter
Was as another Nature dumbe, out-went her,
Motion, and Breath left out.

Post. This is a thing
Which you might from Relation likewise reape,
Being, as it is, much spoke of.

Iach. The Roofe o'th'Chamber,
With golden Cherubins is fretted. Her Andirons
(I had forgot them) were two winking Cupids
Of Siluer, each on one foote standing, nicely
Depending on their Brands.

Post. This is her Honor :
Let it be granted you haue seene all this (and praise
Be giuen to your remembrance) the description
Of what is in her Chamber, nothing saues
The wager you haue laid.

Iach. Then if you can
Be pale, I begge but leaue to ayre this Iewell : See,
And now 'tis vp againe : it must be married
To that your Diamond, Ile keepe them.

Post. Ioue ————
Once more let me behold it : Is it that
Which I left with her?

Iach. Sir (I thanke her) that
She stript it from her Arme : I see her yet :
Her pretty Action, did out-sell her guift,
And yet enrich'd it too : she gaue it me,
And said, she priz'd it once.

Post. May be, she pluck'd it off
To send it me.

Iach. She writes so to you? doth shee?

Post. O no, no, no, 'tis true. Heere, take this too,
It is a Basiliske vnto mine eye,
Killes me to looke on't : Let there be no Honor,
Where there is Beauty : Truth, where semblance : Loue,
Where there's another man. The Vowes of Women,
Of no more bondage be, to where they are made,
Then they are to their Vertues, which is nothing :
O, aboue measure false.

Phil. Haue patience Sir,
And take your Ring againe, 'tis not yet wonne :
It may be probable she lost it : or

Who knowes if one her women, being corrupted
Hath stolne it from her.

Post. Very true,
And so I hope he came by't : backe my Ring,
Render to me some corporall signe about her
More euident then this : for this was stolne.

Iach. By Iupiter, I had it from her Arme.

Post. Hearke you, he sweares : by Iupiter he sweares.
'Tis true, nay keepe the Ring ; 'tis true : I am sure
She would not loose it : her Attendants are
All sworne, and honourable : they induc'd to steale it?
And by a Stranger? No, he hath enioy'd her,
The Cognisance of her incontinencie
Is this : she hath bought the name of Whore, thus deerly
There, take thy hyre, and all the Fiends of Hell
Diuide themselues betweene you.

Phil. Sir, be patient :
This is not strong enough to be beleeu'd
Of one perswaded well of.

Post. Neuer talke on't :
She hath bin colted by him.

Iach. If you seeke
For further satisfying, vnder her Breast
(Worthy her pressing) lyes a Mole, right proud
Of that most delicate Lodging. By my life
I kist it, and it gaue me present hunger
To feede againe, though full. You do remember
This staine vpon her?

Post. I, and it doth confirme
Another staine, as bigge as Hell can hold,
Were there no more but it.

Iach. Will you heare more?

Post. Spare your Arethmaticke,
Neuer count the Turnes : Once, and a Million.

Iach. Ile be sworne.

Post. No swearing :
If you will sweare you haue not done't, you lye,
And I will kill thee, if thou do'st deny
Thou'st made me Cuckold.

Iach. Ile deny nothing.

Post. O that I had her heere, to teare her Limb-meale :
I will go there and doo't, i'th'Court, before
Her Father. Ile do something. *Exit.*

Phil. Quite besides
The gouernment of Patience. You haue wonne :
Let's follow him, and peruert the present wrath
He hath against himselfe.

Iach. With all my heart. *Exeunt.*

Enter Posthumus.

Post. Is there no way for Men to be, but Women
Must be halfe-workers? We are all Bastards,
And that most venerable man, which I
Did call my Father, was, I know not where
When I was stampt. Some Coyner with his Tooles
Made me a counterfeit : yet my Mother seem'd
The *Dian* of that time : so doth my Wife
The Non-pareill of this. Oh Vengeance, Vengeance!
Me of my lawfull pleasure she restrain'd,
And pray'd me oft forbearance : did it with
A pudencie so Rosie, the sweet view on't
Might well haue warm'd olde Saturne ;
That I thought her
As Chaste, as vn-Sunn'd Snow. Oh, all the Diuels!
This yellow *Iachimo* in an houre, was't not?

Signature 214.

This acrostic is found on the last page of *The Tragedie of Cymbeline* (see p. 521), which is wrongly numbered 993 instead of 399 (i. e. the number points to the left). Note the first few lines: —

> Make no Collection of it. Let him shew
> His skill in the construction, etc., etc.,
> Read, and declare the meaning.

Now note the last six lines on the same column, and the first line on the next column: —

Cym. This hath some seeming.
→ *Sooth.* THELOFTYCEDARROYALLCYMBELINE
PERSONATESTHEEANDTHYLOPTBRANCHESPOINT
→ THYTWOSONNESFORTHWHOBYBELARIUSSTOLNE
FORMANYYEARESTHOUGHTDEADARENOWREUIUD
→ TOTHEMAIESTICKECEDARIOYNDWHOSEISSUE
——————————————————————————————
PROMISESBRITAINEPEACEANDPLENTY.

Treat this explanation by the Soothsayer as a string of letters.

Note the initials $\frac{F}{T}$ at the heads of the last two lines on the column.

Begin to read on the T at the bottom left-hand corner; upwards; to the right; in the usual sequence, throughout the five lines and back again, spelling TINEVNI NOCAB SICNUARF, i. e. Frauncis Bacon Invenit, you will arrive at the F of the word 'For,' at the head of the second line from the bottom of the column.

Now note that this Soothsayer's explanation seems to have been arranged so that it will yield the same result if the *whole* speech is used. Read from T, to the right; downwards; and back, throughout the speech, continuously; spelling as before, you will again arrive at the F of the word 'For.'

The acrostic figures here are alike, and circular: —

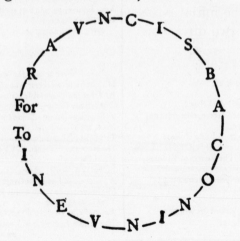

Signature 215.

This acrostic is also found on the last page of *The Tragedy of Cymbeline.* (See p. 521.)

Begin to read from the initial F of the word 'FINIS'; to the right; upwards; on the initials of the words of the text; up the right-hand column and then up the left; spelling FRAVNCIS BACON, you will arrive at the initial N of the word 'name.'

The acrostic figure here is:—

The fit and apt Construction of thy Name

O
C
A
B
S
I
C
N
V
A
R
FINIS.

As this acrostic runs from point to word instead of from point to point, I regard it as a 'weak' acrostic; though definite enough in its way. It is the more remarkable when you find that if you begin to read from the initial F of 'FINIS'; to the left; upwards; on the initials of the words of the text; up the right-hand column and down the left-hand column; spelling FRAVNCIS BACON, you will again arrive at the initial N of the same word 'name.' The acrostic is thus keyed in two directions.

Signature 216.

While we are dealing with this last page of the Folio we may as well note that the 'Letter of the Oracle' also contains an acrostic. In the last signature but one (No. 214) the Soothsayer has given us the meaning of it.

Begin to read from the last letter E of the 'Oracle'; to the left; upwards; on all the letters of all the words; spelling ERAEPSEKAHS MAILLIW (= William Shakespeare), you will arrive at the large

W which begins the first word of the 'Oracle.'

The acrostic figure here is: —

W^{Hen}

I

L

L

I   (Y in Lyons = I in Lion's.)

A

M

S

H

A   (Y in Ayre = I in Air.)

K

E

S

P

E

A

R

_{ti}E

NOTE. — For information as to the use of acrostics in oracles, refer to Graf's article, mentioned in Appendix II, p. 615.

For the use of the letter I in the place of the letter Y, in acrostics, see the acrostic showing STANLEI (Stanley), down the face of each of seven stanzas. See *Political, Religious, and Love Poems, etc.* (Early English Text Society), edited by F. J. Furnivall.

Make no Collection of it. Let him shew
His skill in the construction.

Luc. *Philarmonus.*

Sooth Heere, my good Lord.

Luc Read, and declare the meaning.

Reades

WHen as a Lyons whelpe, shall to himselfe vnknown, without seeking finde, and bee embrac'd by a peece of tender Ayre: And when from a stately Cedar shall be lopt branches, which being dead many yeares, shall after reuiue, bee ioynted to the old Stocke, and freshly grow, then shall Posthumus end his miseries, Britaine be fortunate, and flourish in Peace and Plentie.

Thou *Leonatus* art the Lyons Whelpe,
The fit and apt Construction of thy name
Being *Leonatus*, doth import so much
The peece of tender Ayre, thy vertuous Daughter,
Which we call *Mollis Aer*, and *Mollis Aer*
We terme it *Mulier*; which *Mulier* I diuine
Is this most constant Wife, who euen now
Answering the Letter of the Oracle,
Vnknowne to you vnsought, were clipt about
With this most tender Aire.

Cym. This hath some seeming.

Sooth. The lofty Cedar, Royall *Cymbeline*
Personates thee: And thy lopt Branches, point
Thy two Sonnes forth: who by *Belarius* stolne
For many yeares thought dead, are now reuiu'd
To the Maiesticke Cedar ioyn'd; whose Issue
Promises Britaine, Peace and Plenty.

Cym. Well,
My Peace we will begin: And *Caius Lucius*,
Although the Victor, we submit to *Cæsar*,
And to the Romane Empire; promising
To pay our wonted Tribute, from the which
We were disswaded by our wicked Queene,
Whom heauens in Iustice both on her, and hers,
Haue laid most heauy hand.

Sooth. The fingers of the Powres aboue, do tune
The harmony of this Peace: the Vision
Which I made knowne to *Lucius* ere the stroke
Of yet this scarse-cold-Battaile, at this instant
Is full accomplish'd. For the Romaine Eagle
From South to West, on wing soaring aloft
Lessen'd her selfe, and in the Beames o'th'Sun
So vanish'd; which fore-shew'd our Princely Eagle
Th'Imperiall *Cæsar*, should againe vnite
His Fauour, with the Radiant *Cymbeline*,
Which shines heere in the West.

Cym. Laud we the Gods,
And let our crooked Smoakes climbe to their Nostrils
From our blest Altars. Publish we this Peace
To all our Subiects. Set we forward: Let
A Roman, and a Brittish Ensigne waue
Friendly together: so through *Luds-Towne* march,
And in the Temple of great Iupiter
Our Peace wee'l ratifie: Seale it with Feasts.
Set on there: Neuer was a Warre did cease
(Ere bloodie hands were wash'd) with such a Peace.
Exeunt.

FINIS.

Printed at the Charges of W. Jaggard, Ed. Blount, I. Smithweeke, and W. Aspley, 1623.

CHAPTER XIII

Richard II. Quarto edition of 1597.

Romeo and Juliet. Quarto edition of 1597.

Romeo and Juliet. Quarto edition of 1599.

Romeo and Juliet. Folio edition of 1623.

Richard III. Quarto edition of 1597.

Richard III. Quarto edition of 1602.

Titus Andronicus. Quarto edition of 1600.

Hamlet. Quarto edition of 1603.

Hamlet. Quarto edition of 1604.

Othello. Quarto edition of 1622.

The nine Quartos with which I deal in this chapter must serve, for the present, as an indication of what may be sought in the rest. The mere bulk to which this book has grown has limited my work on the Quartos.

For purposes of presentation I have used the numberings which have hitherto been given to these Quartos. It is probable that some of them are incorrectly numbered, and that corrections will be made in view of the discovery in Sweden of a copy of *Titus Andronicus* dated 1594,[1] and of Mr. W. W. Greg's examination of the water-marks of some copies.[2]

[1] See W. Keller's account of the edition, and of Ljungren's collation of it with the Quarto of 1600, in the *Jahrbuch der Deutschen Shakespeare-Gesellschaft*, pp. 211–12, 1905.

[2] See *The Library*, New Series, nos. 34 and 36, October and April, 1908.

Signature 218.

This signature is found in the last two (facing) pages of *The Tragedie of King Richard the Second,* as it is printed anonymously in the Quarto of 1597. (See pp. 526-27.)

Note that the initial of the first word on the penultimate page is the O of the word ' Our,' and that the initial of the last word of the play is the capital letter B of the word ' Beere.'

Begin to read from the capital B of the word ' Beere '; to the right or to the left; upwards; through the text of the two pages; using *all* the *capitals* of *all the words* on the page; spelling Bacono, you will arrive at the capital O of the word ' Our ' at the top left-hand corner of the penultimate page.

The acrostic figure here is: —

Our towne of Ciceter in Gloucestershire,

N

O

C

A

In weeping after this vntimely Beere

Note that the initials of the last two words of the play are the B F, or, if read upwards, the F B of the words ' Finis ' and ' Beere.'

Signature 219.

In dealing with *The Tragedie of Romeo and Juliet*, I shall show you the signature as it appears in the first known Quarto, published anonymously in 1597, so that you may compare it with the signature in the second known Quarto, published anonymously in 1599.

The second known Quarto contains revisions and additions which rendered necessary another cipher. Note that the last paragraph of the play as it is printed in the second known Quarto is printed *verbatim* with the same paragraph as it was printed twenty-four years later in the first Folio.

We will now take the so-called first Quarto of 1597, on its last page.

Begin to read from the initial B of the word 'By,' which is the first word on the page of the text; to the right; downwards; on the initials of the words of the text; spelling BACONO, you will arrive at the initial O of the word ' on.'

Now begin to read from the initial F of the word 'FINIS'; to the right; on the initials of the words of the text; spelling FRANCISCO, you will arrive again at the same initial O of the word ' on.'

The acrostic figure here is:—

By me, or by my meanes, etc.

A

C

O

N

Can I bestowe On her, thats all I haue.

C

S

I

C

N

A

R

FINIS

of Romeo and Iuliet.

By me, or by my meanes let my old life
Be sacrificd some houre before his time.
To the most strickest rigor of the Law.

   Pry: VVe still haue knowne thee for a holy man,
VVheres *Romeos* man, what can he say in this?

   Balth: I brought my maister word that shee was dead,
And then he poasted straight stom *Mantua,*
Vnto this Toombe. These Letters he deliuered me,
Charging me early giue them to his Father.

   Prin: Lets see the Letters, I will read them ouer.
VVhere is the Counties Boy that calld the VVatch?

   Boy: I brought my Master vnto *Iuliets* graue,
But one approaching, straight I calld my Master.
At last they fought, I ran to call the VVatch.
And this is all that I can say or know.

   Prin: These letters doe make good the Fryers wordes,
Come *Capolet,* and come olde *Mountagewe.*
VVhere are these enemies? see what hate hath done,

   Cap: Come brother *Mountague* giue me thy hand,
There is my daughters dowry: for now no more
Can I bestowe on her, thats all I haue.

   Moun: But I will giue them more, I will erect
Her statue of pure golde:
That while *Verona* by that name is knowne.
There shall no statue of such price be set,
As that of *Romeos* loued *Iuliet.*

   Cap: As rich shall *Romeo* by his Lady lie,
Poore Sacrifices to our Enmitie.

   Prin: A gloomie peace this day doth with it bring.
Come, let vs hence,
To haue more talke of these sad things.
Some shall be pardoned and some punished:
For nere was heard a Storie of more woe,
Than this of *Iuliet* and her *Romeo.*

FINIS.

Signature 220.

Let us now turn to the so-called second Quarto (1599. Anonymous), where we see at once that the revision of the text has changed the face of the page and has necessitated the use of a new cipher.

I reproduce the facsimile from both the second Quarto, and the first Folio, so that the reader may compare them with the first Quarto. (See pp. 532–33.)

The acrostic is contained in the text of the last speech by the Prince.

For convenience I print the letters of the Prince's parting words, as if they were strung on a sixfold string, and I have placed arrow-marks for guidance.

```
  A GLOOMING PEACE THIS MORNING WITH IT BRINGS ←
→ THE SUN FOR SORROW WILL NOT SHEW HIS HEAD
  GO HENCE TO HAUE MORE TALKE OF THESE SAD THINGS ←
→ SOME SHALL BE PARDONED AND SOME PUNISHED
  FOR NEUER WAS A STORIE OF MORE WO ←        Note the cipher at
→ THEN THIS OF IULIET AND HER ROMEO         the end of each line.
```

Begin to read from the initial T, which begins the last line of the play; to the right; upwards; throughout the speech and back again continuously; on all the letters of all the words; spelling backwards TINEVNI NOCAB SICNVARFF (i. e., Ffrauncis Bacon Invenit), you will arrive at the letter F of the word 'For,' which begins the last line but one.

The acrostic figure here is: —

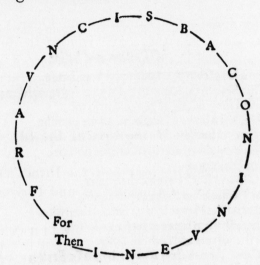

Note that the last page of the play in the Folio is wrongly numbered 79. It should be 77.

of Romeo and Iuliet.

See what a scourge is laide vpon your hate ?
That heauen finds means to kil your ioyes with loue,
And I for winking at your discords too,
Haue lost a brace of kinsmen, all are punisht.

Cap. O brother *Mountague,* giue me thy hand,
This is my daughters ioynture, for no more
Can I demaund.

Moun. But I can giue thee more,
For I will raie her statue in pure gold,
That whiles *Verona* by that name is knowne,
There shall no figure at such rate be set,
As that of true and faithfull *Iuliet.*

Capel. As rich shall *Romeos* by his Ladies lie,
Poore sacrifices of our enmitie.

Prin. A glooming peace this morning with it brings.
The Sun for sorrow will not shew his head:
Go hence to haue more talke of these sad things,
Some shall be pardoned, and some punished.
For neuer was a Storie of more wo,
Then this of *Iuliet* and her *Romeo.*

F I N I S.

I married them; and their stolne marriage day
Was *Tybalts* Doomesday: whose vntimely death
Banish'd the new-made Bridegroome from this Citie:
For whom (and not for *Tybalt*) *Iuliet* pinde.
You, to remoue that siege of Greefe from her,
Betroth'd and would haue married her perforce
To Countie *Paris*. Then comes she to me,
And (with wilde lookes) bid me deuise some meanes
To rid her from this second Marriage,
Or in my Cell there would she kill her selfe.
Then gaue I her (so Tutor'd by my Art)
A sleeping Potion, which so tooke effect
As I intended, for it wrought on her
The forme of death. Meane time, I writ to *Romeo*,
That he should hither come, as this dyre night,
To helpe to take her from her borrowed graue,
Being the time the Potions force should cease.
But he which bore my Letter, Frier *Iohn*,
Was stay'd by accident; and yesternight
Return'd my Letter backe. Then all alone,
At the prefixed houre of her waking,
Came I to take her from her Kindreds vault,
Meaning to keepe her closely at my Cell,
Till I conueniently could send to *Romeo*.
But when I came (some Minute ere the time
Of her awaking) heere vntimely lay
The Noble *Paris*, and true *Romeo* dead.
Shee wakes, and I intreated her come foorth,
And beare this worke of Heauen, with patience:
But then, a noyse did scarre me from the Tombe,
And she (too desperate) would not go with me,
But (as it seemes) did violence on her selfe.
All this I know, and to the Marriage her Nurse is priuy:
And if ought in this miscarried by my fault,
Let my old life be sacrific'd, some houre before the time,
Vnto the rigour of seuerest Law.
    Prin. We still haue knowne thee for a Holy man.
Where's *Romeo's* man? What can he say to this?
    Boy. I brought my Master newes of *Iuliets* death,

And then in poste he came from *Mantua*
To this same place, to this same Monument.
This Letter he early bid me giue his Father,
And threatned me with death, going in the Vault,
If I departed not, and left him there.
    Prin. Giue me the Letter, I will looke on it.
Where is the Counties Page that rais'd the Watch?
Sirra, what made your Master in this place?
    Page. He came with flowres to strew his Ladies graue,
And bid me stand aloofe, and so I did:
Anon comes one with light to ope the Tombe,
And by and by my Maister drew on him,
And then I ran away to call the Watch.
    Prin. This Letter doth make good the Friers words,
Their course of Loue, the tydings of her death:
And heere he writes, that he did buy a poyson
Of a poore Pothecarie, and therewithall
Came to this Vault to dye, and lye with *Iuliet*.
Where be these Enemies? *Capulet*, *Mountague*,
See what a scourge is laide vpon your hate,
That Heauen finds meanes to kill your ioyes with Loue;
And I, for winking at your discords too,
Haue lost a brace of Kinsmen: All are punish'd.
    Cap. O Brother *Mountague*, giue me thy hand,
This is my Daughters ioynture, for no more
Can I demand.
    Moun. But I can giue thee more:
For I will raise her Statue in pure Gold,
That whiles *Verona* by that name is knowne,
There shall no figure at that Rate be set,
As that of True and Faithfull *Iuliet*.
    Cap. As rich shall *Romeo* by his Lady ly,
Poore sacrifices of our enmity.
    Prin. A glooming peace this morning with it brings,
The Sunne for sorrow will not shew his head:
Go hence, to haue more talke of these sad things,
Some shall be pardon'd, and some punished.
For neuer was a Storie of more Wo,
Then this of *Iuliet*, and her *Romeo*.   *Exeunt omnes*

Gg

FINIS.

Signature 221.

This acrostic is found on the first page of *The Tragedy of King Richard the Third*, as it is printed in the Quarto of 1597, published anonymously.

Note the large initial of the first line, and the initials of the lines which are indented.

$$N\begin{matrix} O \\ M \\ A \\ I \end{matrix}$$

Reading upwards we have I AM O; which may mean *I am, cipher*.

Note also that the last words on the page are 'I am.'

Begin to read from the words 'I am'; to the right; upwards; and thereafter continue on the initials of the words of the text; spelling FFRANCIS BACON, you will arrive at the large **N** which begins the text of the first line.

The acrostic figure here is:—

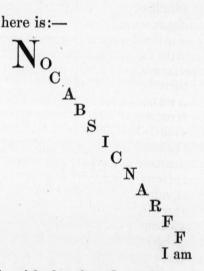

Compare this acrostic with that found on the corresponding page of the same play in the Quarto of 1602. (See p. 536.)

Enter Richard Duke of Glocester, solus.

NOw is the winter of our difcontent,
Made glorious fummer by this fonne of Yorke:
And all the cloudes that lowrd vpon our houfe,
In the deepe bofome of the Ocean buried.
Now are our browes bound with victorious wreathes,
Our bruifed armes hung vp for monuments,
Our fterne alarmies changd to merry meetings,
Our dreadfull marches to delightfull meafures.
Grim-vifagde warre, hath fmoothde his wrinkled front,
And now in fteed of mounting barbed fteedes,
To fright the foules of fearefull aduerfaries,
He capers nimbly in a Ladies chamber,
To the lafciuious pleafing of a loue.
But I that am not fhapte for fportiue trickes,
Nor made to court an amorous looking glaffe,
I that am rudely ftampt and want loues maiefty,
To ftrut before a wanton ambling Nymph:
I that am curtaild of this faire proportion,
Cheated of feature by diffembling nature,
Deformd, vnfinifht, fent before my time
Into this breathing world fcarce halfe made vp,
And that fo lamely and vnfafhionable,
That dogs barke at me as I halt by them:
Why I in this weake piping time of peace
Haue no delight to paffe away the time,
Vnleffe to fpie my fhadow in the funne,
And defcant on mine owne deformity:
And therefore fince I cannot prooue a louer
To entertaine thefe faire well fpoken daies,
                    A 2   I am

Signature 222.

This acrostic is found on the first page of *The Tragedie of King Richard the Third*, as it is printed in the Quarto of 1602.

We shall use the capital letters only.

Begin to read from the large 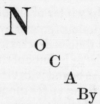 at the beginning of the first line; to the right; downwards; on *all* the capitals used on the page; spelling backwards NOCAB, you will arrive at the capital B of the word 'By' at the lower right-hand corner of the page.

The acrostic figure here is:—

       N
         o
           C
             A
               By

If you prefer to read from the O, or cipher, which follows the 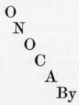 ; to the left or to the right; downwards; on capitals; then the signature becomes ONOCAB, i. e. Bacono.

The acrostic figure here is:—

       O
        N
         O
          C
           A
            By

It is interesting and instructive to compare this signature with that in the same play in its corresponding place in the first Folio.

Enter Richard Duke of Glocester, solus.

NOw is the winter of discontent,
Made glorious sommer by this sonne of Yorke :
And all the cloudes that lowrd vpon our house,
In the deepe bosomie of the Ocean buried.
Now are our browes bound with victorious wreathes,
Our bruised armes hung vp for monuments,
Our sterne alarums changd to merry meetings,
Our dreadfull marches to delightfull measures.
Grim-visagde warre, hath smoothde his wringled front,
And now in stead of mounting barbed steeds,
To fright the soules of fearefull aduersaries,
He capers nimblie in a Ladies chamber,
To the lasciuious pleasing of a Loue.
But I that am not shapte for sportiue trickes,
Nor made to court an amorous looking glasse,
I that am rudely stampt, and want loues maiestie
To strut before a wanton ambling Nymph:
I that am curtaild of this faire proportion,
Cheated of feature by dissembling nature,
Deformd, vnfinisht, sent before my time
Into this breathing world halfe made vp,
And that so lamely and vnfashionable,
That dogs barke at me as I halt by them:
Why I in this weake piping time of peace
Haue no delight to passe away the time,
Vnlesse to spie my shadow in the Sunne,
And descant on mine owne deformitie :
And therefore since I cannot proue a louer
To entertaine these faire well spoken daies,
I am determined to proue a villaine,
And hate the idle pleasures of these daies :
Plots haue I laid, inductions dangerous,
A 2   By

Signature 224.

This acrostic is found on the page preceding the last page of the Quarto edition of *The most lamentable Romaine Tragedie of Titus Andronicus,* published anonymously in 1600.

Note the initials of the first two lines on the page; they are $\begin{smallmatrix}B\\F\end{smallmatrix}$ of the words $\begin{smallmatrix}But\\For\end{smallmatrix}$

Note the initial F of the first word of the last line.

Begin to read from the initial F of the word 'For'; to the right; upwards; on the initials of the words of the text; spelling FRANCISCO, you will arrive at the initial O of the word ' of.' Continue to read from the initial O of the word ' of '; to the right; upwards; on the initials of the words of the text; spelling ONOCAB, you will arrive at the initial B of the word ' But '; thus keying the cipher from the initial of the first word of the last line to the initial of the first word of the first line.

The acrostic figure here is: —

```
        But gentle people giue me ayme a while,
        A
            C
                O
                    N
        and learne  Of vs
                    C
                   S
                 I
               C
             N
           A
         R
        For the offence he dies, this is our doome.
```

of Titus Andronicus.

But gentle people giue me ayme a while,
For nature puts me to a heauie taske,
Stand all a loofe, but Vnkle draw you neere,
To shed obsequious teares vpon this trunke,
Oh take this warme kisse on thy pale cold lips,
These sorrowfull drops vpon thy bloodslaine face,
The last true duties of thy noble sonne.

   Marcus. Teare for teare, and louing kisse for kisse,
Thy brother *Marcus* tenders on thy lips,
Oh were the summe of these that I should pay,
Countlesse and infinite, yet would I pay them.

   Lucius. Come hither boy come, come and learne of vs
To melt in showers, thy Grandsire lou'd thee well,
Many a time he daunst thee on his knee,
Sung thee a sleepe, his louing breast thy pillow,
Many a matter hath he told to thee,
Meete and agreeing with thine infancie,
In that respect then, like a louing child.
Shed yet some small drops from thy tender spring,
Because kind nature doth require it so,
Friends should associate friends in griefe and woe.
Bid him farewell, commit him to the graue,
Doe them that kindnes, and take leaue of them.

   Puer. Oh Grandsire, Grandsire, eu'n with all my hart,
Would I were dead so you did liue againe,
O Lord I cannot speake to him for weeping,
My teares will choake me if I ope my mouth.

   Romaine. You sad *Andronicie* haue done with woes,
Giue sentence on this execrable wretch,
That hath beene breeder of these dire euents.

   Lucius. Set him breast deepe in earth and famish him,
There let him stand and raue and cry for foode,
If any one releeues or pitties him,
For the offence he dies, this is our doome.

                                  Some

The acrostic figure here is: —

The Tragicall Historie oF

R
A
N
C
I
S
C
O
B
A
C
O
N

O Farewell honest souldier, etc.

R
A
N
C
I
S
C

And wil nOt let beliefe take hold of him,

N
O
C
A
B   (Printer's Signature.)

The Tragicall Hiſtorie of
HAMLET
Prince of Denmarke.

Enter two Centinels.

1. STand : who is that?
2. STis I.
1. O you come moſt carefully vpon your watch,
2. And if you meete *Marcellus* and *Horatio*,
The partners of my watch, bid them make haſte.
1. I will : See who goes there.
            Enter Horatio and Marcellus.
Hor. Friends to this ground.
Mar. And leegemen to the Dane,
O farewell honeſt ſouldier, who hath releeued you?
1. *Barnardo* hath my place, giue you good night.
Mar. Holla, *Barnardo.*
2. Say, is *Horatio* there?
Hor. A peece of him.
2. Welcome *Horatio*, welcome good *Marcellus.*
Mar. What hath this thing appear'd againe to night.
2. I haue ſeene nothing.
Mar. *Horatio* ſayes tis but our fantaſie,
And wil not let beliefe take hold of him,
Touching this dreaded ſight twice ſeene by vs,
            B   There-

Signature 227.

This signature is found on the first page of *The Tragedie of Hamlet Prince of Denmarke*, in the Quarto edition of 1604.

Note the change that has taken place in the text of the page. Compare it with the previous facsimile. The former signature has been obliterated. But scan the last line of this page in the so-called second Quarto. It runs: —

F r a n. *Barnardo* hath my place; giue you good night.
FRAN BA.......... ....C. .... .O .... N.......

Begin to read from the initial B of 'Barnardo'; along the line; on all the letters; spelling BACON, you will arrive at the initial N of the last word, 'night.'

If you choose to include the name of the *dramatis personae*, you will have the name as it is signed to the 'Dedication' of the first edition of the *Essayes*, namely, FRAN BACON.

The Tragedie of

HAMLET

Prince of Denmarke.

Enter Barnardo, and Francisco, two Centinels.

Bar. VVHose there?
Fran. Nay answere me. Stand and vnfolde your selfe.
Bar. Long liue the King.
Fran. Barnardo.
Bar. Hee.
Fran. You come most carefully vpon your houre,
Bar. Tis now strooke twelfe, get thee to bed *Francisco*,
Fran. For this reliefe much thanks, tis bitter cold,
  And I am sick at hart.
Bar. Haue you had quiet guard?
Fran. Not a mouse stirring.
Bar. Well, good night :
  If you doe meete *Horatio* and *Marcellus*,
  The riualls of my watch, bid them make hast.
        Enter Horatio, and Marcellus.
Fran. I thinke I heare them, stand ho, who is there?
Hora. Friends to this ground.
Mar. And Leedgemen to the Dane,
Fran. Giue you good night.
Mar. O, farwell honest souldiers, who hath relieu'd you?
Fran. *Barnardo* hath my place; giue you good night.   *Exit Fran.*
        B.   *Mar.*

Signature 228.

This acrostic is found in the last page of *The Tragedie of Othello,* as it is printed in the Quarto of 1622.

Begin to read from the initial N of the word 'No,' which is the first word of the first line; to the right; downwards; on the terminals of the words of the text; spelling NOCAB SICNARF, you will arrive at the initial F of the word 'FINIS.'

Here we have an acrostic on terminals of all words on the page, beginning on the initial of the first word of the first line, and ending on the initial of the first (and only) word of the last line.

The acrostic figure here is: —

No more of that: I pray you in your letters,
  O
   C
    A
     B
      S
       I
        C
        N
         A
          R
           FINIS.

The Moore of Venice.

No more of that : I pray you in your letters,
When you ſhall theſe vnlucky deedes relate,
Speake of them as they are ; nothing extenuate,
Nor ſet downe ought in malice, then muſt you ſpeake,
Of one that lou'd not wiſely, but too well :
Of one not eaſily iealous, but being wrought,
Perplext in the extreame ; of one whoſe hand,
Like the baſe *Indian*, threw a pearle away,
Richer then all his Tribe : of one whoſe ſubdued eyes,
Albeit vnuſed to the melting moode,
Drops teares as faſt as the *Arabian* trees,
Their medicinall gum ; ſet you downe this,
And ſay beſides, that in *Aleppo* once,
Where a *Malignant* and a *Turband Turke*,
Beate a *Venetian*, and traduc'd the State ;
I tooke by'th throate the circumciſed dog,
And ſmote him thus.   *He ſtabs himſelfe.*
    Lod. O bloody period.
    Gra. All that's ſpoke is mard.
    Oth. I kiſt thee ere I kild thee, no way but this,
Killing my ſelfe, to die vpon a kiſſe.   *He dies.*
    Caſ. This did I feare, but thought he had no weapon,
For he was great of heart.
    Lod. O Spartane dog,
More fell then anguiſh, hunger, or the Sea,
Looke on the tragicke lodging of this bed :
This is thy worke, the obiect poiſons ſight,
Let it be hid : *Gratiano*, keepe the houſe,
And ceaze vpon the fortunes of the Moore :
For they ſucceed to you, to you Lord Gouernour,
Remaines the cenſure of this helliſh villaine,
The time, the place, the torture : O inforce it,
My ſelfe will ſtraite aboord, and to the State,
This heauy act with heauy heart relate.
                          Exeunt omnes.

FINIS.

CHAPTER XIV

ACROSTICS MADE IN AN IDENTICAL WAY, BY JOHN MILTON, BEN JONSON, JOSEPH HALL, AND (?) RICHARD BARNFIELD

Signature 229.

MILTON'S poem, which appears (unsigned) in the second Folio of Shakespeare's *Comedies, Histories and Tragedies,* contains one important difference from its wording in the first collected edition of Milton's *Poems* published in 1645; so I print facsimiles from both editions. (See p. 553.)

We find that Milton has used the same method as that used by Ben Jonson in his poem in the first Folio.

Observe the word 'bones' at the end of the first line of the poem.

Begin to read from the letter B of the word 'bones'; to the left; on the outside letters of the poem; reading clean around the poem; spelling BACONO, you will arrive at the letter O of the word 'bones,' having entirely encircled the poem. (This Italianate form cannot be here regarded as the ablative.)

Begin to read from the letter O of the word 'bones'; to the right; on the outside letters of the poem; clean around the poem; spelling ONOCAB (= Bacono), you will arrive at the letter B of the word 'bones,' having again entirely encircled the poem.

I reproduce the outside letters showing the reading in the second Folio. The spelling is different in the *Poems* of Milton (Edition of 1645), but does not alter the result.

```
WHATNEEDEMYSHAKESPEAREFORHISHONOURDBONES
T                                       S
O                                       D
V                                       D
D                                       E
W                                       E
T                                       T
H                                       T
F                                       T
T                                       T
H                                       E
T                                       E
T                                       G
D                                       G
A                                       E
THAT KINGS FOR SUCH A TOMBE WOULD WISH TO DIE
```

Signature 230.

Now note that if you begin to read from the initial B of the word 'bones'; to the left; downwards; on all the letters of all the words; spelling BACON, you will arrive at the initial N of the word 'Name.'

The acrostic figure here is:—

Bones
A
C
O
Name.

Now note that if you begin to read from the initial F of the word 'Fame'; to the left; upwards; through the poem and back again; on all letters of all words; spelling FRAN BACON, you will again arrive at the initial N of the word 'Name.'

The acrostic figure here is:—

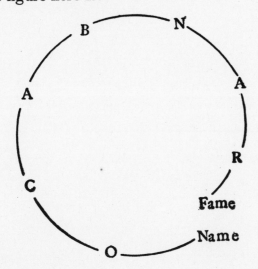

Signature 231.

The reader will now observe that the reading of the fourth line from the bottom of the poem runs, in the second Folio version:—

Then thou our fancy of her selfe bereaving.

And that in the facsimile from the *Poems* of Milton, it runs:—

Then thou our fancy of it self bereaving.

The change of the word 'her,' in the Folio of 1632, to the word 'it' looks like a revision by Milton for his collected edition of 1645. This revision throws another acrostic into the poem, as follows.

Begin to read *from the only letter F* in the last line; to the right; upwards; on all the letters of all the words; spelling Ffrauncis Bacon, you will arrive again at the initial N of the word 'name.'

The acrostic figure here is:—

That Kings For such a Tomb would wish to die.

An Epitaph on the admirable Dramaticke Poet, VV. SHAKESPEARE.

What neede my Shakespeare for his honour'd bones,
The labour of an Age, in piled stones
Or that his hallow'd Reliques should be hid
Vnder a starre-ypointing Pyramid?
Deare Sonne of Memory, great Heire of Fame,
What needst thou such dull witnesse of thy Name?
Thou in our wonder and astonishment
Hast built thy selfe a lasting Monument:
For whil'st to th'shame of slow-endevouring Art,
Thy easie numbers flow, and that each part,
Hath from the leaves of thy unvalued Booke,
Those Delphicke Lines with deepe Impression tooke
Then thou our fancy of her selfe bereaving,
Dost make us Marble with too much conceiving;
And so Sepulcher'd in such pompe dost lie
That Kings for such a Tombe would wish to die.

2d Folio Version.

On Shakespear. 1630.

What needs my Shakespear for his honour'd Bones,
The labour of an age in piled Stones,
Or that his hallow'd reliques should be hid
Under a Star-ypointing Pyramid?
Dear son of memory, great heir of Fame,
What need'st thou such weak witnes of thy name?
Thou in our wonder and astonishment
Hast built thy self a live-long Monument.
For whilst toth'shame of slow-endevouring art,
Thy easie numbers flow, and that each heart
Hath from the leaves of thy unvalu'd Book,
Those Delphick lines with deep impression took,
Then thou our fancy of it self bereaving,
Dost make us Marble with too much conceaving;
And so Sepulcher'd in such pomp dost lie,
That Kings for such a Tomb would wish to die.

On

Poems of Mr. John Milton, 1645.

NOVÆ

SOLYMÆ

Libri Sex.

LONDINI,
Typis Joannis Legati.

MDCXLVIII.

Signature 234.

My friend Richard T. Holbrook, professor of Mediæval French and Italian literature in Bryn Mawr College, has written a valuable little book on Milton's relation to the music and musicians of his time.[1] I have had the privilege of reading this book in manuscript and the still more generous one of quoting freely from those passages which throw light on my own work. Indeed, I am indebted to my friend for the suggestion that acrostics might be found in Milton's Italian poems. Professor Holbrook offers both acrostic and circumstantial evidence to show that Leonora Baroni was the name of the woman to whom Milton addressed these poems. Masson dismisses, as a fancy for which there is no real ground, the surmise that they were addressed to this attractive and famous singer.[2]

Donna Leonora's initials were L. B. Now it is not to be supposed that the good-looking John Milton was an anchorite, or that he was ignorant of the literary devices and tricks of type so common among the Italian wits of that day. It is even possible that he had seen a book, issued at Venice in 1623 and again at Naples in 1628, entitled *Il Teatro delle glorie della signora Adriana Basile.* Adriana was a Neapolitan singer, famous from about 1600 to about 1640. This book contains poems by a score of authors, some of them of noble birth, and in several languages, — Latin, Greek, Spanish, and Italian. Among others, Francesco Massa lauds Adriana and her husband, Muzio Baroni, in fourteen hexameters, the *initials* of which form the name of Muzio (Mutius), and the *finals* that of Adriana Basile (Basilis).[3]

But we must face the possibility that Milton knew little and cared less about such 'toys' as acrostics.[4] If that was the case, it is interesting to discover that he saw fit to use, or devise, those which you have already seen, and those, very skilfully concealed, which follow.

[1] *A Poet and his Music.* By Richard T. Holbrook. (Not yet published.)

[2] *The Poetical Works of John Milton:* edited, with Memoir, etc., by David Masson, vol. i, p. 62. Also, *Life of John Milton.* Masson, vol. i, pp. 774–5. 1859.

[3] See A. Ademollo, *La bell'Adriana,* etc. Città di Castello, 1888, pp. 320–323.

[4] But what about that outrageous practical joke which Milton, at the age of 37, played on William Marshall in the Greek inscription under Milton's own portrait in the first collected edition of his own poems in 1645?

In the light of the purely historical (non-acrostic) part of Professor Holbrook's argument that the unknown Italian lady may well have been Leonora Baroni, it is interesting to note that the typographical opening of the first Italian sonnet is composed of the word *Donna*, and the initials $\frac{L}{B}$ (See p. 564.) Their position in the sonnet itself is: —

(See p. 564.)

DONNA

L

B

Professor Holbrook tells me that, according to an opinion given to him by an accomplished mathematician, the combination D L B at the beginning of the sonnet [1] might occur, by chance, once in eight thousand sonnets. The calculation is based on the theory of chances. The greater the number of letters occurring as initials at the beginning of the verses, the smaller would be the chance that a given combination, or monogram, would fall at the very beginning and nowhere else.

Now begin to read from the initial D of the word 'Donna,' to the right; on all the letters of all the words; spelling DONNA LEONORA, you will arrive at the letter A, with which the line ends.

Begin to read from the initial L of the first word of the second line; to the right; upwards; on all the letters of all the words; spelling LEONORA, you will again arrive at the last letter A on the first line; thus meeting and keying the previous reading.

The acrostic figure here is: —

DONNA LEggiadra il cui bel nOme hoNORA

L'hErbOsa val di rheNO, e il nobil vaRco

---

[1] This sonnet is the first poem in a sequence of six poems, all of them being sonnets, save the third, which is a canzone. There are eighty-five lines in these six poems, as may be readily seen, with the monogram D L B at the head, where we should expect it to be.

Signature 235.

Begin again to read from the initial B in the group $\begin{matrix} \text{DONNA} \\ \text{L} \\ \text{B} \end{matrix}$ to the right; upwards; spelling BARONI, you will arrive at the letter I of the word 'il' on the second line. (See p. 564.)

Begin to read *from the only letter B* on the first line; to the right, *or to the left;* downwards; spelling BARONI, you will arrive again at the letter I of the word 'il' on the second line; thus keying the signature BARONI.

The acrostic figure here is: —

> Bel nome honora
> A
> R
> O
> N
> Il nobil, etc.
>
>   N
>   O
> R
> A
> Ben e colui, etc.

Signature 236.

Now observe the words *L' entrata* (twelfth line). They may mean 'the beginning,' or 'the entrance.' (See p. 564.)

Begin to read from the initial I of the word ' *il* ' (first line); to the right; downwards; on the terminals of all the words; spelling INORAB ARONOEL (Leonora Baroni), you will arrive at the letter L of the words ' *L' entrata* ' (twelfth line).

The acrostic figure here is:—

Donna leggiadra I
              N
              O
              R
              A
              B
              A
              R
              O
              N
              O
              E
           L' entrata,

The English of this may be rendered, ' Fair Lady, Leonora Baroni.' One may be permitted to wonder whether Milton disclosed his acrostic skill to Mary Powell.

NOTE.—This is a pretty play with the words, rather than an acrostic: it combines both.

Signature 237.

Let us now turn to the second Italian sonnet, by Milton. (See p. 564.)

Begin to read from the initial L of the first word of the second line; to the right; on all the letters of all the words; spelling LEONORA, you will arrive at the letter A at the end of the word 'pastorella,' which is the last letter on the line.

Begin to read from the last letter (A of the word 'sera') of the first line; to the left; downwards; on all the letters of all the words; spelling A LEONORA, you will again arrive at the last letter A in the word 'pastorella.'

Begin to read from the last letter (A of the word 'bella') of the third line; to the left; upwards; on all the letters of all the words; spelling A LEONORA, you will again arrive at the last letter A in the word 'pastorella.'

The acrostic figure here is: —

```
                              serA
                                 L
                                 E
                                 O
                                 N
                                 O
                                 R
   L' avEzza giOviNetta pastORellA
                                 R
                                 O
                                 N
                                 O
                                 E
                                 L
                              bellA
```

Signature 238.

Leonora Baroni was commonly spoken of as L'Adrianella, or simply as Adrianella. We are therefore not altogether surprised to find that the first two lines of the second Italian sonnet contain still another acrostic. (See p. 564.)

Begin to read from the letter A which is the end of the word 'sera' in the first line; to the left; downwards; spelling ADRIANELLA, you will arrive at the last letter of the second line, thus:—

QUAL IN COLLE ASPRO, AL IMBRUNIR DI SERA,
............n........................a..............i r....d............A   ←—≪

L'AVEZZA GIOVINETTA PASTORELLA
............e..ll a

Or, if you prefer to see the two lines laid out as a string of letters, the acrostic can be shown like this:—

ARES ID RINURBMI LA ORPSA ELLOC NI LAUQ L'AVEZZA GIOVINETTA PASTORELLA.
A........d.r.i.............a.................n.................e.............................ll a.

Observe that these two lines contain precisely fifty-nine letters. Counting from the end of either line will show you that the letter A of the word 'Qual' is the centre of this string.

Now turn to the next signature.

Signature 239.

Again observe the first two lines of the second sonnet. (See p. 564.) They run:—

QUAL IN COLLE ASPRO, AL IMBRUNIR DI SERA
L'AVEZZA GIOVINETTA PASTORELLA

As a working hypothesis let us suppose that Milton is playing with the types of these lines. Let us bear in mind that the meaning of 'qual' is *who*, or *one who*. The middle letter of these two lines is the A of 'Qual' (Qua may mean '*Here*,' '*In this place*'). Let us therefore suppose that there is a *double entente* in the word 'Qual,' and look at these two lines of type as a cipher, or circle of letters, divided after the letter L of the word 'Qual.' We find that if you begin to read from the letter L of the word 'Qual'; to the left; downwards, and around the circle of letters; spelling LEONORA BARONI, you will arrive at the letter I of the word 'in'; and thus meet the letter L from which you started.

The acrostic figure here is:—

```
 L    i n o           r     a          B                       a
 L I-N-C-O-L-L-E-A-S-P-R-O-A-L-I-M-B-R-U-N-I-R-D-I-S-E-R-A - A
A                                                              L
 i                                                            )
U                                                             L
 Q-L-A-V-E-Z-Z-A-G-I-O-V-I-N-E-T-T-A-P-A-S-T-O-R-E
         e          o       n                      o r
```

The observant reader will note that when we join these two lines at the ends in this way we get the word 'Qual' at one end, and the word 'ella,' at the other. This result may not be intentional. It is worth mentioning.

Compare these tricks of type with that used by Tasso when honouring another Leonora. I quote again from *A Poet and his Music*, by Professor R. T. Holbrook: 'In his *Life of Torquato Tasso* (*Vita di Torquato Tasso*, etc. In Venetia, MDCXXI), the Marquis Giovanni Battista Manso (1560?–1645), who had been Tasso's host at Naples in 1592 and entertained Milton early in 1639, declares that no one had ever discovered the identity of the lady so greatly loved by Tasso, although in many parts of his rimes he artfully disclosed her name, which was Leonora, and especially in the sonnet which begins, *Rose, che l' arte inuidiosa ammira* [Roses that envious Art admires], wherein he thus concludes: . . . *E di si degno cor tuo strale onora* [And honour thine arrow with so worthy a heart], where with the last syllable of the word "stra*le*" [i. e. Le] and with the following "onora," he composed the name of Leonora; and in many other places likewise, in which, playing on the words "ora" and "aura," he stealthily reveals the name of his lady.'

NOTE.—See Milton's second epigram, *Ad Leonoram Romae Canentem.*

For my relief; yet hadst no reason why,
Whether the Muse, or Love call thee his mate,
Both them I serve, and of their train am I.

I I.

Donna leggiadra il cui bel nome honora
L'herbosa val di Rheno, e il nobil varco,
Ben è colui d'ogni valore scarco
Qual tuo spirto gentil non innamora,
Che dolcemente mostra si di fuora
De suoi atti soavi giamai parco,
E i don', che son d'amor saette ed arco,
La onde l'alta tua virtù s'infiora.
Quando tu vaga parli, o lieta canti
Che mover possa duro alpestre legno,
Guardi ciascun a gli occhi, ed a gli orecchi
L'entrata, chi di te si truova indegno ;
Gratia sola di sù gli vaglia, inanti
Che'l disio amoroso al cuor s'invecchi.

III.

Qual in colle aspro, al imbrunir di sera
L'avezza giovinetta pastorella
Va bagnando l'herbetta strana e bella
Che mal si spande a disusata spera

Fuor

Fuor di sua natia alma primavera,

Cosi Amor meco insu la lingua snella

Desta il fior novo di strania favella,

Mentre io di te, vezzosamente altera,

Canto, dal mio buon popol non inteso

E'l bel Tamigi cangio col bel Arno.

Amor lo volse, ed io a l'altrui peso

Seppi ch'Amor cosa mai volse indarno.

Deh! foss'il mio cuor lento e'l duro seno

A chi pianta dal ciel si buon terreno.

Canzone.

Ridonsi donne e giovani amorosi

   M'accostandosi attorno, e perche scrivi,

Perche tu scrivi in lingua ignota e strana

Verseggiando d'amor, e come t'osi?

Dinne, se la tua speme sia mai vana,

E de pensieri lo miglior t'arrivi;

Cosi mi van burlando, altri rivi

Altri lidi t'aspettan, & altre onde

Nelle cui verdi sponde

Spuntati ad hor, ad hor a la tua chioma

L'immortal guiderdon d'eterne frondi

Perche alle spalle tue soverchia soma?

   Canzon dirotti, e tu per me rispondi

Signature 240.

This acrostic is found in *Epigramme XXXVII. On Chev'rill The Lawyer*, by Ben Jonson (see p. 568).

Begley hazards the guess that *Chev'rill The Lawyer* was a hit at Francis Bacon (*Is it Shakespeare*, p. 92), and my friend John Macy shows me that if we begin to read from the initial N of the first word of the first line; to the right; downwards; on all the letters of all the words, spelling NOCAB SICNARF (Francis Bacon), we shall arrive at the initial F of the first word of the last line.

The acrostic figure here is:—

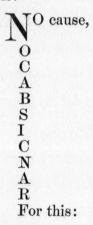

N O cause,

O
C
A
B
S
I
C
N
A
R

For this:

The reader will observe the way the letters are bunched around the large initial N. They are arranged thus; independently of the cipher:—

N^{O ca}
B

The capital letters of the stanza also tell a story. They are:—

N^O   C
    B
A   F

    F

Here we have F F B A C O N, without much difficulty.

There is no reason to suppose that this was a malicious squib. I have heard as personal and pungent wit applied by one member to another of a club of friendly acquaintances. They were fond of hard hitting in those days. It may have been written and handed around in manuscript with real malice. We do not know.

Signature 241.

This acrostic is found in *Epigramme LIIII* by Ben Jonson, as it appears in the Folio edition of his works dated 1616. (See below.)

Begin to read from the terminal N of the word 'On' in the title *On Chev'ril;* to the left; on the terminals; downwards; spelling NOCAB, you will arrive at the initial terminal B of the word ' barre.'

Begin to read from the terminal N of the word 'men,' which is the last word of the stanza; to the left; upwards; on the terminals; spelling NOCAB, you will arrive again at the initial terminal B of the word ' barre.'

Begin to read from the terminal N of the last word of the stanza; to the left; upwards; on all the letters of all the words of the stanza and its title; spelling NOCABACON, you will arrive at the terminal N of the word 'On' in the title.

In both instances the acrostic figure is : —

ON CHEV'RIL
O
C
A
Barre
A
C
O
meN

LIIII

ON CHEV'RIL.

CHev'ril cryes out, my verſes libells are;
　　And threatens the Starre-chamber, and the barre:
What are thy petulant pleadings, Chev'ril, then,
　　That quit'ſt the cauſe ſo oft, and rayl'ſt at men?

The *Epigramme* as here printed is a literal and typographical copy of its rendering in the Folio of 1616, in the Lenox Library, New York.

XXXVII.

ON CHEV'RILL THE LAWYER.

NO caufe, nor client fat, will CHEV'RILL leefe,
    But as they come, on both fides he takes fees,
And pleafeth both. For while he melts his greace
For this: that winnes, for whom he holds his peace.

XXXVIII.

TO PERSON GVILTIE.

Facsimile from the first Folio edition of Ben Jonson's Works. Published in 1616.

XXXVII.

ON CHEV'RILL THE LAWYER.

NO caufe, nor client fat, will CHEV'RILL leefe,
    But as they come, on both fides he takes fees,
And pleafeth both. For while he melts his greafe
For this: that winnes, for whom he holds his peace.

Facsimile from the second Folio edition of Ben Jonson's Works. Published in 1640.

Signature 242.

This acrostic is found in *Epigramme LVI. On Poet-Ape,* by Ben Jonson (see pp. 572–573).

I print this *Epigramme* in facsimile from the first Folio (1616) of the *Works* of Ben Jonson, and also in facsimile from the second Folio, which was published in 1640. Bacon was Attorney-General in 1616, and had been dead fourteen years at the date of the second Folio. It is therefore interesting to observe the dropped letters at the end of the last word of the poem as it appears in the latter edition. I am told by Mr. Robert Seaver of The Riverside Press that these letters were probably dropped by intention, as the improbability of so even a typographical result by accident would be too great to admit of another explanation.

Let us take the hint, if it is one, and drop, or disregard the silent ' e's ' of the words at the ends of the lines of the poem.

Begin to read from the terminal F of the word ' chief(e) '; which is the last word of the first line; to the left; on terminals; downwards; spelling FRAN BACON, you will arrive at the terminal N of the word ' own(e).'

Begin to read from the initial F of the word ' From,' which is the first word of the last line; to the right; upwards; on terminals; spelling FRAN BACON, you will again arrive at the terminal N of the word ' own(e).'

The acrostic figure here is:—

Poore Poet-Ape, that would be thought our chieF(e)

```
                                        R
                                      A
                                    N
                                  B
                                A
                              C
                            O
He takes up all, makes each mans wit his owN(e)
                            O
                          C
                        A
                      B
                    N
                  A
                R
                From locks of wooll, etc.
```

Begin to read from the initial F of the word 'From,' which is the first word of the last line; to the right; upwards; on the terminals; spelling FFRAUNCIS BACON, you will arrive at the terminal N of the word 'ON' in the title 'ON POET–APE.'

ON POET–APE.
O
C
A
B
S
I
C
N
U
A
R
F
From locks of wooll, etc.

The epigram *On Poet-Ape*, read in the light of the acrostics which are found running through it, is subject to much interpretation. We seem to have Bacon here charged with taking up all, and with making each man's wit his own. We seem to see him charged with buying up reversions of old plays and with re-writing them. Jonson seems to have supposed that Bacon made money out of his literary work. He takes the attitude, not unknown in these days, that a man was doing a contemptible thing when he bought plays or manuscripts written by other men, re-wrote them, and turned them out under other than the original author's name. It is possible that when these squibs were written, Ben Jonson was not aware of the vast plans for the advancement of learning which Bacon was maturing, and of the important part which the Drama might play in Bacon's great scheme. We know that Jonson came to know and to revere Bacon at a later period, and to write of him in his *Scriptorum Catalogus* (*Discoveries*) that he ' hath filled up all numbers, and performed that in our tongue, which may be compared or preferred either to insolent Greece, or haughty Rome . . .: so that he may be named, and stand as the mark and ἀκμή of our language.' Readers will be interested to compare this praise of Francis Bacon with similar praise of Shakespeare in Ben Jonson's poem *To the memory of my beloued, The Avthor Mr. William Shakespeare*, in the first Folio, which I give in facsimile on pp. 324 and 325.

LVI.

ON POET-APE.

POore POET-APE, that would be thought our chiefe,
    Whose workes are eene the fripperie of wit,
From brocage is become so bold a thiefe,
    As we, the rob'd, leaue rage, and pittie it.
At firft he made low fhifts, would picke and gleane,
    Buy the reuerfion of old playes; now growne
To'a little wealth, and credit in the *scene*,
    He takes vp all, makes each mans wit his owne.
And, told of this, he flights it. Tut, such crimes
    The fluggifh gaping auditor deuoures;
He markes not whofe 'twas firft: and after-times
    May iudge it to be his, as well as ours.
Foole, as if halfe eyes will not know a fleece
    From locks of wooll, or fhreds from the whole peece?

Facsimile from the first Folio edition of Ben Jonson's *Works*. Published in 1616.

LVI.
ON POET-APE.

POore POET-APE, that would be thought our chiefe,
  Whose Works are eene the frippery of wit,
From brocage is become so bold a theefe,
  As we, the rob'd, leave rage, and pitie it.
At first he made low shifts, would pick and gleane,
  Buy the reversion of old Playes; now growne
To'a little wealth, and credit in the *Scene*,
  He takes up all, makes each mans wit his owne.
And, told of this, he slights it. Tut, such crimes
  The sluggish gaping auditor devoures;
He markes not whose 'twas first: and after-times
  May judge it to be his, as well as ours.
Foole, as if halfe eyes will not know a fleece
  From locks of wooll, or shreds from the whole peece?

LVII.
ON BAUDES, AND USURERS.

IF, as their ends, their fruits were so the same,
  Baudry', and Usury were one kind of game.

LVIII.
TO GROOME IDEOT.

IDEOT, last night, I pray'd thee but forbeare
  To reade my verses; now I must to heare:
For offring, with thy smiles, my wit to grace,
Thy ignorance still laughs in the wrong place.
And so my sharpnesse thou no lesse dif-joynts,
  Than thou did'st late my sense, loosing my points.
So have I seene at CHRIST-masse sports, one lost,
  And, hood-wink'd, for a man, embrace a post.

LIX.
ON SPIES.

Facsimile from the second Folio edition of Ben Jonson's *Works*. Published in 1640.

LIB. II.

SAT. I.

22

FOr shame write better *Labeo*, or write none,
Or better write, or *Labeo* write alone,
Nay call the *Cynick* but a wittie foole,
Thence to abiure his handfome drinking bole:
Becaufe the thirftie fwaine with hollow hand,
Conuei'ed the ftreame to weet his drie weafand,
Write they that can, tho they that cannot, doe:
But who knowes that, but they that do not know.
Lo what it is that makes white rags fo deare,
That men muft giue a tefton for a queare.
Lo what it is that makes goofe-wings fo fcant,
That the diftreffed Semfter did them want,
So, lauifh ope-tyde caufeth fafting-lents,
And ftarueling *Famine* comes of large expence.
                                        Might

LIB. II.

23

Might not (fo they where pleaf'd that beene aboue)
Long '*Paper-abftinence* our death remoue?
Then manic a *Lollerd* would in forfaitment,
Beare *Paper-fagots* ore the Pauement.
But now men wager who fhall blot the moft,
And each man writes. *Ther's fo much labour loft,*
That's good, that's great : Nay much is fildome well,
Of what is bad, a litil's a greate deale.
Better is more: but beft is nought at all.
Leffe is the next, and leffer criminall.
Little and good, is greateft good faue one,
Then Labco, or write little or write none.
Tufh but fmall paynes can be but little art,
Or lode full dric-fats fro the forren mart.
With *Folio-volumes,* two to an Oxe hide,
Or elfe ye *Pamphleter* go ftand a fide,
Reade in each Schoole, in euerie margent coted,
In euerie Catalogue for an auour noted.
There's happineffe well giuen, and well got,
Leffe gifts, and leffer gaines I weigh them not.
                                            So
                                        C 4

LIB. II.

24

So may the Giant rome and write on high,
Be he a Dwarfe that writes not their as I.
But well fare *Strabo*, which as stories tell,
Contriu'd all *Troy* within one Walnut shell.
His curious ghost now lately hither came.
Arriuing neere the mouth of luckie Taine:
I saw a *Pismire* strugling with the lode,
Dragging all *Troy* home towards her abode.
Now dare we hither, if we durst appeare,
The subtile *Stithy-man* that liu'd while eare:
Such one was once, or once I was mistaught,
A Smith at *Vulcans* owne forge vp brought,
That made an Iron-chariot so light,
The coach-horse was a Flea in trappings dight.
The tame-lesse steed could well his wagon wield,
Through downes and dales of the vneuen field.
Striue they laugh we: meane while the black storie
Passes new *Strabo*, and new *Straboes Troy*.
Little for great:and great for good:all one:
For shame or better write, or *Labeo* write none.   But

LIB. I.

25

But who coniur'd this bawdie *Poggies* ghost,
From out the *stewes* of his lewde home-bred coast:
Or wicked *Rablais* dronken reuellings,
To grace the mis-rule of our Tauernings?
Or who put *Bayes* into blind *Cupids* fist,
That he should crowne what Laureats him list?
Whose words are those, to remedie the deed,
That cause men stop their noses when they read?
Both good things ill, and ill things well: all one?
For shame write cleanly *Labeo*, or write none.

SAT.

Signature 244.

This acrostic is found in *An Ode,* a poem printed in *Poems: In diuers humours.*   I have already remarked upon the reasons which have led some scholars to ascribe this book to Barnfield (see footnote to p. 15; and text of p. 174). The version which I use is that found in Arber's reprint. I have been unable to obtain a facsimile (see p. 581.)

Begin to read on the initial A of the first word of the first line; to the right; downwards; on the initials; spelling ANTONIO, you will arrive at the initial O of the word 'of' in the line: —

Carelesse of thy sorrowing.

Begin to read from the initial F of the first word of the last line; to the right; upwards; on the initials; spelling FRANCISCO, you will arrive again at the initial O of the word 'of' in the line: —

Carelesse of thy sorrowing.

The acrostic figure here is: —

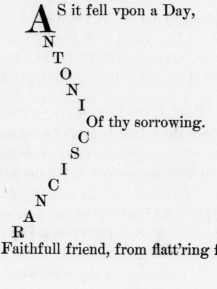

A S it fell vpon a Day,
N
T
O
N
I
C Of thy sorrowing.
S
I
C
N
A
R
Faithfull friend, from flatt'ring foe.

Signature 245.

This acrostic is also found in *An Ode* (see p. 581).

Begin to read from the initial A of the first word of the first line of the poem; to the right; downwards; on the terminals; spelling ANTONIO BACONO, you will arrive at the initial O of the word 'on,' in the line: —

None takes Pitty on thy paine.

Begin to read from the initial F of the first word of the last line of the poem; to the right; upwards; on the terminals; spelling FRANCISCO BACONO, you will again arrive at the initial O of the word 'on,' in the line quoted above.

The acrostic figure here is: —

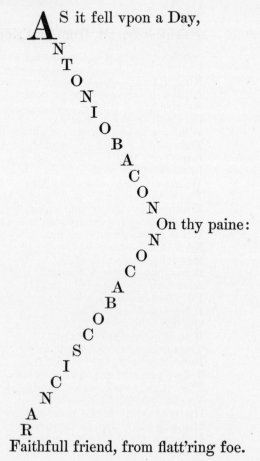

An Ode.

AS it fell vpon a Day,
In the merrie Month of May,
Sitting in a pleasant shade,
Which a groue of Myrtles made,
Beastes did leape, and Birds did sing,
Trees did grow, and Plants did spring:
Euery thing did banish mone,
Saue the Nightingale alone.
Shee (poore Bird) as all forlorne,
Leand her Breast vp-till a Thorne,
And there sung the dolefulst Ditty,
That to heare it was great Pitty.
Fie, fie, fie, now would she cry
Teru Teru, by and by:
That to heare her so complaine,
Scarce I could from Teares refraine:
For her griefes so liuely showne,
Made me thinke vpon mine owne.
Ah (thought I) thou mournst in vaine;
None takes Pitty on thy paine:
Senslesse Trees, they cannot heere thee;
Ruthlesse Beares, they wil not cheer thee.
King *Pandion*, hee is dead:
All thy friends are lapt in Lead.
All thy fellow Birds doe singe,
Carelesse of thy sorrowing.
Whilst as fickle Fortune smilde,
Thou and I, were both beguilde.
Euerie one that flatters thee,
Is no friend in miserie:
Words are easie, like the winde;
Faithfull friends are hard to finde:
Euerie man will bee thy friend,
Whilst thou hast wherewith to spend:
But if store of Crownes be scant,
No man will supply thy want.
If that one be prodigall,
Bountifull, they will him call.
And with such-like flattering,
Pitty but hee were a King.
If hee bee adict to vice,
Quickly him, they will intice.
If to Woemen hee be bent,
They haue at Commaundement.
But if Fortune once doe frowne,
Then farewell his great renowne:
They that fawnd on him before,
Vse his company no more.
Hee that is thy friend indeed,
Hee will helpe thee in thy neede:
If thou sorrowe, hee will weepe;
If thou wake, hee cannot sleepe:
Thus of euerie griefe, in hart,
Hee, with thee, doeth beare a Part.
These are certaine Signes, to knowe
Faithfull friend, from flatt'ring foe.

CHAPTER XV

INSTANCES OF WORK ACKNOWLEDGED BY FRANCIS BACON IN WHICH SIMILAR ACROSTIC SIGNATURES ARE FOUND CONSTRUCTED BY THE SAME METHOD AS ARE THOSE WHICH HAVE PRECEDED

Essayes — Religious Meditations — Places of perswasion and disswasion — A Translation of Certaine Psalmes

Signature 246.

I NOW turn to the little volume by Francis Bacon which contains the three small books, each with an anonymous title-page, entitled, *Essayes, Religious Meditations, Places of perswasion and disswasion* (published 1597). In his 'Dedication' to 'his deare Brother' Anthony, which is given in facsimile on pages 28–29, Bacon does not say in so many words that the three books had been going around *anonymously* in manuscript, 'as they passed long agoe' from his pen; and by the phrase 'retiring and withdrawing mens conceites' he may have meant simply 'not printing.' He does say, however, 'These fragments of my conceites were going to print. To labour the staie of them had bin troublesome, and subiect to interpretation; and to let them passe had beene to adventure the wrong they mought receiue by vntrue Coppies, or by some garnishment, which it mought please any that should set them forth to bestow vpon them. Therefore I helde it best discreation to publish them my selfe as they passed long agoe from my pen.' It is a fair supposition that these essays had been anonymous in their manuscript form, though we have no direct evidence that they were. That the first printed edition is without name on its three title-pages leads one to suppose that Bacon had prepared them for anonymous publication and had inserted the signed dedication before going to press.

Be that as it may: I was curious to know if Bacon had put his mark of identification on the essays, in his usual manner, and by his usual method. There is no indication that he did so, until we come to the last essay in the first book, *Essayes*. Here we find that there is no word on the first page with an initial N except the word 'Negociating' in the title. As the first word of the title begins with an initial O, we are on the track of a possible signature.

Begin to read on the initial F of the word 'FINIS' at the end; to the right; upwards; throughout the essay; on the initials of the words of the text; spelling F BACONO, FR BACONO, or FRA BACONO, you will arrive at the initial O of the word 'Of,' which is the first word of the title. Thus we have here a signature from the first letter of the first (and only) word on the last line to the first letter of the first word of the first line.

The acrostic figure here is: —

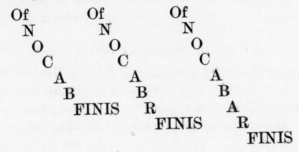

Signature 247.

Now note the words 'backe againe,' which begin the last line of the first page of the essay.

Begin to read from the initial B of the word 'backe'; to the right; upwards; on the initials of the text; spelling BACONO, you will arrive at the initial O of the word 'Of' in the title.

The acrostic figure here is: —

> Of Negociating.
> N
> O
> C
> A
> Backe againe

Begin to read from the initial O of the word 'Of' in the title; downwards; to the right; on the initials of the words of the text; spelling backwards ONOCAB, you will arrive at the initial B of the word 'backe.' Thus this signature is keyed forwards and backwards from the initial of the first word of the first line to the initial of the first word of the last line.

The acrostic figure here is: —

> Of Negociating.
> N
> O
> C
> A
> Backe againe

Note that these results are accomplished by the simple expedient of banishing the initial N from the words of the first page of text excepting the initials of the words of the title.

Of Negociating.

IT is generally better to deale by speech then by letter, and by the mediation of a thirde then by a mans selfe. Letters are good when a man woulde draw an answere by letter backe againe, or whē it may serue for a mans iustification afterwards to produce his owne letter. To deale in person is good when a mans face breedes regard, as commonly with inferiours. ¶ In choyce of instrumēts it is better to choose men of a plainer forte that are like to doe that that is comitted to them, and to reporte backe againe faithfully the successe, then

C 4

then those that are cunning to contriue out of other mens businesse somewhat to grace themselues, and will helpe the matter in reporte for satisfactions sake.

¶ It is better to found a person with whome one deales a farre off, then to fal vppon the pointe at first, except you meane to surprise him by some shorte question. ¶ It is better dealing with men in appetite then with those which are where they would be. ¶ If a man deale with an other vppon conditions, the starte or first performance is all, which a man can not reasonably demaunde, except either the nature of the thing be such which must goe before, or else a man can perswade the other partie that he shall still neede him in some other thing, or else that he bee counted the honester man. ¶ All practise is to discouer or to worke: men discouer themselues in trust, in pasion, at vnwares & of necessitie, when they would haue somewhat donne, and cannot find an apt precept. If you would worke any man, you must either know his nature, and

and fashions and so leade him, or his ends, and so winne him, or his weaknesses or disaduantages, and so awe him, or those that haue interest in him and so gouerne him. ¶ In dealing with cunning persons, we must euer consider their endes to interpret their speeches, and it is good to say little to them, and that which they least looke for,

FINIS.

Signature 249.

This acrostic also is found in the last of the 'Meditationes Sacræ.'

Begin to read from the capital O, or cipher, which stands next to the ornamental letter; to the right; downwards; on all the letters of all the words; spelling backwards Onocab Ocsicnarf, i. e. Francisco Bacono, you will arrive at the initial F of the word 'Finis.'

The acrostic figure here is: —

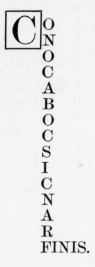

Meditationes Sacrae. 15

do & ecclesiæ custodia, & traditio per manus scripturarum demandata est, sed anima Tabernaculi est testimonium.

FINIS.

Meditationes Sacrae.

De ecclesia & Scripturis.

Proteges eos in tabernaculo tuo a contradictione linguarum.

Contradictiones linguarum vbiq; occurrunt extra tabernaculum Dei. Quare quocunq; te verteris, exitum controuersiarum non reperies nisi huc te receperis. Dices, verum est, nempe in vnitatem ecclesiæ. Sed aduerte. Erat in tabernaculo Arca, & in Arca Testimonium vel tabulæ legis. Quid mihi narras corticem Tabernaculi, sine nucleo testimonij? Tabernaculum ad custodiendum & tradendum testimonium erat ordinatum. Eodem modo

do

they are of no lesse vse to quicken and strengthen the opinions and per-swasions which are true: for reasons plainely deliuered, and alwaies after one manner especially with fine and fastidious mindes, enter but heauily and dully; whereas if they be varyed and haue more life and vigor put into them by these fourmes and insi-nuations, they cause a stronger ap-prehension, and many times sud-dainely win the minde to a resolu-tion. Lastly, to make a true and safe iudgement, nothing can be of grea-ter vse and defence to the minde, then the discouering and reprehen-sion of these coulers, shewing in what cases they hold, and in what they deceiue: which as it cannot be done, but our of a very vniuersall knowledge of the nature of things, so being perfourmed, it so cleareth mans iudgement and election, as it is the lesse apt to slide into any error.

A Table of Coulers, or

apparances of good and euill, and their degrees as places of perswasion and disswasion; and thur seuerall fallaxes, and the elenchis of them.

Cui cetrae partes vel sectae secundas vna-mae vter deserunt, cum singule princi-patum sibi vendicent melior reliquis vi-detur, nam primas quaeque ex zelo vi-detur sumere, secundas autem ex vero & merito tribuere.

SO Cicero went about to pique the Secte of Acade-miques which suspended all assecuration, for to be the best, for sayth he, aske a Stoicke which Philosophie is true, he will preferre his owne: Then aske him which appro-cheth next the truth, he will confesse the Academiques. So deale with the E-picure that will scant indure the Stoicke to be in sight of him, as soone as he hath placed himselfe, he will place the Aca-demiques next him.

So if a Prince tooke diuers competi-tors to a place, and examined them se-uerallie whome next themselues they would rather commend, it were like the ablest man, should haue the most second votes.

The fallax of this couler happeneth oft in respect of enuy, for men are ac-customed after themselues and their owne faction to incline to them which are soffest, and are least in their way in despite and derogation of them that hold them hardest to it. So that this couler of melioritie and preheminence is oft a signe of eneruation and weake-nesse.

? *Cuius excellentia vel exuperantia me-lior, id toto genere melius.*

APpertaining to this are the fourmes: Let vs not wander in generalities: Let vs compare particular with particular, &c.

This

This appearance though it seeme of strength and rather Logicall then Rhetoricall, yet is very of a fallax.

Sometimes because some things are in kinde very casuall; which if they escape, proue excellent, so that the kinde is inferior, because it is so subiect to perill, but that which is excellent being proued is superior, as the blossome of some of March and the blossome of May, whereof the French verse goeth,

Bourgeon de Mars enfant de Paris,
Si un eschape, il en vaut dix.

So that the blossome of May is generally better then the blossome of March; and yet the best blossome of March is better then the best blossome of May.

Sometimes, because the nature of some kindes is to be more equall and more indifferent, and not to haue very distant degrees, as hath bene noted in the warmer clymates, the people are generally more wise, but in the Northerne climate the wits of chiefe are greater. So in many Armies, if the mar-

F *ter*

A Table of the Coulers

eer should be tryed by duell betweene two Champions, the victory should go on one side, and yet if it be tryed by the grosse, it would go of the other side; for excellencies go as it were by chance, but kindes go by a more certaine nature, as by discipline in warre.

Lastly, many kindes haue much refuse which counteruale that which they haue excellent; and therefore generally mettall is more precious then stone, and yet a dyamond is more precious then gould.

3 *Quod ad veritatem refertur maius est quam quod ad opinionem. Modus autem & probatio eius quod ad opinionem pertinet, hæc est, quod quis si clam putaret sore, facturus non esset.*

SO the Epicures say of the Stoicks felicitie placed in vertue, That it is like the felicitie of a Player, who if he were left of his Auditorie and their applause, he would streight be out of hart and countenance, and therefore they call

---

call vertue *Bonum theatrale.* But of Riches the Poet sayth:

Populus me sibilat,
At mihi plaudo.

And of pleasure.

Grata sub uno
Gaudia corde premens, vultu simulata pudorem.

The fallax of this couler is somewhat subtile, though the answere to the example be readie, for vertue is not chosen propter auram popularem. But contrariwise, *Maxime omnium teipsum reuerere.* So as a vertuous man will be vertuous in *solitudine,* and not onely in *theatro,* though percase it will be more strong by glory and fame, as an heate which is doubled by reflexion; But that denieth the supposition, it doth not reprehend the fallax whereof the reprehension is a low, that vertue (such as is ioyned with labor and conflict) would not be chosen but for fame and opinion, yet it followeth not that the chiefe motiue of the election should

F 2 not

not be reall and for it selfe, for fame may be onely *causa impulsiua*, and not *causa constituens*, or *efficiens*. As if there were two horses, and the one would doo better without the spurre then the other: but agayne, the other with the spurre woulde farre exceede the doing of the former, giuing him the spurre also; yet the latter will be iudged to be the better horse, and the fourme as to say, *Tush, the life of this horse is but in the spurre*, will not serue as to a wise iudgemente: For since the ordinary instrument of horsemanship is the spurre, and that it is no manner of impediment nor burden, the horse is not to bee accounted the lesse of, which will not doo well without the spurre, but rather the other is to be reckoned a delicacie then a vertue, so glory and honor are as spurres to vertue: and although vertue would languish without them, yet since they be alwayes at hand to attend vertue, vertue is not to be layd the lesse, chosen for it selfe, because

because it needeth the spurre of fame and reputation: and therefore that position, *Nota eius rei quod propter opinionem & non propter veritatem eligitur, hoc est quod quis si clam putaret fore facturus non esse* is reprehended.

4 *Quod rem integram seruat bonum, quod sine receptu est malum. Nam se recipere non posse impotentiæ genus est, potentia autem bonum.*

HEreof *Aesope* framed the Fable of the two Frogs that consulted together in time of drowth (when many plashes that they had repayred to were dry) what was to be done, and the one propounded to goe downe into a deepe Well, because it was like the water woulde not fayle there, but the other aunswered, yea but if it do faile how shall we get vp againe? And the reason is, that humane actions are so vncertayne and subiecte to perills, as that seemeth the best course

course which hath most passages out of it.

Appertaining to this perswasion the fourmes are, you shall ingage your selfe. On the other side, *Tantum quantum voles sumes ex fortuna*, you shall keepe the matter in your owne hands. The reprehension of it is, *That proceeding and resoluing in all actions is necessarie*: for as he sayth well, *Not to resolue, is to resolue*, and many times it breedes as many necessities, and ingageth as farre in some other sort as to resolue.

So it is but the couetous mans disease translated into power, for the couetous man will enioy nothing because he will haue his full store and possibilitie to enioy the more, so by this reason a man shoulde execute nothing because hee shoulde be still indifferent and at libertie to execute any thing. Besides necessitie and this same *iacta est alea* hath many times an aduantage, because it awaketh the powers of the minde, and strengtheneth indeuor, *Ceteris pares necessitate certe superiores estis.*

5 *Quod*

Quod ex pluribus constat et diuisibi-lius est maius quam quod ex paucioribus et magis vnum: nam omnia per partes considerata maiora videntur; quare et pluralitas partium magnitudinem prae se fert; fortius autem operatur plurali-tas partium si ordo absit, nam inducit similitudinem infiniti et impedit com-prehensionem.

THis cowler seemeth palpable, for it is not pluralitie of partes without maioritie of partes that maketh the to-tall greater, yet neuerthelesse it often carries the minde away, yea, it decey-ueth the sence, as it seemeth to the eye a shorter distance of way if it be all dead and continued, then if it haue trees or buildings or any other markes whereby the eye may deuide it. So when a great moneyed man hath deui-ded his chests and coines and bags, hee seemeth to himselfe richer then hee was, and therefore a way to amplifie any thing, is to breake it, and to make

an anatomie of it in seuerall partes, and to examine it according to seuerall circumstances. And this maketh the greater shew if it be done without or-der, for confusion maketh things mus-ter more, and besides what is set downe by order and diuision, doth demon-strate that nothing is left out or omit-ted, but all is there; whereas if it be without order, both the minde compre-hendeth lesse that which is set downe, and besides it leaueth a suspition, as if more might be sayde then is ex-pressed.

This cowler deceyueth, if the minde of him that is to be perswaded, do of it selfe ouer-conceiue or preiudge of the greatnesse of any thing, for then the breaking of it will make it seeme lesse, because it maketh it appeare more according to the truth, and there-fore if a man be in sicknes or payne, the time will seeme longer without a clocke or howre-glasse then with it, for the minde doth value euery mo-ment, and then the howre doth ra-ther

ther summe vp the moments then de-uide the day. So in a dead playne, the way seemeth the longer, because the eye hath preconceyued it shorter then the truth: and the frustrating of that maketh it seeme longer then the truth. Therefore if any man haue an ouergreat opinion of any thing, then if an other thinke by breaking it into se-uerall considerations, he shall make it seeme greater to him, he will be decey-ued, and therefore in such cases it is not safe to deuide, but to extoll the entire still in generall.

An other case wherein this cowler deceyueth, is, when the matter broken or deuided is not comprehended by the sence or minde at once in respect of the distracting or scattering of it, and being intire and not deuided, is comprehended, as a hundred poundes in heapes of fiue poundes will shewe more, then in one grosse heape, so as the heapes be all vppon one table to be seene at once, otherwise not, or flowers growing scattered in di-uers

uers beds will showe, more then if they did grow in one bed, so as all those beds be within a plot that they be obiect to view at once, otherwise not; and therefore men whose liuing lieth together in one Shire, are commonly counted greater landed then those whose liuings are dispersed though it be more, because of the notice and comprehension.

A third case wherein this couler deceiueth, and it is not so properly a case or reprehension as it is a counter couler being in effect as large as the couler it selfe, and that is, *Omnis compositio indigentiae cuiusdam videtur esse particeps*, because if one thing would serue the turne it were euer best, but the defect and imperfections of things hath brought in that help to piece them vp as it is sayd, *Martha Martha attendis ad plurima, vnum sufficit.* So likewise hereupon *Aesope* framed the Fable of the Fox and the Cat, whereas the Fox bragged what a number of shifts and deuises he had to get from the houndes, and the

the Catte saide she had but one, which was to clime a tree, whichin proofe was better worth then all the rest, whereof the prouerbe grew, *Multa nouit Vulpes sed Felis vnum magnum.* And in the morall of this fable it comes likewise to passe: That a good sure friend is a better helpe at a pinch, then all the stratagems and pollicies of a mans owne wit. So it falleth out to bee a common errour in negociating, whereas men haue many reasons to induce or perswade, they striue commonly to vtter and vse them all at once, which weakeneth them. For it argueth as was said, a neednes, in euery of the reasons by it selfe, as if one did not trust to any of them, but fled from one to another, helping himselfe onely with that. *Et quae non prosunt singula multa iuuant.* Indeed in a set speech in an assemblie it is expected a man shoulde vse all his reasons in the case hee handleth, but in priuate perswasions it is alwayes a great errour.

A fourth case wherein this colour may bee reprehended is in respecte of that

that same *vis vnita fortior*, according to the tale of the French King, that when the Emperours Amb. had recited his maysters stile at large which consilleth of many countries and dominions: the French King willed his Chauncellor or other minister to repeate and say ouer Fraunce as many times as the other had recited the seuerall dominions, intending it was equiualent with them all, & beside more compacted and vnited.

There is also appertayning to this couler an other point, why breaking of a thing doth helpe it, not by way of adding a shew of magnitude vnto it, but a note of excellency and raritie; whereof the fourmes are, *Where shall you finde such a concurrence? Great but not compleat*, for it seemes a lesse worke of nature or fortune to make any thing in his kinde greater then ordinarie, then to make a straunge composition.

Yet if it bee narrowly considered, this colour will bee reprehended or incountred by imputing to all excellencies in compositions a kind of pouertie

or

or at least a casualty or ieopardy, for frō that which is excellent in greatnes somwhat may be taken, or there may be decay; and yet sufficiencie lett, but from that which hath his price in compositiō on if you take away any thing, or any part doe fayle all is disgraced.

6. Cuius priuatio bona, malum, cuius priuatio mala, bonum.

THe formes to make it conceyued that that was euill which is chaunged for the better are, *He that is in bell thinkes there is no other beauen, Satis quercus, Acornes were good till bread Was found* &c. And of the other side the formes to make it conceyued that that was good which was chaunged for the worse are, *Bona magis carendo quàm fruendo sentimus, Bona à tergo formosissima, Good things neuer appear in their full beautie, till they turne their backe and be going away,* &c. The reprehension of this colour is, that the good or euill which is removed

removed may be esteemed good or euill cōparatiuely and not positiuely or simply, So that if the priuation bee good, it follows not the former condition was euill, but lesse good, for the flower or blossome is a politiue good, although there remoue of it to giue place to the fruite be a comparatiue good, So in the tale of Esope; when the olde fainting man in the heat of the day cast downe his burthen & called for death, & when death came to know his will with him, said it was for nothing but to helpe him vppe with his burthen agayne: it doth not follow that because death which was the priuation of the burthen was ill, therefore the burthen was good. And in this parte the ordinarie forme of *Malum necessarium* aptly reprehendeth this colour, for *Priuatio mali necessarij est malum,* and yet that doth not conuert the nature of the necessarie euill, but it is euill.

Againe it commeth sometimes to passe, that there is an equalitie in the chaunge or priuation, and as it were a *Dilemma boni* or a *Dilemma mali,* so that the

the corruption of the one good is a generation of the other, *Sortis pater equus vterque est:* And contrarie the remedy of the one euill is the occasion and cōmencement of an other, as in Scilla and Charibdis.

7. Quod bono vicinum, bonum; quod a bono remotum malum.

SVch is the nature of thinges, that things contrarie and distant in nature and qualitie are also seuered and disioyned in place, and thinges like and consenting in qualitie are placed, and as it were quartered together, for partly in regarde of the nature to spredde, multiplie and infect in similitude, and partly in regard of the nature to break, expell and alter that which is disagreeable and contrarie, most thinges do eyther associate and draw neere to themselues the like, or at least assimulate to themselues that which approcheth neer them, and doe also diue away, chase and

and exterminate their contraries, And that is the reason commonly yeelded why the middle region of the aire should be coldest, because the Sunne and stars are eyther hot by direct beames or by reflection. The direct beames heate the vpper region, the reflected beames from the earth and seas heate the lower Region. That which is in the middest being furthest. distant in place from these two Regions of heate are most distant in nature that is coldest, which is that they tearme colde or hot, *per antiperistasin*, that is inuironing by contraries, which was pleasantly taken holde of by him that said that an honest man, in these daies must needes be more honest then in ages heretofore, *propter antiperistasin* because the shutting of him in the middest of contraries must needs make the honesty stronger and more compact in it selfe.

The reprehension of this colour is, first many things of amplitude in their kind doe as it were ingrosse to themselues all, and leaue that which is next them

then

them most destitute, as the shootes or vnderwood that grow neare a great and spread tree, is the most pyned & shrubbie wood of the field, because the great tree doth depriue and deceiue them of sappe and nourishment. So he saith wel, *Diuitis serui maximè serui*: And the comparison was pleasant of him that compared courtiers attendant in the courtes of princes, without great place or office, to falling daies, which were next the holy daies, but otherwise were the leanest dayes in all the weeke.

An other reprehension is, that things of greatnes and predominancie, though they doe not extenuate the thinges adioyning in substance, yet they drowne them and obscure them in shew and appearance. And therefore the Astronomers say, that whereas in all other planets coniunction is the perfectest amitie: the Sunne contrariwise is good by aspect, but euill by coniunction.

A third reprehension is because the euill approcheth to good sometimes for concealement, sometimes for protection, and

G

and good to euill for conuersion and reformation. So hipocrisie draweth neer to religion for couert & hyding it selfe. *Sæpe latet vitium proximitate boni*, & Sanctuary men which were commonly inordinate men & malefactors, were wont to be neerest to priestes and Prelates and holy men, for the maiestie of good thinges is such, as the confines of them are reuered. On the other side our Sauiour charged with neerenes of Publicanes and rioters said, *The Phisitian approcheth the sicke, rather then the whole.*

Quod quis culpa sua contraxit, maius malum; quod ab externis imponitur, minus malum.

THe reason is because the sting and remorse of the mind accusing it selfe doubleth all aduersitie, contrarywise the considering and recording inwardly that a man is cleare and free from fault and iust imputation, doth attemper outward calamities. For if the euill bee in

the

the fence and in the conscience both, there is a gemination of it, but if euill be in the one and comfort in the other, it is a kind of compensation. So the Poets in tragedies doe make the most passionate lamentations, and those that forerunne final dispaire, to be accusing, questioning and torturing of a mans selfe.

Seqionum clamat causa, caput{que} malorum, & contrariwise the extremities of worldlie persons haue beene annihilated in the consideration of their owne good deseruing. Besides when the euill commeth from without, there is left a kinde of euaporation of griefe, if it come by humane iniurie, eyther by indignation and meditating of reuenge from our selues, or by expecting or foreconceyuing that *Nemesis* and retribution will take holde of the authours of our hart, or if it bee by fortune or accident, yet there is left a kinde of expostulation against the diuine powers.

Atque Deos atque astra vocat crudelia mater.

But where the euill is deriued from a

G 2   mans

---

mans own fault there all strikes deadly inwards and suffocateth.

The reprehension of this colour is first in respect of hope, for reformation of our faultes is in *nostra potestate*, but amendment of our fortune simplie is not. Therefore *Demosthenes* in many of his orations sayth thus to the people of *Athens, That which hauing regarde to the time past is the worst pointe and circumstance of all the rest, that as to the time to come is the best. What is that? Euen this, that by your sloth, irresolution, and misgouernement, your affaires are growne to this declination and decay. For had you vsed and ordered your meanes and forces to the best, and done your partes euery Way to the full, and notwithstanding your matters should haue gone backwards in this manner as they doe, there had been no hope left of recouerie or reparation, but since it hath beene onely by your owne errours &c.* So *Epictetus* in his degrees faith, *The Worst state of man is to accuse externe things, better then that to accuse a mans selfe, and best of all to accuse neyther.*

An

Another reprehension of this colour is in respect of the wel bearing of euils, wherewith a man can charge no bodie but himselfe, which maketh them the lesse.

Lene fit quod bene fertur onus. And therefore many natures, that are eyther extreamely proude and will take no fault to themselues, or els very true, and cleauing to themselues (when they see the blame of any thing that falles out ill must light vpon themselues) haue no other shift but to beare it out wel, and to make the least of it, foras wee see when sometimes a fault is committed, & before it be known who is to blame, much adoe is made of it, but after if it appeare to be done by a sonne, or by a wife, or by a neere friend, then it is light made of. So much more when a man must take it vpon himselfe. And therefore it is commonly seene that women that marrie husbandes of their owne choosing against their friends consents, if they be neuer so ill vsed, yet you shall seldome see them complaine but to set

G 3

Quod opera & virtute nostra partum
est maius bonum; quod ab alieno bene-
ficio, vel ab indulgentia fortunæ dela-
sum est minus bonum.

THe reasons are first the future hope, because in the fauours of others or the good windes of fortune we haue no state or certainty, in our endeuours or abilities we haue. So as when they haue purchased vs one good fortune, we haue them as ready and better edged and inured to procure another.

The formes be, *you haue wonne this by play, you haue not onely the water, but you haue the receit, you can make it againe if it be lost &c.*

Next because these properties which we inioy by the benefite of others carry with them an obligation, which seemeth a kinde of burthen, whereas the other which deriue frō our selues, are like the freest patents *absq; aliquo inde reddendo,* and

and if they proceede from fortune or prouidence, yet they seeme to touch vs secretly with the reuerence of the diuine powers whose fauours we tast, and therfore worke a kind of religious feare and restraint, whereas in the other kind, that come to passe which the Prophet speaketh, *Lætantur & exultant, immolant plagis suis, & sacrificant reti suo.*

Thirdely because that which cometh vnto vs without our owne virtue, yeeldeth not that commendation and reputation, for actions of great felicitie may drawe wonder, but praiselesse, as Cæsar said to Cæsar: *Quæ miremur habemus, quæ laudemus expectamus.*

Fourthly because the purchases of our own industrie are ioyned commonly with labour and strife which giues an edge and appetite, and makes the fruition of our desire more pleasant, *Suauis cibus a venatu.*

On the other side there bee fowre counter colours to this colour rather then reprehensions, because they be as large as the colour it selfe, first because felicitie

felicitie seemeth to bee a character of the fauour and loue of the diuine powers, and accordingly worketh both confidence in our selues and respecte and authoritie from others. And this felicitie extendeth to many casuall things, whereunto the care or virtue of man cannot extend, and therefore seemeth to be a larger good, as when Cæsar sayd to the sayler, *Cæsarem portas & fortunam eius,* if he had lande, *& virtutem eius,* it had beene small comfort against a tempest otherwise then if it might seeme vpon merite to induce fortune.

Next, whatsoeuer is done by vertue and industrie, seemes to be done by a kinde of habite and arte, and therefore open to be imitated and followed, whereas felicitie is imitable : So wee generally see, that things of nature seeme more excellent then things of arte, because they be imitable, for *quod imitabile est potentia quadam vulga-* *tum est.*

Thirdly, felicitie commendeth those things which cometh without our owne

owne labor, for they seeme gifts, and the other seemes penyworths: whereupon *Plutarch* sayth elegantly of the actes of *Timoleon*, who was so fortunate, compared with the actes of *Agesilaus* and *Epammondas*, *That they were like Homers verses they ranne so easily and so well*, and therefore it is the word we giue vnto poesie, terming it a happie vaine, because facilitie seemeth euer to come from happines.

Fourthly, this same *prater spem, vel prater expectatum*, doth increase the price and pleasure of many things, and this cannot be incident to those things that procede from our owne care, and compasse.

10 *Gradus priuationis maior videtur quam gradus diminutionis, & rursus gradus inceptionis maior videtur quam gradus incrementi.*

IT is a position in the Mathematiques that there is no proportion betweene some-

somewhat and nothing, therefore the degree of nullitie and quidditie or act, seemeth larger then the degrees of increase and decrease, as to a monoculos it is more to loose one eye, then to a man that hath two eyes. So if one haue lost diuers children, it is more griefe to him to loose the last then all the rest, because he is *spes gregis*. And therefore *Sybilla* when she brought her three books, and had burned two, did double the whole price of both the other, because the burning of that had bin *gradus priuationis*, and not *diminutionis*.

This couler is reprehended first in those things, the vse and seruice whereof resteth in sufficiencie, competencie, or determinate quantitie, as if a man be to pay one hundreth poundes vpon a penaltie, it is more for him to want xii pence, then after that xii pence supposeth to be wanting, to want ten shillings more: So the decay of a mans estate seemes to be most touched in the degree when he first growes behinde, more then afterwards when he proues nothing

nothing worth. And hereof the common fournes are, *Serra in fundo parsimonia*, and as good neuer awhit, as neuer the better, &c. It is reprehended also in respect of that notion, *Corruptio vnius, generatio alterius*, so that *gradus priuationis*, is many times lesse matter, because it giues the cause, and motiue to some new course. As when *Demosthenes* reprehended the people for harkning to the conditions offered by King Phillip, being not honorable nor equall, he saith they were but elements of their sloth and weakenes, which if they were taken away, necessitie woulde teach them stronger resolutions, So Doctor *Hector* was wont to Dames of London, when they complayned they were they could not tell how, but yet they could not endure to take any medicine, he would tell them, Their way was onely to be sicke, for then they would be glad to take any medicine.

Thirdly, this couler may be reprehended, in respect that the degree of decrease

metre, a fine feeling for imaginative effect in words, and a vein of poetic passion. (*Lord Bacon's Works*, vol. vii, p. 267.)

Let us now turn to the last Psalm in the book, where we may reasonably expect a signature.

Begin to read from the cipher **O** which begins the first line; to the right; downwards; on *all* the letters of *all* the words, as if they are on a string; spelling backwards ONOCAB OCSICNARF, you will arrive at the initial F of the word 'FINIS,' i. e. the initial of the first (and only) word of the last line.

The signature thus runs from the *first* letter of the *first* line to the *first* letter of the *last* line.

O Sing a new Song, to our God above,
N
O
C
A
B
O
C
S
I
C
N
A
R
FINIS

The acrostic figure here is similar to that of the Walsingham specimen on pages 54–55, with the exception of the secrecy of its interior letters.

We have Bacon's word for it that these translations were the exercise of a spell of sickness. As he was a prey to sickness now and again throughout his life, we do not know to what sickness he refers: presumably it was a recent attack (he was then about 64), but we do not know. I wish we did, for it is worth remark that the book contains *seven* Psalms, and that in the printer's preface to the *Complaints*, published thirty-four years before the Psalms, mention is made of *The Seven Psalms* which the supposed author of the *Complaints* had then written. I draw no conclusions, but present the facts, which may be of interest hereafter.

As I have been unable to see the first edition of this little book, I have fallen back on the third edition of the *Resuscitatio*, published in 1671, which will serve our purpose. (*Resuscitatio*, pt. 2, p. 26.)

And as thou didſt by us, ſo do by thee.
Yea happy he, that takes thy Childrens Bones,
And daſheth them againſt the Pavement Stones.

The Tranſlation of the 149 Pſalm.

O Sing a new Song, to our God above,
　　Avoid profane ones, 'tis for holy Quire:
Let Iſrael ſing Songs of holy Love
To him that made them, with their Hearts on fire:
　　Let *Sions* Sons lift up their voice, and ſing
　　Carols and Anthems to their Heavenly King.

Let not your voice alone his praiſe forth tell,
But move withal, and praiſe him in the Dance;
Cymbals and Harps let them be tuned well,
'Tis he that doth the Poors eſtate advance:
　　Do this not onely on the Solemn days,
　　But on your ſecret Beds your Spirits raiſe.

O let the Saints bear in their Mouth his Praiſe,
And a two edged Sword drawn in their Hand,
Therewith for to revenge the former Days,
Upon all Nations, that their Zeal withſtand;
　　To bind their Kings in Chains of Iron ſtrong,
　　And manacle their Nobles for their wrong.

　　Expect the time, for 'tis decreed in Heaven,
　　Such Honour ſhall unto his Saints be given.

FINIS.

CONCLUSION

A HISTORICAL study of the life and work of Francis and Anthony Bacon in the light of these acrostics will entail the reproduction of many documents which are not so well known in this connexion as they may be in the future. I hope that it may be possible for me to complete and publish a volume of that nature which I have already begun.

I wish that the present work be regarded merely as an entrance to a field which has hitherto been closed to most students. The reader will have seen that it extends over a period of about sixty years, and that it uncovers about two hundred and fifty signatures. I have no doubt that I have overlooked many signatures which will be seen by those who have the patience to follow my plough. Even while this volume was going through the press friends discovered several acrostics which had escaped my vigilance, in *Venus and Adonis, Lucrece, Shake-speare's Sonnets*. Furthermore it can hardly be hoped that so large a book, composed of so much technical matter, will be free from errors; but it is as correct as my own care and the generous help of friends could make it.

It has been my desire throughout that each reader shall be allowed to draw his own inferences, and make his own interpretations, and I hope that I have been consistent in my plan merely to give the reader materials with which to work, and a practical method of investigation.

EPILOGUE

Ipse certè (vt ingenuê fatear) soleo aestimare hoc
Opus magis pro partu Temporis, quàm Ingenij. Illud
enim in eo solummodò mirabile est; Initia Rei, & tantas
de ijs quae inualuerunt Suspiciones, alicui in mentem
venire potuisse.   Caetera non illibentèr sequuntur.
  Nouum Organum. Epistola Dedicatoria. 1620.

FINIS.

APPENDIX

I

FURTHER REMARKS ON FALSE NAMES AND PEN–NAMES, AND ON THE SURVIVAL OF WORKS WHICH SEEM TO CONTAIN NO NAME [1]

As has been said in the text (p. 16, note 2), so far as I am aware no competent investigator has ever undertaken the task of studying systematically the immense catalogues of anonymous and pseudonymous writings, including both printed books and manuscripts. This task would be so enormous as to baffle all but those rare minds which are not dismayed at the very outset by the immensity of the field to be investigated, and by the endless difficulties necessarily involved in the research. Such a study could never be complete. To perform this task ideally well it would be necessary to ascertain what motives and other causes have led to the existence of anonymous and pseudonymous works during all the periods for which data exist. The conclusions given in this book were derived mainly from the consideration of well-known examples such as are to be found scattered through literary or political histories.

My own reading, and conversations with well-read friends, have convinced me that very little is generally known about anonymous and pseudonymous literature, notwithstanding its bulk and its importance. At the risk of repetition let us sum up a few important facts. The *Iliad* and the *Odyssey* are anonymous, though tradition attributes them to Homer. The desire to fasten these works upon some definite author led, even in ancient times, to the writing of biographies which were widely believed till they were exploded by modern research. Until only a generation ago various familiar fables were unhesitatingly attributed to Æsop, whose life was definitely described in literary histories and other serious works. The author is hardly less shadowy than Homer.

When *Beowulf* and the *Chanson de Roland* were completed, each probably aroused for its supposed author some small part of the admiration that it won for itself. To some contemporaries, at least, the authors of these poems were probably known; but who has chronicled their names? The chante-fable, *Aucassin and Nicolete*, and the farce, *Maistre Pierre Pathelin*, are ranked high among the masterpieces of the Middle Ages. Their authors also may once have been known, but where shall we find their names? So it is with all the other mediæval French farces that have survived; with nearly all the epics; with most of the *fabliaux;* with the *Cent Nouvelles Nouvelles*, and other collections of tales;

[1] Written in collaboration with Mr. R. T. Holbrook.

with the *Roman de Renard;* with a large number of *chansons,*[1] and other forms of artistic and popular poetry. The older English drama is almost wholly anonymous; so, too, is a large part of the Elizabethan drama. We are equally in the dark as to the authors of the *English and Scottish Popular Ballads,* and many titles might be added to the list.[2] But many other mediæval works have come down to us under a pseudonym, or under the name of some one generally (often erroneously) supposed to be the author. For mediæval pseudonymity two striking examples may suffice: the series of 232 sonnets, known as *Il Fiore,* is ascribed to Dante (1265–1321) by Francesco D'Ovidio and other scholars (see *Nuovi Studi Danteschi. Se possa 'Il Fiore' essere di Dante.* Naples, 1907). These sonnets are in fact signed structurally with the name 'Durante,' which may be the poet's genuine name, though it is possibly only a fanciful appellation, or a suggestive pseudonym. 'The simple faith of our childhood in a Sir John Mandeville, really born at St. Albans, who travelled, and told in an English book what he saw and heard, is shattered to pieces. We now know that our Mandeville is a compilation, as clever and as artistic as Mallory's *Morte d'Arthur,* from the works of earlier writers, with few, if any, touches added from personal experience; that it was written in French, and rendered into Latin before it attracted the notice of a series of English translators (whose own accounts of the work they were translating are not to be trusted), and that the name of Sir John Mandeville was a *nom de guerre* borrowed from a real knight of this name who lived in the reign of Edward II. Beyond this it is difficult to unravel the knot, despite the ends which lie temptingly loose. A Liège chronicler, Jean d'Outremeuse, tells a story of a certain Jean de Bourgogne revealing on his deathbed that his real name was Sir John Mandeville; and in accordance with this story there is authentic record of a funeral inscription to a Sir John Mandeville in a church at Liège. Jean de Bourgogne had written other books and had been in England, which he had left in 1322 (the year in which "Mandeville" began his travels), being then implicated in killing a nobleman, just as the real Sir John Mandeville had been implicated ten years before in the death of the Earl of Cornwall. We think for a moment that we have an explanation of the whole mystery in imagining that Jean de Bourgogne (he was also called Jean à la Barbe, Joannes Barbatus) had chosen to father his compilation on Mandeville, and eventually merged his own identity in that of his pseudonym. But Jean d'Outremeuse, the recipient of his deathbed confidence, is a tricky witness, who may have had a hand in the authorship himself, and there is no clear story as yet forthcoming. But the book remains, and is none the less delightful for the mystery which attaches to it . . . ' (Quoted from A. W. Pollard, *The Travels of Sir John Mandeville.* 'Bibliographical Note.') He who reads thoughtfully will not fail to catch the venom of the argument.

Mediæval sculpture, architecture, and painting manifest similar tendencies.

---

[1] See Gaston Paris, *Littérature française au moyen âge;* Joseph Bédier, *Les légendes épiques,* and *Les Fabliaux;* Holbrook, *The Farce of Master Pierre Patelin,* 'Introduction.'

[2] See E. K. Chambers, *The Mediæval Stage.* F. B. Gummere, *The Popular Ballad.*

Nearly all the great buildings of the Middle Ages are anonymous, though some of them are ascribed to architects of whom little or nothing is known. Dante, the chronicler Giovanni Villani (d. 1348), Petrarch (1304–1374), Antonio Pucci (about 1310–1390), and Boccaccio (1313–1375), with his legendary account, to which we may add two or three of the earliest Dante commentators, are, so far as we know, with the exception of the anonymous writers of three or four archives, the only contemporaries of Giotto (1266?–1337) who have recorded his name, and the critics are still speculating as to what are his authentic works.

More recent times afford names in an overwhelming plenty. François Marie Arouet le jeune (AROUET. L. J.) may possibly have been indulging in a whim when he changed this name into the anagram 'Voltaire.' This world-famous writer, as is well known, published a large number of writings under this pseudonym, which, later, when he had felt his power, became the only name by which he was universally known. Before him, François Rabelais (1490?–1560) had devised for himself the anagram Alcofribas Nasier, under which he published *Pantagruel* and other works. How many readers have forgotten that Villon's real name was François de Montcorbier? Jean Baptiste Poquelin chose to call himself Molière, though apparently with no intent to mislead any one as to his identity. However, many actors and some playwrights have had other reasons for choosing the names under which they have appeared in public.

Defoe is almost too well known to be cited. Dean Swift has been shown to have made political attacks under a pseudonym the secrecy of which was well maintained. Milton before him had pursued similar tactics as a pamphleteer; furthermore, a part of the first edition of his greatest poem (1667) bore this title, *Paradise Lost, a Poem in Ten Books; the author J. M.* The 1637 edition of *A Maske (Comus)* contains this statement in the dedication signed by his friend Henry Lawes, 'Although not openly acknowledg'd by the Author, yet it [this poem] is an off-spring, so lovely, and so much desired, that the often Copying of it hath tir'd my pen to give my severall friends satisfaction, and brought me to a necessity of producing it to the publike view . . .' (see p. 24, *supra*, with note 2).

In other times, and for other reasons, masking names were used by Pietro Aretino, Erasmus, Theodor Beza (the correspondent of Bacon's learned mother), Sir Philip Sidney, and Isaac Casaubon. Spinoza was born with the name Baruch, but few of us remember it.

Who to-day can tell us who Junius was? In spite of the strenuous efforts of the Government to ascertain the identity of this author, and of the researches of many modern writers, the facts are still unknown. But Junius was merely the most prominent of many pamphleteers who wrote in that time anonymously or under pseudonyms. Most journalism has been carried on anonymously or pseudonymously.

William Prideaux Courtney (see p. 16, note 3) has about fifteen hundred entries of anonymous and pseudonymous works and authors. Most of the publications mentioned by him were issued during the past one hundred and fifty years; he tells us that even so many were necessarily a mere selection from a much greater

number. Newman, Manning, Matthew Arnold, as Mr. Courtney shows, as well
as Lamb, Godwin, and Tennyson, all had reasons for pulling the wool over the
eyes of their contemporaries. An idea of the possible number of books issued
in one language, under a false name, a pen-name, *nom de guerre*, or under no
name at all, may be gained from a perusal of the *Deutsches Pseudonymen-Lexi-
kon* and from the statement in Mr. Courtney's book, that the *Deutsches Anony-
men-Lexikon* will contain over fifty thousand entries. This national work is
being compiled by Messrs. Holzmann and Bohatta, who will bring it down to the
year 1850, in four volumes. The latest edition of *Wer ist's?* is said to contain
no less than three thousand pseudonyms.

II[1]

THE USE OF ACROSTICS IN ANCIENT TIMES

IN the historical introduction to this book the use of acrostics in ancient times has barely been touched upon, and indeed there was no reason to deal at length with the vogue they had in remote antiquity, in the early Christian period, nor even in the Middle Ages and the Renaissance. This book is what its title indicates, and the 'Specimens' given in *Part I* have no other aim than to familiarise the reader with illustrative facts. Whoever wishes to pursue this subject further may begin with a careful and richly documented article on acrostics in Greek and Latin literature, to be found in *Pauly's Real-Encyclopädie der Classischen Alter-tumswissenschaft. . . . Neue Bearbeitung. . . . Herausgegeben von Georg Wis-sowa.* (See vol. i, s. v. *Akrostichis*, cols. 1200–1207. Stuttgart, 1893.) The author of this article (Graf) emphasises the importance of acrostics in determining the true authorship of works, the names of persons to whom they may be addressed, etc. His scholarship has made it unnecessary for me to amplify my sketch, in so far as it deals with the use of acrostics in ancient times. In an article entitled, and well entitled, 'The acrostic as a critical aid' ('Das akrostichon als kritisches hilfsmittel'), *Zeitschrift für deutsche Philologie*, vol. 30, pp. 212–244 (anno 1900), Mr. Arthur Kopp gives further evidence that the composing of acrostics is not an isolated phenomenon, but a common fact in European literature. The many examples that he cites from the still greater number that he knows of, or whose presence he suspects, are all German, and nearly all are of a commonplace sort; but his mind was open to the light, and his observations reach far beyond the boundaries of Germany. The fallacy of judging an old custom insignificant, because *we* happen to think it silly, is properly laid bare by Mr. Kopp. I gladly and gratefully add some of his enlightening remarks to what has been said else-where in this book. He says: 'The slight esteem in which acrostics are held is not purely modern. Even in the pre-classic period [i. e. for Germany, before 1750], they had only a sporadic vogue. Johann Christian Guenther [1695–1723] liked acrostics, especially in his earlier years, and not a few of his poems bear witness thereto. *The investigations devoted to Guenther have afforded striking examples to show how useful acrostics may be scientifically, however much they may be despised as an aid to art.* [The italics are mine.] How many rambling, false surmises with regard to Leonore [*Altera* Torquatum cepit Leonora poetam!] would con-tinue to be started if the poem "My trust is firmly founded on two pillars that do not totter," with the name "Magdalena Eleonora Jachmannin" in the initials

[1] I owe the matter in this appendix to the generosity of Mr. R. T. Holbrook.

of the lines (*Poem*, p. 70) were not at hand!' — and here follows another good example of biographical import.

We have already seen that the acrostics presumably used by Francis Bacon and the men who knew his method not only require far less time to make than the commonplace sort used by Guenther, but that the Baconian acrostic is so well hidden as to have escaped discovery for more than three centuries.

Mr. Kopp goes on as follows: 'Incidentally these examples from Guenther prove besides that a poem, through being an acrostic, is not necessarily bad on that account, nor need it pursue a forced train of thought in affected phrases. The very poems above mentioned, in acrostic, have regularly, though no one recognised the presence of acrostics, been counted among the finest productions of Guenther's Muse.

'In Guenther's period there was, in general, no great inclination to this play; the young poet stood alone in this respect [an assumption: his contemporaries may have successfully hidden their acrostics]; there was, however, a time in German poetry when the acrostic may be said to have grown luxuriantly over everything; particularly in the half-century from 1575 to 1625.' [These years, it will be noticed, cover the Elizabethan period and the active days of Bacon's life.] 'To be sure, what predominated was the freer form, according to which names were built for the most part with the initial letters of stanzas, on which account it was unnecessary to begin every verse with a definite letter. Oftenest, as one might expect, it is feminine baptismal names that are eternalised in the acrostics in honour of various sweethearts; less frequently, with the addition of family names. Occasionally, however, the author has woven his own name in as well. The poems in which the name of the poet can be deciphered can be turned to good account in various ways for literary history; all acrostics, however, are of great importance to text criticism . . .' Though Mr. Kopp says 'all acrostics,' the reason he gives applies in the main only to the most commonplace forms of acrostics. It appears that in Nuremberg, a city devoted to the highest art as well as to artistic fads, the making of acrostics had a special vogue. Even Hans Sachs followed the fashion in his later days, and put acrostics into some of his best poems; but naïvely provided his readers with all necessary clues. If no great poets, save possibly Hans Sachs, practised this art in Germany during the period of Queen Elizabeth, the reason may be that Germany's great poets had not yet been born.

Mr. Kopp's final paragraph is so significant (one might almost say, prophetic) that I will quote it all: 'The aim of these lines was to prove, by a fairly good number of examples, how acrostics may be employed to discover new facts, not only in literary history, but in textual criticism [and, as his own article shows, in biography]. If the yield here was not to be despised, there need be no doubt that further fine fruits are only waiting to be plucked by the sagacious scholar in this field. Let us hope, therefore, that investigators, even though acrostic poems are distasteful to them, will nevertheless pay them more heed than they may have thought needful hitherto.'

III

THE SPELLING OF FRANCIS BACON'S NAMES AND TITLES

THE following list shows the forms under which the name of Francis Bacon appeared during his lifetime, or in his authorised works issued after his death:—

1. S^r ffrancis Bacon Kn^t. — *Essays.* Harleian MS. 5106.
2. M^r frauncis. — Northumberland MS. Burgoyne's edition.
3. M^r ffrauncis Bacon. — do.
4. M^r ffr Bacon. — do.
5. ffran Bacon. — Letter to Tobie Matthew, beginning 'Doe not think me forgetful.'
6. B. Fra. — Letter to Burghley, 1580–1584. Spedding, vol. viii, p. 13.
7. Mr. Frauncis Bacon. — In a list of New-Year's gifts given to the Queen at Richmond in 1599–1600. Spedding, vol. ix, p. 163.
8. Fra. Bacon. — Letter to the King, 1612. Spedding, vol. xi, p. 305.
9. F. B. — Letter to the King, 1612. Spedding, vol. xi, p. 280.
10. Francis Bacon. — Opinion, etc., 1613. Spedding, vol. xi, p. 388.
11. Franc. Bacon. — Decree on the Præmunire Question, 1616. Spedding, vol. xii, p. 394.
12. F. Bacon. — Letter to Anthony Bacon, 1596. Spedding, vol. ix, p. 37.
13. Fr. V. — Letter to Buckingham, 1619. Spedding, vol. xiv, p. 50.
14. Fr. Verulam. Canc. — Letter to Buckingham, 1619. Spedding, vol. xiv, p. 51.
15. Fr. Bacon. — Certificate touching the wools of Ireland, 1616. Spedding, vol. xiii, p. 3.
16. Fr. St. Alban, Can. — Letter to the King of Denmark, 1620. Spedding, vol. xiv, p. 166.
17. Fr. St. A. — Letter to Buckingham, 1621. Spedding, vol. xiv, p. 317.
18. S. Albans. — Letter to Father Baranzan, 1622. Spedding, vol. xiv, p. 377.
19. Fra. Baconus. — Epist. Dedicatoria, *De Sapientia Veterum*, 1638.
20. D^s Franciscus Bacon. — Border on portrait by Simon Pass. Spedding, vol. i, p. xv.
21. Sr Frauncis Bacon. Knight. — Inscription under portrait by Simon Pass. Spedding, vol. i, p. xv.

IV

BOOKS ON CIPHERING AND DECIPHERING

I ADD this Appendix because books on these subjects are little known. I am inclined to suspect that they are understood least by those who talk and write most glibly about the results of their use by others. It is much to be regretted that even a slight knowledge of the arts of ciphering and deciphering has not been hitherto deemed necessary to the student of the literature in which they may often play so important a part.

It is a common error to suppose that the most recondite ciphers are the most difficult to decipher, and that a cipherer will use methods mechanically difficult in proportion to his desire for secrecy. The more commonplace the page of type or manuscript containing the cipher, and the more the cipherer makes use of the everyday methods of the printer or the scribe, the more chance has he of escaping notice, if that be his purpose.

In his article on *Cryptography*, Poe has correctly said that ability in these arts is proportioned to analytic power, and that in the case of two persons of acknowledged equality as regards ordinary mental efforts, it will be found that, while one cannot unriddle the commonest cipher, the other will scarcely be puzzled by the most abstruse. The mere literary man is prone to regard such problems as convincing in proportion to his ability to comprehend them, and it is to be regretted again that a literary training should have come to connote (as a rule) an ignorance of mathematics.

The writers whose inventions or collections of ciphers are most likely to have been used by public officials of the sixteenth and early seventeenth centuries were Trithemius (1500), Vigenère (1587), Porta (1563), Selenus (1624). A very complete bibliography of these and other writers, and their later editions, is to be found in Joh. Ludw. Klueber's *Kryptographik. Lehrbuch der Geheimschreibekunst (Chiffrir- und Dechiffrirkunst) in Staats- und Privatgeschäften.* (Tuebingen, 1809.) This is the best general account of the art that I have seen.

There are articles in the encyclopædias, but they are necessarily secondary as sources of information. Blair's article in *Rees's Encyclopædia* is the ablest that I have seen in English. There are also later books by Frenchmen, and others, but for our purpose I suspect that the early collections will prove the most useful. The chief object in consulting them in connexion with acrostics is to gain an insight into the possible habits of the minds of men who used ciphers in their daily work.

The Riverside Press
CAMBRIDGE · MASSACHUSETTS
U · S · A

Date Due